BLACK HISTORY FOR EVERY DAY OF THE YEAR

*Other books by David Olusoga for
Macmillan Children's Books*

Black and British: A Short Essential History

Black and British: An Illustrated History

Other books by David Olusoga for Picador

The Kaiser's Holocaust

The World's War

Black and British: A Forgotten History

Cult of Progress

A House Through Time

DAVID OLUSOGA

BLACK HISTORY FOR EVERY DAY OF THE YEAR

MACMILLAN

YINKA OLUSOGA   KEMI OLUSOGA

Published 2024 by Macmillan Children's Books
an imprint of Pan Macmillan
The Smithson, 6 Briset Street, London EC1M 5NR
EU representative: Macmillan Publishers Ireland Ltd, 1st Floor,
The Liffey Trust Centre, 117–126 Sheriff Street Upper
Dublin 1, D01 YC43
Associated companies throughout the world
www.panmacmillan.com

ISBN 978-1-5290-6620-3

5 7 9 8 6 4

A CIP catalogue record for this book is available from the British Library.

Printed and bound by CPI Group (UK) Ltd, Croydon CR0 4YY

MIX
Paper | Supporting
responsible forestry
FSC® C116313

CONTENTS

For our mum, Marion Olusoga-Ndebele.

AUTHORS' NOTE

What you hold in your hand is the start of a journey through time and space. Each of the 366 daily entries in this book is a portal into the life of a person, group of people, place or event that is part of Black history and part of global history. Some you might already have heard of, and can now learn more about, but others will possibly be new to you.

In these pages you will see hope and connection, ingenuity and creativity, alongside tales of racism and oppression, resistance and celebration. Read this book in whichever way you want. You might start on 1 January, or whichever date this book comes into your possession, and read a page a day for a year. You might look up your birthday, and other occasions that are important to you, to see what happened on each date. Where entries have links to other entries in the book we will let you know. Inevitably, space in this book is limited, so please also look upon each entry as a starting point, giving you the information you need to research and find out more about the particular people, groups, places and events that spark your interest.

At the back of the book you will find twelve timelines. These showcase some groups of related entries that will help you to explore particular themes in the book. These include such themes as the Victorian anti-slavery movement that sought to end slavery once and for all, the Black contribution to the First and Second World Wars, and the work of Black creatives from the Harlem Renaissance to the Black Arts Movement. You will also find a glossary that explains some key terms that are used in the entries and their use in the context of talking about Black history. When you come across a word, acronym or phrase in bold text, please look for it in the glossary for an explanation and wider information.

We have made some decisions about language in the book that we would like to draw your attention to. We use the term Black with a capital B to make it clear that we are writing about a group of people with shared African heritage and culture, not just a colour. We also use the terms 'enslaved person' and 'enslaved people' to remind us that people living under slavery were human and that slavery was a state forced upon them, and not who they were.

Don't forget to look closely at the illustrations that you will find dotted around the book, on the inside covers, at the start of each month, on pages within each month, and in the timelines. In them you will find more interesting details that link to the entries and that celebrate Black history and creativity in visual form.

Whichever way you read this book, we hope that you enjoy it and share some of what you learn with your friends and family.

David, Yinka and Kemi Olusoga

1 JANUARY ~ THE YEAR OF AFRICA

Ahmadou Ahidjo, prime minister of Cameroon, announced his country's liberation from its French colonists on 1 January 1960. By the end of the year that became known as the Year of Africa, sixteen more colonies had wrested back control of their own lands and people from European colonizers.

The sweeping changes that engulfed the continent over this year had many causes but represented the culmination of decades of work from the Pan-Africanist movement. After fourteen European nations had carved up Africa for exploitation at the Berlin Conference (see 15 November), Henry Williams founded the African Association to try to unite Africans, both in the colonies and in the diaspora, against this existential threat. The first grand meeting of this anti-colonialist movement took place in London in 1900 attended by, among others, W. E. B. Du Bois, Samuel Coleridge Taylor and Dr John Alcindor (see 23 February, 15 August and 16 July).

The Pan-African movement gathered real steam after the World Wars. The Europeans had relied heavily on troops from their colonies to bolster their forces. Africans had fought for their colonial rulers and now justly felt that they had earned the right to independence. Unrest spread and resistance to colonial rule began to take form. In the 1950s, revolution in Egypt forced British and French forces out, liberating both Egypt and its neighbour Sudan, and Algeria began a long, bloody yet ultimately successful war of independence. Kenya too fought its occupation in the Mau Mau Rebellion (see 23 July) which was brutally put down by the British ruling powers, who unleashed a campaign of systematic violence and torture against the country's civilians. It was becoming increasingly clear that the days of empire and colonialism were numbered.

After Kwame Nkrumah's (see 1 July) victory in a hard fought battle for Ghanaian independence (see 6 March), he made it his mission to nurture other independence movements across the continent. In December 1958, Nkrumah organized the first of three meetings of the All-African Peoples'

British prime minister Harold Macmillan meeting Sir Abubakar Tafawa Balewa of Nigeria, January 1960

Conference, the successor to the Pan-African Congress (see 21 October). He brought movement leaders, unions and community representatives to the event in Accra, including Patrice Lumumba of the Democratic Republic of Congo (see 24 June), Kenneth Kaunda of Zambia, Hastings Banda of Malawi, and Tom Mboya of Kenya. The conference resolved that 'the political and economic exploitation of Africans by Europeans should cease forthwith' and Nkrumah outlined a four-step pathway for an Africa free from colonial interference:

> 1. the attainment of freedom and independence;
> 2. the consolidation of that freedom and independence;
> 3. the creation of unity and community between the free African states;
> 4. the economic and social reconstruction of Africa

The colonial powers could now see that the end of their overt rule in Africa was at hand. Originating in a memo from the British Ministry of Colonies, the phrase 'Year of Africa', reached the ears and conciousness of the public in a speech from British prime minister Harold Macmillan. In France, General Charles de Gaulle made efforts to protect French interests by rebranding the colonies as 'territories' and offering them self-governance with a route to full independence. The abundance of natural resources in Africa had sustained the wealth of Europe over centuries and an end to colonial rule was a direct threat to the economic status quo. The Europeans were reluctant to grant a full and genuine independence to their former colonies and so top officials were often installed and received military backing from the outgoing power. This uncomfortable situation resulted in much unrest and a high number of **coups d'état** for many of the nations in the years following their independence.

Patrice Lumumba signs the document granting independence to the Democratic Republic of Congo

At the end of 1960, the **UN General Assembly** approved the Declaration on the Granting of Independence to Colonial Countries and Peoples. There were no votes against it, but Australia, Belgium, the Dominican Republic, France, Portugal, Spain, the Union of South Africa, the United Kingdom and the United States all chose to abstain.

TIMELINE OF THE YEAR OF AFRICA, 1960

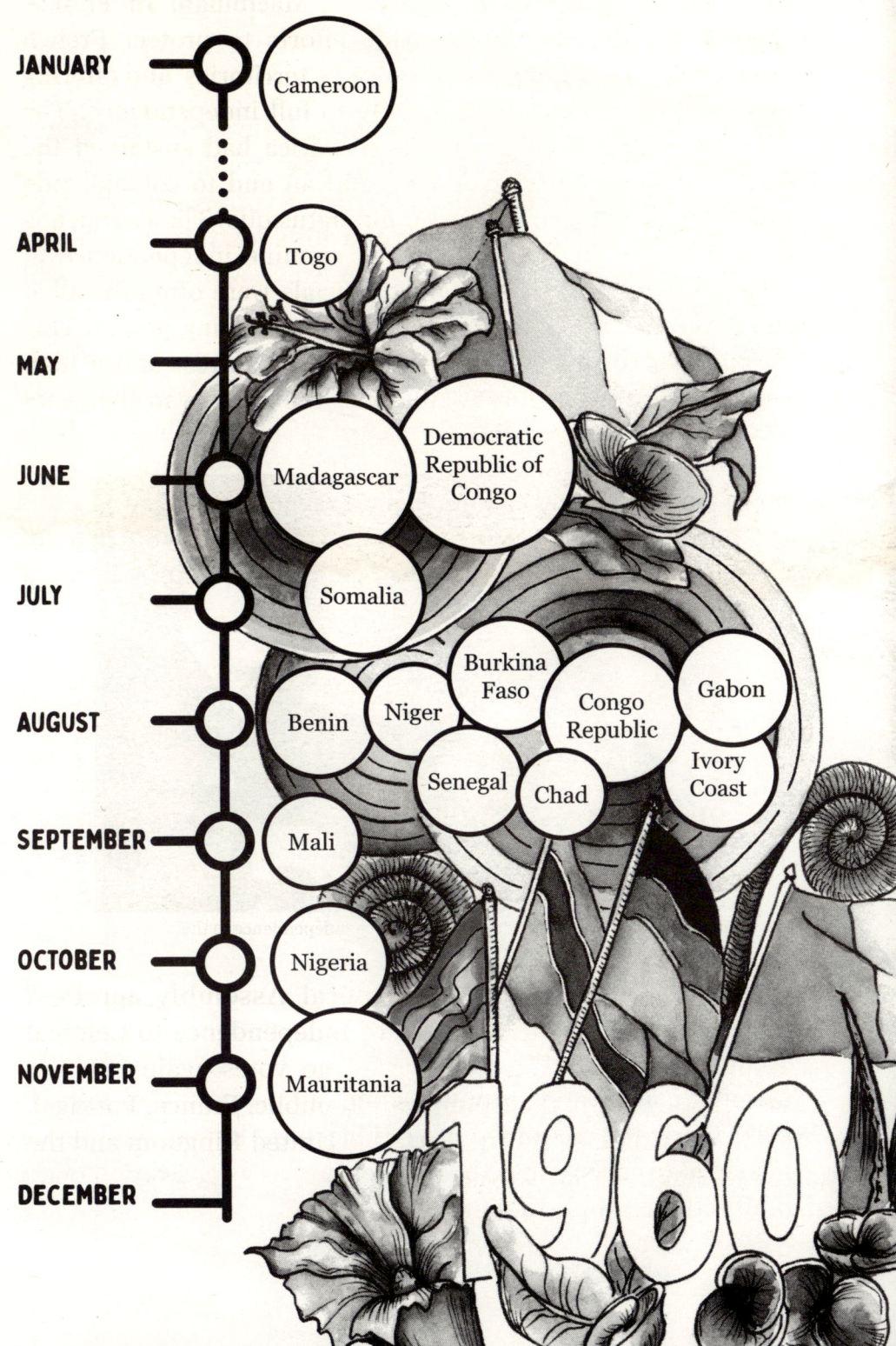

JANUARY — Cameroon

APRIL — Togo

MAY

JUNE — Madagascar, Democratic Republic of Congo

JULY — Somalia

AUGUST — Benin, Niger, Burkina Faso, Senegal, Chad, Congo Republic, Gabon, Ivory Coast

SEPTEMBER — Mali

OCTOBER — Nigeria

NOVEMBER — Mauritania

DECEMBER

1960

2 JANUARY ~ KAAPSE KLOPSE

Kaapse Klopse is an annual carnival held in Cape Town, South Africa, on 2 January.

Dutch settlers colonized Southern African in 1652 and established 2 January as a New Year tradition when the enslaved were granted a day off work. South Africa was then colonized by the British during the 19th century, in a violent process that established a society in which white settlers, who were only 20% of the population, ruled over everyone else.

After the British abolished slavery in 1834, 2 January also became a day of celebration for non-white populations in Cape Town. This coincided with the rise of minstrelsy shows, a form of Victorian entertainment where white singers wore blackface make-up and clothes to mimic and exaggerate the features and behaviour of Black people (see 8 May). By the late 1800s, many clubs (or klopse) would come together to perform in these celebrations on 2 January.

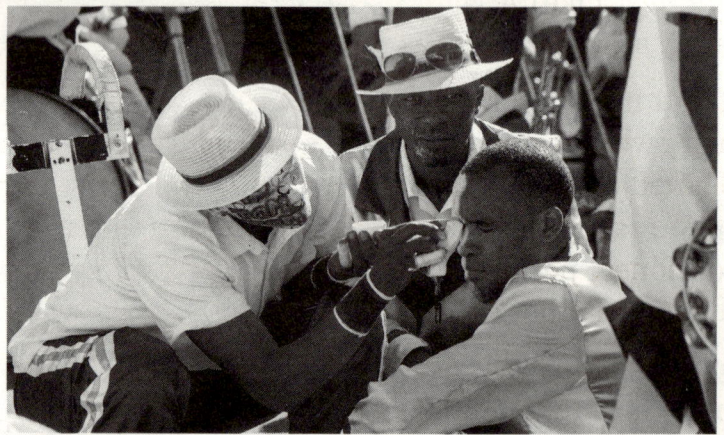

Shutterstock/Ravi Santana

Second New Year, Cape Town, South Africa – 2 January 2017
Minstrels celebrating the Carnival and marching at Bo Kaap neighborhood

Despite controversy around some aspects of the festival, particularly the continued use of blackface, Kaapse Klopse has managed to survive into the 21st century as a celebration of the multi-ethnic people of the Cape.

3 JANUARY - ARETHA FRANKLIN

On 3 January 1987, the African American singer-songwriter Aretha Franklin, the Queen of Soul, became the first woman to be inducted into the Rock & Roll Hall of Fame.

As a child, Franklin performed gospel songs in the church where her father was the minister, and at the age of just eighteen she became a professional singer. In a career that lasted over fifty years, she sold over 75 million records, won eighteen Grammy Awards and became one of the most successful artists of all time. Some of her most famous songs, such as her versions of 'Respect' and '(You Make Me Feel Like) A Natural Woman', reflect and celebrate her identity as a Black woman.

Throughout her life, Franklin was involved in the Civil Rights movement, which campaigned for equal rights for Black people in the United States of America, and she supported the rights of Indigenous peoples across the world. She attended protests, donated money, performed at fundraising benefits and spoke up in support of other campaigners.

In 2005, Franklin was awarded the Presidential Medal of Freedom. In 2019, one year after her death, she was awarded a Pulitzer Prize Special Citation for her contribution to American music and culture.

4 JANUARY – THOMAS WYNDHAM'S JOURNEY TO WEST AFRICA

In the Tudor era (1485–1603) the English began to travel further south, beyond the Mediterranean Sea, exploring the west coast of Africa. The Portuguese had been trading in Africa for years and the English were keen to try to break into that trade and establish connections with African rulers.

One of the first English explorers was Thomas Wyndham, a former pirate, who had the advantage of having a Portuguese second-in-command, Anthony Anes Pinteado. With the support and money of London merchants and King Edward VI, Wyndham and Pinteado left for West Africa in 1553. This was supposed to be a trading expedition, and while they did trade with Africans for gold and pepper, Wyndham also attacked and raided Portuguese ships, taking their goods; which included enslaved people. Rather than heading back for England, Wyndham ignored advice from Pinteado and continued sailing around the African coast. This was a big mistake. Wyndham, Pinteado and two thirds of their crew died from fever.

In 1555 Richard Eden wrote about Wyndham's journey, in a book called *Decades of the New World*. He spoke to the survivors of the journey and examined the ship's logs. In his book, Africa was described as dangerous, and its people as superstitious, violent and uneducated. Eden's account of the voyage, and of the Africans Wyndham encountered in the court of the Oba of Benin, was extremely biased and negative. Despite this, Wyndham's journey was a huge financial success, and his investors, including the king, encouraged other sailors to begin their own trading expeditions to Africa in the years that followed.

5 JANUARY - GEORGE WASHINGTON CARVER

George Washington Carver was an African American scientist and inventor, born into slavery just before the American Civil War (1861–65). His father died before he was born, and his mother and sister were kidnapped and sold by raiders. After the abolition of slavery, Carver and his brother were brought up by their previous owners. Black children were not allowed to attend the local school, so at the age of ten Carver moved into a foster home in order to attend a school ten miles away. Over the next few years he moved to new schools and new foster families, and eventually gained a high school diploma. He got a place at a university in Kansas, but when he arrived they would not let him in because he was Black.

After discovering a talent for working with plants, Carver took out a loan to pay for his education and got a place at a college in Iowa to study for a degree in botany. He was their first Black student and, after completing both his undergraduate and master's degree there, he became their first Black staff member. In 1897 Carver became the head of the Agriculture Department at the new Tuskegee Institute, a private university originally set up as a college for African American students. He stayed there for forty-seven years and became internationally famous for his work on crop rotation and caring for the environment.

Carver died on 5 January 1943. Later that year president Roosevelt ordered the creation of the George Washington Carver National Monument in Missouri. He was the first African American, and the first person who was not a president, to have a national monument dedicated in his honour.

6 JANUARY - ERNIE CHAMBERS

Nebraska Unicameral Information Office, Attribution, via Wikimedia Commons

On 6 January 1971, Ernie Chambers took office as a state senator in Nebraska, USA. He went on to hold that position for forty-six years, making him Nebraska's longest-serving state senator.

Chambers was politically active from an early age. During a heatwave in 1966, his home city of Omaha had two outbreaks of rioting. Both times, Chambers was a spokesperson representing the African American youth in talks with the authorities to bring the riots to a close. That year, while he was working as a barber, Chambers was filmed for the documentary *A Time for Burning*, where he spoke on the issue of race relations with the police in Omaha. In the late 1960s, Chambers ran unsuccessfully for election to the Omaha School Board and Omaha City Council, before his successful campaign of 1970 saw him elected as a state senator.

Chambers is a lifelong atheist. A 2015 survey found that he was the USA's only elected state government member who was a non-believer. During his long political career, Chambers has campaigned against racial and sexual discrimination. He successfully led Nebraska to become the first American state to stop investing money in South Africa during the time of apartheid.

7 JANUARY - RAYFORD W. LOGAN

The historian and activist Rayford W. Logan was born in Washington DC on 7 January 1897. He excelled at school, and won a scholarship to attend Williams College for his undergraduate degree. After graduating in 1917, he served during the First World War, in the 93rd Division, an all-Black unit. He was captain of his high school army cadets and a member of his college's Student Army Training Corps, but was denied commision as an officer due to his colour. After the war Logan remained in France and became active in the Pan-African movement. He befriended W. E. B. Du Bois (see 23 February) and in 1921 helped to organize the second Pan-African Congress in Paris.

Returning to America, he helped organize voter registration campaigns and citizenship schools, to support Black people to exercise their right to vote in elections. He also began his academic career, earning a master's degree and then a PhD from Harvard. In 1932 Logan was appointed to the Black Cabinet, an advisory group of president Franklin D. Roosevelt. It was Logan who drafted the president's executive order that ended the ban on Black people serving in the US Armed Forces during the Second World War (see 26 July).

In 1938 Logan became a history professor at Howard University. He was also a member of NAACP, and its expert on colonial affairs. In 1980 he was awarded the organization's Spingarn Medal for his outstanding achievements as an educator and writer. He died 4 November 1982, aged eighty-five.

8 JANUARY - DAME SHIRLEY BASSEY

Shirley Veronica Bassey was born in Cardiff on 8 January 1937. Her father was Nigerian and her mother was from Teesside in the north of England.

Growing up, Bassey developed a love of singing, and by the time she was fourteen she was already performing for audiences in the pubs and clubs of Cardiff. At the age of eighteen she was a professional singer, performing first in London and then in the USA. She then began her career as a recording artist and had her first hit, 'The Banana Boat Song', in 1957. In 1958 she became the first Welsh artist to get a number one single in the UK charts with 'As I Love You'.

She rose to international fame and became perhaps best known for the theme songs that she recorded for three of the James Bond movies: *Goldfinger*, *Diamonds Are Forever* and *Moonraker*. In 2020 she became the first female artist to have had albums in the UK charts for seven consecutive decades.

> **DID YOU KNOW?**
>
> Bassey has always remained proud of her Welsh upbringing, and in 2016 the Royal Welsh College of Music and Drama named one of its studios the Shirley Bassey Studio in recognition of her generosity in supporting young Welsh singers.

9 JANUARY - ALTHEIA JONES-LECOINTE

Altheia Jones-Lecointe is a biomedical research scientist, most famous for her political activism in Britain in the 1960s and 70s as leader of the British Black Panther movement. She was born on 9 January 1945 in Port of Spain, Trinidad.

She moved to Britain to study for a PhD in advanced chemistry and became involved in the British Black Panther movement, an organization that aimed to tackle racism and discrimination against Black and Asian heritage communities in Britain. She married fellow activist Eddie LeCointe, and together with other members they worked on raising the profile of the organization.

In 1970 Jones-LeCointe and eight fellow activists were named the Mangrove Nine (see 16 December) after they were arrested at a protest outside the Mangrove restaurant in Notting Hill in London. The Mangrove had been targeted and repeatedly raided by police in the months leading up to the protest, despite there being no evidence of criminal activity taking place at the restaurant.

The Mangrove Nine were charged with a number of offences, including conspiring to start a riot. Jones-LeCointe and fellow activist Darcus Howe decided to represent themselves during their trial, and in her closing speech to the jury Jones-LeCointe argued that the police had been persecuting the Black community in Notting Hill. The jury found them not guilty of trying to start a riot, and although Jones-LeCointe and three others were convicted of assault, the judge suspended their sentences and they did not have to go to prison. In 2020, the story of Jones-LeCointe and the trial of the Mangrove Nine was included in the British film series *Small Axe* by the director Steve McQueen (see 30 November), about the history of the Black community in London.

10 JANUARY - DR MARTIN LUTHER KING JR

On 10 January 1957 a twenty-seven-year-old pastor invited dozens of church ministers and Black leaders to a meeting at his church, the Ebenezer Baptist Church in Atlanta, Georgia. The group that they established that day was the **Southern Christian Leadership Conference (SCLC)**, a civil rights organization committed to achieving change via non-violent direct action. The young pastor was elected its first president, a role that he held until his untimely and violent death. His name was the Rev. Dr Martin Luther King Jr.

Dr King was born in Atlanta on 15 January 1929. A gifted child, he graduated high school and started college at the age of just fifteen. After gaining a degree in sociology, he entered theological school and qualified as a pastor. After gaining a **doctorate** at the age of twenty-five, he became pastor at the Dexter Avenue Baptist Church in Montgomery, Alabama.

Martin Luther King at the Civil Rights March on Washington, DC, August 28, 1963

US Information Agency. Press and Publications Service. (ca. 1953 – ca. 1978)
US National Archives: NWDNS-306-SSM-4C(51)13

Montgomery was about to become famous as the city in which Rosa Parks refused to give up her seat on her bus journey home, sparking the Montgomery Bus Boycott, which Dr King organized (see 1 December). His leadership, arrest and imprisonment during the boycott raised his profile, demonstrating the effectiveness of non-violent direct action. With the SCLC, King mobilized Black churches and organizations across the South to challenge **segregation** and Black voter disenfranchisement.

The SCLC conducted a series of civil disobedience campaigns. In Birmingham, Alabama, the response was brutal. Dr King was arrested there in 1963, drawing criticism from people who argued that the campaign was 'untimely' and 'unwise'. In response he wrote his famous Letter from Birmingham Jail, arguing that:

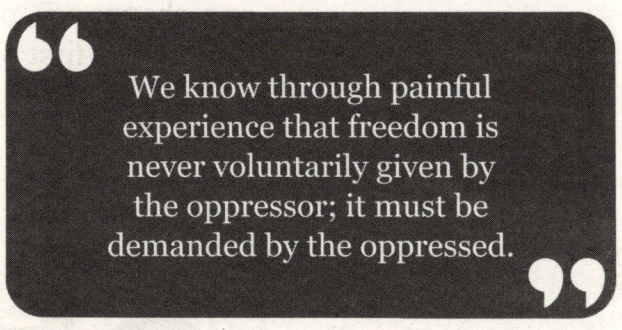

> We know through painful experience that freedom is never voluntarily given by the oppressor; it must be demanded by the oppressed.

Dr King and the SCLC helped to organize a national protest, the March on Washington for Jobs and Freedom, which took place in August 1963 (see 28 August). His speech that day became one of the most famous in history, prompting the passing of the 1964 Civil Rights Bill which prohibited racial segregation in public places. Later that year the Nobel Committee awarded Dr King its 1964 Peace Prize.

A year later, Dr King and the SCLC were in Selma, Alabama, supporting local voter registration campaigns. After the protestors were met with violence, Dr King led a march from Selma to Montgomery, and later that year President Johnson passed the Voting Rights Act of 1965, outlawing disenfranchisement of Black voters (see 7 March).

In the mid-1960s, America's involvement in the Vietnam War entered a new phase, prompting Dr King to voice his opposition to the conflict. This, plus his 1968 Poor People's Campaign with its call to restructure the economy to support working people, led to a dip in his popularity and increased surveillance by the FBI, but he continued campaigning. On 3 April 1968, in Memphis, Tennessee he gave his final speech. In it he said:

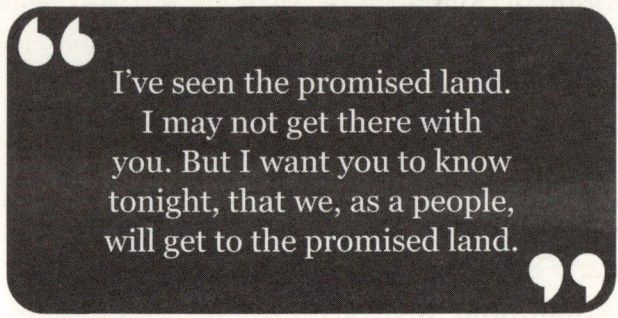

> I've seen the promised land. I may not get there with you. But I want you to know tonight, that we, as a people, will get to the promised land.

At one minute past six on the evening of Thursday 4 April, at just thirty-nine years of age, he was assassinated.

His widow, Coretta Scott King, established the Martin Luther King, Jr Center for Nonviolent Social Change in 1968 to carry on his work. In 1977 Dr King was posthumously awarded the **Presidential Medal of Freedom**, and in 1994 he and his wife received the Congressional Gold Medal. Calls to establish Martin Luther King Jr Day began in 1968. It was signed into law in 1984 and by 2000 was being celebrated in all fifty states, on the third Monday of January each year, to commemorate the extraordinary life of Dr King.

11 JANUARY ~ SISTER ROSETTA THARPE

Sister Rosetta Tharpe, a guitarist, singer and songwriter, pioneered rock and roll music in America. She was born Rosetta Nubin in Alabama in 1915 to musical parents who picked cotton for work. By the age of six she was performing gospel music in church, and she started travelling with her mother as part of a religious musical troupe.

In the 1930s Rosetta Tharpe became a recording star. She played electric guitar, which was at that time very unusual for a woman. She played in nightclubs such as the Cotton Club in Harlem, and was often criticized for playing gospel music alongside jazz and blues performers. She continued her trailblazing career during the Second World War, recording songs to entertain the troops overseas. Her 1944 song 'Strange Things Happening Every Day' is considered by some people to be the first ever rock and roll record.

In recent years there has been more recognition of her influence on popular music, and in 2008 the state of Pennsylvania declared 11 January to be Sister Rosetta Tharpe Day. In 2018 she was finally inducted into the Rock & Roll Hall of Fame.

> **DID YOU KNOW?**
>
> Sister Rosetta Tharpe's guitar was a Les Paul SG Custom '61, made by the Gibson guitar company. In 2002, to introduce Tharpe to a whole new generation of listeners and players, Gibson made a new version of this guitar and released *Shout, Sister, Shout!*, a short documentary about her life.

12 JANUARY - JUANA RAMÍREZ

12 January marks the birth date of the Venezuelan national hero, rebel commander Juana 'La Avanzadora' Ramírez. She was born in 1790 to an enslaved African woman who had been bought by General Andrés Rojas (likely her father), an officer of the Spanish forces ruling the colony of Venezuela.

Monument to Juana Ramírez

Ramírez had worked as a laundress in the city of Maturín up until 1810, when Venezuela began its war for independence from Spain. She immediately joined the rebel forces where her intelligence and skill propelled her through the ranks to become commander of a one-hundred strong, all-women artillery unit. She and her unit gained a reputation for fearlessness in the many battles they fought around Maturín. In 1813 they were called to the Battle of Alto de los Godos against the superior forces of General Domingo de Monteverde. Although seriously outnumbered, the rebels won, thanks, in part, to a courageous and dramatic charge against the Spanish led by a sword-wielding Ramírez. It was this deed that earned her the nickname 'La Avanzadora' (The Advancer).

Over the course of the war, as she continued to organize and fight, Ramírez's reputation grew to legendary proportions. But not long after her death in 1856, her name faded from history. A century and a half later Ramírez's reputation was resurrected and her deeds officially recognized. On 23 October 2015 her remains were moved and interred in Venezuela's National Mausoleum of Heroes in a state ceremony. Ramírez is one of only a handful of women and the first Black woman to receive this honour.

13 JANUARY ~ SHONDA RHIMES

Shonda Rhimes, a Golden Globe-winning television producer and screenwriter, was born in Chicago on 13 January 1970. She was the youngest of six children. Both of her parents worked in higher education, her mother as a professor and her father in university administration. Rhimes studied screenwriting at university, where she graduated top of her class.

Rhimes became famous in 2005 as the showrunner – the person who creates a television show, produces it and leads the team of writers – of the medical drama *Grey's Anatomy*. Rhimes then set up her own television production company, Shondaland, and has gone on to create, write and produce many popular television shows including the political drama *Scandal* and the global streaming hit *Bridgerton*.

Bridgerton is based on a series of books written by Julia Quinn, set in Georgian England, which Rhimes discovered when she went on holiday. The books follow the lives of eight siblings, each book focusing on how a particular sibling falls in love and marries. Rhimes has reimagined the stories, making the Bridgerton world multi-ethnic, where people of colour from the **British Empire** are part of society across all of the social classes.

> **DID YOU KNOW?**
>
> *Bridgerton* includes characters inspired by real-life people, such as Queen Charlotte, who some people have argued was of mixed ancestry, and the Black Georgian boxer Bill Richmond (see 17 October).

14 JANUARY ~ MALORIE BLACKMAN

Children's author Malorie Blackman was born in 1962 in London. Her books have always featured characters from diverse backgrounds, but her book *Noughts and Crosses* (published in January 2001) was her first story to focus on race and racism. It is set in an alternate reality, where Africans colonized and enslaved Europeans.

Racism and discrimination exist in the book, but are reversed – Crosses are the dark-skinned people who are privileged, while Noughts are light-skinned people whom society treats as racially inferior. The book is written from the perspectives of Callum (a Nought) and Sephy (a Cross) and explores themes of interracial relationships, racial oppression and resistance. The book was a huge success and won many awards, and Blackman went on to write more books set in the Noughts and Crosses universe.

Blackman's books are popular across the world, and have been translated into a number of different languages. In 2013 she became the UK's Children's Laureate – a two-year role that is awarded to celebrate the achievements of a writer or illustrator of books for children and young people, which allows them to be an ambassador for children's literature. In her time as Laureate, Blackman established the Young Adult Literature Convention and helped to set up Project Remix, an initiative that inspires teenagers to develop their own creative projects.

> **❝**
> You're a Nought and I'm a Cross and there's nowhere for us to be, nowhere for us to go where we'd be left in peace . . . That's why I started crying. That's why I couldn't stop. For all the things we might've had and all the things we're never going to have.
>
> Malorie Blackman, *Noughts and Crosses* **❞**

15 JANUARY ~ JOSEPH KNIGHT

The case of Knight vs. Wedderburn was a legal dispute that started in Edinburgh in 1772 when an enslaved African man, Joseph Knight, heard about the outcome of the Somerset case in England (see 21 June), which seemed to suggest that slavery was not legal on English soil.

Knight had been born in Africa and was captured by slave traders as a boy. He was then transported across the Atlantic and sold into captivity in the Caribbean. He was bought by a man called John Wedderburn, who brought him to Scotland in 1769 to work as a slave in his household.

Although Scotland had different laws from England, the Somerset ruling inspired Knight to demand payment for his work from John Wedderburn. Wedderburn refused, and so Knight left his house and started living as a free man.

Incensed by this behaviour, Wedderburn had Knight arrested and took him to court to demand his return to enslavement. Wedderburn won that case, but Knight took the case to a higher court and the decision was overturned in Knight's favour. Legal challenges continued between the two until 1777. On 15 January 1778 the Justices of the Peace court in Perth, Scotland, made their final judgement on the case of Knight vs. Wedderburn, ruling that slavery was illegal in Scotland.

On 16 January 2006 Ellen Johnson Sirleaf was inaugurated as president of Liberia, becoming Africa's first elected female head of state.

Sean Hurt, CC BY 2.0 via Wikimedia Commons

Johnson Sirleaf was born in Liberia's capital city, Monrovia, in 1938. In the 1960s she attended university in the US, eventually gaining a master's degree from Harvard. She returned to Liberia in the early 1970s where she became first the assistant minister of finance in the treasury department, and later the minister of finance, before the government was overthrown in a coup d'état in 1980. Johnson Sirleaf spent many years living in exile, working in banking and then for the United Nations Development Programme. She returned to Liberia to run for president in 1997 and was finally elected in 2005.

Johnson Sirleaf served two full terms as president, before she retired and oversaw the first peaceful, democratic transition of power in Liberia in seventy-three years. In 2011 she was awarded the Nobel Peace Prize for her role in securing the end of the fourteen-year-long civil war in Liberia.

17 JANUARY ~ MICHELLE OBAMA

Michelle LaVaughn Robinson Obama was born on 17 January 1964 on the South Side of Chicago.

After studying sociology and African American studies, and then graduating from Harvard Law School, she worked as an attorney in Chicago, where she met her future husband, Barack Obama, when she was assigned to be his mentor. As her career developed, her commitment to social and charitable projects led her to work for non-profit organizations before moving into student services and community-focused roles at the University of Chicago.

She became world famous as the first Black First Lady of the United States when her husband successfully ran for the office of president in the 2008 election (see 4 November). As First Lady she took on her own projects, such as 'Let's Move!', which focused on healthy eating and exercise for children in the USA, and 'Let Girls Learn' which championed education for girls across the world. She also used her platform to showcase the work of American and African fashion designers.

Obama's autobiography, *Becoming*, was an award-winning bestseller. Since 2020 Obama has also hosted her own podcast and co-founded a production company with her husband that aims to give a platform to diverse voices, stories and perspectives.

In 2018, 2019 and 2020, Obama was voted the most admired woman in America in a Gallup poll, and in 2020 she was inducted into America's National Women's Hall of Fame.

18 JANUARY - THE NEW CROSS FIRE

In the early hours of 18 January 1981, thirteen young Black people were killed when a fire swept through a house in the New Cross area of London. They had been attending a birthday party. The eldest victim was twenty-two and the youngest was just fourteen. One survivor died by suicide two years later.

The police did not begin a proper investigation into the cause of the fire. Over the following weeks they dismissed appeals from the families of the victims, who wanted the fire investigated as a potentially racially motivated attack. Media coverage of the fire was not sympathetic to the victims and their families, and did not support their calls for justice. The New Cross Massacre Action Committee was established to campaign on behalf of the families and community. They organized the Black People's Day of Action (see 2 March) in which around 20,000 Black protesters marched for over eight hours, from Deptford in south London to central London, to bring attention to the case and to demand a proper police investigation. Although it was on the whole peaceful, some press outlets unfairly reported it as a riot rather than a protest march.

Two inquests have been held to examine the New Cross Fire, one in 1981 and one in 2004. Both recorded an open verdict, which means that the jury agreed that the deaths of the victims were suspicious, but that they couldn't agree who was guilty of the crime. The New Cross Fire is remembered as a turning point, when different generations of Black people came together to expose and challenge racist attitudes within the British police and media.

19 JANUARY - EARTHA KITT

Eartha Kitt was a singer, dancer, actor, activist and author of African American and Native-American descent. She was born in South Carolina in January 1927 and had a very eventful life – between 1956 and 2001 she wrote four autobiographies!

Kitt began her career in the 1940s when she appeared in Broadway musicals, before becoming a recording artist. By the 1950s she had several Top 30 records in the US charts, and by the 1960s she was acting in roles such as Catwoman in the *Batman* television series.

Kitt became a civil rights activist, campaigning for peace and racial justice in the 1950s and 60s, and later for LGBTQ+ rights in the 1990s and 2000s. However, statements she made during a question and answer session at the White House on 19 January 1968, criticizing America's involvement in the Vietnam War, had a very negative effect on her career. After that offers of work disappeared for over a decade.

In 1978, however, Kitt returned to Broadway and won two Tony awards for her performances in *Timbuktu!* and *The Wild Party*.

She died in 2008, aged eighty-one.

In the 2000s Kitt voiced the role of Yzma, the villain in the Disney movies *The Emperor's New Groove* and its sequels.

DID YOU KNOW?

20 JANUARY - AMANDA GORMAN

Amanda Gorman is an award-winning African American poet and activist. As a child she had a speech impediment, and she continues to be very sensitive to sound and has difficulties processing it. Her mother, an English teacher, who Gorman cites as the major influence in her life, encouraged her love of words, and her talent was soon recognized. In 2017, at the age of nineteen, she was named America's first National Youth Poet Laureate. This is a title given annually to a young person to recognize the quality of their poetry and skill with spoken word performance, and their active commitment to activism and social justice.

Gorman was only 22 years old when she wrote and performed the poem 'The Hill We Climb' at the inauguration of America's 47th president, Joe Biden, on 20 January 2021. This made her the sixth poet to perfom at an inaurguarion and also the youngest inaugural poet in the history of the US.

Chairman of the Joint Chiefs of Staff from Washington DC United States, CC BY 2.0, via Wikimedia Commons

Amanda Gorman recites her inaugural poem, 'The Hill We Climb', during the 59th presidential inauguration ceremony in Washington, Jan. 20, 2021

In 2016 Gorman founded One Pen One Page, an organization to promote creative writing and its power to make social change. Aimed at young people, the organization partners with other groups around the world in order to support literacy on a global scale.

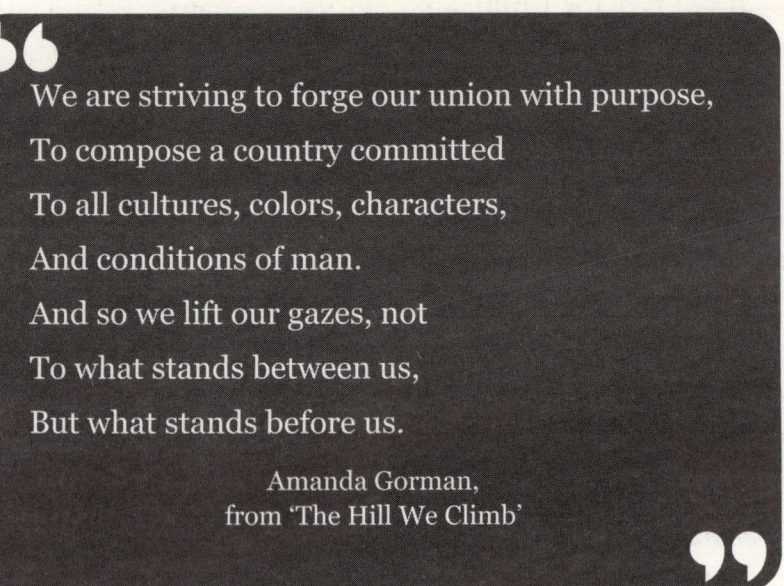

> We are striving to forge our union with purpose,
>
> To compose a country committed
>
> To all cultures, colors, characters,
>
> And conditions of man.
>
> And so we lift our gazes, not
>
> To what stands between us,
>
> But what stands before us.
>
> Amanda Gorman,
> from 'The Hill We Climb'

21 JANUARY - THE FREE BREAKFAST PROGRAM

In January 1969, eleven children enjoyed a free breakfast at St Augustine's church in Oakland, California. Within a week there were ten times that number. Within a year the Black Panthers' Free Breakfast for Children Program had spread to a further twenty-three cities and had fed around 20,000 children.

Established by Bobby Seale and Huey P. Newton in 1966, the Black Panther Party for Self Defense was initially founded as a reaction to police violence and oppression, but soon the community began to turn to the organization for help in other areas. The Free Breakfast Program was just one of the Survival Programs the Panthers put in place to provide support to Black communities where they were being failed by the government. The programs included free ambulances, free clothing, dental treatment and research into sickle cell anaemia where over half a million people were tested for the condition.

The positive publicity that the Breakfast Program in particular gave the Black Panthers was worrying to those who regarded the party as a danger to national security. In May 1969, J. Edgar Hoover, the director of the FBI. expressed those concerns in a message sent through the organization stating that it was the greatest threat to their efforts against the Panthers. To smash the program, the FBI, with assistance from local law enforcement agencies, spread disinformation, intimidated parents and children and raided buildings, destroying food and resources. The attacks were devastating and despite the best efforts of the volunteers, the program closed down in the early 1970s.

Although the program did not last, it had highlighted a need to provide meals for children living in poverty. In 1975 the US government expanded its funding to provide lunches and breakfasts for children in public schools.

22 JANUARY ~ GEORGE FOREMAN

George Foreman is an African American sportsman, famous for his career as a heavyweight boxer and, later in his life, as an entrepreneur.

Born on 10 January 1949 in Texas, Foreman had a difficult childhood. He dropped out of school at the age of fifteen and began training as a boxer while working in the Job Corp. His talent was quickly recognized and in 1968 he represented the USA at the summer Olympics, where he won the heavyweight gold medal. A year later he turned professional. He became World Heavyweight Champion on 22 January 1973, after defeating Joe Frazier in a match in Jamaica, billed as *The Sunshine Showdown*. He successfully defended his title twice before losing it in October 1974 to Muhammad Ali in Zaire, Africa, in a fight known as *The Rumble in the Jungle* (see 25 February).

Foreman retired from boxing for the first time in 1977. He had a near-death experience after a boxing defeat, which led him to become a Christian and to train to become a minister. However, after ten years he returned to boxing, partly to help raise money to fund a youth centre he had established. In 1994, at the age of forty-five, he beat Michael Moorer in Las Vegas to become the oldest Heavyweight Champion in history. In 1997 he retired from boxing for the final time, with a record of seventy-six wins and only five losses!

Outside of his boxing career, Foreman is best known as an entrepreneur and the promoter of the internationally best-selling George Foreman Grill.

23 JANUARY - JORDAN PEELE

Jordan Peele is an African American actor, comedian, producer and director. As one half of a comedy duo with Keegan-Michael Key, Peele worked on the comedy sketch shows *Mad TV* and *Key & Peele* in the 2000s and 2010s.

In 2012 he founded his own production company, Monkeypaw Productions. He has produced many TV programmes including *The Twilight Zone*, and is now most famous for his work in film.

On 23 January 2017, Peele's first film as a director, *Get Out*, premiered at the Sundance Film Festival. *Get Out* is a horror film that tells the story of a young Black man who travels with his white girlfriend to meet her family for the first time. The film was highly praised for its originality and quality, and it was nominated for Best Picture, Best Director and Best Actor at the Academy Awards in 2018. It won in the Best Original Screenplay category, making Peele the first Black recipient of the award.

© Daniel Benavides (2019), Wikimedia Commons

24 JANUARY - ROBERT L. JOHNSON

Robert L. Johnson is an African American businessman and entrepreneur who founded the company Black Entertainment Television (BET).

Launched in January 1980, BET showed a mix of music videos featuring Black recording artists and Black comedy programmes. Over the years it added other programmes including news, a talk show and reality TV.

When Johnson sold BET in 2001 he became America's first Black billionaire. In 2002 he bought the basketball team the Charlotte Bobcats, becoming the first African American owner of an American major sports league team. Johnson is also a philanthropist who has raised funds for causes such as hurricane relief in the Bahamas and the charity Malaria No More.

> Graphic designer Cheryl D. Miller designed the original BET logo. An award-winning pioneer of the **decolonization** of graphic design, her work includes **NASA**'s 1992 poster of Dr Mae Jemison, the first Black female astronaut (see 20 September).

DID YOU KNOW?

25 JANUARY - HUE AND CRY ADVERTISEMENTS

In recent years, newspapers from the past have been digitally scanned and made available to read online. In these digitized sources historians have found hundreds of advertisements in the newspapers of Georgian Britain for the sale of enslaved African people.

They have also found 'hue and cry' advertisements for the capture and return of 'runaway slaves'. In British law, a 'hue and cry' is an appeal for bystanders to help capture someone who has broken the law, so these advertisements show us that enslaved African people who attempted to leave their owners were being treated as criminals.

ELOPED from Mr. SAMUEL DELPRATT, Merchant, at Briftol, and come to London, A NEGRO MAN, about 17 or 18 Years old, Five Feet Five or Six Inches high, had on when he left Briftol, a brown Livery Coat lined with Red, red Button Holes and Collar, red Waiftcoat, a Pair of old Leather Breeches pieced at the Knee, a black Leather Cap, and a Pair of black ribbed Stockings, anfwers to the Name of JOHN; if he fhould offer to fhip himfelf as a free Man, on Board any Ship, by directing a Line to the Jamaica Coffee Houfe, for Capt. William Tomlinfon, or to Mr. Jofeph Malpas, Jeweller, in Wood Street, Cheapfide, whatever Expence in ftopping the faid Negro fhall be repaid with Thanks, and Six Guineas Reward.

Hue and cry advertisement for return of enslaved person – Joshua Steele
Covent Garden Journal, London, 25 January 1752, p.4

This example, published in the *Covent Garden Journal* on 25 January 1752 is a 'hue and cry' advertisement for the return of an enslaved man named Joshua Steele.

26 JANUARY – PUBLIC ENEMY

On 26 January 2020 the hip-hop group Public Enemy were presented with a Lifetime Achievement Award from the Rock & Roll Hall of Fame. The group was founded in 1985 by Chuck D and Flavor Flav, who met at university in New York.

From the beginning, Public Enemy's music was inventive and political – it addressed racism in America – and experimented with sound, drawing together the diverse musical influences of jazz, funk and metal.

Public Enemy's third album, *Fear of a Black Planet*, released in 1990, is their most successful. The single 'Fight the Power' from that album is one of the most influential hip-hop songs of all time, and was used by the African American director Spike Lee as the theme song for his 1989 film *Do the Right Thing* (see 26 August).

In 2013, Public Enemy members Chuck D, Flava Flav, Professor Griff and Terminator X were inducted into the Rock & Roll Hall of Fame by Spike Lee and actor Harry Belafonte (see 1 March), and hailed as a band whose musical, political and philosophical influence has been revolutionary.

Public Enemy performing in Hamburg, March 2000

27 JANUARY - MARY SEACOLE

On 27 January 1855 a Dutch ship set sail from London for Constantinople (which is now known as Istanbul). One of the passengers was forty-nine-year-old Mary Jane Seacole. Her destination was the Crimea in Eastern Europe, where Britain was engaged in a war against Russia.

Born Mary Jane Grant in Jamaica in 1805, she was the daughter of a white Scottish man and a free Black Jamaican woman. Her father was a lieutenant in the British Army and her mother ran a boarding house and was also a healer – or 'doctress' – who used traditional herbal remedies to treat her patients. Seacole followed in her mother's footsteps as a healer. In 1836 she married an Englishman, Edwin Horatio Hamilton Seacole, but he died just five years later. In 1854 she visited England and heard of the appeal being made for nurses to travel to the Crimea to serve in army hospitals. Seacole wrote to the War Office asking to join the next group of nurses who were being sent to the Crimea, but her offer was rejected. She suspected that she was rejected due to racial prejudice. Undeterred, Seacole decided to make her own way there and on arrival she opened what she named the 'British Hotel' to offer food, treatment and a place for ill and injured soldiers to recover and rest.

Seacole told the story of her contribution to the Crimean War in her autobiography, *Wonderful Adventures of Mrs. Seacole in Many Lands.*

28 JANUARY – RICHMOND BARTHÉ

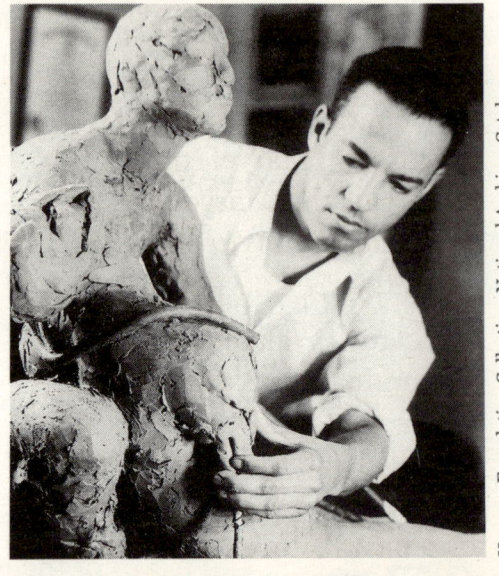

The sculptor and painter Richmond Barthé was born 28 January 1901 in Bay St Louis, Mississippi. He was interested in art from an early age and in 1924 his talent prompted fellow worshippers at his local Catholic church to raise the funds to pay for his tuition at the School of the Art Institute of Chicago. His first art exhibitions in 1927 and 1928 were successful, winning him commissions (including a bust of Toussaint L'Ouverture – see 20 May) that allowed him to continue and complete his studies.

Barthé graduated in 1929 and moved to New York to establish his own art studio in 1930. He quickly became involved in the artistic and literary community of the Harlem Renaissance. Barthé's work was figurative, and most of his subjects were Black. Unable to afford to pay models to sit for him, his early work took inspiration from actors, dancers and singers. Over the next two decades, Barthé's career flourished, and he won a Rosenwald fellowship in 1930 and the Guggenheim Fellowship in 1940. Bronzes by Barthé and paintings by Jacob Lawrence became the first works by African American artists to enter the permanent art collections of New York's Whitney Museum and Metropolitan Museum of Art.

In 1949 Barthé moved to Jamaica, where he lived and worked for twenty years, before spending his last years in California. He died on 5 March 1989, at the age of eighty-eight.

29 JANUARY ~ BLACK PANTHER

On 29 January 2018 the superhero film *Black Panther* was released.

The character of King T'Challa, aka Black Panther, first appeared in Marvel comics in 1966 and he had been introduced as part of the Marvel cinematic universe in the film *Captain America: Civil War* in 2016.

Black Panther tells the story of T'Challa returning to his homeland Wakanda to be crowned king. The film had a predominantly Black cast, led by the late Chadwick Boseman in the role of T'Challa, and it was the first Marvel film to have a Black director (Ryan Coogler). The film was critically acclaimed, and was the first superhero movie to be nominated for a Best Picture Oscar.

The costume and visual designs for the kingdom of Wakanda drew on a range of African influences, with a futurist twist, and the Wakandan language devised for the film was based on Xhosa, one of the languages of South Africa. *Black Panther* broke box office records, becoming the highest grossing film by a Black director.

> **DID YOU KNOW?**
>
> Fashion designer Ozwald Boateng (see 5 May) created some of the clothing for the film. Known for his African influenced work, he said it was an honour to have his pieces included.

30 JANUARY - CLAUDIA JONES

The writer and political activist Claudia Jones was born in Trinidad and moved to the USA at the age of eight. After leaving school, Claudia became an active member of the Young Communist League, and she often wrote for their newspaper. She went on to write and edit a number of political newspapers, and was a member of a number of communist organizations. Communism was regarded with deep suspicion by the American government at that time and her involvement in these organizations eventually led to her imprisonment. By 1955 the authorities decided that she had to leave the USA and she was deported to Britain in 1955.

Claudia continued her political work in her new country with England's growing African-Caribbean community. In March 1958 she founded *The West Indian Gazette*, Britain's first major Black newspaper. The paper reported the news, published essays and shared reviews and ideas about the arts and culture of the West Indian community. Later that year, after the horror of the racial attacks in Notting Hill (see 29 August) and in Nottingham (see 23 August), Claudia helped to organize an indoor carnival to celebrate Caribbean culture. It was held in St Pancras Town Hall on 30 January 1959 and televised on the BBC. Money from the sale of the event's souvenir brochure went towards paying the police fines of young people, both Black and white, who had been caught up in the Notting Hill riots. Over the years the Caribbean Carnival eventually became the Notting Hill Carnival, which is now the second largest street carnival in the world (see 31 August).

31 JANUARY – THE SONS OF AFRICA

In the year 1787 a group of Black Britons founded an anti-slavery group called the Sons of Africa. The group, led by Olaudah Equiano and Ottobah Cugoano (see 6 April and 24 September), was made up of men who had either been enslaved themselves or who were descendants of enslaved Africans.

The Sons of Africa campaigned for the abolition of slavery – they wrote letters, made speeches, attended meetings and were the authors of pamphlets, newspaper articles, poems and books, often sharing the details of their experiences of enslavement.

Enslaved people aboard a ship being shackled before being put in the hold. A wooden engraving by Joseph Swain

Not many records remain of their activities, but we do know the names of some of the members: Joseph Almze, Cojoh Ammere, James Bailey, Boughwa Gegansmel, Jasper Goree, Thomas Jones, George Robert Mandeville, Thomas Oxford, William Stevens and George Wallace. The role that the Sons of Africa played in the abolitionist movement was critically important. They provided eyewitness testimony to the brutal realities of slavery, and were also living proof of the humanity, intelligence and worth of Black people, challenging the racist assumptions that were often used to justify and excuse the trade in enslaved Africans.

1 FEBRUARY - LANGSTON HUGHES

The African American writer, poet and political activist Langston Hughes was born on 1 February 1901 in Joplin, Missouri. In the 1920s and 30s he became one of the leaders of a vibrant intellectual and cultural movement known as the Harlem Renaissance.

Hughes began writing poetry as a child and wrote his most famous poem, 'The Negro Speaks of Rivers', the summer after he finished high school. At the heart of Hughes's writing was a focus on racial pride and valuing Black culture. As well as being a poet, Hughes was a correspondent for several African American newspapers, and he wrote plays and books for both adults and children. Some of his work also featured on jazz poetry albums. On his 1958 album *Weary Blues* Hughes recited his poetry with musical accompaniment from jazz musicians Charles Mingus and Leonard Feather.

Hughes died in 1967 and his ashes were laid to rest underneath the floor in the Schomburg Center for Research in Black Culture in Harlem.

> I been scared and battered.
> My hopes the wind done scattered.
> Snow has friz me,
> Sun has baked me,
>
> Looks like between 'em they done
> Tried to make me
>
> Stop laughin', stop lovin', stop livin'—
> But I don't care!
> I'm still here!
>
> Langston Hughes, 'Still Here'

2 FEBRUARY - THE GREENSBORO FOUR

On 1 February 1960, in the town of Greensboro, North Carolina, four African American students – David Richmond, Franklin McCain, Jibreel Khazan (Ezell Blair Jr.) and Joseph McNeil – walked into an F. W. Woolworth store. They bought items they needed and then headed to the shop's lunch counter. In the southern United States at that time, **segregation** policies meant that sitting and being served food at the lunch counter was reserved for white people only.

The four students had decided to make a stand. Once they reached the lunch counter they sat down and each asked the server for a coffee and a doughnut. As expected, they were refused service. A Black Woolworth's employee advised them to move, as did the store manager. The police were called and when they arrived an officer came up to the four young men. He got out his nightstick (a metal weapon carried by American

(From left) Joseph McNeil and Franklin McCain, two of the Greensboro Four who the day before had sat at the 'whites only' counter of a Woolworth store, came back on 2 February, 1960, with two others – Billy Smith and Clarence Henderson.
Jack Moebes/*Greensboro News & Record*

45

police officers) and walked behind where the men sat, hitting it against his hand threateningly. Still, the four men remained peacefully sitting in their chairs. Eventually, the manager, Clarence L. Harris, decided to close the store early, and the men left.

A photograph of the four men, taken on the first day of the protest, helped the protest spread. It appeared in the *Greensboro Record* newspaper on 2 February.

The men returned to the shop the next day along with sixteen more friends, and they warned the manager that each day they would be joined by more students. After this, the protest and reports about it started to grow day after day. By 4 February there were several hundred students taking part in the lunch counter sit-in, protesting against the racist law. By the second week, the protest had spread to other cities in the south and thousands of young people were taking part. Later that month students began a boycott of stores that had segregated lunch counters, causing sales in those stores to fall dramatically.

Eventually, on 25 July 1960, Harris, the manager of the Greensboro store, decided to end segregation at the store's lunch counter. He asked the store's lunch counter manager, Rachel Holt, to select some of the store's Black employees to change out of their work clothes, sit at the lunch counter and order some food. So, Geneva Tisdale, Susie Morrison, Anetha Jones and Charles Bess became the first Black people to be served at a Woolworth's lunch counter. No reporters were invited and no photographs were taken of this historical moment. In the following months many other stores desegregated their lunch counters, but it wasn't until the 1964 Civil Rights Act that laws were passed to ban the segregation of public facilities in America (see 2 July).

3 FEBRUARY - THE 6888 BATTALION

In 1945 the United States Army found itself with a problem. Millions of parcels and letters, posted by Americans to their loved ones serving in Europe in the Second World War, had not been delivered. Not hearing from their loved

Photographs of American Military Activities, National Archives Catalog

ones back home meant that the morale of the American soldiers was suffering. To solve the problem, the 6888 Battalion, a unit of 855 female African American soldiers, was sent to Britain to sort the post. They arrived on 3 February 1945.

The post sorting went on twenty-four hours a day, with the unit split over three eight-hour shifts, seven days a week. By the end of the war they had processed 17 million pieces of mail. Army authorities had estimated that it would take six months, maybe even a year, to clear the postal backlog in Europe – but the 6888 managed to do this work in just three months!

The 6888 Battalion had been formed in 1944 and was the brainchild of African American educationalist Dr Mary McLeod Bethune (see 10 July). At that time the US army was racially segregated, and Bethune was keen that more African American women should get the opportunity to play their part in the war. The unit was led by Major Charity Adams, who was the first African American officer in the Women's Army Auxiliary Corps, the women's branch of the US Army.

On 20 February 2019, the 'SixTripleEight' received the Meritorious Unit Commendation for Meritorious Service during Military Operations for their work to solve the US Army's postal crisis in 1945–6.

4 FEBRUARY ~ TSITSI DANGAREMBGA

Tsitsi Dangarembga is a writer and film-maker from Zimbabwe. She was born on 4 February 1959 in what was at that time Southern Rhodesia. Her family moved to England for a few years but returned in 1965, as colonial rule ended and Southern Rhodesia became Zimbabwe.

© David Clarke, Ayebia Clarke Publishing Ltd. Wikimedia Commons

Dangarembga's first book, *Nervous Conditions*, was highly praised, winning the Commonwealth Writers' Prize in 1989. It is part of a series of three books that make up her Tambudzai Trilogy. The books explore the journey of Zimbabwe from the end of colonial rule to the present day, through the life of a girl called Tambu and her family.

After training as a film director in Berlin, Dangarembga founded Nyerai Films, and also the Institute of Creative Arts for Progress in Africa. This organization helps to train and mentor African film-makers, and promote African film internationally.

Much of Dangarembga's work focuses on politics, and she has been a consistent critic of the Zimbabwean government. In 2020, amid growing public discontent, the government launched a crackdown on opposition and activists. Dangarembga was arrested while attending a peaceful anti-corruption protest but was charged and later convicted of incitement to commit violence. After a campaign by Amnesty International and PEN International (a human rights organization that promotes freedom of expression and international writing) the High Court overturned her conviction in May 2023. She continues to speak out against the government.

5 FEBRUARY - NILE RODGERS

Nile Rodgers is an award-winning musician, record producer and composer. He was born in New York on 19 September 1952. Rodgers played flute and clarinet before settling on guitar at sixteen. As a teenager, alongside developing his musical talent, he began to take a keen interest in politics and activism.

In 1970 Rodgers met musician Bernie Edwards and in 1972 they formed the Big Apple Band. They changed their name to Chic in 1977 and had chart success with singles 'Le Freak', 'I Want Your Love' and 'Good Times'. They were invited to work as record producers and began producing hit records with artists such as Sister Sledge. After Chic was disbanded in 1979 Rodgers became one of the world's most highly sought after record producers, working with artists such as David Bowie, Madonna, Diana Ross and Mick Jagger. He also produced soundtracks for films and video games.

Following the September 11 terror attacks in America, in which nearly 3,000 people were killed, Rodgers recruited over 200 musicians and celebrities to record the single 'We are Family'. In 2002 he set up the We Are Family Foundation with his partner, Nancy Hunt. The organization works to promote peace and understanding and to nurture the talents and ideas of children and young people.

Rodgers has received many awards for his work, including being inducted into the Songwriters Hall of Fame in 2016 and the Rock & Roll Hall of Fame in 2017. On 5 February 2023, he was given a Grammy Lifetime Achievement Award in recognition of his outstanding contribution to music.

© Raph_PH/WikiCommons

6 FEBRUARY - BOB MARLEY

The musician and songwriter Robert Nesta Marley was born on 6 February 1945 in Nine Mile, Jamaica. He began making music with his school friend Neville Livingston, who later became known as Bunny Wailer. In the early 1960s they started a band with their friend Peter Tosh, which they eventually called The Wailers. Their music style was reggae, but with heavy ska and rocksteady influences. Over the next twenty years Marley recorded numerous songs both with the band and as a solo artist. He became recognized as a pioneer of reggae music and recorded global hits such as 'Redemption Song' and 'Revolution'.

Marley became a **Rastafarian** in the 1960s, and this influenced his music and lyrics. He was also a proud Jamaican and a campaigner for social justice there. In 1976 he planned a free concert called Smile Jamaica aiming to bring people together and promote peace. The government then moved the country's general election to the same date. This angered Marley and made him a target for some rival political parties who thought that the concert would help the government win the election. On 3 December 1976 he survived an assassination attempt and, two days later, the concert went ahead and Marley performed.

Marley was also a strong opponent of **apartheid** in South Africa and he supported African independence movements. In 1978 the **United Nations** awarded him the Peace Medal of the Third World and in 1981 he was awarded the Jamaican Order of Merit.

Marley died from cancer at the age of thirty-six. He had been ill for four years, although he continued to work during this time. He was given a state funeral in Jamaica. In 2001 he was posthumously given a Grammy Lifetime Achievement Award and in 2019 English Heritage placed a blue plaque on the London home in Chelsea where he had lived in 1977 while recording the best-selling album *Exodus* with The Wailers.

7 FEBRUARY - THE KINGDOM OF KUSH

The ancient kingdom of Kush was located in Nubia, in Africa. Today its territories lie under the southern region of Egypt and northern Sudan. It flourished from around 1070 BCE to around 550 CE, and was an important trading nation, independent from the Persian, Greek and Roman empires.

Laurent de Walick/WikiCommons

The Kushite civilization had its own language, technology, religion and a strong economy. It was famous for the skills of its archers, some of whom went to serve in armies in neighbouring countries. It also had its own distinct style of architecture and art – like the Egyptians, the Kushites built temples and pyramids, but they decorated them in their own unique way, carving scenes of African life deep into the walls. They were also famous for their very fine pottery, which was painted and stamped with patterns made from geometric shapes, plants and animals.

In the 720sBCE reports reached Kush that Kushite soldiers serving in the Egyptian army were being mistreated. Kush decided to invade its neighbour Egypt, and won a victory that gave it imperial control over Egypt. Kushite rulers took on the title of pharaoh. For the next fifty years they revived the practice of building pyramids for themselves as rulers over Egypt. In 677BCE the Kushites were defeated by the Assyrians, bringing their rule over Egypt to an end. In around 330CE Kush was finally invaded by the Kingdom of Axum (see 3 October), a kingdom that lay to the south, in what today covers parts of Ethiopia, Eritrea, Djibouti and Sudan. Kush had finally lost its independence and became part of the Aksumite Empire.

8 FEBRUARY - JACQUES FRANCIS

Jacques Francis was born around 1527 and is thought to have come from Arguin Island, in what is now Mauritania. He was an expert salvage diver who likely trained to dive in the waters around the island, to depths of seven to nine metres, to collect valuable pearls and shells from the seabed.

In 1546 Francis was employed by a salvage master called Peter Paulo Corsi. Francis was to be the lead diver in a team hired to salvage weapons from the wreck of the *Mary Rose* – King Henry VIII's favourite ship – which had sunk off Portsmouth in 1545. Several previous attempts to salvage her valuable weaponry had failed, but Francis and his diving team successfuly retrieved much of it.

A year later a group of Italian merchants accused Corsi of illegally salvaging metals from a wreck in Southampton. Jacques Francis was called to give testimony in defence of his master, and in 1548 he became the first known African to give evidence in an English court of law. As he was a foreigner, a Black man and a non-Christian, this was highly unusual.

Francis gave a dignified testimony. However, one of Corsi's accusers tried to discredit him, saying that he was an uncivilized slave who had no right to speak in an English court. 'A morisco, born where they are not christened, and slave to ... [Corsi] ... no credit nor faith ought to be given to his sayings, as in other strange Christian countries it is to no such slave given'. This objection was rejected by the High Court, who accorded Jacques Francis the same legal rights as any Englishman in a rare acknowledgement of a Black man's humanity in Tudor times.

9 FEBRUARY - THE BENIN BRONZES

The Benin Bronzes are a group of sculptures, plaques and royal ornaments made by skilled artists in the Kingdom of Benin, in what is now Edo State in Nigeria. They were cast in bronze and brass and carved from ivory. Thousands of these bronzes were created from the 13th century onwards at the palace of the Oba of Benin, and they were displayed and used as part of the ceremonial life of the court (see 17 November).

On 9 February 1897 British armed forces entered Benin City. Over the next nine days they ransacked the city, including the Oba's palace. Thousands of the Benin Bronzes were seized. Some were given to the British Museum, and other museums and collectors across Europe and America acquired the rest. The artistic quality of the bronzes meant that they became collector's items.

Nigeria gained its independence in 1960 and since then a campaign to return the Benin Bronzes to their homeland has grown. Since 2020 some European and American museums and universities have begun to return Benin Bronzes so that they can be displayed in Nigeria. The new Edo Museum of West African Art will house returned bronzes as well as modern and contemporary art.

10 FEBRUARY - STUART HALL

On 10 February 2014, Professor Stuart Hall, Britain's most celebrated Black intellectual, died. He was a pioneer who helped to develop the academic discipline of **cultural studies**. Hall was an anti-racist campaigner who argued that many cultures contribute to society, and therefore they should all be valued by it. His work examined and challenged how things like film, television, newspapers, magazines, art and photography all shape the way that race and identity are viewed and understood.

Hall was born in Jamaica in 1932. He was descended from African, European and Indian ancestors. In later years he described how being the darkest member of his family had impacted him due to **colourism**.

At nineteen, Hall was awarded a scholarship to study at the University of Oxford. He moved to England, where he stayed for the rest of his life. He got his **master's degree** and began a **PhD**, but left to become a high school teacher in London before completing it.

In 1964 Hall helped to set up the Centre for Contemporary Cultural Studies at the University of Birmingham. He was known for being an encouraging teacher and colleague. In 1991 he presented a television series, *Redemption Song* (named after Bob Marley's song), about the people and histories of the islands of the Caribbean. He had a strong love of the arts and in his later years he worked with and supported young artists. After his death, the Stuart Hall Foundation was established to continue his legacy, providing a supportive community for anti-racist scholars and artists.

11 FEBRUARY ~ TAYTU BETUL

Taytu Betul was a noblewoman, born in Northern Ethiopia in 1851. She was married several times, the first time when she was just ten years old. It was her final marriage that made her famous, when she married King Menelik of Shewa. In 1889 he became emperor of Ethiopia and she became his Empress, taking the title of Etege Taytu Betul, Light of Ethiopia.

Betul was a clever, educated and resourceful woman and as Empress she played an important role in resisting European colonization during the Scramble for Africa in the late 19th century (see 15 November). Italy had already colonized neighbouring Eritrea and Somalia, and were in dispute with Ethiopia over the terms of the Treaty of Wuchale. The treaty was supposed to promote cooperation, but the Ethiopians discovered that the Italians thought that it gave them the right to make Ethiopia a protectorate, controlled by Italy. Betul tore the treaty up and she and her husband resisted Italy's attempts to renegotiate it. The Italians then invaded Ethiopia and Betul supplied her own troops and marched to battle with her husband, dressed in the uniform of a cavalry commander. She devised the military strategy that defeated the Italians

The Battle of Adwa: The Last Rally Of General Dabormid, 1896

at the Battle of Adwa in 1896. Following the battle, the two countries signed the Treaty of Addis Ababa, which recognized Ethiopia as an independent country. The following year France and Britain signed similar treaties with Ethiopia.

Betul and her husband did not produce an heir, and she died in exile on 11 February 1918 in Addis Ababa, the new capital city of Ethiopia that she had founded with her husband.

12 FEBRUARY ~ MALCOLM X IN SMETHWICK

This image was taken on 12 February 1965, showing Malcolm X standing among the red-brick terraced houses of Smethwick

In February 1965 the African American civil rights campaigner Malcolm X visited the town of Smethwick in the Midlands region of the United Kingdom. He was a prominent campaigner in the Black civil rights struggle in the United States.

Malcolm X had become a Muslim in 1963 (see 21 February) and in 1964 he completed the Hajj, a sacred pilgrimage to Mecca. He had developed a passion for promoting African unity and had started visiting campaigners against racism in other countries.

Malcom X had heard about a British election campaign held in 1964 in the town of Smethwick. Peter Griffiths, who had won the election, had repeatedly used racist words and slogans in his campaign. So, in 1965, Malcolm X decided to come to the United Kingdom to visit British anti-racism activists and to see for himself the racism and hostile attitudes that this election campaign had tapped into. He met with local anti-racism campaigners and together they walked the streets, and he was shocked by the racist name-calling and exclusion he witnessed there. He returned to America where, just nine days later, on 21 February 1965, he was assassinated.

13 FEBRUARY - JOHN BLANKE

In February 1511, during the reign of King Henry VIII, a very important celebration took place – the Westminster Tournament, held to celebrate the birth of Henry's son. This event provides us with the earliest portrait of a Black person living in Britain whose name we also know. That name is John Blanke, and his portrait appears in a document called the Westminster Tournament Roll.

John Blanke was a trumpeter in the court of the Tudor king. His duties included playing fanfares and providing music at court events. The Westminster Tournament was a joust, followed by a banquet.

John Blanke depicted in the Westminster Tournament Roll

The Westminster Tournament Roll is a series of thirty-six paintings sewn together into a roll that is over eighteen metres long. John Blanke appears in the images of two processions during the tournament, riding on horseback alongside five other trumpeters. Like his fellow trumpeters, Blanke plays a long trumpet in the pictures, decorated with an embroidered cloth hanging, and wears a yellow and grey uniform. While his colleagues don't wear anything on their heads, he wears a brown and yellow head covering in one of the paintings and a green and gold one in the other. These head coverings indicate that Blanke was possibly a Muslim or had been brought up in Muslim society.

14 FEBRUARY - FREDERICK DOUGLASS

Frederick Augustus Washington Bailey, one of the most important anti-slavery campaigners of the 19th century, chose his own birthday, 14 February, and his own name.

Separated from his mother during his childhood, as an adult he escaped enslavement in 1838 and fled to the northern American states. With his wife Anna Murray, a free Black woman, he moved to Massachusetts. There he rejected his slave surname of 'Bailey', and became a preacher. He began speaking at anti-slavery meetings and writing on the subject. His first book, *The Narrative of the Life of Frederick Douglass, an American Slave*, was published in 1845, and became a bestseller. This made Douglass famous – but it also put him at risk of being hunted down by bounty hunters who could capture and return him to his former owner, Thomas Auld, who still considered himself to be the legal owner of Douglass. So Douglass decided to leave Massachusetts and go to Britain.

Douglass's time in Britain was extremely busy, but he appreciated living in a society where he did not have to worry about being re-enslaved. He travelled widely, speaking at hundreds of events and raising public awareness about the anti-slavery movement. His presence and charisma as a speaker was crucial in persuading many Britons that despite

Portrait of Frederick Douglass © MET museum, Wikimedia Commons

the end of slavery in the **British Empire** in 1833, there was still a moral duty to campaign to end slavery across the globe.

It was on one of these trips that a controversial but life-changing event occurred. In Newcastle, in the north-east of England, a group of his supporters led by Anna Richardson and her sister-in-law Ellen Richardson decided to raise the funds to buy Douglass his freedom from his American owner. This was controversial as many anti-slavery campaigners felt that paying for another human was always morally wrong, whatever the circumstances. However, the sisters-in-law argued that this was practical help that would enable Douglass to continue his work unhindered by fear on either side of the Atlantic. Auld agreed to the sale, and Douglass was legally freed on 12 December 1846.

Douglass returned to America after eighteen months in Britain to continue campaigning for the release of the 3 million Africans who were still enslaved on American soil. As well as his freedom, during his stay in Britain his supporters had raised the funds to establish his own abolitionist newspaper, the *North Star*.

Douglass wrote a further two autobiographies, *My Bondage and My Freedom* in 1855, and the *Life and Times of Frederick Douglass*, first published in 1881. After the American Civil War he continued to campaign for the rights of African Americans who had been freed from enslavement, and he was active in promoting women's rights too.

Douglass died on 20 February 1895, at the age of seventy-seven. A campaigner until the very end, he spoke at a women's **suffrage** meeting the night he died, and received a standing ovation.

Douglass continues to be remembered and honoured across the world. In 1999 the Frederick Douglass Book Prize was established at Yale University. In 2002 he was named as one of the 100 Greatest African Americans, and in the same year the Frederick Douglass Memorial was unveiled in Central Park in New York. He is also remembered in Britain for his campaigning visits – in 2019 Newcastle University opened the Frederick Douglass Centre, close to where Douglass had stayed on his visit to the city of Newcastle upon Tyne in 1846.

If there is no struggle there is no progress. Those who profess to favor freedom and yet deprecate agitation are men who want crops without plowing up the ground; they want rain without thunder and lightning. They want the ocean without the awful roar of its many waters.

This struggle may be a moral one, or it may be a physical one, and it may be both moral and physical, but it must be a struggle. Power concedes nothing without a demand. It never did and it never will.

From a speech given by Frederick Douglass at Canandaigua, New York on 3 August 1857 to commemorate the twenty-third anniversary of Britain's emancipation of slaves in the West Indies

15 FEBRUARY - NOLLYWOOD

Nollywood, aka Nigerian Hollywood, is the nickname given to the Nigerian film industry, which is one of the biggest and most important in the world.

Nollywood includes films made in Nigerian English as well as in Nigerian ethnic languages such as Yoruba and Hausa. In recent years a new branch of Nollywood has arrived, called Nollywood USA. These are films by film-makers from the Nigerian diaspora.

Nigerian cinema has a long history that began years before the term Nollywood became popular. The earliest feature film made in Nigeria was *Palaver* in 1926, in Nigeria's colonial era. After Nigeria gained its independence from the British Empire the Nigerian film industry began to grow, experiencing a golden age during the 1960s. The 1990s brought a second golden age to Nollywood, and another period of rapid growth. Films were produced for both cinema release and for the new and expanding home viewing market. By the mid-2000s, only Hollywood in the USA was making more films per year than Nollywood.

Kunle Afolayan at the 2014 Africa Magic Viewers Choice Awards

Today, although the Nigerian film industry is a bit smaller than it was, high-profile directors such as Kunle Afolayan and Omoni Oboli are making high quality films for both cinema and for home-streaming platforms.

16 FEBRUARY ~ PAUL GILROY

Paul Gilroy is a British academic working in the study of race and racism and examining Black history and culture in the diasporas.

Gilroy was born on 16 February 1956. His mother was the teacher and writer Beryl Gilroy (see 30 August), a Windrush Generation migrant from British Guiana who had arrived in Britain in 1951. His white English father, Partick Gilroy, was a scientist. After completing his undergraduate degree at the University of Sussex, Paul Gilroy moved to the Centre for Contemporary Cultural Studies at the University of Birmingham to study for his PhD, where his supervisor was Stuart Hall (see 10 February). He completed his doctorate in cultural studies in 1986.

Professor Gilroy has worked as an academic in Britain and America. He was the head of his department at Yale University and is the founding director of the Sarah Parker Remond Centre for the Study of Racism and Racialisation at University College, London. He is the author of the award-winning book *The Black Atlantic: Modernity and Double Consciousness*. In 2014 he was elected as a fellow of the British Academy and of the Royal Society of Literature, and in 2018 he was elected an international honorary member of the American Academy of Arts & Sciences. In 2019 he was awarded the Holberg Prize for his outstanding contribution to knowledge.

17 FEBRUARY - PRINCE

Born in Minneapolis in 1958, Prince Rogers Nelson, later known just as Prince, demonstrated his musical genius from an early age. He wrote his first song at the age of seven, using his father's piano, and by his teens was learning to play guitar. He started his career as a singer-songwriter in the late 1970s and by the 1980s he had had great success with his album *1999*. His video for the single 'Little Red Corvette' became one of the very first music videos by a Black artist to be played frequently on the new music channel, MTV.

Prince became one of the bestselling artists of all time, selling over 150 million records. His music commented on subjects that were important to him, like poverty, violence, the AIDS crisis and war. He helped to create organizations that supported Black children and young people and donated money and time to support Black victims of violence and police brutality.

Sadly, towards the end of his life, Prince became addicted to painkillers. He died in 2016. During his lifetime he had won many honours, including seven Grammy Awards, and on 17 February 2022 he was inducted into the Black Music and Entertainment Walk of Fame for his outstanding lifetime contribution.

> **DID YOU KNOW?**
>
> In 1984 Prince starred in and wrote the soundtrack for the film *Purple Rain*. The song 'Purple Rain' spent 24 weeks at No. 1 on the US Billboard music charts and for a time Prince had the number one film, album and single in the US.

18 FEBRUARY - AUDRE LORDE

Audre Lorde was an American writer, feminist and civil rights activist. She was born in Harlem on 18 February 1934, a child of Caribbean immigrants. From an early age Audre was fascinated by poetry. She used it to explore and communicate her ideas about her identity, and her first poem was published when she was in high school.

Over the course of her life Lorde published nine volumes of poetry, covering topics of racism, sexism, politics and violence. She was also a gifted spoken word performer, and when she made public appearances she would introduce herself by saying 'I am a Black, lesbian, mother, warrior, poet.'

She was politically active in many women's activist groups, and in 1980 she co-founded Kitchen Table: Women of Color Press. Her most famous essay, 'The Master's Tools Will Never Dismantle the Master's House', was published in 1984. It is still regularly quoted today by anti-racist activists who are taking action to dismantle racist systems. Lorde argued that educating people about oppression is the responsibility of everyone, and not the job of those being oppressed.

Illness and disability were also themes in Lorde's writing. She had very poor eyesight from birth and was classed as legally blind, and in 1977 she developed breast cancer. She explored her experience of diagnosis and treatment in her work titled *The Cancer Journals*.

Lorde died from liver cancer on 17 November 1992, but continues to be recognized and honoured. In 2001 an annual literary award for lesbian poetry – The Audre Lorde Award – was established in her honour. In 2019 she was one of the fifty LGBTQ+ American trailblazers to be inducted on the National Wall of Honor at the Stonewall National Monument in New York.

19 FEBRUARY ~ US BLACK HISTORY MONTH

Black History Month is an annual event in the United States of America, held throughout the month of February to celebrate and educate people about African American History.

Its origins lie in the 1920s with Negro History Week, the brainchild of the African American historian Carter G. Woodson and the Association for the Study of Negro Life and History. This annual event was celebrated in the second week of February, alongside anniversaries of the birth of president Abraham Lincoln and of the African American anti-slavery campaigner Frederick Douglass (see 14 February). African American newspapers supported Negro History Week from the start, but it was only over time that departments of education across America started to observe and promote it in their schools.

In 1970 Black students and faculty at Kent State University expanded on the idea and celebrated the first Black History Month. It involved a programme of talks and cultural events that celebrated the contributions of African Americans to American society, history and culture. Within six years this new, longer event was being celebrated in schools, colleges and universities across the country.

In 1976 the United States held celebrations to mark America's two centuries as a nation. President Gerald Ford officially recognized Black History Month as part of this national period of celebration. Since then Black History Month has continued to grow in the United States, and has inspired other Black communities in countries such as Canada, the United Kingdom, Ireland and Germany to introduce their own versions.

20 FEBRUARY - SAM KING

Sam King was born on 20 February 1926 in Portland, Jamaica. He volunteered for military service during the Second World War, enlisting as an engineer in the Royal Air Force in 1944. After the war he returned to Jamaica, but found it difficult to get work on the island. In 1948, in a newspaper called *The Gleaner*, he saw an advertisement for tickets to London aboard the ship the *Empire Windrush*. King decided to buy a ticket for this historic journey, becoming one of what is now known as the **Windrush Generation** (see 22 June).

After arriving in Britain on the *Windrush*, King re-enlisted in the Royal Air Force where he served until 1953. His next career move took him to the Post Office, where he worked for the next thirty-four years as a postman. When he was not working, King was very active in the community. In 1959 he worked with Claudia Jones to help organize a Caribbean-style carnival held in St Pancras Town Hall (see 30 January). They also worked together to establish the *West Indian Gazette*, a newspaper written by and for the West Indian community. King became involved in local politics and served as a local councillor before being elected as mayor of the London Borough of Southwark in 1983. He made history as the borough's first Black mayor.

King's identity as one of the Windrush Generation was very important to him. In 1996 he co-founded the Windrush Foundation with Arthur Torrington, which aimed to preserve the memories of the Windrush Generation and celebrate their contribution to British life. In 1998, as part of national events to celebrate the fiftieth anniversary of the arrival of the *Windrush*, King was awarded an MBE. He was listed in the 2020 edition of 100 Great Black Britons.

21 FEBRUARY ~ MALCOLM X

In the 1960s Malcolm X was one of the most famous African American civil rights leaders. He was born Malcolm Little in 1925 in Nebraska. His father was African American and his mother was from Grenada. He had a difficult childhood – his parents were active campaigners against racism and were often the targets of threats and harassment from racist groups like the Ku Klux Klan and the Black Legion. These groups believed in white supremacy and used violence to intimidate Black people in America.

During his childhood, Little's father was run over and killed in a suspected racist attack. His mother later became mentally

Marion S. Trikosko, Library of Congress

Portrait of Malcolm X taken while he waits for a press conference to begin, March 26, 1964

ill and was placed in a psychiatric hospital. Little and his siblings were taken into care, split up and sent to different homes. Although Little was intelligent and wanted to become a lawyer, his teachers did not encourage him and he dropped out of school before he could graduate. As a young adult, Little moved from state to state and worked in different jobs, not all of them legal. Eventually, he was arrested and found guilty of robbery. He was given an eight-to-ten year jail sentence and sent to prison. But it was in prison that his life was to change.

This was firstly thanks to the influence of one of his fellow prisoners, John Bembry. Bembry encouraged Little to begin his own self-education, using the time in prison to read and think about new ideas. Secondly, Little's brother, Reginald, visited and told him about a new religious movement called the **Nation of Islam**. This movement was arguing for the civil rights of Black people in America and campaigning for a return to Africa for Americans of African descent, to free them from the impact of racism. Little was inspired by the leader of the Nation of Islam to convert to Islam, renounce his criminal past and take up a new name: Malcolm X. The group used the surname X instead of the surnames that African Americans had been given by the white owners of their enslaved ancestors.

When he left prison in 1952, X became a minister in the Nation of Islam and soon became an impressive speaker, recruiting others to join the organization. He was invited to speak to leaders of African countries at the **United Nations** in New York. This brought him to the attention of the **FBI**, who put him under surveillance. By 1964, X had begun to reject some of the ideas from the Nation of Islam and its leader Elijah Muhammad, who believed that white people could not be part of the struggle against racism in America. X soon left the organization.

X wanted to work with other civil rights leaders and so he founded a new non-religious group called the Organization of Afro-American Unity (OAAU). The OAAU promoted the idea of pan-Africanism, or unity between people of African descent across the world. In 1964 and 1965 Malcolm X travelled overseas, visiting countries in Africa and Europe, including Britain (see 12 February). He was excited by examples he saw of Black and white people working together to challenge racism.

Malcolm X returned to the United States, where he told an interviewer that the Nation of Islam was trying to kill him because he had left the organization. Two days later, on 21 February, Malcolm X was assassinated. He was speaking at the Audubon Ballroom in Manhattan, New York, when a man rushed to the stage and shot him once in the chest, followed by two other men who shot him multiple times. Several men connected to the Nation of Islam were eventually arrested and convicted of his murder. However, some of these convictions have since been questioned, and exactly who it was who ordered the killing of Malcom X remains a mystery. He was buried on 27 February 1965 at Ferncliff Cemetery in New York. Black civil rights activists came together to mourn him and to raise money to support his widow, Betty Shabazz, and his children.

22 FEBRUARY - ROBERT GORDON

Robert Gordon was born into slavery in the early 1800s. He worked for a wealthy coal merchant in Virginia and did the job so well that his master put him in charge of the coal yard. Gordon saw an opportunity to sell unwanted coal dust – called 'slack' – to local manufacturers and he managed to save enough money to buy his freedom in 1846. He was thirty-four. He decided to move to Cincinnati, a city where he'd heard that Black people could do well.

ROBERT GORDON & CO.,

COAL YARD

SIXTH STREET, EAST OF BROADWAY,

At the Canal, North side,   **CINCINNATI, O.**

☞ The best Youghiogheny and Pomeroy Coal always on hand. All orders promptly attended to.

An advert for Gordon's business in Williams Cincnnati Directory of 1859

Gordon bought a Cincinnati property in 1848 and soon opened his own coal yard. However, the local white coal merchants did not appreciate the competition from a Black man, and they plotted to ruin Gordon, dropping their prices in order to bankrupt him. Gordon outsmarted them by hiring light-skinned 'mulatto' (an historic term indicating a person of mixed Black and white ancestry) agents – who could pass for white men – to buy up their cheap coal, which he sold on for a higher price. He continued to run his successful coal business until 1865, when he retired and began investing in property.

Gordon eventually became one of the richest Black men in Ohio and he used his wealth to help establish several Black schools.

23 FEBRUARY - W. E. B. DU BOIS

The African American academic and activist W. E. B. Du Bois was born William Edward Burghardt Du Bois on 23 February 1868. Brought up in a mostly white community in Great Barrington, Massachusetts, he attended an integrated school and excelled at his studies. His local church raised funds for his university tuition fees and he left for Fisk University, in Nashville, Tennessee where, for the first time, he experienced the racism of the Jim Crow laws. After Fisk, Du Bois attended Harvard, studying for both another undergraduate degree and a postgraduate degree. While there he won a scholarship that allowed him to travel to Germany in 1892 to attend the Friedrich Wilhelm University. He wrote that the experience gave him the perspective of being 'outside of the American world, looking in'. On his return he completed a PhD, becoming the first African American to earn one at Harvard.

© Cornelius Marion Battey, Library of Congress

Du Bois started an academic career, eventually becoming a professor of history, sociology and economics at Atlanta University. He became an advocate for equal rights for Black people, for women's right to vote and a campaigner against white supremacy. In 1909 he co-founded the National Association for the Advancement of Colored People (NAACP). A year later he left Atlanta University to become the NAACP's director of publicity and research, and editor of its monthly magazine, *The Crisis*. He was committed to pan-Africanism and decolonization across the world and became a peace activist, campaigning for nuclear disarmament. Du Bois died in Ghana on 27 August 1963, aged ninety-five.

24 FEBRUARY - THE MACPHERSON REPORT

On 24 February 1999 the Macpherson Report was published in Britain, which detailed the conduct of the police during their investigation into the murder of the Black teenager Stephen Lawrence in April 1993 (see 22 April).

Lawrence was an eighteen-year-old studying for his exams. One evening, while waiting at a bus stop, he was attacked and stabbed to death by a group of young white men. The police investigation that followed was deeply flawed. In 1997 Stephen Lawrence's parents made an official complaint about the attitudes of some of the leading officers, which appeared to reflect racist attitudes, and the home secretary ordered a public inquiry.

The inquiry found that the original police investigation into Lawrence's murder had been incompetent and that senior police officers had failed in their leadership. The report stated that the **Metropolitan Police** Service had become 'institutionally racist'.

It explained that the failures in the investigation had happened not just through officers being deliberately racist, but because of ignorance, thoughtlessness and racist stereotyping that resulted in a police service that was not treating people fairly. Police officers had failed to provide first aid to Stephen when they arrived at the crime scene, failed to follow up on clues at the scene of the murder and failed to arrest suspects.

The Macpherson Report made seventy recommendations for change within the Metropolitan Police and advised that similar change was needed in other organizations. The National Health Service, schools and the judicial system were all asked to review their practices, and tackle cultural ignorance and racist attitudes to make sure that they were providing a fair and professional service to people of all racial backgrounds.

25 FEBRUARY – MUHAMMAD ALI

Ira Rosenberg, Library of Congress

On 25 February 1964, with all the odds stacked against him, a twenty-two-year-old African American boxer beat the reigning heavyweight boxing champion, Sonny Liston. That new champion was Cassius Clay from Kentucky. As a new member of the Nation of Islam, Clay soon renounced the surname he'd inherited from his enslaved ancestors who had been named by white owners, and took on the name he would be known by for the rest of his life – Muhammad Ali.

Boxing and politics were the two forces that shaped Ali's life. In 1966 he was called up to fight in the Vietnam War, but Ali refused to fight for moral reasons. This decision led to him being stripped of his boxing titles and banned from competing for five years (see 20 June). On his return to boxing Ali took part in some of the most famous matches of the 20th century, such as the *Fight of the Century* in 1971 and *The Thrilla in Manila* in 1975, both against Joe Frazier, and *The Rumble in the Jungle* against George Foreman in 1974 (see 22 January).

Ali was recognized as the greatest heavyweight boxing champion of all time, earning the nickname 'The Greatest'. A showman who revelled in trash-talking his opponents and making bold claims about his own talent, Ali was proud of his Black identity and released albums of spoken word poetry. However, in 1984, Ali announced that he had developed Parkinson's disease, which affected his movement and speech. In retirement Ali did charitable work, especially in Africa. In 1999, he was named Sportsman of the Century by *Sports Illustrated* magazine, and one of the 100 Most Important People of the 20th Century by *Time* magazine. He died on 3 June 2016 aged seventy-four.

26 FEBRUARY - NEIL DEGRASSE TYSON

Neil deGrasse Tyson is an American astrophysicist, author and broadcaster. He was born in the city of New York in 1958. As a child he became fascinated by astronomy after a visit to the Hayden Planetarium, where he soon began taking astronomy classes. By the age of fifteen he was already giving lectures on the subject. Tyson went on to gain a PhD in astrophysics, and he returned to the Hayden Planetarium in 1994, working as a researcher before becoming its youngest ever director in 1995.

In the 2000s Tyson became famous as a public scientist. He had an ability to explain complex ideas to the public clearly and with humour, in television documentaries, on the radio and on the internet. He has even played himself on TV, including appearances on the science-fiction adventure series *Stargate Atlantis* and sitcom *The Big Bang Theory*.

In 2006 he supported the arguments for Pluto to be reclassified and labelled a space object instead of a planet. Exhibits at the Hayden Planetarium were amended to reflect this change in Pluto's status, which was eventually confirmed by the International Astronomical Union.

On 26 February 2015, Tyson was presented with the National Academy of Sciences' Public Welfare Medal for his role in engaging and exciting the public in the wonders of science. In 2017 he was awarded the Stephen Hawking Medal for Science Communication.

27 FEBRUARY ~ MOONLIGHT

Moonlight is a 2016 film with an all-Black cast that tells the life story of Chiron, a young African American man struggling with his identity, relationships and sexuality.

At the 2017 Golden Globes film awards, *Moonlight* received six nominations and won in the Best Motion Picture – Drama category.

Moonlight was nominated in eight categories in the Academy Awards – Best Picture, Best Director (Barry Jenkins), Best Supporting Actor (Mahershala Ali), Best Supporting Actress (Naomie Harris), Best Adapted Screenplay (Barry Jenkins and Tarell Alvin McCraney), Best Cinematography (James Laxton) and Best Film Editing (Joi McMillon – the first Black woman to be nominated for an Oscar for editing – and Nat Sanders).

At the Academy Awards ceremony on 27 February 2017, Mahershala Ali won the Oscar for Best Supporting Actor, becoming the first Muslim to win an acting Oscar. Barry Jenkins and Tarell Alvin McCraney won for Best Adapted Screenplay. *Moonlight* won the award for Best Picture, becoming the first film featuring an all-Black cast and the first LGBTQ+ film to win the Oscar for Best Picture.

> Mahershala Ali won Best Supporting Actor for a second time in 2018 for his role as Don Shirley in the film *Green Book*, making him the first Black actor to win two Academy Awards in the same category.

DID YOU KNOW?

28 FEBRUARY - KETANJI BROWN JACKSON

Ketanji Brown Jackson is the first Black woman to be appointed to the United States **Supreme Court**. Born Ketanji Onyika Brown in 1970 in Washington DC, she graduated from Harvard Law School in 1996 and married, changing her name to Ketanji Brown Jackson. After years of legal experience Jackson was nominated by President Obama in 2009 to serve on the US Sentencing Commission and in 2012 to serve as a district judge.

On 28 February 2022 Jackson was nominated by president Biden for a vacancy on the United States Supreme Court. The Senate held confirmation hearings for her nomination in March and April 2022 and she was finally sworn in as an associate justice on 30 June 2022.

DID YOU KNOW?

In her confirmation hearings, Jackson acknowledged the work of her trailblazing predecessor Judge Constance Baker Motley. The first African American female federal judge, Motley started her career working for the **NAACP**. She was involved in many high-profile civil rights cases including as defence for the Freedom Riders (see 4 May) and the protesters of the Birmingham Children's Crusade (see 2 May). Her appointment as a federal judge was protested by a Mississippi senator who was angered by her instrumental involvement in the movement to **desegregate** education, but she was eventually confirmed in 1966.

29 FEBRUARY - ALICE BALL

Alice Ball was an African American chemist, born in Seattle in 1892. Her interest in the use of plants to produce medical treatments led to an invitation from Harry T. Hollmann to join his workforce. Hollmann worked at Hawaii's Leprosy Investigation Station and wanted Ball to investigate possible treatments for leprosy based on oil from the chaulmoogra tree. In 1915, at the age of just twenty-three, Ball devised a method of extracting chaulmoogra oil and turning it into an injection for leprosy patients. It was far more effective than the existing available treatments. Her discovery would save countless lives around the world.

Just a year after her discovery, and before she could publish her research, Ball sadly died due to lung damage caused by accidentally inhaling chlorine gas. Her former university research supervisor, Arthur L. Dean, took credit for Ball's idea without naming her, and the method of extracting injectable chaulmoogra oil became known as 'the Dean method'. Hollmann challenged this and wrote a paper in 1922 that credited Ball for the innovation. In the 1970s, University of Hawaii professors Kathryn Takara and Stanley Ali started a campaign to put the record straight and to give her the rightful credit for the invention of 'Ball's Method'. In 2000, 29 February was declared as 'Alice Ball Day' in Hawaii in memory of her life-saving work.

1 MARCH ~ HARRY BELAFONTE

Harry Belafonte was a Jamaican-American singer and actor, famous also for his activism during the American civil rights movement. He was born Harold George Bellanfanti Jr to Jamaican parents in Harlem, New York, in 1927, but spent eight years of his childhood living in Jamaica with his grandmother. Returning from serving in the Navy during the Second World War, he was given tickets to a play at the American Negro Theater in New York. This inspired him to become an actor and led to his friendship with fellow actor Sidney Poitier (see 24 March).

To pay for acting lessons Belafonte worked as a nightclub singer, providing backing vocals for artists including the jazz musicians Charlie Parker and Miles Davis, before becoming a recording artist in his own right. His music ranged from the blues and folk songs to show tunes, but he became most famous for singing calypso songs that reflected his Caribbean ancestry. He released over forty albums in a career spanning seven decades, winning two Grammy awards and, in 2000, a Grammy Lifetime Achievement Award.

In the 1950s he began his acting career on stage. He won a Tony award in 1954 for his performance in *Murray Anderson's Almanac*. In 1953 and 1954 he starred in his first two films, *Bright Road* and *Carmen Jones*, alongside the actress Dorothy Dandridge and mostly Black casts. He also acted and sang on television, winning an Emmy Award in 1959 for the programme *Revlon Revue: Tonight with Belafonte*.

Alongside his singing and acting career, Belafonte was a committed humanitarian and political activist, following the example of his friend and mentor Paul Robeson (see 9 April). He became a supporter of Dr Martin Luther King Jr and donated money to the civil rights movement, including

Sidney Poitier and Harry Belafonte at the Civil Rights March on Washington

the Freedom Riders in 1961 (see 4 May). In 1963 he bailed Dr King out of jail after his arrest during non-violent action in Birmingham, Alabama. He then helped to organize the March on Washington at which Dr King delivered his 'I have a dream' speech (see 28 August). One of the programmes he helped to fund in the 1950s was the African American Students Foundation. It was a grant from that organization that allowed Barack Obama Sr to travel from Kenya to Hawaii to study in 1959, leading to the birth of Barack Obama Jr, America's 44th president (see 4 November).

Across the decades Belafonte supported humanitarian causes, particularly in Africa: he campaigned against apartheid in South Africa, and became a UNICEF Goodwill Ambassador in 1987, raising money for African Education. He also campaigned for HIV/AIDS education and treatment. Belafonte was recognized for his contribution to American culture and received the Kennedy Center Honors in 1989 and the National Medal of Arts in 1994. On 23 February 2000 he was presented with a Lifetime Achievement Award at the Academy Awards. He died on 25 April 2023 aged ninety-six.

2 MARCH - BLACK PEOPLE'S DAY OF ACTION

After thirteen young Black people died in the New Cross Fire (see 18 January) it seemed to many local Black people that the police and the media were not taking the matter seriously. The community realized that they were going to have to come together to protest. A week after the fire, on 25 January 1981 at a public meeting, the New Cross Massacre Action Committee was formed. The activist and publisher John La Rose was elected as its chairman. The group made the decision to ask Black community groups and leaders to come together on 2 March 1981 for the Black People's Day of Action. They chose a working day instead of the weekend to show just how serious they thought the injustice to the victims of the fire was.

2 March was a rainy day, and the 20,000 people who answered the call marched for eight hours through the wet London streets chanting 'Thirteen dead, nothing said'. The route was planned carefully, taking the protestors from the scene of the fire across London and ending at the **Houses of Parliament**. As they passed through Fleet Street, where the newspapers who had done little to report the fire had their offices, there were some scuffles when people shouted racist abuse at the marchers. They also passed the Royal Courts of Justice to make the point that no progress had been made by the police to bring those responsible for the fire to justice. Once they reached the Houses of Parliament they handed over a petition to the government and the commissioner of the **Metropolitan Police** that stated their concerns. The few stories about the march in the newspapers the next day blamed the protestors for the scuffles on Fleet Street instead of focusing on the reasons for the march. Despite this, the sheer scale of the protest made it a turning point in the history of the struggle against racial injustice in the United Kingdom.

3 MARCH - SERETSE KHAMA

Seretse Goitsebeng Maphiri Khama was born in Bechuanaland on 1 July 1921. His father was the chieftain of the Bamangwato people. When he was four his father died, leaving Khama to become chieftain. However, as he was still a child his uncle Tshekedi Khama took on the task of ruling the Bamagwato.

Khama was sent to school in South Africa and then studied law at the University of Oxford. While there his life took an unexpected change of direction. One evening in 1947 Khama met a young English woman called Ruth Williams at a dance. They quickly fell in love and a year later decided to get married, but both of their families strongly disapproved. In fact, they got married earlier than planned when Khama became worried that his uncle was going to try to stop the wedding from happening.

In 1949 Khama returned to Bechuanaland, ready to take up his role as chieftain, but only if he could have his wife at his side. At a meeting the Bamangwato people confirmed him as their chieftain, and his uncle went into exile in South Africa. However, when Khama went back to London to collect his wife, the South African authorities banned the mixed race couple from entering Bechuanaland. The Bamangwato people asked the British government for help, but instead the British ordered them to choose someone else to replace Khama as chieftain. When they refused, the British set up a replacement government instead. The Khamas were only allowed into Bechuanaland in 1956 on the condition that Khama gave up his claim to the chieftainship, which he did.

In 1961 Khama started the Bechuanaland Democratic Party, and became its leader. In an election on 3 March 1965 he won the vote, becoming the prime minister of Bechuanaland. A year later, Bechuanaland became the independent country of Botswana, and Khama became its first president.

4 MARCH - FÉDON'S REVOLUTION

On the night of 2 March 1795, on the Caribbean island of Grenada, an uprising against British rule began. First colonized by the French, the island had become a British colony in 1783. Over the years the French-speaking free Black and mixed race population of the island became more and more dissatisfied with the British, and some of them began training for and plotting their rebellion, encouraged by a recent revolution against French rule in the Caribbean island of Haiti (see 22 August).

The rebellion was led by Julien Fédon, the son of a French jeweller who had emigrated to Grenada, and a freed Black woman. He owned a plantation, which he fortified, and he had recruited over a hundred people to his cause; some formerly enslaved, some of mixed heritage. On 2 March 1795 his rebel forces attacked the towns of Gouyave and Grenville. They looted plantations, burned down houses, freed the enslaved and took hostages. People flocked to join the rebels and on 4 March Fédon issued a proclamation demanding that the British surrender.

Over the next three months the struggle for control of the island cost many lives. The British Navy blockaded the island, guarding it with ships to stop reinforcements and supplies from reaching the rebels. When his brother was killed in the fighting, Fédon ordered the execution of forty-eight British hostages. Eventually, on 19 June, under the command of General Abercromby, the British defeated the rebels. Fédon was never captured and it is unclear whether he survived and managed to escape. Many of his fellow rebels were executed by the British, and those of them who were enslaved were killed without being given a trial. Fédon is remembered in Grenada and the Caribbean as an important historical figure whose rebellion inspired the struggle for the end of slavery.

5 MARCH ~ THE ABRAHAM LINCOLN BRIGADE

In 1936 the Spanish Civil War broke out when General Franco's fascists staged a coup d'état. The international Communist Party issued a call to arms and 40,000 volunteer fighters joined the International Brigades to fight the fascists.

Around 2,800 Americans volunteered for the Abraham Lincoln Brigade and, of those, around ninety were African Americans. The US Communist Party supported the fight for civil rights and offered practical help and legal assistance to many African Americans. When the call came to fight against fascism many African Americans saw it as their duty to respond.

They found that their treatment in Spain differed greatly from how they were treated at home. Their forces were integrated and people were allocated positions based on their ability, with Black officers commanding white troops. The Spanish civilians welcomed them as equals. They received wide support on the home front too, and both Paul Robeson (see 9 April) and Langston Hughes (see 1 February) visited Spain to highlight the anti-fascist efforts.

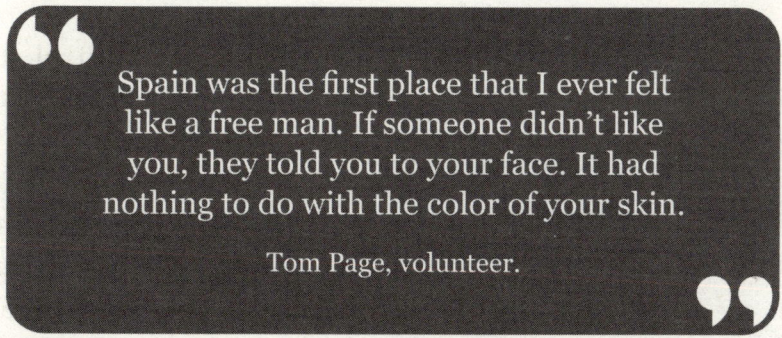

> Spain was the first place that I ever felt like a free man. If someone didn't like you, they told you to your face. It had nothing to do with the color of your skin.
>
> Tom Page, volunteer.

By 5 March 1939 the anti-fascist forces had accepted defeat and began proceedings to negotiate peace. Many of the African American volunteers went on to continue the fight against fascists in the Second World War, but found that discrimination reemerged when they enlisted in the US's segregated army.

6 MARCH - GHANA'S INDEPENDENCE DAY

At midnight on 6 March 1957, in the city of Accra on the west coast of Africa, the British flag was lowered and a new flag was raised in its place. It was the flag of a new country called Ghana, the first sub-Saharan African nation to win its independence from a European colonizer.

The new country consisted of four previous colonial territories – the Gold Coast, Ashanti, the Northern Territories and British Togoland (which had been ruled over by the British since the expansion of the British Empire in Victorian times). Independence meant these territories became a unified nation, with the right to govern itself. Independence Day marked the end of a long struggle for the Ghanaian people. Kwame Nkrumah, the man who had led that political struggle, had been arrested and imprisoned before being elected as the country's prime minister in 1952 (see 1 July). He had struggled not only for Ghana's independence, but for the liberation of Africa and cooperation between all the nations.

The teacher and artist Theodosia Salome Okoh designed the flag for the new nation. It consists of three horizontal stripes – red representing the blood of those who died for independence, gold for the mineral wealth of the country, and

green for the country's rich and fertile grasslands. On top of the gold stripe is a black star which represents the people and the cause of African emancipation from colonial rule.

7 MARCH - THE SELMA TO MONTGOMERY MARCHES

In January 1965 a campaign of non-violent protests was organized to demonstrate against policies of the state of Alabama, which were denying Black voters their right to register to vote. Three civil rights campaigning groups were involved – the Dallas County Voters League (DCVL), the SNCC and Dr Martin Luther King Jr's SCLC. On 18 February, at one of their protests, a state trooper shot and killed twenty-six-year-old Jimmie Lee Jackson as he tried to protect his mother.

A march from Selma to the state capital Montgomery was planned to protest Jackson's killing. It was led by John Lewis (see 17 July), of the SNCC, and Hosea Williams of the SCLC. Six hundred protestors set off from Selma on 7 March. On reaching the Edmund Pettus Bridge they were met by state troopers and police. When they defied an order from Selma's Sheriff Jim Clark and Major John Cloud to go home, Cloud ordered his troops to attack. State troopers attacked with clubs and tear gas and mounted troopers chased them down as they fled. Many demonstrators, including SNCC leader John Lewis, were severely beaten. The clash was broadcast on television news and the incident became known as 'Bloody Sunday'.

Peter Pettus, Library of Congress

Civil rights march from Selma to Montgomery, Alabama in 1965

That evening Dr Martin Luther King Jr (see 10 January) called for religious leaders all over America to join the protesters and continue the march to Montgomery. Hundreds responded to his call. Two days later he led over 2,000 marchers back to the Edmund Pettus Bridge. Blocked again by police and state troopers, Dr King stopped the march, led the protestors in prayer, and turned back the way they had come, avoiding violence. That night, however, a white protestor, James Reeb, who was a religious minister, was beaten to death by racist thugs. The Alabama governor George Wallace tried to have the march legally banned but on 15 March President Lyndon B. Johnson went on television to tell America that he supported the Selma protests. He announced that he would introduce a new bill to Congress to protect the voting rights of African Americans.

On 21 March the protestors set off again from Selma. This time they were protected by troops from the US Army and the Alabama National Guard. Walking for twelve hours a day, with more people joining each day, the marchers camped each evening in fields by the road. On 24 March they reached Montgomery County. As they camped that evening, a Stars for Freedom rally was held, organized by the singer, actor and activist Harry Belafonte (see 1 March). It included performances and speeches from celebrities including Nina Simone (see 10 September), Tony Bennett, James Baldwin (see 2 August), Sammy Davis Jr (see 6 June), Lena Horne, Joan Baez and Leonard Bernstein. The marchers reached the state capitol building in Montgomery the following day, where a crowd of 50,000 supporters gathered to hear the words of Dr King and the other leaders.

The Selma marches directly led to the Voting Rights Act of 1965, which was passed in August that year. The Act banned states from making people pass literacy tests before they could vote, and gave the national government powers to inspect voter registration practices across the country.

8 MARCH - ANDREW WATSON

Andrew Watson was born on 24 May 1856 in Demerara in the South American **colony** British Guiana (which is now the independent country of Guyana). His mother was a Black woman, Anna (or Hanna) Watson (née Rose). His Scottish father, Peter Miller Watson, was

Watson (third from right, back row), Glasgow Select Team 1880

Unknown photographer, Public domain, Wikimedia Commons

a very wealthy white plantation owner and sugar merchant. When he was very young, Watson's father took him and his sister to live in Britain. Watson was sent to private boarding schools and he soon demonstrated a talent for sport. When he was thirteen his father died, and Watson and his sister inherited part of the large fortune that the Scottish side of his family had made through its ownership of the plantation and enslaved Africans, shipping, insurance and banking.

Watson was able to continue his education, and he attended the prestigious Heath Grammar School in Halifax. He went on to study natural philosophy and mathematics at Glasgow University and engineering at the University of Liverpool. However, he did not complete his studies, choosing instead to become a footballer. Staying in Glasgow, he played for Parkgrove Football Club before moving to Queen's Park FC. His success led to him being called up to play for the Scottish national team as its captain. He played three international matches, two against England and one against Wales, winning all of them and becoming the first Black footballer to captain a team at the international level. He died on 8 March 1921.

9 MARCH - MIRIAM MAKEBA

The singer, actress and civil rights activist Miriam Makeba was born in the township of Prospect, outside of Johannesburg in 1932. She began her career as a singer in South Africa but came to international attention after appearing in the award-winning documentary film *Come Back Africa*. She was invited to perform all over the world and in 1959 left South Africa for London and then New York. Makeba recorded American jazz and folk songs, traditional African songs and songs she wrote herself, often in the South African languages of Xhosa and Zulu (see 31 July). She was the first female artist to make African music globally popular, and became known as Mama Africa.

Despite this, in 1960, when she tried to go home to South Africa to attend her mother's funeral, Makeba found that the government had cancelled her passport and that she was banned from the country because of her anti-apartheid politics. She settled in America and became part of a New York community of artists and activists, which included her friend Harry Belafonte (with whom she won a Grammy Award in 1965, making her the first African artist to do so – see 1 March), and her fellow South African musician Hugh Masekela (who became her second husband).

On 9 March 1963, Makeba gave a speech in New York to the United Nations General Assembly. The UN knew that many South Africans who were seeking to bring apartheid to an end – including Nelson Mandela (see 18 July) – were being imprisoned. Makeba used her speech to call on the countries of the world to stop trading with South Africa in order to put pressure on its government to end apartheid. After the speech the South African government took away Makeba's citizenship and banned her music. Undeterred, Makeba addressed the UN again in 1976 and continued campaigning until her triumphant return to South Africa in June 1990.

10 MARCH ~ HARRIET TUBMAN

Harriet Tubman was born into slavery with the name Araminta Ross in the early 1820s in Maryland, USA. From the age of five she was rented out by her owner to work as a servant in other households. During her childhood she suffered many whippings and beatings from her masters. At the age of twelve, she was seriously injured when an overseer threw a two-pound metal weight at another enslaved person who was trying to escape, but it hit her across the head instead. The results

Harvey B. Lindsley, Library of Congress

of that injury were lifelong, causing headaches and narcolepsy (a condition that causes a person to fall asleep suddenly and frequently throughout the day).

In 1844 she married a free Black man called John Tubman and changed her first name to Harriet. Five years later she escaped enslavement by travelling in secret via the Underground Railroad to the northern states where slavery was not legal (see 18 September). After her own escape in 1849 Tubman became a guide on the Underground Railroad, helping around seventy enslaved people, including members of her family, to freedom. Her husband John, however, refused to go with her to the north and married another woman instead.

Tubman's skill became legendary. She never lost a 'passenger' and eventually a reward of $40,000 was offered to anyone who could capture her. Then, in 1861, the American Civil War, between the Confederate states of the south and the Union states of the north, started. Straightaway Tubman put her huge knowledge of the secret routes through the southern states and her skill with herbal medicines to use on the side of the Union.

She worked as scout for the Union troops, supporting them on military assaults by guiding them along secret pathways. She would also disguise herself as an old woman to work as a spy and gather information in areas under Confederate control. She made herbal remedies to treat Union soldiers at their camp at Port Royal.

At the end of the Civil War Tubman settled in the town of Auburn in New York state. She cared for her parents and rented out rooms to earn extra income. She went on to marry one of her boarders, a young Union soldier called Nelson Davis, and in 1874 they adopted a daughter, called Gertie. Tubman became involved in the women's suffrage movement and campaigned alongside the white suffrage leaders Susan B. Anthony and Elizabeth Cady Stanton for votes for women. Tubman's friends and supporters were keen to help her financially. Tubman and the white historian and author Sarah Hopkins Bradford worked together on an authorized biography of Tubman's life, earning Tubman some much needed income.

Tubman's contribution during the Civil War had not been acknowledged by the authorities. During the 1890s her friends and supporters began campaigning for this to be changed and for Tubman to receive a proper pension. Eventually, in 1897, Congress and the president approved a pension of $20 a month, for being the widow of Davis, who had been a Union soldier, and for Tubman's service as a nurse. She received no official recognition of her service as a scout and as a spy in her lifetime.

Tubman spent her remaining years campaigning for women's suffrage. She also opened a home for the elderly near her home in Auburn. She died on 10 March 1913 and was buried at Fort Hill Cemetery, with military honours. In 2013, a century after her death, president Obama announced the creation of the Harriet Tubman Underground Railroad National Monument.

11 MARCH - LORRAINE HANSBERRY

On 11 March 1959 history was made at the Ethel Barrymore Theatre in New York, when the first Broadway play written by an African American woman was performed. The playwright was Lorraine Hansberry and at the time she was only twenty-nine years old.

Her play, *A Raisin in the Sun*, was named from a line in the Langston Hughes poem 'Harlem: A Dream Deferred' (see 1 February), and tells the story of a working-class Black family in Chicago. Its cast was led by the actor Sidney Poitier (see 24 March). The director was Lloyd Richards who, that night, became the first African American to direct a Broadway play. The play was nominated for four Tony awards and was named the best play of 1959 by the New York Drama Critics Circle, making Hansberry the youngest American to win that award. In 1961 it was turned into a film, starring the original Broadway cast.

Hansberry was the youngest child born to an accomplished African American family living on the South Side of Chicago. She became interested in theatre and politics and moved to New York to study. She started writing for *Freedom*, a monthly African American newspaper that featured

columns by its co-founder, the singer and activist Paul Robeson (see 9 April) and articles by the scholar and activist W. E. B. Du Bois (see 23 February). Hansberry identified as a lesbian but homosexuality was illegal in New York at that time (see 3 July). In 1953 she married fellow activist Robert Nemiroff and, although their romantic relationship ended a few years later, he remained one of her closest friends.

Her only other play to be performed during her lifetime was *The Sign in Sidney Brustein's Window*. It closed on the day she died at the tragically early age of thirty-four from pancreatic cancer. In 1969 Nina Simone (see 10 September) and Weldon Irvine co-wrote the song 'To Be Young, Gifted and Black' about Hansberry, who had been godmother to Simone's daughter.

> The Hansberry vs. Lee Supreme Court case of 1940, that helped make housing discrimination illegal, was brought by Lorraine Hansberry's parents. Her family had moved to an all-white area and their home was attacked. Eight-year-old Hansberry had almost been hit in the head by a brick that was flung through the window. The Illinois court said that the white neighbours had the right to force the Black family out, but Hansberry's father took their fight all the way to the Supreme Court and won.

DID YOU KNOW?

12 MARCH - FLOELLA BENJAMIN

Floella Benjamin has enjoyed a long and successful career as a British television presenter, actress, author and producer. She is also an activist for children and their wellbeing. She was born Floella Karen Yunies Benjamin in Pointe-à-Pierre, Trinidad, in 1949. In the late 1950s her Trinidadian parents made the decision to move to Britain. Her father left for Britain in 1958 and her mother in 1959. Benjamin and some of her siblings stayed in Trinidad, looked after by relatives until they were sent to rejoin the family in 1960. Benjamin still regards the fifteen months she spent apart from her parents as the most difficult part of her life. When they came to Britain, the family encountered prejudice and racist abuse – Benjamin has written about this in her books for both children and adults.

Once she left school, Benjamin became an actress. At first she worked on the stage in musicals and plays, before going on to become a presenter on British children's television programmes *Play School* and *Play Away*. She was one of very few Black people on British screens at the time. She soon became beloved by her audience and worked on screen and behind the scenes to improve representation of diversity in programmes, toys and books for children.

Benjamin has won many awards for her work and her involvement in charities. In 2001 she was awarded an OBE and in 2010 she became a baroness in the House of Lords. In a ceremony on 12 March 2020 she was awarded the title of Dame Commander of the Order of the British Empire for her services to charity.

She served for ten years as the chancellor of Exeter University and at the end of her term of office in 2016 a statue of her was erected on campus. This was the first statue of a named Black woman to be erected in the United Kingdom.

13 MARCH - DR HAROLD MOODY

Harold Arundel Moody, a pioneering doctor and civil rights activist, was born in Kingston, Jamaica in 1882. At twenty-one he travelled to London to study medicine and applied to work as a hospital doctor and then a medical officer. In both cases he was told that he was being denied the post because of the colour of his skin. But Moody was a very determined person, and in February 1913 he set up his own medical practice at his home in Peckham in south London. Later that same year he married Olive Tranter, a white nurse whom he had met during his training. Moody began to build up his practice. Unlike some other local doctors, he was willing to treat the poor, often for free. As he gained a reputation for being an excellent and very caring doctor, more people started to come to him for treatment, until eventually he had to expand into a bigger house.

Moody also helped Black people who came to him for support due to difficulties they were encountering with racist attitudes and policies. Moody and his wife hosted several famous Black activists at his home, including Paul Robeson (see 9 April), Kwame Nkrumah (see 1 July) and Jomo Kenyatta, who would later become Kenya's first president.

On 13 March 1931 Moody formed the League of Coloured Peoples (LCP). This was a civil rights organization which aimed to support Black Britons and promote interracial understanding. The organization provided invaluable support to Black students and migrants coming to the country from Africa and the Caribbean to help them find accommodation and jobs. It also published a journal called *The Keys*. The title was inspired by a lecture delivered by James Aggrey, who used the idea of piano keys to argue that for harmony to happen, white and black must come together.

14 MARCH – MUDDY WATERS

On 14 March 1972, Muddy Waters, the man who electrified the blues, won the first of six Grammy awards for his album *They Call Me Muddy Waters*. Born in 1913, McKinley Morganfield was raised by his grandmother in Mississippi, and she was the one who first nicknamed him Muddy. His friends later referred to him as Muddy Waters. He showed musical promise early on with the harmonica, but everything changed when he was seventeen and bought his first acoustic guitar.

In 1941 the folklorist Alan Lomax came across Waters when he was in the southern states looking for country blues musicians. He recorded Waters in his home in 1941 and 1942. When Waters received copies of the recordings he decided to pursue a career as a musician. In 1943 he moved to Chicago and began working in the city's nightclubs as a full-time professional musician. Playing in such noisy venues meant that Waters needed a louder instrument; he bought his first electric guitar.

© Lionel Decoster, CC BY-SA 4.0, via Wikimedia Commons

Waters spent years on tour, all over America and Europe. By the 1970s and 80s his groundbreaking electric blues, and his virtuoso guitar playing, were influencing a number of rock musicians and bands including Led Zeppelin, Cream, Free, AC/DC, ZZ Top and the Rolling Stones (who are named after Waters' 1948 hit song).

Muddy Waters performing in Paris, 1976

15 MARCH - JOSEPH JENKINS ROBERTS

Joseph Jenkins was born on 15 March 1809 in Norfolk, Virginia. He was born free and was of mixed ancestry – the son of a Welsh father and mixed race mother who had previously been enslaved. When he was still a child his mother Amelia married a free Black man called James Roberts, who ran a successful boating business, and the family took on his surname. They moved to Petersburg where Roberts at first worked at his stepfather's business, and then became an apprentice in a barber's shop owned by a minister called William Colson. Colson would later partner with Roberts in an export company.

Roberts married in 1828 and the following year emigrated with his wife and child, and his mother and younger brothers, to Liberia on the west coast of Africa. The family had heard of the work of the American Colonization Society (ACS), which saw free Black people and former slaves as a potential problem for America, and so it was establishing Liberia as a **colony** where they could be encouraged to move to.

Once in Liberia, Roberts continued to run his American export business, and was soon trading between Liberia and America. He also became involved in local trade. In 1833 Roberts was appointed as high sheriff of the colony of Liberia, responsible for negotiating peace and trade with the colony's neighbours. By 1839 he had become the vice-governor and by 1841 he was governor, making him the first man with African heritage to hold that office. In 1847 Roberts declared Liberia independent and was elected its first president. He was re-elected three times, serving from 1847 to 1856, and then serving a further two terms between 1872 to 1876. Between his stints as president he was a major general in the army, president and law professor at Liberia College and a diplomat. He died on 24 February 1876. Today both the town of Robertsport and Liberia's main airport are named after him, and his face appears on Liberia's $10 bill.

On 16 March 1827 a group of free Black men in New York published the first issue of *Freedom's Journal*. The group of men who created the newspaper had decided that it was time for African Americans to tell their own story. This was the first newspaper in America owned and published by African Americans. Later in the same year the American state of New York abolished slavery.

Vol. 1 No.1, March 16, 1827

Freedom's Journal was founded by Rev. John Wilks, John Brown Russwurm and Samuel Cornish. Russwurm in particular understood the power of the media and its role in constructing how African Americans were seen and treated. He wanted *Freedom's Journal* to challenge negative stereotypes and to instil pride in its African American readership.

The newspaper only lasted for two years but it inspired many other African American leaders and anti-slavery campaigners, including people like James Forten (see 2 September) and Frederick Douglass (see 14 February), to set up their own newspapers to continue the fight for abolition and the cause of civil rights.

17 MARCH ~ JOHN BOYEGA

John Adedayo Bamidele Adegboyega, known as John Boyega, is an award-winning British actor most famous for his major role as Finn, a Stormtrooper who escapes from the First Order and joins the rebellion in the *Star Wars* franchise. He won a Golden Globe Best Supporting Actor (Television) Award for his role as Black Metropolitan Police Officer

© Gage Skidmore, Wikimedia Commons

Leroy Logan, who founded the UK's Black Police Association, in Steve McQueen's *Small Axe* anthology (see 30 November).

Born in London on 17 March 1992, to Nigerian parents, Boyega discovered his love of acting at primary school. As a young adult he trained at the Identity School of Acting, a drama school established by the agent Femi Oguns to train actors from diverse backgrounds.

Alongside acting, Boyega runs his own production company and is an outspoken activist against racism. In June 2020, in the aftermath of the death of George Floyd (see 25 May), Boyega took to the stage at an event at London's Hyde Park and gave a rousing speech to the crowd. His speech ended with a call for action:

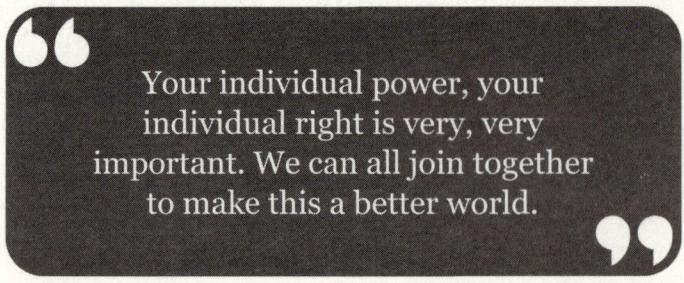

> **"** Your individual power, your individual right is very, very important. We can all join together to make this a better world. **"**

18 MARCH - THE COLOURED ALIEN SEAMEN ORDER

During the First World War – and for centuries before that – sailors from the British Empire served in the Royal Navy and in Britain's merchant navy transporting goods and people. Some of these sailors settled and established communities in British port towns and cities such as Liverpool, Cardiff, South Shields, Hull and London. Some married local white British women and had children. In 1919, however, when many servicemen returning from war could not find work or housing, these sailors became targets for violence and racist discrimination. In 1920 the Aliens Order was passed, requiring all 'aliens' (people who did not have British nationality) seeking to work or live in Britain to register with the police.

On 18 March 1925 the Special Restrictions (Coloured Alien Seamen) Order was passed by the British government. It targeted 'coloured' (non-white) sailors living in Britain. The order required them to produce proof of British nationality. If they could not, they would be classed as aliens, as would their families, even though most of their wives were white women born in Britain. Passports had only become a recent requirement for travel and many Black, Asian and Arab sailors did not have them. Despite having fought for and been long settled in the country, they could not prove their claim to British nationality, as the government refused to recognize alternative forms of identification. Those who could not prove their claim had to register with the police and were prevented from getting jobs. They and their families were threatened with deportation.

The order was in part intended to stop other sailors from the British Empire from coming to Britain, however it also meant that for seventeen years many families lived in poverty and fear of deportation. It remained in force until 1942 when Britiain needed to bolster its navy during the Second World War.

19 MARCH - THE BOHEE BROTHERS

James and George Bohee were two Black Canadian banjo-playing siblings who enjoyed an international musical career in the 19th century, as part of a minstrel troupe (see 8 May).

Photo of the brothers, James on the left and George on the right, from the book *Minstrel Memories*, 1928

The Bohee siblings were born in New Brunswick in the mid-1800s but moved with their family to Boston, where they started their careers as musicians. In 1881 they moved to London, initially performing in the Black minstrel troupe Haverly's Genuine Colored Minstrels. Afterwards they decided to stay in Britain and form their own act, The Bohee Operatic Minstrels. This was a group of thirty musicians, Black and white, and with them the Bohees toured Britain. On arrival in a new town or city, the troupe would drum up custom for their shows by holding flamboyant parades in the streets while wearing their full costume.

The banjo was a very popular musical instrument in Britain at the time, across all sections of society. Banjos were an important part of minstrel music, and the Bohee Brothers were both very talented banjo-players. They wrote their own songs and their performances were lively, and they often danced as they played. Their skills at the finger-picking style of banjo-playing became so renowned that James Bohee set up a banjo-instruction school in London, drawing customers from all walks of life. By far the most famous of his customers was the Prince of Wales, Queen Victoria's eldest son and the future King Edward VII.

20 MARCH - UNCLE TOM'S CABIN

Uncle Tom's Cabin, by the white American author and abolitionist Harriet Beecher Stowe, is the story of two enslaved Black people, Harry and Uncle Tom, who are about to be sold by their owner Arthur Shelby to pay off debts he owes on his farm. Harry decides to make a dash for freedom, escaping to the northern states and then to Canada with his mother. Uncle Tom is left behind and is eventually sold to the brutal owner of another plantation. There he bears the violent abuse of his new owner Simon Legree, before being beaten to death after two of the enslaved women on the plantation escape and he refuses to tell his owner where they have gone. At the end George Shelby, the son of Uncle Tom's original owner, arrives to try to buy him back. Shocked to find that Uncle Tom is dead, he returns home and frees all of the enslaved people on his land.

The story was published as a novel on 20 March 1852, becoming an instant international bestseller. The author personally sent a copy to Prince Albert, the husband of Queen Victoria, asking him to pass it to the Queen.

THE AUCTION SALE. Page 174.

From Uncle Tom's cabin : or, life among the lowly 1852 (1850s). Public Domain

When Beecher Stowe visited Britain in 1853 she was presented with a petition in support of the abolition of slavery in the USA that was signed by over half a million British women.

Although the book delivered an anti-slavery message, its stereotypes of Black characters have been criticized. The way in which Uncle Tom just accepts his brutal treatment and forgives those who carry it out is particularly controversial. The term 'Uncle Tom' is used by some people to describe Black people who accept racist treatment and turn their backs on the struggle against racism.

21 MARCH - THE SHARPEVILLE MASSACRE

On 21 March 1960, in the South African township of Sharpeville, sixty-nine people were killed and 180 people injured when police opened fire on protestors outside the police station. The crowd had gathered to protest the **pass laws**, which were an important part of the **apartheid** regime in South Africa at the time. In the 1950s rules became even more focused on keeping the races apart, and the police used the pass laws to intimidate and imprison opponents of the apartheid system.

Thousands of people gathered to protest in Sharpeville and through the day the crowd grew. By the afternoon the crowd was moving closer to the police station and police started using tear gas. At around 1 p.m. the police tried to arrest a protestor, and the crowd surged forward. The police opened fire, shooting into the crowd. Many of those killed and wounded were hit while trying to flee.

The Sharpeville Massacre was reported around the world and led to protests in South Africa. It marked a turning point in attitudes towards South Africa and apartheid abroad. The **United Nations** passed Resolution 134 condemning what had happened and began isolating South Africa from the international community. Today in South Africa, 21 March is a public holiday that commemorates the Sharpeville Massacre and celebrates human rights.

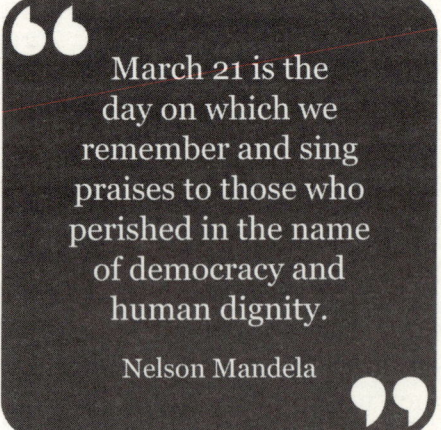

> March 21 is the day on which we remember and sing praises to those who perished in the name of democracy and human dignity.
>
> Nelson Mandela

22 MARCH – SURYA BONALY

The French figure skater Surya Bonaly was born on 15 December 1973 in Nice, France. Her birth mother was from Reunion Island, a French overseas territory in the Indian Ocean, and her birth father came from Ivory Coast. She was adopted as a baby and grew up in the French countryside.

Focus on Sport/Getty Images

Inspired by her mother, who was a physical education teacher, Bonaly had a very active childhood. She took up ice-skating at the age of two and by the age of four was also a keen gymnast. Combining her skills from gymnastics with her ice-skating would be very important to her later success. At the age of eleven she was recruited to train with the French national figure skating team and the family moved with her to Paris.

Bonaly went on to become a French national champion nine times, European champion five times and world silver medal winner three times. She represented France at the Olympic Games in 1992, 1994 and 1998. At the Winter Olympics of 1998 she became the first and only Olympic skater to land a backflip on one blade.

Retiring after the 1998 Olympics, Bonaly continued to skate professionally in ice shows, but retired from performing in 2015. She is an activist, encouraging racial diversity and tackling racism in sport. She also advocates for animal rights, and has taken part in campaigns against seal hunting, bullfighting and the use of fur in fashion. In 2019 she was made a commander of the Legion of Honour, which is France's highest honour.

23 MARCH - YASUKE, THE BLACK SAMURAI

Almost 500 years ago an African man called Yasuke became the first Black Samurai in Japan. The Samurai were elite Japanese warriors, highly trained in martial arts, weaponry and horse-riding. Yasuke arrived in Japan in 1579 as the bodyguard for the Italian Jesuit missionary Alessandro Valignano, but historians think he was originally from Mozambique.

When Yasuke entered the city of Kyoto in March 1581 he caused a sensation. Locals crowded onto the streets to see this tall, African stranger. A powerful Japanese warlord called Oda Nobunaga heard the news and arranged a meeting. Nobunaga was impressed by Yasuke's strength and power.

The two men soon found that they had much in common. Yasuke underwent martial arts training and quickly learned to speak Japanese. Before long, Nobunaga honoured him with Samurai status and Yasuke became his weapon-bearer in battle. However, in 1582, Nobunaga was attacked by one of his generals and decided to take his own life in an act of seppuku – an honourable death. Yasuke continued to fight with Nobunaga's son but was eventually captured. It is not known what happened to Yasuke afterwards.

Yasuke is now remembered as a legendary warrior of Japanese history. In 2021 he became the inspiration for a Japanese-American Netflix anime series which re-imagines his story in a magical alternate reality.

DID YOU KNOW?

24 MARCH - SIDNEY POITIER

The actor, director, civil rights activist and diplomat Sidney Poitier was born in 1927 in Florida. He spent his childhood in the Bahamas before coming to America in 1942, aged fifteen, and moving to New York a year later. After a year in the US Army, Poitier auditioned twice to join New York's American Negro

Theatre. He quickly established himself as a respected stage and film actor, and became a successful director in the 1970s. He believed in the arts as a platform for social change, and most of his work addressed the issue of racial prejudice. In 1958 he became the first Black male actor to be nominated for an Academy Award for his role in the film *The Defiant Ones*, and he won the Best Actor Academy Award in 1963 for his role in *Lilies of the Field*. In 1959 he played the lead role in the debut Broadway play by Lorraine Hansberry (see 11 March), *A Raisin in the Sun*, and in 1961 returned to the role in the film version.

Like his lifelong friend Harry Belafonte (see 1 March) Poitier was a committed civil rights activist. He donated time and money to support the movement, attending events including the 1963 March on Washington (see 28 August). He was appointed as the Bahamas' ambassador to Japan in 1997 and to UNESCO in 2002.

On 24 March 2002 Poitier received an Academy Lifetime Achievement Award presented by Denzel Washington 'in recognition of his remarkable accomplishments as an artist and as a human'. In 2009 president Obama awarded Poitier the Presidential Medal of Freedom. Poitier died on 6 January 2022 aged ninety-four, and on 19 January theatres in Broadway, where his career had begun, dimmed their lights in tribute to his memory.

25 MARCH ~ WALTER TULL

Walter Tull was born in 1888, in the town of Folkestone, on the south coast of England. His father Daniel was born in Barbados, the son of a Black enslaved woman, and moved to Britain in 1876, where he met Tull's white mother, Alice Palmer. When Tull was a young boy his parents died, and he and his brother were sent to live in a children's home in the East End of London.

After leaving school Walter trained to become a printer, but his real passion was playing football. He was playing for a club in Clapton when he was spotted by a talent scout in 1908. He then joined the First Division London team Tottenham Hotspur.

© Bob Thomas/Popperfoto/Getty Images.

Portrait of Walter Tull as footballer of note playing for Tottenham Hotspur, 1909

In the summer of 1909 he travelled to South America and played for Tottenham during a tour of Argentina and Uruguay. Aged twenty-one he was being paid £4 per week, the most a footballer could earn under the rules of the early 20th century. But the newspapers from the time tell us that Walter's experiences at Tottenham Hotspur were not happy. He began his first season very well, but at a game against Bristol City, in October 1909, he was subjected to racism from the Bristol

City fans. One newspaper reported what had happened under the headline, 'Football and Colour Prejudice'. That traumatic experience shocked Tull and his teammates. After that he struggled to play and spent much of the season on the bench. In 1911 Tull was recruited by a new team, Northampton, where he had a better experience, scoring twelve goals in his first nine matches.

By 1914 Walter's reputation had grown and Glasgow Rangers were interested in bringing him to Scotland to play for them. But that summer Tull's life – like the lives of millions of people across the world – was changed dramatically when the First World War began. Walter joined the British Army, becoming part of the 17th Battalion of the Middlesex Regiment, known as the 1st Footballers' Battalion, as it was made up of players. His commanding officer, Major Frank Buckley, had been a player for Manchester United.

After training, the regiment was sent to France to fight the German Army on the Western Front, a line of trenches that stretched hundreds of miles, all the way across France and Belgium. The Western Front was defended by soldiers from Britain, France and Belgium, and their overseas colonies. In 1916, after fighting on the Western Front, Walter was treated for what today we call post-traumatic stress disorder. He was brought home to recover before returning to the Western Front, where he took part in the latter stages of the famous Battle of the Somme.

In February 1917 Walter returned to Britain. He travelled up to Scotland and there began training to become an officer, having been recommended for promotion by his commanders. This recommendation was highly unusual because it was against the rules of the British Army at the time. The British Army's Manual of Military Law, published in 1914, described men who were not white as 'alien soldiers' and under those laws a man who was mixed-race, like Tull, was not allowed to become an officer or have 'any actual command or power' over other soldiers. To become an officer in the British Army soldiers had to have been born in Britain but also be 'of pure European descent' – which meant they had to be white. But by 1917 Britain needed many more new officers because so many had died fighting on the Western Front. Walter Tull had years of experience as a soldier, he was respected and fit. So it seems that when it came to Tull, the Army's racist laws were put aside, and he was allowed to do his training, becoming a second lieutenant in May 1917.

Later that year he took part in fighting in Italy and was so effective as a soldier that he was recommended for the Military Cross – a distinguished medal in the British army awarded to recognize acts of exemplary gallantry.

In 1918 Walter was back on the Western Front. In March of that year the German Army launched their Spring Offensive, a huge attack on the trenches defended by the French and British armies. They fired more than one million shells, and hundreds of thousands of their soldiers rushed forward to attack. It was during this German offensive, in what became known as the First Battle of Bapaume, that Walter Tull was killed fighting near the French village of Favreuil. He was just twenty-nine years old. His body was never recovered from the battlefield, despite attempts by men of his unit to do so. Today Walter Tull's name is among the 34,785 names engraved into the Arras Memorial in Nord-Pas-de-Calais, in France – the names of soldiers who died but whose bodies were never found.

26 MARCH – JACKIE ROBINSON

On 26 March 1984, Rachel Robinson, Jackie Robinson's widow, accepted his **Presidential Medal of Freedom** at the White House.

Robinson was the first Black player to break the **colour bar** in major league baseball. From his first game with the Brooklyn Dodgers on 15 April 1947 (now celebrated as Jackie Robinson Day) he faced continued abuse from fans and other players, including his own team. The Dodgers' manager held firm, and once Robinson's outstanding ability began to benefit the team, the abuse died down. He was named Rookie of the Year in 1947, and League MVP in 1949. He was the first Black player inducted into the National Baseball Hall of Fame in 1962.

After retiring in 1957, Robinson threw his weight behind the civil rights movement. He had been court-martialled in 1944 during his army career, for refusing to move on a **segregated** bus, but was eventually acquitted. Robinson reprised this incident in 1959 when he refused to leave a whites-only waiting room at an airport. One thousand people marched on the airport and it was **desegregated** soon after. Dr King acknowledged that Robinson's public profile and popularity greatly helped the civil rights movement. Robinson also continued to champion Black baseball players and protested the lack of Black managers right up until his death on 24 October 1972 at just fifty-three years old.

> Jackie Robinson's older brother Matthew 'Mack' Robinson finished 0.4 seconds behind Jesse Owens at the Berlin Olympics (see 3 August), taking the silver medal in the 200m final.

DID YOU KNOW?

27 MARCH - ADE ADEPITAN

Ade Adepitan is an athlete, Paralympic medal winner, disability advocate, actor, presenter and author. He was born in Lagos, Nigeria, on 27 March 1973. As a very young child he caught polio, a viral infection that can cause serious health complications and even death. It damaged Adepitan's legs and meant that he needed to use leg callipers and wheelchairs to move around.

© Garry Knight, Wiki Commons

At the age of three, Adepitan came to live in the UK, settling in London with his family. At school he was very interested and capable at sport. When he was twelve he took up wheelchair basketball, and by the age of twenty he was offered a chance to play professional wheelchair basketball for two years in Spain. In 2000 he was selected to play on Great Britain men's wheelchair basketball team at the Olympics in Sydney. Four years later he was on the team again at the 2004 Summer Paralympics in Athens, where the team won a bronze medal. A year later he won gold as part of Team GB at the 2005 Paralympic World Cup in Manchester.

Alongside his athletic career Adepitan also has a successful career in television. He is an actor and author, and he also presents programmes for adults and for children about disability, travel and sport.

28 MARCH ~ LILIAN BADER

Lilian Bader was born in 1918 in Liverpool to an Irish-British mother and a Barbadian father. Her father had served in the British Merchant Navy during the First World War. When the Second World War started, Lilian was inspired to follow in her father's footsteps and join the war effort.

Bader joined the Navy, Army and Air Force Institute (NAAFI) at Catterick Camp in Yorkshire in 1939. She completed seven weeks of training before she was asked to leave when the authorities there discovered her father's Caribbean background.

In 1940 she heard that some people from the West Indies had been able to join the Royal Air Force. So, on 28 March 1941, Bader enlisted in the Women's Auxiliary Air Force (WAAF), a military service whose job it was to support the Royal Air Force. She thrived in the WAAF, where she became a Leading Aircraft Woman and eventually was promoted to the rank of Acting Corporal.

Bader served in the WAAF until 1944 when she left to have her first child. After the war, once her children had grown up, she studied for a degree and became a teacher. Today she is remembered for her contribution to British life and her refusal to accept rejection and injustice.

29 MARCH - HENRY 'BOX' BROWN

Henry 'Box' Brown was an enslaved African American, born on a plantation in the state of Virginia in around 1815. When he was fifteen his owner allowed a local tobacco factory to hire him. He moved from the plantation into a rented house, married an enslaved woman called Nancy, and they had three children. Brown made regular payments to his wife's owner so that she would not be sold and moved away from him. However, one day he came home from work to find that his wife and children were gone, sold by her owner.

This experience changed Brown, and in 1849, at the age of thirty-three, in a daring and imaginative move, he decided to escape to freedom. Aided by a free Black man named James C. A. Smith and a white man named Samuel A. Smith, on 29 March 1849 Brown had himself nailed into a wooden box in the city of Richmond, Virginia and mailed to Pennsylvania, a northern state where slavery was not legal. The small box (0.91 x 0.81 x 0.61 metres) was labelled 'Handle with Care' and 'This Side Up'. After a twenty-seven-hour ordeal Brown was safely delivered to the offices of the Pennsylvania Anti Slavery Society. Finally a free man, Brown moved to Massachusetts. He became an anti-slavery speaker and got to know Frederick Douglass (see 14 February). It was there that he got his nickname and became known as Henry 'Box' Brown.

Fearful of re-enslavement after Congress passed the second Fugitive Slave Act in 1850, Brown moved to Britain and gave speaking tours across the country, bringing the wooden box with him as a prop. In 1851 he re-enacted his escape in the north of England and posted himself from the city of Bradford to the neighbouring city of Leeds. Brown married an English woman, Jane, and lived in Manchester with her and their children. Eventually he returned to America with his family and spent the rest of his life as a performer.

Brown was not the only person to escape enslavement by means of a box. Around eight years later a young Black woman, Lear Green, made her way to freedom in an old chest.

Enslaved since childhood, at eighteen years old Green met and fell in love with freed Black man William Adams. He wanted to marry her but she refused as she knew that any children she had would also be enslaved. Desperate to be with her, Adams and his mother hatched a plan to smuggle Green out of Baltimore in an old wooden sailor's chest. They lined it with pillows and blankets and left some food and water for Green for the eighteen-hour steamship journey. Although a freed Black woman, Adams' mother was confined to the ship's deck, but this allowed her to stay with the chest and open it to allow Green some fresh air.

Green made it to Philadelphia and then moved on to New York where she and Adams were married.

30 MARCH ~ CHRIS SMALLS

On 30 March 2020, Chris Smalls, an assistant manager at an Amazon warehouse, led a walkout in Staten Island, New York. He had raised concerns about safe working conditions during the Covid-19 pandemic but, instead of discussing the matter with him, Amazon fired him. Smalls gained huge support on social media and he and his co-worker Derrick Palmer fought back by rallying local Amazon workers and organizing protests. On one occasion Amazon had Smalls and others arrested when they delivered food and union materials to the warehouse car park.

On 20 April 2021 the Staten Island workers voted to support Smalls in establishing the Amazon Labor Union – the first ever workers' union at the billion-dollar company. This was a huge victory for workers' rights. Smalls, who is now president of the ALU, currently works to help people take similar action in their own workplaces.

© Legoktm, Wikimedia Commons

Chris Smalls was named one of *Time* magazine's most influential people of 2022.

31 MARCH ~ TONI MORRISON

Toni Morrison was an American author, most well known for her fifth novel *Beloved*. Based on the true and tragic story of an enslaved woman, Margaret Garner, on the run from slave hunters with her young daughter, the book was highly praised by critics and fellow authors. On 31 March 1988 *Beloved* was awarded the **Pulitzer Prize** for Fiction.

Morrison started out working in publishing, editing books by authors including Angela Davis (see 13 October) and Muhammad Ali (see 25 February). She did not begin her own writing career until she was thirty-nine, when she published her first book *The Bluest Eye*, while she was still working in publishing. *Beloved* was the first book she wrote after leaving that job. It is one of three linked novels, followed by *Jazz* and *Paradise*. Morrison wrote eleven novels and several children's books along with her son Slade. She also wrote essays and speeches and taught creative writing at several universities.

Morrsions's writing has focused on stories of Black people and the Black community. The importance of her work was recognized in 1993 when she became the first Black woman to win the **Nobel** Prize for Literature. She was also named a Living Legend by the **Library of Congress**, and in 2012 was granted the **Presidential Medal of Freedom**.

Toni Morrison died at the age of eighty-eight on 5 August 2019.

> If there's a book that you want to read, but it hasn't been written yet, then you must write it.

APRIL

1 APRIL - GIL SCOTT-HERON

Poet and musician Gil Scott-Heron was born on 1 April 1949. Born in Chicago, he was raised in Tennessee by his grandmother Lily Scott. She was a musician and civil rights activist and introduced her grandson to the work of Langston Hughes (see 1 February), effectively shaping Scott-Heron's career. He moved to New York to study and met musician Brian Jackson. They began working together and put music to Scott-Heron's poetry.

Scott-Heron's work was part of a budding music genre characterized by biting political commentary recited over jazz and blues influenced music. His most well known and most sampled track, 'The Revolution Will Not Be Televised', appeared on his first album in 1970. Along with other artists like The Last Poets, his work served as a blueprint for hip-hop. Scott-Heron's activism also made a lasting mark. He campaigned alongside Stevie Wonder (see 21 May) to make Dr King Jr's birthday a holiday and was a vocal critic of South African apartheid.

Over his lifetime Scott-Heron published several novels and anthologies of his poetry alongside his prolific musical output. His final album *I'm New Here* was released in 2010 to critical acclaim. Scott-Heron died the following year and was granted a posthumous Grammy Lifetime Achievement Award in 2012.

> **DID YOU KNOW?**
>
> Scott-Heron's father, Gilbert St Elmo Heron, became the first (and only) Black professional soccer player in the United States when he joined the Detroit Wolverines in 1946. He went on to be the first Black player for Celtic FC in Scotland.

2 APRIL - WINNIE MANDELA

© Superikonoskop, Wikimedia Commons

Winifred Madikizela-Mandela, born in 1936, was a leading anti-apartheid activist in South Africa. A former social worker, she married the leader of the African National Congress, Nelson Mandela, in 1958. That same year, while she was pregnant with her first child, she was one of over one thousand women arrested for protesting against the passbook system. During this first period in detention she nearly miscarried her baby but received medical attention from fellow detainee Albertina Sisulu, who was a trained midwife. She was detained by the authorities on many more occasions during her turbulent life. Her longest imprisonment was 491 days, during which she was kept in solitary confinement, tortured and beaten.

During her husband's many years of imprisonment (1962–90), Mandela became an important spokesperson of the anti-apartheid movement. She fought for justice for her husband and for all Black South Africans, while raising two daughters on her own.

After the end of apartheid, Mandela was elected Head of the ANC Women's League in 1993 and held several government positions during her life. She is now a controversial figure in South African politics because of her involvement in criminal activities in her later years. Winnie Mandela died on 2 April 2018 at the age of eighty-one.

3 APRIL - MICHELLE OGUNDEHIN

The award-winning writer, author, TV presenter and influencer Michelle Ogundehin was born in Manchester in 1967 to a Nigerian father and British mother. She trained as an architect at London's Bartlett School before beginning her career as a writer at *Tate Art* magazine. She joined *Elle Decoration* magazine in 1997, becoming editor in chief in 2004, and over the thirteen years she worked there the magazine won many awards. She runs her own design business and is often a presenter on British television, appearing on *Great Designs* and *Interior Design Masters*.

While at *Elle Decoration*, Ogundehin used her reach and influence to champion the design industry and look after the rights of designers. At the beginning of April in 2012, she started a campaign to help designers keep ownership of their work. In Britain, artists, film-makers and authors keep the copyright of their work for their lifetime and for seventy years after their death. This means that if anyone wants to use any of their art, they have to pay the artist, or their surviving family, to be allowed to use it, and to name the artist that they have borrowed from. For designers of objects (like furniture) this protection only lasted for twenty-five years, so people could make cheap copies of their work and would not have to pay or name the original designer. Ogundehin campaigned for designers to get the same copyright protections as artists, and by the end of May that same year the law was changed.

4 APRIL ~ MAYA ANGELOU

Marguerite Annie Johnson was born on 4 April 1928 in St Louis, Missouri. She would become known to the world as Maya Angelou, a writer, poet, performer, director, activist and teacher. As a child she was abused by her mother's boyfriend and consequently was mute for five years. Her love of poetry, and her teacher's encouragement to read poems out loud, led her to recover her voice and start speaking again.

Maya Angelou reciting her poem *On the Pulse of Morning* at the inauguration of President Bill Clinton in Washington DC, 20 January 1993

Angelou's adult life was highly creative. In the early 1950s she trained as a dancer, performing with the choreographer Alvin Ailey (see 10 November). She was soon performing as a dancer and singer in the opera *Porgy and Bess*, touring Europe before returning to America and releasing her first record in 1957. In the late 1950s she began to focus on her writing and also became a civil rights activist and a close friend of Dr Martin Luther King Jr (see 10 January). She lived in Africa during the early 1960s, in Egypt and then in Ghana, where she wrote for the *African Review* and the *Ghanaian Times*. While in Ghana, Angelou met and befriended Malcolm X (see 21 February). She returned to America to support X's Organization of Afro-American Unity, and was devastated when X was assassinated.

Angelou's first book, the autobiography *I Know Why the Caged Bird Sings*, was published in 1969. She went on to write another six acclaimed autobiographies, as well as poetry collections, plays and films. She also began writing music for film and television and returned to acting.

Angelou continued to work until her death in May 2014. She received many honours, including the **Presidential Medal of Freedom**, awarded to her by Barack Obama in 2010.

DID YOU KNOW?

Angelou was making history even before she became famous. In 1943, encouraged by her mother and attracted by the smart uniforms, fifteen-year-old Angelou lied about her age and experience to secure a job with the Market Street Railway Company, becoming one of San Francisco's first Black female streetcar conductors. She wrote about her time on the streetcars in *I Know Why the Caged Bird Sings* in which she recalls swinging from the back of the clattering car on her Market Street route. Angelou spent five months in the job before returning to school.

5 APRIL - LENNY HENRY

Lenny Henry is a British comedian and actor. In 1985 he co-founded the charity Comic Relief to raise money to help people in Britain and around the world. The first fundraising event, *Comic Relief Utterly Utterly Live*, was a show held over 4, 5 and 6 April in 1986 at the Shaftesbury Theatre in London. Two years later it became Red Nose Day, with a telethon on 8 February 1988. Henry hosted the event live on British television, introducing comedy sketches and charity reports, accompanied by a range of comedians and celebrities.

Henry was born in Dudley in 1958, to parents who had come to Britain from Jamaica. When he was still at school he discovered his talent for comedy and impressions. At the age of just sixteen he appeared on and won the British television show *New Faces*, which was a national talent competition. The victory launched his career on television and on the stage. He went on to star in *The Fosters*, Britain's first comedy series with a largely Black cast, and became a presenter on the children's Saturday morning show *Tiswas*.

In the 1980s he was given his own television show, *The Lenny Henry Show*, which featured him playing a range of Black characters he had invented and doing spoofs of famous films and music videos. Henry's career has been very varied. By 2009, in his early fifties, Henry was establishing himself as an actor, and he made his Shakespearean debut playing Othello.

Having left school at sixteen, Henry returned to academic study in his forties. He was awarded a knighthood in 2015, and in 2016 became chancellor of Birmingham City University. He is now visiting professor of media diversity and chancellor at the university and is a member of the Sir Lenny Henry Centre for Media Diversity, which campaigns for accurate representation of all sections of society throughout the UK media.

6 APRIL - OLAUDAH EQUIANO

Oluadah Equiano, who was buried on this day in London in 1797, is believed to have been born around 1745 in what is now Nigeria. When he was about eleven years old he was captured by African slave traders and sold into slavery. He was shipped across the Atlantic Ocean, first to Barbados and then to a plantation house in the American colony of Virginia. He was then sold to a British naval officer called Michael Pascal. Pascal renamed him Gustavus Vassa, after a 17th-century Swedish king, and put him to work as a sailor. He worked on board ships that transported the goods grown by enslaved labour. For over twenty years he sailed across the West Indies, along the coasts of Northern and Central America, to Europe and even as far as Turkey.

During his twenty years at sea he became literate and very skilled at trading goods. By the 1780s he had saved enough money to buy his freedom and move to London. Once there his life became very different. He married a white British woman called Susannah Cullen and started a family. By 1783 he had become involved in the early abolitionist movement alongside campaigners like Granville Sharp. Soon he was a full-time campaigner who gave powerful anti-slavery speeches at abolitionist events.

Equiano wrote a book, published in March 1789, called *The Interesting Narrative of the Life of Olaudah Equiano*. It became a bestseller and was republished several times in Britain. An American edition was published and the book was also translated into German, Russian and Dutch. With his friend Ottobah Cugoano (see 24 September) and other Black Britons, Equiano founded a group called the Sons of Africa to continue the fight for the abolition of slavery (see 31 January).

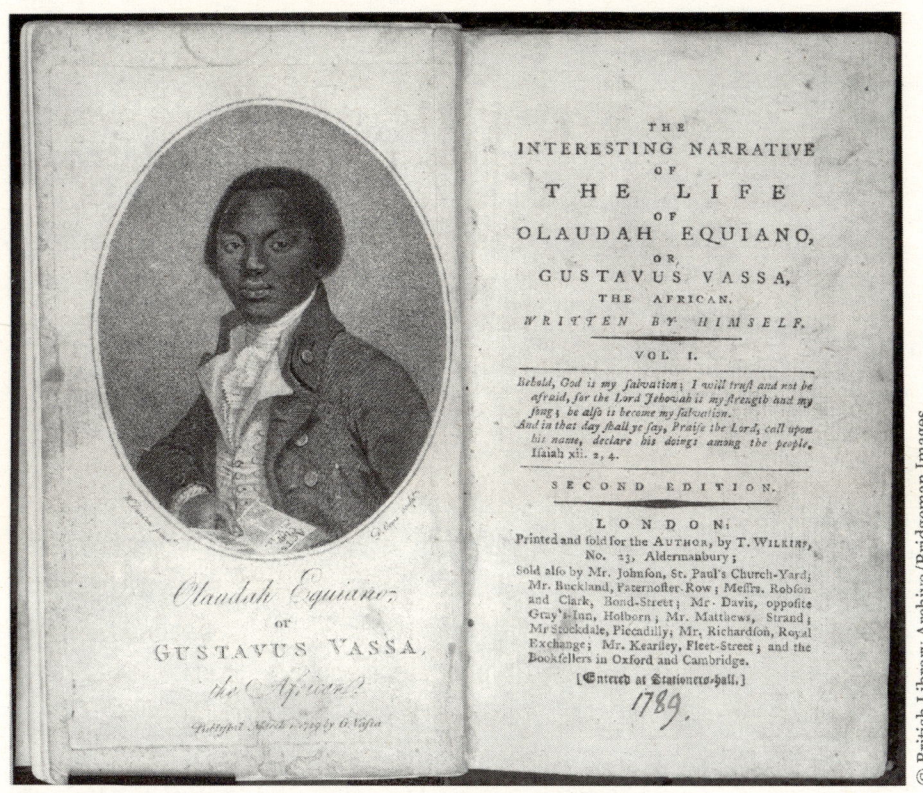

Title page from *The Interesting Narrative of the Life of Olaudah Equiano, or Gustavus Vassa, the African*. Published 1789

Equiano died on 31 March 1797 and his death was reported in newspapers in Britain and America. In recent years Equiano's life and his contribution to the abolitionist movement has been remembered. Until recently it was not known where Equiano was buried, but some historical detective work in 2019 discovered that he was buried at Whitefield's Tabernacle on Tottenham Court Road in London. The church was destroyed by bombs during the Second World War and the site now lies under a park. In 2021 his book, *The Interesting Narrative of the Life of Olaudah Equiano*, was republished and today historians continue to research his fascinating life.

7 APRIL - TACKY'S REVOLT

Tacky's Revolt is the name given to the uprising of enslaved people on the island of Jamaica in the 1760s. The treatment of enslaved people in the British colony of Jamaica was particularly brutal. The Jamaica Slave Code of 1664 made it legal to punish them with extreme violence and even death. It is thought that Tacky was from an Akan-speaking kingdom on Africa's Gold Coast and had royal connections before becoming enslaved. He led the violent rebellion that began on Easter Monday.

Just before daybreak on the morning of 7 April 1760, enslaved people rose up and took control of their plantations. They seized guns and gunpowder and killed many of the white slave masters. Encouraged by the rebellion's early success, more enslaved people came to join Tacky's forces.

On 9 April 1760 the British lieutenant governor of Jamaica sent soldiers to quash the rebellion. They were supported by Maroon soldiers from the island. The Maroons were a group of Africans who had successfully freed themselves from slavery during the First Maroon War in the 1730s. They had won their freedom but had signed a treaty to help the British fight against other rebellions. Tacky was forced to go on the run and on 14 April he was captured and killed. Over the next few months, Tacky's remaining followers were either killed, died by suicide or were taken to court and then executed. Even so, smaller uprisings continued for the rest of the year and, Tacky's Revolt became the inspiration for later rebellions, both on the island of Jamaica and beyond.

8 APRIL - KOFI ANNAN

In 1997 Kofi Atta Annan became the first Black secretary general of the United Nations (UN).

Born in Ghana on 8 April 1938, he studied at universities in Ghana, the USA and Switzerland. In 1962 he began his career at the UN – the international organization established at the end of the Second World War to promote peace and cooperation between countries all around the world. As their secretary general, Annan was the person in charge of the organization.

Hecker / MSC (2018), Wikimedia Commons

In 2001 Annan was awarded the Nobel Peace Prize in recognition of his work to promote peace around the world and his commitment to human rights.

In 2006, after ten years of working for the UN, Annan retired from his role, but he continued to work for international peace and human rights. He founded the Kofi Annan Foundation, which aims to make the world a fairer, more peaceful place.

9 APRIL - PAUL ROBESON

The American singer, actor, lawyer, professional football player and political activist Paul Robeson was born in Princeton, New Jersey on 9 April 1898, the son of a former slave. He was academically gifted and a talented sportsman, graduating as valedictorian from Rutgers College before gaining a law degree from Columbia University. After short careers as an American football player and then as a lawyer, he became a singer and a stage and film actor, and an important figure in the Harlem Renaissance. With his new career came the opportunity to travel internationally, and these experiences had a profound effect on Robeson.

Paul Robeson leading Moore Shipyard workers in singing the 'Star Spangled Banner' during their lunch hour, September 1942, Oakland, California

African American Activities in Industry, Government, and the Armed Forces, National Archives Catalog

In 1928 Robeson came to perform at the London premier of the musical *Showboat*, and he stayed in Britain until 1939. It was there that he began learning about socialism and communism from friends, including the authors H. G. Wells and Aldous Huxley. On the street one day in 1929 Robeson encountered a group of Welsh miners. They had taken part in Britain's general strike of 1926 and had been blacklisted from employment ever since. They sang protest songs as they had marched to London looking for work. Robeson immediately joined the march and donated money to their cause, beginning a connection to Wales that lasted the rest of his life. Robeson campaigned tirelessly against fascism and imperialism, for the rights of the working classes and the rights of colonized countries to rule themselves.

Following the Second World War, and back in America, Robeson co-founded the monthly Black newspaper *Freedom*, with W. E. B. DuBois (see 23 February). Named after *Freedom's Journal* (see 16 March), *Freedom* ran from 1950 to 1955 and provided a platform for Robeson to share his anti-imperialist and pro-labour movement views. However, Robeson suffered for his political views. He was called before the HUAC and was blacklisted from stage and screen work. His passport was revoked from 1950 until 1958, stopping him from travelling abroad to earn his living. Robeson's health and career never properly recovered and he died on 23 January 1976, aged seventy-seven.

Robeson's contribution to culture and politics has since come to be recognized and honoured. In 1978 Robeson was posthumously given an award by the United Nations General Assembly for his personal contribution to the international campaign against apartheid, and twenty years later he was awarded a Lifetime Grammy Award. Buildings and roads have been named after him and some of his residences in the USA and elsewhere bear plaques in his memory.

10 APRIL - OPERATION SWAMP

Operation Swamp was the codename given by the **Metropolitan Police** to a six-day policing operation in Brixton, an area of London with a large Black community, which started on 6 April 1981. There was high unemployment in the area, robbery and burglary rates had been rising, and the police decided to increase their presence on the streets and to make use of the 'sus laws'. Also known as '**stop and search**', these laws allowed police to stop anyone they suspected of being on the streets intending to commit a crime, and to search them. The use of stop and search was very unpopular, particularly because the police were tending to use it far more on Black people.

In the afternoons and evenings, over one hundred police officers in plain clothes were on the street. They stopped and searched around one thousand people, and made around one hundred arrests for a range of offences, very few of which were for robbery or burglary. The operation took place just three months after the New Cross Fire and one month after the Black People's Day of Action (see 18 January and 2 March), at a time when distrust of the police by the Black community was running high.

On 10 April, the fifth day of the exercise, an officer saw a young Black man who was bleeding from a stab wound. At first the young man ran from the officer, but he was then put in a taxi, and eventually into a police car to go to hospital. Concerned that the man was being arrested instead of being helped, a crowd surrounded the police car and pulled him out.

That night untrue rumours spread that instead of trying to help a young man who had been stabbed, the police had stopped him from getting treatment and he had died. By the next morning tensions were high and Brixton was about to be the location of the worst race riots in British history.

11 APRIL - THE BRIXTON RIOTS

On 11 April 1981, the sixth day of Operation Swamp (see 10 April), the police responded to rising tensions with the Black community in Brixton by putting even more officers on the street.

11 April 1981, during the 1981 Brixton Riot in London, police with riot shields line up outside the Atlantic Pub, on the corner of Atlantic Road and Coldharbour Lane, Brixton

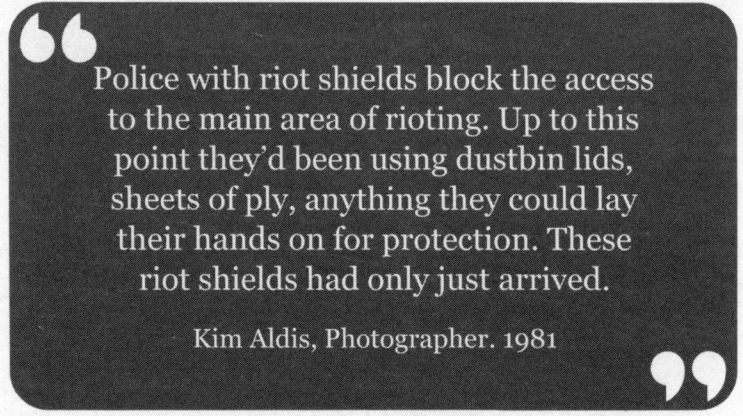

> " Police with riot shields block the access to the main area of rioting. Up to this point they'd been using dustbin lids, sheets of ply, anything they could lay their hands on for protection. These riot shields had only just arrived.
>
> Kim Aldis, Photographer. 1981 "

At around four that afternoon, two police officers stopped and searched a taxi in Railton Road, Brixton. They were soon surrounded by a crowd of people, some of whom started throwing things. The confrontation spread and shops in nearby streets were looted. Within hours the unrest became a riot, and police officers from all over London were sent to stop it. People fought police officers in the street, some throwing bricks and bottles at police cars and fire engines that had been sent to the scene. Other members of the community tried to talk to the rioters and the police to bring calm to the situation.

The riot was over by the afternoon of 12 April. Hundreds had been hurt – police officers, firefighters and community members – cars and buildings had been burned and looted. Months later, similar riots took place elsewhere in the UK, including Birmingham, Liverpool and Manchester.

Lord Scarman, a British law lord, was asked to lead an inquiry into the riots, and in November 1981 his report was published. Scarman had found evidence that the police had indeed overused their stop and search powers on the Black community, and his report called for a new code of behaviour for the police. This led to the creation of the Police Complaints Authority, which investigates allegations of police wrongdoing brought to it by members of the public. Scarman also called on the government to tackle the problems of unemployment and chronic lack of investment that were affecting these communities, but his recommendations were ignored, and rioting would break out again in Brixton in the 1980s and 90s.

Lord Scarman, 1983

12 APRIL ~ THE PHILADELPHIA FREE AFRICAN SOCIETY

In the late 1700s Philadelphia was becoming a destination for many freed people. The Black population was growing and two men, Richard Allen and Absalom Jones, recognized that these people would need some help with their new lives. They founded the Free African Society on 12 April 1787.

The Society worked as both a church and a mutual aid organization. For a monthly fee of one shilling, people could join up and then, if ever they fell on hard times, they could rely on the society to offer support. It also offered help with literacy and food programmes for widows and children.

During an outbreak of yellow fever in 1793 the Society gave medical aid to all in the city, nursing the sick, transporting people to quarantine sites and burying the dead. Allen and Jones wrote an account of their work in *A Narrative of the Proceedings of the Black People during the late awful calamity*.

Excluded from worship in white churches, the Society was also founded to provide a place of worship for all Black people, no matter what type of Christianity they followed. Eventually this led to the break-up of the society as the founders disagreed on how worship should be organized; Allen left and established the Bethel African Methodist Episcopal church in 1794.

Although the Free African Society didn't last long, it inspired the creation of many other aid organizations for Black people.

> Allen and Jones were asked to stay and help with the yellow fever outbreak because many physicians wrongly believed that Black people were immune to it.
>
> **DID YOU KNOW?**

13 APRIL - KATHERINE JOHNSON

We are surrounded by computers – devices that store and process data, and can perform complicated calculations in a blink of an eye. So it is perhaps a bit surprising to learn that in 1953 a gifted mathematician called Katherine Johnson was about to start a job as a 'computer'. Her new job was with NACA, which would soon change its name to NASA. The complex mathematical work she would do in the coming years would play a vital role in making space exploration possible.

Katherine Johnson was born Creoloa Katherine Coleman in White Sulfur Springs, West Virginia in 1918. From an early age she loved learning and was especially fascinated by numbers. The county the Coleman family lived in did not provide high school education for its Black students, but her parents were willing to do everything they could to support their children's education, so she and her three older siblings attended a school over one hundred miles away. During the school year, she and her siblings and their mother lived in Institute, while her father stayed to work in Sulfur Springs. She was only ten when she started high school and graduated four years early, at the age of fourteen. At the age of fifteen she became a student at West Virginia State College, which was one of America's HBCUs. The degree involved studying numerous subjects, but soon

her talent for mathematics was clear and she completed every mathematics course in the college. She graduated **summa cum laude** with a degree in French and mathematics in 1937.

Despite her high grades she was not able to go straight into graduate study. At that time the graduate colleges in West Virginia did not accept Black students, so instead she became a teacher. Two years later, in 1939, she married her first husband, James Goble. That same year West Virginia decided to open its graduate colleges to Black students and she and two male graduates were selected for places at West Virginia University. After attending her first class, however, she decided to leave and devote her time to raising a family. Thirteen years later her husband became ill, and so she went back to work as a teacher. Then, at a family party, a relative told her about the new jobs being advertised at NACA and that they were open to Black women. She applied and began work as a computer in 1953. Once again, her mathematical talent got her noticed and she was soon working with a team of aeronautical engineers on projects involving high speed aircraft.

In 1958 she married her second husband, taking his surname of Johnson, and that same year, when NACA became NASA, she

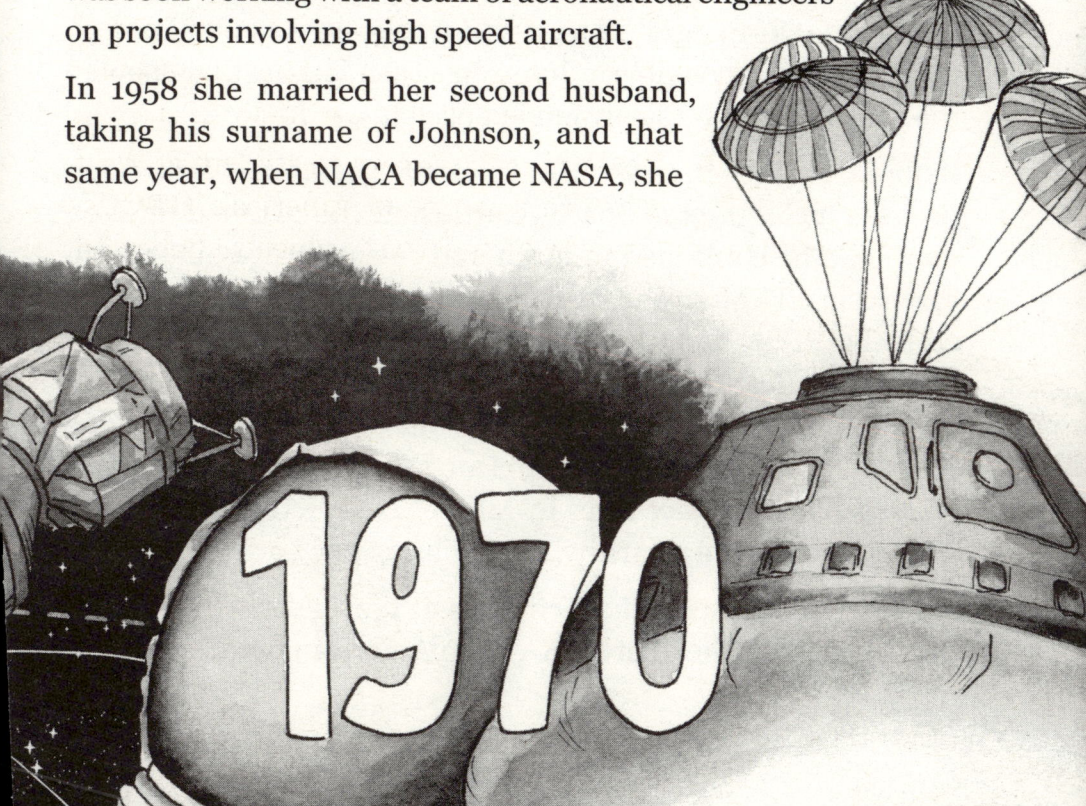

became part of the Space Task Force. America had entered what became known as the 'space race' and Johnson's skill as a computer was going to be crucial to their success. She worked on complicated and precise mathematical calculations of trajectories – the paths moving objects take when they travel. Johnson excelled at her job and it was her calculations that decided the trajectory of the *Freedom 7*, America's first crewed space flight in 1961.

By the early 1960s the first electronic computers were introduced at NASA. But in 1962, when astronaut John Glenn was due to pilot America's first crewed spacecraft, *Friendship 7*, which would go into orbit around earth, he asked for Johnson to go through all of the calculations herself to check that the electronic computer had got them right. She checked them, confirmed that they were correct, and Glenn became the first American to orbit the earth. Johnson went on to provide the calculations for the lunar landing of Apollo 11, when humankind first stepped onto the surface of the moon on 20 July 1969. On 13 April 1970, when Apollo 13 was damaged on its way to the moon, it was Johnson's calculations that enabled the astronauts to be safely guided back to earth.

Before retiring from NASA in 1986 Johnson worked on projects including the Space Shuttle and the planned mission to Mars. She continued to teach and to encourage others into careers in STEM and in 2015 president Obama presented her with the **Presidential Medal of Freedom** in recognition of her outstanding contribution to the nation. In 2016 Johnson's career and contribution to science was spotlighted in *Hidden Figures: The Story of the African American Women Who Helped Win the Space Race* by Margot Lee Shetterly. The book was turned into an award-winning film in 2017.

Johnson died on 24 February 2020 at the age of 101, and was described by the head of NASA as an American hero.

14 APRIL – BEYONCÉ AT COACHELLA

On 14 April 2018, the Coachella festival welcomed multiple award-winning artist Beyoncé as its first Black woman headline act. Topping the bill on both weekends, the performances were recorded and made into a film, *Homecoming*, and a live album.

Kevin Winter/Getty Images

Deciding to bring Black culture to Coachella, Beyoncé themed her performance as a tribute to HBCUs, using marching bands and steppers as her backing musicians and dancers. Stepping is a dance style that emerged from Black sororities and fraternities in which the whole body is used to create percussion and rhythm. The show acknowledged other elements of African American history and culture. Beyoncé included a sample of Nina Simone's (see 10 September) 'Lilac Wine' and sang 'Lift Every Voice and Sing' – the African American national anthem. The words of Malcolm X (see 21 February), Toni Morrison (see 31 March) and W. E. B. Du Bois (see 23 February) also made their way into the performance.

Her appearance became Coachella's most watched live-streamed performance of all time, with 41 million views globally.

After the show, Beyoncé added $100,000 to her BeyGOOD scholarship programme, which supports one student at each of eight HBCUs. Her BeyGOOD charity, founded in 2013, has donated to many causes, including hurricane relief and small business support, across the US, Caribbean and Africa.

15 APRIL - BARBADOS SLAVE REVOLT

The Barbados Slave Revolt of 1816 is also known as Bussa's Rebellion, after the enslaved African man who led it. Bussa worked as a ranger at the Bayley plantation on the island. That job put him in charge of the enslaved workforce and gave him responsibilities for maintaining the boundaries of the plantation and dealing with neighbouring estates. The Barbados Slave Code of 1661 (see 16 September) was the first set of laws to be drawn up in a slave colony to control the movement and punishment of enslaved people. For most enslaved people any movement was heavily controlled and could be punished by physical violence, but Bussa's role as a ranger meant that he would have been able to move around more freely. This would have helped him to meet with others to plan the revolt.

The revolt began on 14 April 1816, which was Easter Sunday, at Bayley's Plantation. Bussa and his forces took control of the plantation and the revolt began to spread across the island. On Monday 15 April the authorities declared martial law and gave control of the island to British soldiers and local troops. They came together and brutally put down the revolt. On 16 April, Bussa was killed in battle and his forces were defeated. Afterwards, hundreds of the rebels were executed and many more were transported to other colonies. In the Barbados Slave Code, enslaved people who had fought against a white person could be punished by whipping and mutilation and this was the fate of many of the surviving rebels.

Bussa's Revolt was unsuccessful, but was part of the longer struggle towards the end of slavery in British colonies. In 1998 Bussa was officially recognized as one of the National Heroes of Barbados.

16 APRIL ~ CASTER SEMENYA

South African Caster Semenya is an extremely successful middle distance runner. She holds two gold medals for the 800m from the Olympics, three from the World Championships and two from the Commonwealth Games. On 16 April 2016 she became the first person ever to win all three middle distance races at the South African National Championships.

Tab59, Wikimedia Commons

Semenya was born and raised as female. She is a woman with an intersex condition. These are conditions in which a person develops some physical characteristics that differ from those typically associated with a specific gender.

Before the World Championships in 2009, organizers told her that she would have to take tests to be able to compete. She had assumed they were standard doping tests but they were actually to verify her gender. News of the tests broke, making global headlines just three hours before she had to compete in the 800m final. Semenya went on to win but her victory was overshadowed by gossip about her gender and she became the subject of much abuse and ridicule. World Athletics (the organization that sets competition rules for all athletes) allowed Semenya to keep her title but she was barred from competition until 2010 when new rules on the allowed level of testosterone for women athletes were put in place. They decided that higher levels of the hormone could give a competitive advantage, so Semenya had to take medication to supress her naturally high testosterone in order to compete. The medication made her ill and when in 2018 the levels were lowered again, she challenged the rules in the European Court of Human Rights. On 11 July 2023 the court ruled in her favour.

17 APRIL - JONATHAN STRONG

Jonathan Strong was an enslaved person who was brought from the slave colony of Barbados to live in Britain. He was to become the focus of one of the earliest court cases to examine whether slavery was legal or illegal on British soil. Strong was thought to have been born in 1747 or 1748, and was brought to Britain by David Lisle, in whose household he lived.

In 1765 Strong was violently beaten by Lisle, kicked out of his house and left for dead in the street. His injuries were extremely severe but somehow he managed to make his way to the surgery of Dr William Sharp. Strong was admitted to St Bartholomew's Hospital where he stayed for months. Dr Sharp's brother, Granville Sharp, helped Strong once he came out of hospital, paying for his clothing and housing and helping him to find work.

Two years later, Strong was seen in the street by Lisle. Despite having literally thrown Strong out on the street to die, Lisle decided that Strong was still his property. He paid some men to watch Strong and to grab him off the street. Strong was then put in jail while Lisle made arrangements to sell him to a man called James Kerr and ship him back to the Caribbean as a slave. Strong wrote a message to Granville Sharp from prison and Sharp rushed to the office of the lord mayor, telling him that Strong was being held illegally. The mayor had Strong brought before him, along with Kerr's lawyer and the captain of the ship that was to take Strong to the West Indies. Although the lawyer produced documents showing that Kerr had bought Strong, the lord mayor's judgement was that he had been illegally imprisoned in the first place as he had not been guilty of any crime. Strong was released, and that is the last that is known of him until his death on 17 April 1773, aged around twenty-five. His early death may well have been due to Lisle's violent treatment of him in 1765.

18 APRIL - ALICE WALKER

Alice Walker became the first African American woman to win the **Pulitzer Prize** for Fiction on 18 April 1983 with her third novel, *The Color Purple*. The story follows Celie, an African American woman (based on Walker's own grandmother) in Georgia in the early 20th century, and the racism and sexism that shape her life. In 1985 the novel was made into a film starring Whoopi Goldberg and Oprah Winfrey. It received eleven **Oscar** nominations but didn't win any awards.

The lives of Black women and theories of Black **feminism** appear often in Walker's writing. She is the author of seven novels, four short story collections, four children's books and many essays and collections of poetry. Walker has also championed the work of other Black women writers, including rediscovering and republishing the works of forgotten writer Zora Neale Hurston.

Walker was a known figure in the civil rights movement. She met Dr King in 1962 and attended the March on Washington in 1963. She also worked for the **NAACP** Legal Defense and Educational Fund in Mississippi. She and her white husband faced discrimination and threats as **segregation** and **miscegenation** laws were still in force there. Walker has continued her activism throughout her career, and still campaigns globally for the rights of both humans and animals.

> 66
>
> ...it is crucial for Black women to hold on to this very special tradition that we have, exemplified by Harriet Tubman [see 10 March], where you free yourself and you go back and you free other people.
>
> 99

19 APRIL ~ GEORGE AFRICANUS

In the 1760s George Africanus was taken from his home in Sierra Leone, West Africa, enslaved and shipped to England. He was believed to be just three years old when he was given as a 'gift' to the Wolverhampton ironmaster Benjamin Molineux. Molineux named him and, unusually for the time, allowed young Africanus to have an education. Later, Africanus became an apprentice brass founder.

Africanus was twenty-one when he moved to Nottingham in 1784. He married Ester Shaw four years later and together they began an employment agency called Africanus's Register of Servants. By 1829 Africanus was able to buy several properties in Nottingham and the business flourished for seventy years.

Thought to be the first Black entrepreneur in Nottingham, George Africanus is now a celebrated figure in the city. On 19 April 2003 a plaque in his memory was erected on the railings at St Mary's Church, where he and his wife are buried.

Memorial plaque to George Africanus at St Mary's Church, Nottingham

The American civil rights and women's rights campaigner Dorothy Height was born in Virginia in 1912. Inspired by the example of her mother to become a political activist, Height had a talent for public speaking and earned a scholarship to attend college. Her first choice, Barnard College, refused to admit her because they would only take two Black students per year. So instead she went to New York University and then Columbia University, qualifying as a social worker.

Adrian Hood via Wikimedia Commons

Mary McLeod Bethune (see 10 July) met Height at a meeting of the National Council of Negro Women (NCNW) and persuaded her to get involved in the organization. Height eventually became its president in 1957 – a position she held for the next forty years. Under her leadership the NCNW provided guidance and support for many important activities of the civil rights campaign, including helping to raise funds for voter registration in the southern states. When Dr Martin Luther King Jr gave his 'I have a dream' speech at Washington in 1963 (see 28 August), Height was on the stage to his left, wearing one of the magnificent hats she had also become known for.

In 1974 Height was the only African American appointed to the National Commission for the Protection of Human Subjects of Biomedical and Behavioral Research. The commission examined the Tuskegee Experiment of 1932–72, where Black men who thought they were receiving medical treatment at the Tuskegee Institute were actually receiving fake medicines while the doctors recorded how their illness got worse. The commission's Belmont Report still informs how fair and respectful academic and medical research is carried out today. Height received the Citizens Medal Award from President Reagan in 1989 and the Congressional Gold Medal in 2004. She died aged ninety-eight in Washington on 20 April 2010.

Over her lifetime Height collected over 250 hats, many of which were made by famous milliner Vanilla Beane. When Height was honoured with a stamp by the United States Postal Service, she was wearing one of Beane's hats. Beane made hats for many other famous people including Maya Angelou.

DID YOU KNOW?

21 APRIL - THE CHAGOS ISLANDERS

In 1966 the British government decided to allow the USA to build a military base on Diego Garcia, one of the Chagos islands. However, the USA wanted the whole archipelago to be cleared and so the British government began forcibly evicting the islanders from their homes and deporting them.

The Chagos islanders are descendants of enslaved Africans taken there by the French in the 1700s. In 1814 the British took control of Mauritius and the Chagos Islands from the French. When they wanted to clear the islands in 1968 they granted independence to Mauritius but kept control of the Chagos Islands, calling it the British Indian Ocean Territory (BIOT). They then misled the UN by claiming that the islands had no permanent population. In April 1973 the last of the islanders left. They have been fighting ever since to return to their homeland.

Many of the islanders moved to the nearby islands of Mauritius and the Seychelles, but some moved to Britain. As the Chagos Islands are part of the British Commonwealth the islanders and any of their children who had been born between 1969 and 1983 were offered British citizenship. This restriction left many ineligible, with family members scattered across several countries. Some islanders have applied for British citizenship but even if resident or born in Britain, their applications can be rejected, and they are left to live with the threat of deportation. The 2012 Hostile Environment policy of the British government (see 29 April) affected many of the Chagos Islanders.

In 2019 the International Court of Justice declared that Britain did not own the islands, and the UN General Assembly gave Britain six months to give the islands back to Mauritius. As of 2024 Britain has not given the islands back and the Chagossians are still fighting to go home.

22 APRIL - THE MURDER OF STEPHEN LAWRENCE

On the night of 22 April 1993, the Black British teenager Stephen Lawrence was murdered by a gang of young white men. Lawrence had spent the evening playing video games with his friend, Duwayne Brooks. At 10 p.m. they left to travel home by bus. Lawrence left his friend at the bus stop and walked down the road to see if he could see a bus coming from around the corner. At that point a group of white youths surrounded Lawrence. They shouted racist slurs, pushed him to the ground and then stabbed him.

Following the attack the police failed to investigate Lawrence's murder properly. Within days they were given the names of five suspects by members of the public, all of whom had been involved in racist knife attacks in the area before. The police, however, did not arrest them until more than two weeks after the murder. When they were eventually charged, the Crown Prosecution Service dropped the charges because the police had not provided enough evidence. The suspects were brought to court in 1994 when the Lawrence family brought a private prosecution, but it failed due to a lack of evidence.

The inquest into Lawrence's death took place in February 1997. The five suspects were all called but refused to answer any questions. The verdict on 13 February was that Lawrence had been murdered in an unprovoked racist attack by five white youths. The following day the five suspects were named on the cover of the *Daily Mail*, which accused them all of murder and said if they were innocent they should sue the newspaper. None of them did. In July 1997 the government invited Lord Macpherson to conduct an inquiry into Lawrence's murder and the police's investigation of it (see 24 February).

In 2006 the case was reopened and reviewed. New evidence in 2012 led to the conviction of two of the five suspects, Gary Dobson and David Norris, for the murder.

23 APRIL ~ ANNIE EASLEY

The mathematician, rocket scientist, computer scientist and STEM ambassador Annie Jean Easley was born on 23 April 1933 in Birmingham, Alabama. She attended university in New Orleans and studied pharmacy for two years. She returned home to Birmingham in 1954, where she supported members of the Black community to pass the literacy tests that were then required in order to be registered to vote.

In 1955 Easley moved to Cleveland. She had hoped to complete her pharmacy degree there, but found that the course had closed. However, she read a newspaper story about twin sisters who worked at NACA (the forerunner of NASA) and decided to apply for a job there. She got the job and became one of only four African Americans in an organization of roughly 2,500 people. Easley faced daily discrimination, receiving lower pay for her work, being overlooked for promotion and not being included in NASA promotional photographs alongside her white peers.

When electronic computers began to replace human ones, Easley adapted, learning the computing languages Fortran and SOAP and studying for a degree in mathematics. Her work researching alternative power technology helped to develop the Centaur rocket project, as well as the technology underpinning the launch of satellites and of the Cassini spacecraft that journeyed to Saturn in 1997. She also served as NASA's equal employment opportunity counsellor and was a STEM ambassador for the organization. Easley died in 2011 and she was inducted into the NASA Hall of Fame in 2015.

24 APRIL - GREAT ZIMBABWE

In the south-eastern hills of Zimbabwe stand the stone ruins of a huge city. They cover more than seven square kilometres and are thought to have once been the site of a royal palace, populated by thousands, and the centre of a thriving trading empire from the 11th to the 15th centuries. The city is called Great Zimbabwe and is believed to have been constructed by the Bantu people, beginning in the 9th century and continuing for another 300 years.

Throughout the 20th century European colonists and, later, the white-minority government of Southern Rhodesia (the former name of Zimbabwe) refused to accept that Great Zimbabwe could possibly have been built by Indigenous Africans. Reclaiming its history was a long struggle but the archaeological evidence was eventually recognized.

In 1980 Southern Rhodesia was renamed Zimbabwe, in honour of this ancient city. Great Zimbabwe is now a national monument and was designated a UNESCO World Heritage Site in 1986.

25 APRIL - ELLA FITZGERALD

Born on 25 April 1917 in Newport News, Virginia, Ella Fitzgerald had a childhood full of tragedy and hardship. After several family deaths, she moved to Harlem to live with her aunt. In 1934 she won a draw to perform at Amateur Night at the Apollo Theatre. She won first prize that night and went on to win several more competitions, and she soon began working with bandleader Chick Webb, singing with his band at the Savoy Ballroom.

William P. Gottlieb, Library of Congress

Fitzgerald began to make records, but it wasn't until she recorded her version of nursery rhyme 'A-tisket, A-tasket' in 1938 that she became famous. It sold a million copies, reached number one and was in the charts for seventeen weeks.

Her career took off. She sang with Dizzy Gillespie's big band, where she started her famous scat singing (singing using noises rather than words), and worked with many other musicians, including Duke Ellington and Louis Armstrong. She began recording her famous songbook series and it was her album *Ella Fitzgerald Sings the Irving Berlin Songbook* that won her the first of thirteen Grammy awards. In 1967 she became the first woman to receive a Grammy Lifetime Achievement Award.

Having suffered her own hard start in life, Fitzgerald often made donations to organizations supporting disadvantaged children. In 1993 she set up her own organization, the Ella Fitzgerald Charitable Foundation, to offer scholarships and assistance for music students, and to help with healthcare and shelter for those in need.

Ella Fitzgerald, 'The First Lady of Song', died 15 June 1996.

26 APRIL - THE TUSKEGEE AIRMEN

On 26 April 1945 the pilots of the 332nd Fighter Group of the United States Army Air Corps (USAAC) flew their final Second World War combat mission in the skies over Europe. The 332nd was the second air unit formed at Tuskegee Army Air Field in Alabama when, after pressure from civil rights organizations, the USAAC trained and recruited African Americans to join the war effort. The United States Armed Forces enforced racial segregation and instead of being deployed into existing units for white men, the Black fighter pilots, bomber pilots, instructors, mechanics, ground crew and support personnel were organized in new Black units. Collectively, the 99th Pursuit Squadron and the 332nd Fighter Group, who both saw active combat, and the 477th Bombardment Group, who finished their training just after the war, became known as the Tuskegee Airmen. Their achievements and struggle would contribute to the decision three years after the war to desegregate the United States military.

Toni Frissell, Library of Congress

Tuskegee Airmen 332nd Fighter Group pilots at Ramitelli, Italy, March 1945 .
Front row, left to right: unidentified airman; Jimmie D. Wheeler (with goggles);
Emile G. Clifton (cloth cap). Standing left to right: Ronald W. Reeves (cloth cap),
Hiram Mann (leather cap); Joseph L. 'Joe' Chineworth (wheel cap), Elwood T. Driver?,
Edward 'Ed' Thomas (partial view); Woodrow W. Crockett (wheel cap)

In 1939, the US Government realized that war was brewing in Europe, and that there was a shortage of trained pilots. After the Civilian Pilot Training Act was passed on 27 June 1939, civilian pilot training for Black pilots began at the Tuskegee Institute in Alabama. Despite its success, Black men still found themselves barred from enlisting and training as pilots in the USAAC. But in January 1941 two university students – Yancey Williams and Spann Watson – filed a lawsuit that would lead to change. Supported by the civil rights organization NAACP, their lawsuit argued that both men had all of the entry requirements (and more) to join the USAAC and that they had been rejected purely because of their race. The lawsuit was settled when, instead of agreeing to accept the men into white units, the War Department agreed to set up a 'separate but equal' unit for Black recruits.

Tuskegee was chosen as the location for this programme and a new air base was built. In the spring of 1941, First Lady Eleanor Roosevelt visited and was taken up in an aircraft piloted by the programme's chief flight instructor C. Alfred 'Chief' Anderson – who has been called the Father of Black Aviation. Media coverage of this visit did a great deal to raise public interest in the programme.

In July the first cohort of twelve Black cadets and a student officer, Captain Benjamin O. Davis Jr (the son of the US Army's first Black brigadier general) arrived to begin their training. Between 1941 and 1946 a total of around 1,000 men were trained as pilots at Tuskegee, and 352 of them went on to see active combat overseas during the Second World War. The first unit formed was the 99th Fighter Squadron, followed by the 332nd Fighter Group. In total they flew over fifteen thousand missions and were responsible for shooting down 112 enemy aircraft. Both units saw active service in the Mediterranean, stationed at military bases in North Africa and then Italy. They provided vital support to the Allied operations against Germany, protecting and escorting bomber aircraft on their way to and from enemy targets. The 332nd earned the nickname the Red Tails thanks to the distinctive red markings on the tail sections of their aircraft and their ability to shoot down enemy planes. By the end of the war the airmen had been given a Distinguished Unit Citation, and between them the pilots had earned ninety-six Distinguished Flying Crosses.

Even when they were on active service, fighting in Europe for their country, the Tuskegee Airmen were not treated equally to their white counterparts. They were given older, heavier planes to fly and flew twice as many combat missions without a rest than was expected of white units. Back in America, the 477th Bombardment Group had been moved from base to base, including locations in the deep south, where they faced racism on and off Army premises. They were refused promotion and not given resources to do their jobs. In March 1945 Colonel Robert Selway, the white commander of the 477th, ordered the creation of two separate officers' clubs, one for 'instructors' and one for 'trainees'. This segregated officers by race, as no matter how much experience they had none of the Black officers had been promoted to the role of 'instructor'.

The Black officers rebelled in April 1945 and over two nights sixty-one of them were arrested for entering the club for instructors. Over one hundred officers complained to the army inspector general, demanding an investigation. Instead of removing the segregation policy, a new policy was written. It stated that the officers were being segregated by race and Selway demanded that the Black officers agree to it. One hundred and one of them refused to sign the policy, and they reported what was happening to the NAACP and the newspapers. Eventually, Selway was removed from command and replaced by Colonel Benjamin O. Davis Jr. The arrested officers were released, but First Air Force Commander Major General Frank Hunter demanded that three of the 477th officers – Lieutenants

Marsden Thompson, Shirley Clinton and Roger Terry – be court-martialled, facing a possible death penalty. They were charged with physically arguing with the white officer who had blocked the door to the instructors' club. The trial produced clear evidence of the racist attitudes and actions of their white commanding officers. Thompson and Clinton were found not guilty, while Terry was found guilty of 'jostling' the officer. His fellow Tuskegee officers raised and paid his fine of $150 between them. The stand taken by the officers of the 477th was courageous and contributed to the decision by president Harry Truman to sign an executive order in 1948, ending segregation in the United States Armed Forces (see 26 July).

Col. Benjamin O. Davis and Edward C. Gleed Tuskegee Airmen Fighter pilots at air base at Ramitelli, Italy, March 1945

Many of the Tuskegee airmen went on to have distinguished military careers. Four of them, including Colonel Davis Jr., became generals. In recent years the contribution of the Tuskegee airmen to the Second World War and to the history of the desegregation of the US Armed Forces has been recognized, and in 2007 they were awarded a Congressional Medal.

27 APRIL – FREEDOM DAY, SOUTH AFRICA

Allan Tannenbaum/Getty Images

Nelson and Winnie Mandela after his release from Victor Verster prison, February 1990

Freedom Day is celebrated in South Africa on 27 April. It commemorates the date of the first national elections held in the country in 1995 following the end of apartheid. During apartheid, white people had the right to vote, 'non-whites' had limited voting rights and Black people had no right to vote at all. The 1994 elections were the first to be held in the country in which citizens from all races had the right to vote. Freedom Day was declared a public holiday later that year and celebrated for the first time in 1997. President Nelson Mandela addressed the South African parliament and said:

> As a new dawn ushered in this day, the 27 April 1994, few of us could suppress the welling of emotion, as we were reminded of the terrible past from which we come as a nation; the great possibilities that we now have; and the bright future that beckons us.

28 APRIL - PRUDENCIA AYALA

Prudencia Ayala, a feminist writer and activist, was born on 28 April 1885 in El Salvador. Her family couldn't afford for her to finish her schooling, so she taught herself while working as a seamstress. She began to write poems and newspaper articles and got involved in political activism, including protesting the 1912 United States' invasion of neighbouring Nicaragua. She wrote many articles criticizing the government and in 1919 she was arrested and put in prison for two months.

In 1930, angered by the fact that women still couldn't vote in El Salvador, Ayala protested by entering the race to become president. She was supported by the Unionist Party and promised that if she won she would make trade unions stronger, would make government more honest, would allow people to follow whatever religion they wished and, most importantly, would grant women the right to vote. The newspapers said that women should stay at home and called her 'Prudence, the crazy'. Eventually the Supreme Court rejected her bid to be president and she had to step down from the race.

Ayala died in 1936 at only fifty-one years old. Two years after her death voting rights were granted to some women as long as they had a school degree. Full voting rights didn't come until 1950.

> **DID YOU KNOW?**
>
> Ayala was left out of history books and her efforts mostly forgotten until new feminist movements in El Salvador rediscovered her. In 2017 she had a street in San Salvador, Avenida Prudencia Ayala, named after her.

29 APRIL - THE WINDRUSH SCANDAL

In 2012 the British government announced its Hostile Environment policy, making employers, banks, landlords and the NHS check people's right to live in the United Kingdom. This policy had a devastating impact on a group of people known as the 'Windrush Generation'.

The Windrush Generation arrived in Britain in the period after the Second World War from countries in the British Commonwealth. The name comes from the ship the *Empire Windrush*, which brought one of the earliest groups from the Caribbean in 1948 (see 22 June). From 1949 to 1973, people arriving from the British Commonwealth and British colonies were automatically British subjects, with the right to live and work in the UK. When they first came to the UK the authorities recorded their arrival on a landing card and these were stored by the Home Office. Two years before the Hostile Environment policy, the Home Office decided to destroy these records. Many of the Windrush Generation were babies or children when they arrived and many had never left the UK, and so they had never needed to get a British passport. But the new policy meant they had to produce at least one official document from every year they had lived in the UK. Many had their right to have a job, a bank account or to receive medical treatment denied. The Home Office wrongly told them they had to leave the UK and many people were deported unjustly.

In 2018 this became known as the Windrush scandal. On 29 April, Amber Rudd resigned as home secretary, admitting that she had misled parliament in her statements about the policy. The British government apologized and announced a compensation scheme for victims of the scandal. However, most victims have still not received money from the scheme.

30 APRIL - HERBIE HANCOCK

Herbie Hancock is a multi-award-winning American jazz pianist and composer. Born 12 April 1940, he started playing piano at seven years old. Although he was first taught classical piano, Hancock began to teach himself how to play jazz by listening to recordings of his favourite artists. He moved to Chicago and began working with other jazz musicians, and in 1963 was invited by Miles Davis (see 26 May) to join his Second Great Quintet. This was the start of a long and successful career, during which Hancock won multiple awards including an Oscar in 1987 for his music in the film *Round Midnight*, and several Grammys.

In 2011 Hancock was asked to be a Goodwill Ambassador for UNESCO. He had already founded the Herbie Hancock Institute of Jazz, dedicated to the worldwide teaching of jazz, and was also a founder of the International Committee of Artists for Peace, and so, with UNESCO, he started International Jazz Day on 30 April 2012. The aim of the day is to celebrate jazz and learn about its past and future, and what it can do to encourage communication across cultures and bring peace. Every year artists offer free online classes in many different languages for anyone who wants to learn about jazz at whatever level, and the day finishes in a global concert with performances from international jazz stars.

MAY

1 MAY - THE SLAVE TRADE ACT

TIMELINE 4

The Act for the Abolition of the Slave Trade of 1807 (also known as the Slave Trade Act) was an important step on the road to the abolition of slavery in the British Empire. The bill proposing the act was introduced to the British parliament by the abolitionist campaigner, William Wilberforce, with the encouragement of the prime minister, Lord Grenville. Wilberforce had introduced many similar bills since 1791, none of which had made it through the House of Commons and House of Lords and into law. However, this time, with the prime minister helping to lead the fight in the House of Lords and the foreign secretary in the House of Commons, Wilberforce was successful.

On 23 February 1807, after a ten-hour debate and with a 283-vote majority, Members of Parliament voted to allow a second reading of the bill. On 25 February the bill received Royal Assent, becoming law. From 1 May 1807 involvement in the Transatlantic Slave Trade became illegal in Britain and its empire. The British Navy, until then, had been protecting British slave ships. From 1807, the Navy's West Africa Squadron had the job of patrolling the Atlantic Ocean, seizing slave ships, arresting the sailors and freeing the enslaved people.

However, it is important to note that the 1807 Act did not free those Black people already enslaved within the British Empire. The use of labour from already enslaved people continued to be legal in the British colonies and Britain continued to buy goods grown with that labour. It would not be until the Slavery Abolition Act of 1833 that this would begin to change (see 22 July).

2 MAY - THE CHILDREN'S CRUSADE

Birmingham, Alabama was still operating Jim Crow laws in the 1960s. In April 1963 the SCLC began a sustained campaign of non-violent protests led by Reverend Ralph Abernathy, Reverend Fred Shuttlesworth and Dr Martin Luther King Jr to force the city to desegregate. It was during these protests that Dr King was arrested (see 10 January). The campaign was met with a ban on further protests, mass arrests and threats to the jobs of participants.

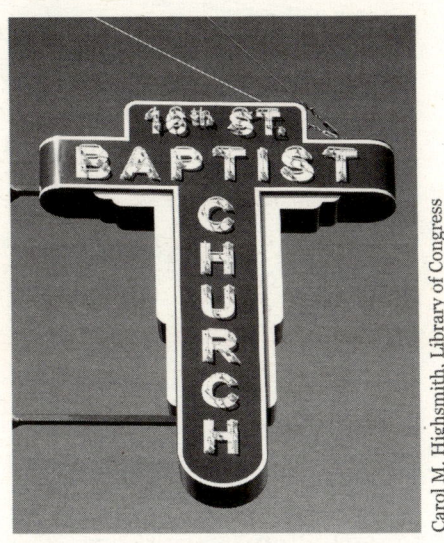

Carol M. Highsmith, Library of Congress

The protest ban began to affect the numbers of participants and SCLC leader James Bevel decided that to keep the protests going they would need the help of the young. Many Black children were already well aware of the struggle through their parents and were proud to be able to participate. They were trained in the tactics of non-violence and on 2 May 1963 over 1,000 children between the ages of seven and eighteen gathered at the 16th Street Baptist church and marched into the city. Hundreds were arrested and the commissioner of public safety, Bull Connor, issued an order for any more protests to be met with force.

Despite the danger, the children continued their protest over the following days. The police sprayed them with water hoses, beat them and set dogs on them. Images of this violence against children began to filter through to a national audience and after eight days, public pressure brought the City of Birmingham to negotiations with the SCLC. On 10 May it was agreed to desegregate the city.

3 MAY ~ MACON B. ALLEN

Macon Bolling Allen was granted his licence to practise law in Massachussetts on 3 May 1845, making him the first African American to practise law and the first to argue before a jury. But Allen had actually passed his first bar exam the year before in Maine.

Previously a teacher, Allen moved to Maine in the 1850s and worked as a legal clerk for abolitionist lawyer General Samuel Fessenden. While there he studied for the bar exam and, after overcoming several obstacles and rejections, passed his exam on 3 July 1844, making him the very first African American lawyer. However, Allen never got to practice law in Maine. He found it impossible to get work and so moved to Boston and took the bar exam there.

Despite facing continued difficulties, Allen pushed on with his career and became justice of the peace in Middlesex County, Massachusetts in 1847. He was only the second African American to hold a judicial position, after Wentworth Cheswell in Newmarket, New Hampshire.

After the Civil War, in 1868, Allen moved to South Carolina and joined with several other African American lawyers to found the country's first African American law firm. He held several judicial positions in South Carolina but returned to his law firm once his time in office was done.

Macon B. Allen died on 15 October 1894. His determination had paved the way for future generations of African American lawyers.

4 MAY - THE FREEDOM RIDERS

Despite the 1960 US Supreme Court Boynton vs. Virginia ruling banning segregation in public buses, waiting rooms and restaurants, some southern American states kept their 'Whites Only' facilities. The Freedom Riders were groups of civil rights activists, mainly college students, who decided to travel by bus to segregated bus terminals and attempt to use facilities such as toilets and waiting rooms.

The first Riders – seven Black men (including John Lewis – see 17 July) and six white men and women – left Washington DC on a Greyhound bus on 4 May 1961. Others joined them along the way. On arrival in Alabama on 14 May, a mob of 200 people attacked and fire-bombed the bus. As the Riders tried to flee the flames, they were beaten with clubs and iron pipes. As news of the attack spread, more volunteers joined the Freedom Riders.

Clashes with mobs and police continued for six months as they rode to other destinations. By September, as they planned a national protest, the Interstate Commerce Commission (ICC) finally issued orders to enforce the 1960 ruling.

5 MAY ~ OZWALD BOATENG

On 5 May 2019 the famous Apollo Theatre in Harlem was host to an 'immersive fashion experience' celebrating one hundred years since the Black American cultural revolution known as the Harlem Renaissance. The British designer Ozwald Boateng, presenting his first women's collection to an audience of stars and students, chose the iconic theatre as his venue for its importance in African American cultural history.

© Miles Warren, WikiCommons

Born in London to Ghanaian parents, Boateng's eye for design led him into the world of fashion. He focused his talents on tailoring and referencing the traditions of Savile Row, the street which has been the centre of bespoke tailoring in Britain since the 18th century. In 1994 he became the first tailor to show a collection at Paris Fashion Week and a year later, at just twenty-eight, became the youngest tailor to open a shop on Savile Row. His unique output has granted him a host of industry awards and positions at top fashion houses.

Boateng's work is recognizable for its fusion of sharp tailoring and bold, bright colour and prints, reflecting his cultural influences from traditional British craftsmanship and traditional Ghanaian art and design. This combination brings him very diverse clients. In 2007 Boateng designed a show at the African Union summit in Accra celebrating both the 200th anniversary of the Abolition Act (see 1 May) and the 50th anniversary of Ghanaian Independence (see 6 March). His work can also be seen on screen, as a favourite of many stars on the red carpet and also in films such as Marvel's *Black Panther* (see 29 January).

6 MAY - BENJAMIN ZEPHANIAH

The poet Benjamin Zephaniah was born in April 1958 in the British city of Birmingham, to a Barbadian father and a Jamaican mother. He was a pioneering writer and performer of dub-poetry from an early age, and moved to London to pursue his career. Dub-poetry traditionally combines poems with reggae music, and Zephaniah also drew on jazz, dubstep and hip-hop in his work. His first book of poetry, *Pen Rhythm*, was published in 1980. He went on to write children's books, books for young adults, radio and stage plays, and an autobiography as well as many more volumes of poetry, including children's poetry.

Zephaniah's work focused on what he called 'street politics' and examined issues of racism, inequality and injustice, in engaging, critical and sometimes humorous ways. He was a **Rastafarian**, and in 1982 he recorded the album *Rasta*, which included a tribute to the then imprisoned South African anti-apartheid campaigner, Nelson Mandela. In 2000 he was poet in residence at the chambers of human rights barrister Michael Mansfield, which produced his *Too Black, Too Strong* poetry volume.

On 6 May 2011, he took the prestigious role of poet-in-residence at Keats House, the former home of one of his favourite poets, John Keats. The same year he was appointed as professor of creative writing at Brunel University London. The *Birmingham Mail* newspaper named him 'The People's Laureate'. Zephaniah died on 7 December 2023 from a brain tumour. He was sixty-five.

© Fred Duval, Shutterstock

7 MAY - JIMMY DURHAM

In May 1899, Jimmy Durham became the first African to join the British Army as a fully enlisted soldier. He was just fourteen years old at the time. Although there were Black **colonial** regiments in the military, no African had been allowed to join up on the same terms as a white recruit before.

As an infant, Jimmy was found in 1885 on the banks of the River Nile following a battle between the British Army and warriors from the Sudan. According to a wounded Sudanese soldier, the two-year-old, whose birth name was Mustapha, had been abandoned by his mother after his father was killed in the previous day's battle. Mustapha was 'adopted' by soldiers in the Durham Light Regiment, who named him James Francis Durham, Jimmy for short. Their commander, Henry de Lisle, wanted to send Jimmy to a **missionary** school once they reached Cairo a year later. But the men appealed to keep Jimmy with them and instead he travelled with the regiment as their unofficial mascot, sailing with them to India in 1887 and to Burma in 1899. It was there that Jimmy was given permission to enlist, and he was formally enrolled as Boy Soldier No. 6758.

When the Regiment returned to England in 1908, Durham married Jane Green, the sister of a sergeant in the Durham Light Infantry. Two years later he died of pneumonia in Ireland. Jimmy Durham was buried with full military honours. His only child, Frances, was born a few weeks afterwards.

8 MAY - MINSTRELSY BROUGHT TO LONDON

In 1836 the American comedian Thomas Dartmouth Rice arrived in Britain. Rice was already famous thanks to the character of Jumpin' Jim Crow that he had developed and performed in America since 1828. Now he was bringing it to Britain.

Jumpin' Jim Crow was a black-faced minstrel act. Although he wasn't the first person to develop this type of character, Rice was the person who made it famous. In order to play minstrel characters, white performers would use materials such as burned cork and greasepaint or shoe polish to paint their faces black. They would wear white make-up around the eyes and mouth and white or red make-up on their lips. They put on thick woolly wigs and wore patchworked and worn-out clothes. The aim was to turn themselves into crude and racist caricatures of enslaved African Americans. Minstrels would sing versions of songs sung by enslaved people and would speak in exaggerated accents and move and dance in 'comical' ways. The effect was to ridicule Black people, making them seem childlike, lazy and unintelligent.

Rice's act became an instant hit with white audiences, and he was invited to perform all over the country. In the years that followed minstrelsy became incredibly popular, and minstrelsy acts were still being performed late into the 20th century.

After the American Civil War, the name Jim Crow became used to refer to the kinds of laws that were passed in many of the southern states of America to deny Black people their civil rights and to segregate them from the white population in public spaces.

9 MAY ~ MARGARET BUSBY

In May 1967 Margaret Busby started Allison and Busby, a new publishing company, with her friend, Clive Allison. She was Britain's youngest and first Black publisher. Born in Ghana in 1944, Busby attended a boarding school in England. She moved back to Ghana briefly but returned to England to study at the University of London where she met and befriended Allison at a party. Allison and Busby quickly became a highly successful company and published the works of many important Black British, African and Caribbean poets and novelists.

Busby was the editorial director at Allison and Busby and, in the 1980s and 90s, at Earthscan Publications (a company devoted to publishing books and journals about sustainable development and climate change). She edited the ground-breaking *Daughters of Africa* anthology in 1992, which included contributions from over 200 women of African descent, including Audre Lorde, Toni Morrison, Alice Walker, Angela Davis, Jackie Kay, bell hooks and Ida B. Wells (see 18 February, 31 March, 18 April, 13 October, 9 November, 15 December and 24 December). When she edited the follow-up, *New Daughters of Africa*, in 2019 for the publisher Myriad Editions, they and the University of London's School of Oriental and African Studies (SOAS) established the 'Margaret Busby New Daughters of Africa Award', a scholarship for Black African women.

Busby has long campaigned for greater diversity in publishing. She has written for radio and the stage, and has been on the judging panel of many literary prizes including the Commonwealth Book Prize and the Orange Award for New Writers, and was the chair of judges for the Booker Prize in 2020. In 2023, Busby became president of English PEN, a human rights organization that promotes freedom of expression and international writing.

10 MAY - ANNIE TURNBO MALONE

Born in Metropolis, Illinois, on 9 August 1869, Annie Turnbo Malone was a pioneer of cosmetic products and a creative entrepreneur. Her parents escaped slavery in Kentucky to raise their family free in Illinois. She first trained as an apprentice hairdresser, then began making her own haircare products for African American women. She sold them door to door, growing her business and eventually employing sales agents.

Malone moved to St Louis, Missouri in 1902 where she opened her own salon. She copyrighted her brand, 'Poro', three years later. In 1918 Malone opened Poro College, a large training centre aimed at the economic betterment of 'Race women'. The facilities and job opportunities that she created were of huge benefit to the local Black community.

By the 1920s Malone was a self-made millionaire who gave generously to many causes. From 1919 to 1943, Malone was board president of the St Louis Colored Orphan's Home, having donated $10,000 to finance their new building. She supported the local Black YMCA and paid for the education of two students in every HBCU.

Malone died aged eighty-seven on 10 May 1957.

> **DID YOU KNOW?**
>
> Madam C. J. Walker was a student at Malone's Poro College. She later worked as a Poro sales representative, but after a move to Denver she developed her own products. She moved again to Pittsburgh where she opened her own college for 'hair culturists'. Walker became America's first self-made millionaire.

11 MAY - AMY ASHWOOD GARVEY

Amy Ashwood Garvey was born in 1897 in Port Antonio, Jamaica. She was an activist and feminist who campaigned for African independence and for the rights of Black women throughout her life.

Together with her then-husband, Marcus Garvey (see 17 August), she co-founded the Universal Negro Improvement Association in New York. In 1934 Ashwood Garvey moved to London and opened a social club which became a well-known meeting place for Black intellectuals. She befriended Claudia Jones (see 30 January) and worked with her on the *West Indian Gazette*, the newspaper Jones founded in 1958, following the Notting Hill race riots (see 29 August).

During her life Ashwood Garvey travelled widely in West Africa and the Caribbean. She was based in London from 1934–60 and set up a community centre in Ladbroke Grove in 1954. After travels around Liberia and the United States Ashwood Garvey finally returned to Jamaica in 1968. She died just one year later and was buried on 11 May 1969. On 5 November 2009, her life and achievements were commemorated with a blue plaque placed at 1 Bassett Road, London W10 where Garvey had once lived.

> **DID YOU KNOW?**
>
> Amy Jaques Garvey, the second wife of Marcus Garvey, was also a **Pan-African** activist and feminist. She fought for the recognition of women within the Black nationalist movement and in 1945 was asked by W. E. B. Du Bois to be co-convener at the Pan-African Congress, the only woman to be offered the position.

12 MAY - ROBERT SMALLS

On the evening of 12 May 1862, on board the **Confederate** transport ship *The Planter*, an enslaved man called Robert Smalls put an incredibly daring plan in motion that would transform his life.

Smalls had been born in Beaufort, South Carolina on 5 April 1839, the enslaved son of Lydia Polite, an enslaved woman, and her owner John McKee. From the age of twelve Smalls was hired out by his owner to work on ships in the Charleston Harbour. By the time the American Civil War broke out he had a wife and children and had become an experienced maritime pilot, with the knowledge and skills to guide and sail ships safely. He was working as a pilot aboard *The Planter* as part of an enslaved crew that was led by three white officers. By April 1862, Smalls was worried that the Confederate side seemed to be winning and would succeed in their goal of establishing a separate slave-owning republic. He began talking with the enslaved crew (except for one man he did not trust) and making plans to escape to the **Union** side of the Civil War and to freedom.

On 12 May 1862, the three white officers left the ship at Charleston's Southern Wharf to spend the night ashore. Smalls asked the captain, Charles C. J. Relyea, for permission for the families of the remaining enslaved crew to visit them on board that night. Relyea agreed on the condition that all family members would be off the ship by the time of the evening curfew, when all Charleston residents needed to be inside their homes. Once the families were on board, Smalls and the enslaved crew members seized their chance. The plan was explained to the families who then pretended to go home but instead went to hide on a steamer ship on Charleston's North Wharf. At three in the morning of 13 May, Smalls and seven of the eight enslaved crew commandeered *The Planter* and they set sail for North Wharf to collect their families.

Next they needed to make it to the Union forces, which meant sailing past six Confederate harbour forts where they would need to convince the guard that Captain Relyea was still in charge and nothing strange was happening. Smalls put on a captain's uniform and a hat. He remained calm, sailing slowly past each fort at the normal distance in the dark. Each time he gave the correct steam whistle signals, impersonating Captain Relyea's mannerisms, and was let through. Once past the final one, Fort Sumter, instead of sailing for the Confederate harbour at Morris Island, he changed course and set sail towards the fleet of the Union Navy. By the time the guards at Fort Sumter realized, *The Planter* was out of range of their guns. Soon the ship was spotted by the Union ship USS *Onward*, who began preparations to fire. Quickly Smalls had the crew take down the Confederate flag and hoist up a white sheet to show that they wanted to surrender. He was able to hand over *The Planter*, its cargo and vital intelligence about Confederate naval security to the Union side. His plan had worked and Smalls had gained freedom for his family, his crew and their families.

Smalls became the first Black man to serve as a pilot in the United States Navy. He was eventually promoted to captain and given command of *The Planter*. He fought in seventeen battles on the ship during the Civil War, winning prize money that enabled him to return to Beaufort in 1864 and buy the house of his former owner in an auction of property that had been seized from fleeing Confederate supporters.

The twelve years after the war became known as the Reconstruction Era – a time when Americans tried to bring the Confederate and Union states together again and rebuild a society without slavery. Smalls now began his second career as an activist and Republican politician after an experience in Philadelphia when he was arrested for riding on a racially segregated streetcar. Smalls immediately rallied support for a boycott and this led to the **desegregation** of public transport in Philadelphia in 1867. He was elected to become a South Carolina state representative in 1868 and a state senator in 1872. In 1874 he was elected to the United States Congress, and went on to serve for five terms in the United States House of Representatives. During his time in Congress, Smalls fought for racial equality, campaigning against racial **segregation** in education, transport and in the armed forces. He retired from national politics in 1887 and was given the post of Collector of Customs in Beaufort, which he held for twenty years.

Smalls died on 23 February 1915 and his military and political careers, and the economic and social success of Beaufort in the Reconstruction Era, were largely forgotten. In the 2000s, however, Smalls and his contribution started to be celebrated. His house is now a National Historic Landmark and in 2017 President Obama issued an executive order to create the Reconstruction Era National Monument in Beaufort, recognizing the contribution of Smalls to American history.

> 66
> My race needs no special defense, for the past history of them in this country proves them to be the equal of any people, anywhere. All they need is an equal chance in the battle of life
>
> Robert Smalls, 1 November 1895
> 99

13 MAY - SLAVERY ABOLISHED IN BRAZIL

The Portuguese arrived in Brazil in 1500 and by the 1540s the country was importing enslaved people. Between the 16th and 19th centuries, Brazil imported about 5 million enslaved African people, more than any other country involved in the Transatlantic Slave Trade. Following the abolition of slavery in Britain's colonies in the 1830, and in the United States at the end of their civil war in 1865, by the late 1860s pressure for its abolition in Brazil was building. The trade in enslaved people was becoming less profitable, and there were slave uprisings and escapes.

Picking coffee in São Paulo 1880–1890

The end of slavery in Brazil was, at first, a slow and gradual process. In 1871, the 'Law of the Free Womb' was passed, which freed all children born to enslaved women after the date of the legislation. At the other end of the spectrum, the Sexagenarian Law of 1885 freed all enslaved people aged sixty and over. However, neither of these laws was strictly enforced. Finally, on 13 May 1888, Law 3,343, the 'Lei Áurea' (the Golden Law), was signed by Isabel, Princess Imperial of Brazil at the Imperial Palace in Rio de Janeiro. It ended slavery in Brazil overnight, setting the enslaved free but also abandoning them with no economic or social support. Within a year, Black people in Brazil were being further marginalized by racist theories of white superiority and Black inferiority, and widespread colourism that favoured light-skinned people over darker-skinned people.

14 MAY ~ THE ENGLISH ARRIVE IN BARBADOS

On 14 May 1625 an English ship called *Olive Blossom* arrived at the island of Barbados. The ship's captain, John Powell, took possession of the island, claiming it for England in the name of King James I.

In 1627 the English established a settlement on the island. John Powell's brother, Henry, led a group of eighty settlers and ten **indentured** labourers. Indentured labourers were impoverished people from Europe who had signed away their freedom for a number of years to work. Some reports state that there were a small number of African people in this first settler group, but that may not be true.

Between 1627 and the early 1640s the Barbados settlement grew tobacco, cotton and spices farmed by indentured labourers from Europe. By the 1640s, however, the growth in the number of plantations and the introduction of sugar production on the island greatly increased the demand for labourers. The plantation owners turned to the import of enslaved Africans to meet this demand. In 1661 the brutal Barbados Slave Code was introduced to keep the enslaved population in fear and under control (see 16 September). By the 1680s there were tens of thousands of enslaved African people living, working and dying in the harsh conditions of the Barbados plantations.

TIMELINE 1

15 MAY ~ THE PROVINCE OF FREEDOM

In 18th-century London, the 'Black Poor' was a name given to a number of Black people living in destitution in areas such as Mile End and Paddington. Some were sailors, and others had previously been enslaved. In the 1780s, the arrival of Black Loyalists who had fought for the British in the American Revolutionary War added to their numbers.

The Committee for the Relief of the Black Poor was set up by a group of abolitionists to help alleviate their suffering. The committee supported a 1787 plan called 'The Sierra Leone Resettlement Scheme', which they saw as an opportunity for the 'Black Poor' to start new lives in a new colony. Others viewed the scheme as an effective way of getting them off the streets of London. The anti-slavery campaigner Granville Sharp (see 17 April) was on the committee and he named the new colony The Province of Freedom.

Three ships containing 411 settlers set sail for West Africa in April 1787, and they included Black men, their white wives and mixed race children. Many died in the awful conditions during the voyage, and others would die later from tropical diseases like malaria. Those who arrived in Sierra Leone on 15 May 1787 established Granville Town (named after Sharp) as their base in the Province of Freedom, but faced a huge challenge to live. By 1778 only 130 of them survived. A second group arrived in 1792, this time Black Loyalists evacuated from Canada. Among them was Harry Washington, who had been the property of America's first president George Washington. They established the new settlement of Freetown, which in time became a functioning community. Freetown is now the capital of Sierra Leone.

16 MAY ~ BROWN VS. TOPEKA

Brown vs. the Board of Education of Topeka was an historic case heard by the Supreme Court in America in 1954. The case began in 1951 when the Board of Education, which ran the public school system in the town of Topeka, Kansas, refused to enrol the daughter of a Black resident called Oliver Brown in the elementary school closest to his house. The school was reserved for white students and the Board insisted that instead of walking to her local school, Brown's daughter

Thurgood Marshall, NAACP Chief Counsel, along with Chalmer Hayes and James Nabrit, lead counsels on two companion cases

would need to get the bus to a school for Black children. Brown, and the parents of another twelve Black families, filed a lawsuit against the Board of Education, arguing that their segregation policy was unlawful. The District Court in Kansas supported the Topeka Board, but Brown took his case to the Supreme Court, supported by the Black civil rights organization NAACP. On 17 May 1954 the Supreme Court issued its verdict on the case. The nine Supreme Court justices had unanimously voted in favour of the Brown family and against segregated public education. In their ruling the justices stated:

> We conclude that in the field of public education the doctrine of 'separate but equal' has no place. Separate educational facilities are inherently unequal.

TIMELINE 7

17 MAY – THE MURDER OF KELSO COCHRANE

On the night of 17 May 1959, Kelso Cochrane was walking home in the Notting Hill area of London. He was followed by a gang of white men who beat him, stabbed him, then left him dying in the street. The police refused to accept that it was a racially motivated killing, and no one was ever charged for his murder.

Cochrane was thirty-two years old and had arrived from Antigua in 1954 to seek a new life in London, finding work as a carpenter. His murder caused an outcry among local Black communities. Claudia Jones (see 30 January), one of the founders of the Notting Hill Carnival, helped set up the Inter-Racial Friendship Co-ordinating Council in the wake of his death and they campaigned for a law to make incitement to racial violence illegal.

More than a thousand people came to pay their respects on the day of Cochrane's funeral. His death became a pivotal moment for Notting Hill, an area where large numbers of immigrants had settled from the 1950s onwards.

On 17 May 2009, a blue plaque was put up in Golborne Road, to mark the fiftieth anniversary of Cochrane's death, and in 2021 Kelso Cochrane's family launched a petition demanding an apology from the government for the serious failings of the police investigation. His family continued to fight for an inquiry into the murder and the handling of the original investigation and in August 2023 appealed for access to the case files. The case files, originally ordered to remain closed until 2054, were released in July 2024. They strongly indicate that Cochrane's murder was indeed a lynching and point to serious failures in the police investigation. Despite this, the case remains classified as unsolved.

18 MAY - GLADYS BROWN WEST

Born in rural Virginia in 1930, Gladys Mae Brown was determined to escape her seemingly pre-determined life as a **sharecropper**. Academically gifted, she won a full scholarship to Virginia State College to study mathematics. She graduated in 1952 and completed a **master's degree** in 1955.

In 1956 Brown took a job at what was then the Naval Proving Ground in Virgina as a programmer and data analyst, and it was here that she met her husband and became Gladys West. One of only a handful of Black employees, West felt driven to prove herself and be taken seriously. Her government position prevented her from joining the protests of the burgeoning civil rights movement and so, hoping to make her contribution to liberation by being a role model, West threw herself into her job. She continued to work on satellite systems and calculations and it was her programming work on a project to generate a detailed and accurate model of the earth that formed the basis of the Global Positioning System (GPS), a technology that informs so much of daily life in the 21st century.

US Navy, Fredericksburg.com, WikiCommons

West's work on GPS went unacknowledged until she mentioned it in a short autobiographical piece for her sorority, who then pushed for recognition. In 2018 West was inducted into the Air Force Space and Missile Pioneers Hall of Fame. In recognition of her part in the development of GPS and her status as a role model for young Black women in STEM, on 18 May 2022 West also received a Webby Lifetime Achievement award from the International Academy of Digital Arts and Sciences.

19 MAY - MEGHAN, DUCHESS OF SUSSEX

On 19 May 2018, a wedding at Windsor Castle in England was televised to millions around the world. The groom was Prince Harry, grandson of Queen Elizabeth II. The bride was Meghan Markle, a mixed-race American actress and philanthropist. Upon their marriage, the Queen bestowed on them the title of the Duke and Duchess of Sussex.

Rachel Meghan Markle was born in 1981 in Los Angeles, California, to a Black mother and white father. She identifies as being of mixed race. Markle attended Northwestern University School of Communication, and graduated with a degree in theatre and international studies in 2003. She then embarked on a career in acting. In 2011, she was cast as the character Rachel Zane in the popular legal drama series, *Suits*. She moved to Toronto, where the series was filmed, engaged in charity work and ran her lifestyle blog, The Tig. In July 2016, Markle was introduced to Prince Harry via mutual friends. The relationship quickly became serious and in November 2016 (shortly before they became engaged) it became public knowledge. Some of the British tabloid press began publishing hostile articles about Markle, which led Prince Harry to issue a statement calling out the 'racial undertones' of some of the articles.

In January 2020 the couple announced their plans to step back from their senior roles in the royal family. They have since established Archewell, an organization combining creative for-profit projects and non-profit charitable activities. The Sussexes now live in California with their children, Prince Archie and Princess Lilibet of Sussex.

20 MAY ~ TOUSSAINT L'OUVERTURE

Toussaint L'Ouverture was born enslaved in the French colony of Saint-Domingue on 20 May 1743. Documents show that by 1776 he was a free man. Like many of the island's freed Black population, L'Ouverture went from being enslaved to renting a small plantation and becoming the owner of other enslaved people. He married his first wife Cécile and started a family. As he began to make money, L'Ouverture bought the freedom of his wife and children and members of their extended family. After just two years his business failed. He lost his money and the plantation he had been renting and in 1782 went back to the plantation he had been enslaved at, this time as a paid worker.

In 1791, L'Ouverture's life changed drastically as he became an important leader of the uprising against slavery and French control of Saint-Domingue that became known as the Haitian Revolution (see 22 August). It was during this time he took on the surname L'Ouverture, or 'opening', as he was famous for creating openings during battle and leading the way to victory or escape. He and the other leaders formed an alliance with Spain, against the French. In order to break this alliance and hold on to Saint-Domingue as a colony, on 4 February 1794, the French government proclaimed slavery illegal to appease the rebel forces. The ploy worked and Saint-Domingue remained a French colony in name, but with L'Ouverture actually in charge. He gave himself the title General-in-Chief of the Army, and then declared himself governor for life.

In 1802, the new French leader Napoleon Bonaparte sent forces to attempt to take back control of Saint-Domingue and reintroduce slavery. The attempt failed but L'Ouverture was captured and taken to France where he died of pneumonia at Fort de Joux prison on 7 April 1803. Although L'Ouverture had lived to see the end of slavery on Saint-Domingue, he died a year before it became the independent state of Haiti.

21 MAY - STEVIE WONDER

At the age of thirteen Stevie Wonder became the youngest artist to ever hit No.1 on the American Billboard chart with his single 'Fingertips'. Released on 21 May 1963, this marked the beginning of a career that has spanned decades and made him one of the best-selling music artists ever.

On 13 May 1950, Stevland Hardaway Judkins was born prematurely, resulting in a condition that left him blind. Discovering a talent for music, he was signed to Motown Records by Berry Gordy (see 28 November) who named him Little Stevie Wonder. Wonder has since collected twenty-five Grammys, an Academy Award and been inducted into the Rhythm and Blues, Rock & Roll, and Songwriters Halls of Fame.

Wonder has also been a vocal activist. In 1980 he released the song 'Happy Birthday', boosting Coretta Scott King's campaign to make Martin Luther King Day a national holiday. It was finally signed into law on 2 November 1983. Wonder was also involved in the anti-apartheid campaign. He was arrested at a protest outside the South African embassy in Washington in 1985, and after dedicating his Oscar win to Nelson Mandela, his music was banned in South Africa. His activism earned him a Nelson Mandela Courage Award and a Lifetime Achievement Award from the National Civil Rights Museum. In recognition of his work for disability rights, he was invited by the UN to become a Messenger of Peace in 2009. Wonder continues to raise funds and awareness for many causes, and is still performing and writing fifty years on from his first hit.

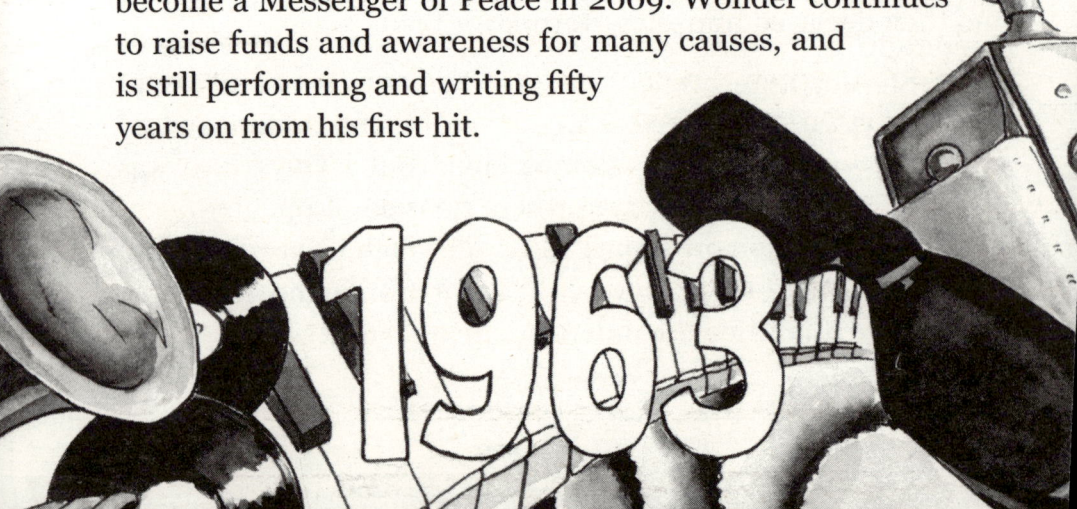

22 MAY - SOCIETY FOR EFFECTING THE ABOLITION OF THE SLAVE TRADE

On 22 May 1787, twelve men met at a print shop in London, to set up the Society for Effecting the Abolition of the Slave Trade. The group included the campaigner Granville Sharp, who had been involved in the cases of Jonathan Strong (see 17 April) and James Somerset (see 21 June); cases that tested whether slavery was legal on British soil. Initially Thomas Clarkson was the leader of the Society, and in 1791 William Wilberforce, an MP, joined him as co-leader.

The group believed that cutting off the supply of enslaved people would bring an end to the slave trade and the appalling **Middle Passage**. The abolitionists also believed that if plantation owners could not replace their enslaved workers, they would be forced to improve conditions and treatment on the plantations and eventually slavery would end.

The Society campaigned to raise funds and public awareness of the horrors of slavery. Members organized events, gave speeches, wrote essays that they published in pamphlets, and they presented signed petitions to the government. Society records show that over 200 women were active subscribers to the organization. They were involved in organizing society activities and events and also set up their own abolitionist groups. The impact of the Society increased with time, reaching huge numbers of people. Between 1787 and 1792, when the population of Britain was just 12 million people, one and a half million people in Britain (nearly 13% of the population) signed petitions against the slave trade. In 1807 the British government finally passed the Act for the Abolition of the Slave Trade (see 1 May). The abolition of slavery itself would take many more years to achieve.

23 MAY – LITTLE RICHARD

Richard Wayne Penniman, better known as Little Richard, was born in 1932 in Macon, Georgia. One of twelve children, poverty and hardship characterized his early life, but church-sponsored piano lessons and a place in the choir gave him the skills that would shape his life. After being thrown out by his father at thirteen years old, he joined a travelling show on the Chitlin' Circuit as a singer, and was given the name Little Richard.

A talent show win in 1951 got him his first record contract, but his career was slow to start. The raucous style for which he became famous only emerged four years later with release of 'Tutti Frutti'. The song was a huge hit and on 23 May 2010, it was included in the Library of Congress in recognition of its cultural importance. Richard was suprised to find his music also appealed to a white audience. His concerts were one of the few places at that time where Black and white audiences were allowed in the same building (although in different sections), leading to fearful warnings from white supremacists about racial mixing.

After only two years of outstanding success, the pioneering musician announced he was quitting popular music and dedicating himself to God and gospel. Always drawn back to the evangelism of his upbringing, Richard returned to and retired from rock 'n' roll several times before his death in May 2020.

> **DID YOU KNOW?**
>
> When Richard was fifteen and working at the Macon City Auditorium, Georgia, one of his favourite musicians, Sister Rosetta Tharpe (see 11 January) was in town to play. She heard him singing and invited him to open for her show.

24 MAY - YINKA SHONIBARE

Yinka Shonibare is one of Britain's leading artists. His work is shown in galleries around the world and one of his more famous pieces, *Nelson's Ship in a Bottle*, occupied the prestigious Fourth Plinth at Trafalgar

© QuentinUK, WikiCommons

Square from 24 May 2010 to 30 January 2012 (the Fourth Plinth is a public art space in central London which hosts a continuous programme of newly commissioned art). In this piece about trade and empire a large glass bottle holds a reproduction of Admiral Nelson's ship with sails made from African patterned fabric. The original location of Trafalgar Square became part of the art as it commemorates Nelson's historic victory at the 1805 battle.

Born in Britain in 1962, Shonibare was raised in Lagos. He returned to Britain at seventeen to complete his school exams, and then went on to study Fine Art at both undergraduate and master's levels. Shonibare's work explores this mixed cultural background and identity, and highlights the complex and violent history between Africa and Europe. He uses a variety of media to construct his art which often references western historical events and literature and infuses them with African imagery.

In 2019 Shonibare launched the Guest Artists Space Foundation in Nigeria with the aim of enabling cultural and creative exchange and research between art and science.

25 MAY - THE MURDER OF GEORGE FLOYD

On 25 May 2020, George Floyd, a forty-six-year-old truck driver who had lost his job during the Covid-19 pandemic, went into a Minneapolis store to buy cigarettes. The sales assistant suspected Floyd of using a counterfeit $20 note and called the police.

Floyd was arrested and handcuffed by officers and forced face down onto the road next to their police car. Two officers restrained him, and another prevented intervention from onlookers. Ignoring Floyd's repeated pleas of 'I can't breathe' and the arrival of an emergency medical team, a white officer called Derek Chauvin knelt on Floyd's neck for eight minutes and forty-six seconds in footage shot by onlookers. This was later confirmed as nine minutes and twenty-nine seconds in police bodycam footage. Floyd was taken to hospital and pronounced dead.

A witness uploaded a phone recording of the arrest on social media. It was viewed by millions. Soon protestors came out on the streets, calling for an end to police brutality. There were violent clashes  with police in Minnesota, where the mayor declared a state of emergency. The protests spread and demonstrations took place all over the USA and across the world as part of the Black Lives Matter movement (see 11 July). On 20 April 2021, Chauvin was found guilty on three murder and manslaughter charges. He was sentenced to twenty-two and a half years in prison.

After a public appeal to raise money for his family and funeral costs, Floyd was buried next to his mother.

Bloomberg/Getty Images

26 MAY ~ MILES DAVIS

Award-winning and hugely influential jazz musician Miles Davis was born in Illinois on 26 May 1926. Davis's family was relatively wealthy, and at the age of thirteen he was gifted a trumpet and trumpet lessons. He went on to gain a place in the renowned Julliard Music School in New York, but his need for novelty and innovation led him to drop out in favour of exploring New York's jazz scene.

IanDagnallComputing/Alamy

Davis's career was defined by his constant musical exploration, which led to the birth of several jazz movements, most notably the fusion jazz of the 1970s which brought him international fame. Often a difficult figure, he constantly pushed himself, his band members and his audience. In 1964 Davis and his Quintet played the Lincoln Day Concert, a fundraiser to support a voter registration drive in Mississippi and Louisiana through SNCC, CORE and NAACP. However, in order to encourage his band to play their best, Davis employed a technique that he called 'creative tension'. He neglected to inform his musicians, right up until they were waiting to go on stage, that their wages for the evening would also be donated to the fund. A huge argument erupted and was played out musically in an intense and experimental performance which can be heard on the two live albums of the event, *My Funny Valentine* and *'Four' and More*.

While this intensity kept him at the top of his professional life, it proved disastrous in Davis's personal life. Drug use and violence plagued him and on 29 September 1991, after several days in a coma, Davis finally died from pneumonia at sixty-five years old.

27 MAY – DIÉBÉDO FRANCIS KÉRÉ

Diébédo Francis Kéré is a Burkinabe architect, renowned for his innovative and sustainable designs.

Born in the tiny village of Gando in 1965, Kéré lived there until the age of seven when his father sent him to live with an uncle in the city to attend school. After finishing his education Kéré moved to Berlin to train as an architect. While studying he began a project to design and build a school for Gando, which would allow children born in his village access to an education. He worked tirelessly to raise the necessary funds and the Gando Primary school was completed in 2001.

Primary School Gando, ©Schulbausteine, WikiCommons

From the start Kéré sought to apply his architectural training to the realities of building within an area of limited resources, both financial and material, and with very different environmental challenges. He used traditional and readily available materials to engineer a modern building which was robust, sustainable and easily maintained. The Gando project was awarded the 2004 Aga Kahn Award for Architecture and the 2009 Global Award for sustainable Architecture.

Now based in Berlin, Kéré continues to design for projects in Burkina Faso but also throughout Africa and the rest of the world. His contribution to architecture was recognized on 27 May 2022 when he became the first African to receive the prestigious Pritzker Architecture Prize, regarded as architecture's highest honour.

28 MAY - SIYA KOLISI

On 28 May 2018, Siya Kolisi became the first Black captain of South Africa's national rugby team. A year later, he led his team to victory against England to win the 2019 Rugby World Cup in Yokohama, Japan, becoming the first Black player to captain a men's World Cup-winning side.

Born Siyamthanda Kolisi in June 1991 in Port Elizabeth, South Africa, by the age of twelve his rugby talent had won him a school scholarship. A few years later he was a member of the South Africa national under-18 rugby union team, and then the under-20s team from 2010–11. He won his first cap for the senior national team in 2013. Alongside his appearances on the national team, Kolisi has played for the rugby union teams Western Province, Stormers and Sharks.

Kolisi is also a philanthropist and in 2020 he and his wife established the Kolisi Foundation, which works to tackle inequalities by supporting under-resourced communities in South Africa. In 2019 *New African* magazine named him in their list of 100 Most Influential Africans. In 2023, the South African Government awarded him the National Order of Ikhamanga for his contributions to rugby.

> **DID YOU KNOW?**
>
> Kolisi is a Global Advocate for the UN Spotlight initiative. In this role he works to promote a healthy version of masculinity and to encourage men and boys to play their part in ending violence against women and girls.

29 MAY - SOJOURNER TRUTH

New York passed its anti-slavery bill in 1827. Enslaved since her birth in 1797, Isabella Baumfree had been promised her freedom in light of the coming law, but it soon became evident that the promise would not be kept. In 1826 she took her infant daughter and escaped her enslavement.

After converting to Christianity, she began preaching at various religious events and festivals, and in 1843 changed her name to Sojourner Truth to reflect her new profession.

Truth's travels brought her into contact with the abolitionist movement, and with encouragement from Frederick Douglass (see 14 February) she turned the focus of her preaching to the evils of slavery. Her autobiography *The Narrative of Sojourner Truth* was published in 1850 and brought her both an income and some fame. Courted by the women's rights movement, on 29 May 1851, Truth delivered her famous 'Aint I a woman?' speech at a convention in Ohio.

Truth's actual words were an articulate and passionate plea that women should not be left behind in the struggle for emancipation. The speech was transcribed and published three weeks later in the *The Anti-Slavery Bugle*. The more well-known version was written twelve years later by Frances Gage, an abolitionist who was president of the 1851 convention. Her version is written in Gage's approximation of a strong southern American dialect and, although it follows the basic outline of Truth's actual speech, it gives a very different impression of Truth as an activist and abolitionist.

Later in life Truth became part of the Freedmen's Bureau, helping formerly enslaved people to start their new lives. She continued to lobby against segregation and for women's rights until her death in 1883.

30 MAY - THE TULSA RACE MASSACRE

In 1906, Black property investor O. W. Gurley bought a forty-acre plot of land in Tulsa, Oklahoma. He named it Greenwood, and over the next fifteen years it became a thriving, prosperous Black neighbourhood, nicknamed 'Black Wall Street'. Today it is remembered as the site of one of the worst incidents of racial violence in American history.

On 30 May 1921 nineteen-year-old Black shoeshiner, Dick Rowlands, got into an elevator with Sarah Page, its seventeen-year-old white operator. What happened next is unclear but it seems likely that the lift jerked, causing Rowlands to fall against Page. The next morning Rowlands was arrested and taken to the Tulsa County Courthouse. That afternoon the *Tulsa Tribune* ran a headline that accused him of assault, and incited its readers to 'nab' Rowlands. A white mob bagan to gather outside. Fearing that Rowlands was about to be **lynched,** Black people arrived at the courthouse where the sheriff had him barricaded on the top floor. After a confrontation, shots were

Mr. Stuart, Library of Congress

fired and the Black crowd began returning to Greenwood. In the early hours of 1 June, Greenwood was looted and burned by the white mob. The governor declared martial law and the National Guard was dispatched to bring order and put out the fires. At the time it was reported that thirty-six people were killed, but today historians estimate it was as many as 300, although the bodies of many victims have never been found. An area covering thirty-five city blocks was destroyed. Hundreds were injured and 10,000 people made homeless.

Mr. Stuart, Library of Congress

The events of the two-day massacre were covered up by the authorities at the time. In 2001 a Race Riot Commission was established to investigate the massacre. They found that the charges against Rowlands were questionable from the start and that the authorities did little to calm the situation. Indeed, white men from the mob were selected to act as deputies and instead of stopping the violence, they joined in the deliberate destruction of 1,256 Greenwood homes, plus churches, businesses, schools, a hospital and a library. While thousands from the Black population of Tulsa were held for days, no one in the white mob was prosecuted for these acts. The Tulsa Reparations Coalition was set up on 7 April 2001 to advise on reparations to the Black community. In 2021, three survivors of the massacre, all aged one hundred or over, filed a reparations lawsuit. This was dismissed in July 2023, and the claimants lost their appeal in June 2024.

31 MAY - USAIN BOLT

On 31 May 2008, Jamaican sprinter Usain Bolt broke the world 100m record, becoming the fastest man in the world. Two months later, he broke his own record again, running 100m in 9.69 seconds, winning the gold medal at the Beijing Olympics. But that wasn't enough for Bolt. One year later, he set a 100m record (9.58 seconds) that has yet to be beaten. He earned the nickname 'the lightning bolt', which was also the name given to his distinctive, and much imitated, victory pose.

©J. Brichto, WikiCommons

Bolt is the only sprinter to win Olympic 100m and 200m titles at three consecutive Olympics (2008, 2012, and 2016). By the time he retired from competition in 2017, he had won eight Olympic gold medals and eleven World Championship gold medals.

1 JUNE - THE LITTLE GEORGE SHIP REVOLT

On 1 June 1730 the *Little George* left West Africa for the colony of Rhode Island with ninety-six captives on board, over half of whom were women and children. On 6 June at four o'clock in the morning, a handful of the captives slipped from their shackles and broke onto the deck where they launched an attack on the crew, killing three watchmen and grabbing their weapons. They managed to imprison the captain, George Scott, and the four remaining crew members in a cabin. In an attempted breakout the crew managed to blow themselves and the cabin up with an improvised grenade. Although badly burned, none of them died and they continued to defend their position until the Africans flooded the cabin and rendered the remaining gunpowder useless. They took control of the *Little George* and sailed back to West Africa, eventually reaching the Sierra Leone River where all ninety-six captives abandoned the ship and the imprisoned crew and presumably returned to their homes. The slavers were eventually rescued by another ship and the captain gave written testimony of the whole event.

The slave trade was an obscenely profitable venture. With an initial outlay of £5–10 per head and plantations buying at £38–88 per head, profits of 600–1000% were not uncommon. To protect such generous profits slavers employed more crew and encouraged the use of violence to subdue the captives. The rebellion of human cargo was a very real threat to business. Of the 36,000 slave voyages roughly one in ten recorded some form of resistance, and while most of these incidents resulted only in the death of the rebels, a significant few resulted in the loss of ships and their crews (see 6 November). A huge number of people were stolen from their homes and transported to the colonies, but it has been suggested that the number could have been almost 40 per cent higher had the ship rebellions not added extra difficulty and cost to this brutal business.

2 JUNE – DR CORNEL WEST

©Darrell Nance, WikiCommons

Dr Cornel West is an African American philosopher and activist, known for his teaching, writing and public speaking on race, gender, religion and class. In June 2023 West entered the field of politics and later began a run as an independent candidate for the presidency on a platform of global social justice.

Born 2 June 1953 in Tulsa, Oklahoma, West was raised in California where as a teen he became heavily involved in the civil rights movement. He went on to study at Harvard where he graduated **magna cum laude**, and then on to Princeton where he became the first African American to gain a **doctorate** in philosophy there.

Over the span of his career West has taught at many high-profile universities and written many books, most notably *Race Matters* and *Democracy Matters*. He has also been involved in political campaigns for several presidential candidates and was initially a supporter of Barack Obama (see 4 November), but has since expressed disappointment with his time in office. West is a seasoned and outspoken activist and is one of the most prominent Black intellectuals operating in the field of academia today.

> **DID YOU KNOW?**
>
> West has also produced music albums with artists including Prince, Bootsy Collins and Andre 3000. He also makes an appearance in the *Matrix* film series.

3 JUNE – JOSEPHINE BAKER

Dancer, activist and spy, Josephine Baker was born Freda Josephine McDonald on 3 June 1906 in St Louis, Missouri. By the time she was a teenager she was already married and working as a street dancer. Baker joined a dance troupe touring the US, then moved to New York, where she danced in a chorus line. Baker's unique comic touches made her stand out and audiences loved her.

In 1925 Baker moved to Paris and soon became one of the most adored performers in France. As the star act at the Folies Bergère musical hall, audiences flocked to see her perform the *Danse Sauvage*. With her short, slicked down hair, and her African-inspired costumes, Baker became an icon of the French art deco movement, and was visited by artists and writers, including Pablo Picasso and Ernest Hemingway. In 1927 she became the first Black woman to star in a major film, *Siren of the Tropics*. She turned her talents to music and released her most successful song, 'J'ai deux amours', in 1931. In 1936 Baker returned to America to star in *Ziegfeld Follies* on Broadway. Despite her fame in France, the show was not a success. Baker came back to France, married and became a French citizen.

When the Nazis invaded and occupied France during the Second World War, Baker became a spy for the Resistance, using her fame as a cover. She obtained and passed on secrets, using invisible ink to write the vital information on her sheet music. She was later awarded the Medal of the Resistance with Rosette and the Legion of Honour by the French government.

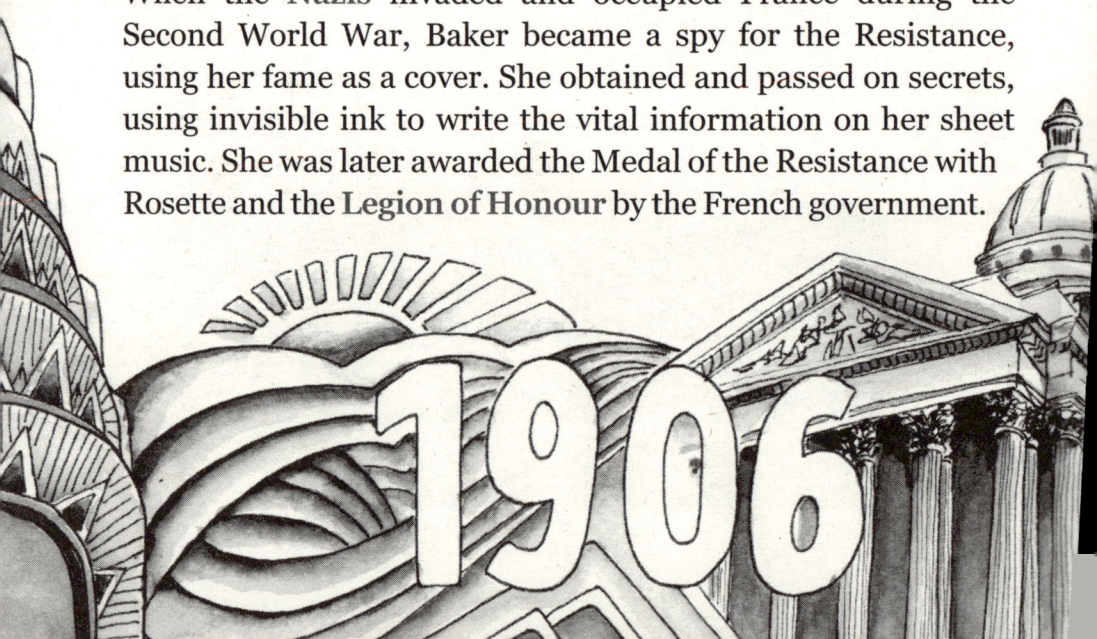

1906

After the war, Baker returned triumphantly to the Folies Bergère. In 1951 she was invited to America to perform in a nightclub in Miami. This time, her shows were a huge success and she embarked on a US tour. Baker refused to play before segregated audiences and as a result received threats from white supremacists. The authorities cancelled her visa, so the tour was cut short and she returned to France. She returned again to America in 1963 when she was invited to speak at the March on Washington (see 28 August). She recounted her own experiences of segregation and her personal battles against racism and encouraged the young to take up the fight.

Josephine Baker in French Air Force uniform in 1948, Studio Harcourt, Paris

©Studio Harcourt, Paris, WikiCommons

Baker gave her final performance in Paris at the age of sixty-eight in April 1975, for which she received a standing ovation. She died days later, on 12 April. More than 20,000 people came to her funeral and she was honoured with a twenty-one-gun salute, making Baker the first American woman buried in France with military honours.

4 JUNE - STOKELY CARMICHAEL/KWAME TURE

In the summer of 1961 the Freedom Riders (see 4 May) set out to enforce the Supreme Court's segregation ban. On 4 June a small group fought their way past protesters and boarded the whites only section of a train bound for Jackson, Mississippi. After reaching Jackson, they went in to a whites only cafeteria and were arrested and jailed. Among this group was teenage activist Stokely Carmichael, the youngest Freedom Rider.

After completing college, Carmichael joined the SNCC to work on voter registration drives and Black political representation. However, he became disillusioned with the lack of progress and, after the rejection of a Black delegation by the Democratic Party, unconvinced by the usefulness of integration as a key aim, Carmichael decided that the only way to liberation was to form an independent Black political group, and so he returned to Alabama where he and other SNCC members organized the Lowndes County Freedom Organization, which took a black panther as its symbol. In 1966 he became chairman of the SNCC and began to move the organization in a more radical direction. His cry of 'Black Power' in a speech made at the end of the March Against Fear (see 25 June) caused a rift with other civil rights groups and ultimately led to the formation of the Black Panther Party.

In the 1970s Carmichael left America to work for African liberation. He changed his name to Kwame Ture in honour of Ghanain leader Kwame Nkrumah (see 1 July) and Sekou Touré of Guinea. Carmichael died of cancer in 1998.

5 JUNE ~ THE MURDER OF CHARLES WOOTTON

In 1919, the year after the end of the First World War, a wave of race riots happened in a number of towns and cities in Britain. During the war, Britain had called on Black men from across its Empire to support the war effort. Many had served in war zones and others had helped to keep Britain's factories, mines and lumberyards working. However, once the war was over, the shortage of jobs and houses for returning soldiers began to cause resentment, and some people were keen to find someone to blame. These tensions led to violence and a series of racially motivated attacks across Britain.

In Liverpool on 4 June 1919 a Black sailor had been stabbed by a Scandinavian sailor when the Black sailor refused to give him a cigarette. On the night of 5 June, trouble started between the two groups of sailors again, and a crowd began to gather. The police arrived and decided to raid a house where many Black sailors were living. One of the men inside was Charles Wootton, a sailor from the island of Bermuda who had served in the Royal Navy during the war. As he left the back entrance of the house, the crowd saw him and began to chase him through the streets, down towards the docks. Once there, the crowd grew and they began pelting him with rocks, forcing him off the dockside and into the river. It was later reported that members of the crowd had shouted 'Let him drown'. A detective came to the scene and climbed down a rope to pull Wootton from the water, but before he could a stone hit Wootton in the head and he sank beneath the waves and drowned.

The inquest into Wootton's death opened and closed in one day, labelling him a police suspect rather than a victim. No one was ever arrested and charged with Wootton's murder.

6 JUNE ~ SAMMY DAVIS JR

On 6 June 1960, singer, dancer and actor Sammy Davis Jr announced his engagement to May Britt, a Swedish actress. Britt saw nothing controversial about their relationship, but Davis was from America where the first anti-miscegenation laws were passed in 1661 and would remain in the constitutions of some states until 2000. Their announcement was met with

Stanley Wolfson, Library of Congress

an onslaught of abuse from both the press and the public. Britt was offered no more films under her studio contract and Davis hired armed guards after the couple received death threats.

At that time Davis was heavily involved in the civil rights movement and he raised millions of dollars for the cause. He also campaigned for John F. Kennedy's successful presidential bid of 1960, but his invite to the inauguration gala was retracted when it became evident he would attend with his white fiancée.

Anti-miscegenation laws in the USA were finally repealed after the case of Mildred and Richard Loving vs. Virginia. In 1958 the couple had left Virginia to marry in Washington DC, where there was no such law. When they returned home they were arrested. Forced to choose between jail time or exile, the couple left Virginia but later filed a lawsuit against the state. In 1967 the Supreme Court ruled the laws unconstitutional. However, Alabama continued to enforce its law until 1970 and did not remove it from its constitution until 2000.

Davis and Britt's marriage did not survive and they divorced in 1968.

7 JUNE ~ THE TOPPLING OF THE COLSTON STATUE

In June of 2020 the world saw a wave of global Black Lives Matter (BLM) protests following the murder of George Floyd in the United States (see 25 May). During a protest on 7 June 2020 in the English city of Bristol, a group of people gathered around a statue of Edward Colston. A rope was tied around the statue and the crowd began to tug it from its stone plinth. Once it crashed to the ground, the statue was sprayed with red and blue paint and one protester put his knee on the statue's neck, echoing how George Floyd had been killed by a police officer who knelt on Floyd's neck for several minutes whilst ignoring pleas to stop. The crowd rolled the statue to Bristol Harbour and pushed it into the water. The statue was pulled out of Bristol Harbour a few days later and placed in storage.

Colston was born in Bristol in 1636 and died in 1721. He had shares in the Royal African Company (RAC) (see 27 September), and became its deputy governor from 1689 to 1690. The RAC was set up in 1660 by James, Duke of York (who became King James II) to run England's slave trade, and some of Colston's vast wealth came from his involvement in the transportation and enslavement of African people. Colston used some of his wealth to set up schools, churches, hospitals and housing for the poor. It was not unitl 1895, 174 years after his death, that politicians and businessmen in Bristol paid for a statue of Colston to be erected.

By the late 1990s, many people in Bristol petitioned the City Council to either remove the statue or place a sign on it that acknowledged Colston's role in the slave trade. No one could agree what to put on a sign and so the statue remained unchanged and in place in May 2020 at the time of the BLM protests. In September 2020 the mayor of Bristol, Marvin Rees, set up the We Are Bristol History Commission to help the people of Bristol understand the shared history of their city.

Th Crisis, March 1914/Wikimedia Commons

Pan-Africanist politician John Archer was born in Liverpool, England on 8 June 1863. The child of an Irish mother and Barbadian father, he was part of a large mixed heritage community, often common in cities built on the profits of the slave trade. After travelling the world with the navy, he finally settled in Battersea, London.

In 1900 Archer attended the Pan-African Conference in London where he met many of the big names of the anti-colonialist movement, including W. E. B. Du Bois (see 23 February), Dr John Alcindor (see 16 July) and composer Samuel Coleridge-Taylor (see 15 August) with whom he forged a lifelong friendship. Inspired to enter the world of politics, Archer joined the Labour League. In 1906 he was elected as a councillor in Battersea and in 1913 he was elected to the office of mayor.

> 66
> You have made history tonight. For the first time in the history of the English nation a man of colour has been elected as mayor of an English borough.
> 99

Throughout his career Archer worked to improve the lives of the working class and to fight for the rights of people of colour. In 1918 he became president of the African Progress Union and in 1921 was a chair of the Pan-African Congress London sessions.

Archer was elected to Battersea council several more times before his death in 1932.

9 JUNE - STEPHEN WILTSHIRE

Stephen Wiltshire is a British artist most famous for his highly detailed cityscapes which are often drawn from memory. His work is held in public and private collections around the world. Diagnosed at three years old as autistic, he developed his prodigious artistic talent as his preferred means of communication. With encouragement from his teacher, he entered his work into many competitions, but at thirteen years old his art reached a national audience when he was featured in a 1987 documentary on savantism. Following a drawing trip to New York to sketch its most iconic buildings, Wiltshire became an international name and his fame grew alongside a list of highly prestigious commissions. In October 2006 he opened his own gallery and studio in London.

Much of Wiltshire's work is available to view in public spaces, and on occasion he has made the process of drawing part of the artwork. A commission in Singapore attracted 150,000 visitors in just five days to watch him create a city panorama. The results of a similar project in New York now cover the walls of the 80th-floor observatory in the Empire State Building.

© Gobierno CDMX, WikiCommons

At a ceremony at Buckingham Palace on 9 June 2006, Stephen Wiltshire received an MBE in recognition of his contribution to the world of art.

10 JUNE - LEWIS HAMILTON

© Governo do Estado de Sao Paulo, WikiCommons

Lewis Hamilton is a British racing driver and the record-holder for most wins, pole positions and podium finishes in Formula One (F1) racing. He was the first Black driver to race in the sport, and the youngest ever F1 World Championship winner.

Born January 1985 in Stevenage, England, Hamilton is of mixed race heritage. He began go-karting at the age of six, and his father nurtured his talent, remortgaging his house to support him financially. At ten, Hamilton became the youngest driver to win the British cadet karting championship and had ambitions to drive for McLaren's Formula One team.

Hamilton worked through the junior motorsport levels and in 1998 won a place in the McLaren driver development programme. Hamilton won his first F1 race on 10 June 2007. He is the world's most successful F1 driver, currently tied with Michael Schumacher at seven drivers' championship titles.

Beyond the racetrack, Hamilton is a social activist. He set up the Hamilton Commission to investigate the lack of racial diversity in the motorsport industry and in the STEM sector. In 2020, following the death of George Floyd (see 25 May) Hamilton wore a Black Lives Matter T-shirt and took the knee (see 1 September) before the Austrian Grand Prix, persuading all of the other white drivers to join him. A week later, during his victory celebration at the next race, he raised his fist in the Black Power Salute. Hamilton was made a knight by Queen Elizabeth II in 2021 for services to motorsport.

11 JUNE ~ DIANE ABBOTT

On 11 June 1987, Diane Abbott was elected as the MP for the constituency of Hackney North and Stoke Newington. Born in London, the daughter of Jamaican parents, Abbott attended grammar school in Harrow, and then studied history at Cambridge University. After graduating she worked in the civil service and as a television researcher, before she got involved in local politics and became a local councillor.

Abbott's 1987 election campaign was difficult. Although she was their candidate, Abbott did not receive much support from the Labour party. At one point a brick was thrown through the window of her campaign office. Many people assumed that the white working-class people in the constituency would not vote for a Black candidate, but Abbott continued her campaign and recruited a team of dedicated volunteers from local communities.

Two weeks after her victory, Abbott attended the state opening of parliament, which marks the formal start of the parliamentary year. Taking her place on the benches in the House of Commons Debating Chamber, she chose to sit in what had been a favourite seat of the MP Enoch Powell, a man who had campaigned for the removal of Black people from Britain. Thirty-seven years later, in July 2024, she became the Mother of the House of Commons, the title given to the longest continuously serving female MP.

12 JUNE ~ HAMILTON

Written by Lin-Manuel Miranda, *Hamilton* is a musical that tells the life story of Alexander Hamilton, one of America's Founding Fathers. Miranda was inspired to write the musical after reading a biography of Hamilton, but has said that he wanted to tell that historical story about 'America then, as told by America now'. As well as more traditional musical theatre influences, *Hamilton* is inspired by a range of musical genres associated with African American and immigrant communities, such as hip-hop, soul, and R&B. Miranda also cast actors of colour in these historic roles, in what is known as colour-blind casting. The music and casting help to emphasize that immigration and diversity are integral to the story of America as a nation.

Barack Obama, after seeing the show with his daughters, greeting the cast and crew of Hamilton at the Richard Rodgers Theatre, New York, 2015

©Pete Souza, WikiCommons

Hamilton premiered in 2015 to rave reviews. In 2016 it was nominated in sixteen categories for the Tony (theatre) awards, and won eleven of them. The album of the show won the 2016 Grammy award for Best Musical Theatre Album. In 2016 *Hamilton* was also awarded the **Pulitzer Prize** for Drama.

13 JUNE - WALTER RODNEY

In October 1968 Jamaica erupted into a large-scale riot, sparked by the government's decision to ban Dr Walter Rodney from returning to Jamaica to his teaching position at the university. It started with a student protest, but quickly escalated. Several people were killed and millions of dollars of damage was done. The events changed Jamaican politics.

Guyanese academic Rodney earned his PhD from the University of London in 1966. He first took a position at the University of Dar es Salaam, Tanzania before moving to Jamaica to teach at the University of the West Indies. A committed Marxist, Rodney saw it as his duty to offer education to those without access to the academic world. He made a point to speak to and connect with the poor and working classes in deprived areas and he published this work as the book *Groundings with My Brothers*. This activism alarmed the Jamaican government and led to his ban from the country.

After a brief time in Cuba, Rodney returned to Tanzania and wrote his most famous work *How Europe Underdeveloped Africa*. The work argues that slavery and colonization not only slowed development but originated the underdevelopment from which the continent is still struggling to emerge.

In 1974 Rodney was offered a position at the University of Guyana. Seeing him as a threat, the government intervened and withdrew the offer, but Rodney still returned to his homeland and joined the Working People's Alliance. He spent the next years writing and giving speeches, and as the WPA gained popularity he found himself the target of death threats and police harassment. On 13 June 1980 Rodney was murdered by a car bomb. His wife, Patricia, suspected government involvement and in June 2021, after forty years of fighting, Guyana's National Assembly accepted that Rodney's murder had been organized by the then president Forbes Burnham.

14 JUNE ~ KHADIJA SAYE

The photographic artist Khadija Saye was born in London in 1992, to Gambian-British parents. As a teenager she won a scholarship to attend Rugby School, a prestigious private boarding school, and she went on to study photography at university. In her work she explored her Gambian heritage, examining themes of identity and place. For her graduation project, Saye produced *Crowned*, a series of photographs celebrating Black hair, which were taken in her home studio in the 20th-storey flat that she shared with her mother.

In 2017 Saye seemed to be on the brink of a promising artistic career. She was among a group of British artists selected to show their work at the Diaspora Pavilion at the Venice Biennale from May to November of that year. The show she created was called *Dwelling: in this space we breathe*, in which she documented traditional spiritual practices of Gambia using a special photographic process to make tintypes, which are photographic images created on thin iron plates.

On the evening of 14 June 2017, a fire broke out at Grenfell Tower, the block of flats where Saye lived. Residents were instructed by authorities to stay put while the fire was dealt with, but this proved to be a deadly mistake. The fire spread to the cladding on the tower, engulfing the whole building in flames. Saye and her mother were among seventy-two residents to die.

A public inquiry into the fire opened in September 2017. At the time of writing it has yet to produce its final report.

15 JUNE - MARCUS RASHFORD

The footballer and campaigner Marcus Rashford was born in Manchester in 1997, the youngest of five children in a working-class family of West Indian descent.

Oleg Bkhambri (Voltmetro) Wikimedia Commons

From the age of five Rashford was a keen footballer, and by the age of seven he had joined Manchester United's football academy. During his childhood his mother worked multiple jobs to look after and feed her children, but still often had to miss meals herself. Her busy work life meant that his siblings had to help to get Marcus to his football training.

By the time he was eighteen, Rashford had earned a place in the Manchester United first team playing in national and international competitions. He had also won a place in the English national football team. In May 2016, he became the youngest player to score a goal for England in their debut match, scoring within just three minutes.

By 2020, Rashford was established as one of the most talented footballers of his generation, but he was also becoming known for his campaigning to support homeless people. Then the Covid-19 pandemic began and Rashford was about to become even more well known for his work as an anti-poverty campaigner.

The lockdown that began in March 2020 brought lots of public attention to the issue of school meals for children. Some children were missing out on free school meals due to the lockdown or were getting really poor-quality meals. Children in poverty were also not getting free school meals during school holidays. Rashford campaigned to bring attention to the issue and to change government policy. On 15 June 2020 he wrote an open letter to the UK government, drawing on his own experiences as a child of how important school meals are to families in poverty. The next day government policy was changed and a commitment to provide free school meals for over a million children in poverty during the holidays was made. In September 2020 Rashford set up the Child Food Poverty Task Force to work with food shops and charities to continue his campaign.

In November 2020 he also set up a book club aimed at getting books to children in poverty. His own book for children, *You Are a Champion: How to Be the Best You Can Be*, was published in 2021 and won the Book of the Year award at the 2022 British Book Awards.

Rashford has received national and international recognition for his campaign work. He became the youngest ever person to be awarded an honorary degree by the University of Manchester in July 2020. In October 2020 he was awarded an MBE by Queen Elizabeth II. He has also been the winner of the inaugural FIFA Foundation Award and has been recognized for his leadership by *Times* and *Forbes* magazines.

Rashford continues to campaign for children in poverty.

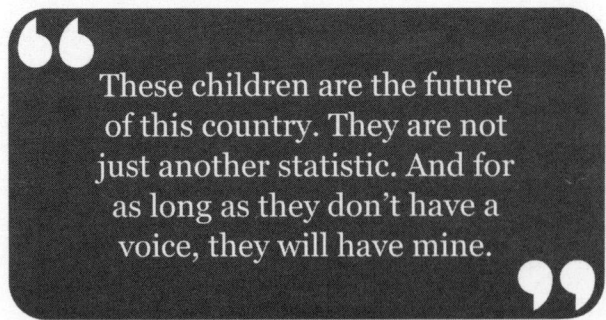

These children are the future of this country. They are not just another statistic. And for as long as they don't have a voice, they will have mine.

16 JUNE ~ HECTOR PIETERSON

Hector Pieterson was a twelve-year-old South African schoolboy who was shot and killed by police during the first day of the Soweto Uprising on 16 June 1976. The Soweto Uprising began as a protest by school children in the Black township of Soweto, against changes that the government was making to education across the country. The Black students wanted to learn in their native African languages such as Xhosa and Zulu, but the government had decided that all high school students were to learn in English and in Afrikaans (the language brought to South Africa by white Dutch settlers).

The Black students gathered for a peaceful protest against the changes. The crowd of children grew and eventually the police arrived. Some began to throw stones at the police who responded by firing tear gas into the crowd. It was after tear gas had been fired that someone (it is not clear who) gave the order for the police officers to shoot their guns into the crowd of children.

In the chaos that followed, children were running and screaming, and some of them were wounded. Pieterson was not the first child to die, but he became famous because of a shocking photograph that was taken that day by the news photographer Sam Nzima. In the photograph the anti-apartheid activist Mbuyisa Makhubo is carrying Pieterson's wounded body in his arms to Nzima's car, with his sister Antoinette Pieterson running by his side. The image shocked the world, and the Soweto Uprisings became a key moment in the fight against apartheid. Today in South Africa 16 June is a public holiday called Youth Day in memory of the children of the Soweto Uprising.

17 JUNE ~ QUINCY JONES

The musician, songwriter, composer and producer Quincy Delight Jones Jr was born in Illinois, Chicago in 1933. He learned the trumpet at school and won scholarships to study music at university. He left his education to begin his musical career in the 1950s, touring as a trumpeter with Lionel Hampton and his orchestra. On the road his talent for arranging music became apparent and soon he was working with renowned artists such as Ray Charles and Count Basie.

In 1961 Jones was appointed vice-president at Mercury Records and became one of the first African Americans to hold a top executive post at a major record company. He composed his first film score for *The Pawnbroker*, which was such a success that he moved to Los Angeles to combine his work as a composer, arranger and producer. Jones launched his record label, Qwest, in 1980 and produced many hit albums, including Michael Jackson's bestselling album *Thriller*. His first film as a producer, *The Color Purple*, was nominated for eleven Oscars, including Best Original Score and Best Original Song. Jones is also a social activist and long-time supporter of NAACP and GLAAD. He founded the non-profit Quincy Jones Listen Up Foundation, a cultural exchange programme that links youth in South Africa and Los Angeles.

Jones has won twenty-eight Grammy awards and an Emmy. In 2013 he was inducted into the Rock & Roll Hall of Fame, and on 17 June 2021, he became one of the Foundational Inductees in the Black Music and Entertainment Walk of Fame.

DID YOU KNOW?

In 1968 Jones became the first African American to receive two Oscar nominations in the same year.

18 JUNE - WORLD ANTI-SLAVERY CONVENTION

From 12 to 23 June 1840, the World Anti-Slavery Convention was held in London. The convention was organized by the British and Foreign Anti-Slavery Society – a group started by the English anti-slavery campaigner Joseph Sturge in 1839. Britain had stopped its involvement in the slave trade with the Abolition of the Slave Trade Act, 1807 (see 1 May) and had passed the Slavery Abolition Act in 1833 (see 22 July) which eventually ended slavery in British colonies. Now anti-slavery campaigners wanted to see the end of slavery everywhere.

The convention brought together over four hundred of the world's leading anti-slavery campaigners. It included speeches, presentations of statistics about slavery around the world, discussion sessions, and the setting up of committees. Speakers included the Black abolitionist campaigner Henry Beckford, who had himself been enslaved.

Despite having a common goal, there was some disagreement. Not all of the people attending the convention were treated equally. Women were not officially allowed to attend the convention or speak in the meetings and could only watch from the balconies above the main hall. Some male delegates, including Charles Lenox Remond, the brother of Sarah Remond (see 14 September), joined the women in solidarity, refusing to take their seats in the main hall.

The artist Benjamin Robert Haydon recorded the convention in a massive oil painting (*The Anti-Slavery Society Convention*, 1840), which is now owned by the National Portrait Gallery in London. The British and Foreign Anti-Slavery Society still survives today, and is now known as Anti-Slavery International.

19 JUNE ~ JUNETEENTH

The Emancipation Proclamation made by President Lincoln on 22 September 1862 was supposed to come into force on 1 January 1863, making enslaved people in the slave-holding Confederate states legally free. While many enslaved people spent the evening of 31 December 1862 waiting for midnight and their freedom (see 31 December), in areas of America still under the control of the Confederates, that freedom would be delayed as the Civil War continued. The last place in America to see the Emancipation Proclamation enforced, two and a half years later, was Galveston in Texas. There, on 19 June 1865, General Gordon Granger of the Union Army issued General Order No. 3 and declared the state's 250,000 enslaved people to be free.

Black communities in Texas began to commemorate the date, and named it Jubilee Day. By the 1890s it had become known as Juneteenth and regarded by many African Americans in the southern states as America's second independence day, celebrated with parties, picnics, barbecues, historical talks and church services.

During the Jim Crow era Juneteenth celebrations declined in popularity, but towards the end of the 1960s, it started to be more widely celebrated by various civil rights groups. Texas became the first state to recognize Juneteenth as a state holiday in 1980 and soon many people were campaigning to make Juneteenth a national holiday. Opal Lee, known as the godmother of Juneteenth, campaigned for decades, leading marches and organizing petitions. In 2021, in recognition of her dedication, Lee was invited to stand next to President Biden when he signed the Juneteenth National Independence Day Bill, finally making it an official federal holiday.

20 JUNE - MUHAMMAD ALI FOUND GUILTY

On 28 April 1967 boxing legend Muhammad Ali refused to be conscripted into the US Army and be forced to fight in the Vietnam War. He took this decision both because of his religious beliefs and because of his moral opposition to the war. Ali felt that to join the fighting would go against his Muslim faith. He said that he was also unwilling, as a Black man, to fight brown people on behalf of a government that denied Black people their human rights.

Ali was immediately stripped of his heavyweight title and faced trial for draft evasion. The US government took him to court and on 20 June 1967 he was found guilty of evading military conscription. He was sentenced to five years in prison, fined $10,000 and banned from boxing for three years. This meant that at the very peak of his potential as an athlete Ali was unable to compete in professional boxing matches. Ali was freed on bail and spent the next four years appealing the verdict. During this time, Ali made several speeches as an anti-war activist, in which he was supported by Dr Martin Luther King Jr.

Ali's boxing licence was finally restored in October 1970. He appealed his prison sentence, taking his case to the Supreme Court, where in 1971 the conviction was overturned because the army had never given its reasons for denying him the status of conscientious objector in the first place. Ali then resumed his boxing career and continued to compete until his retirement from the ring at thirty-nine years old in 1981.

21 JUNE - THE MANSFIELD JUDGEMENT

The Mansfield Judgement was a decision made in a legal case in Britain in 1772 about James Somerset, an enslaved African man, whose fate was determined in a court presided over by Lord Chief Justice Mansfield.

James Somerset was born in West Africa around 1741. When he was about eight years old he was captured and transported to the British colony of Virginia, where he was sold as a domestic slave to Charles Stewart. Somerset had been enslaved by Stewart for almost twenty years by the time he was brought by him to London in 1769. Thousands of Black people lived in London at the time, some enslaved and others free. While in London Somerset was baptized and three white godparents at his church helped expand his knowledge of the Christian faith.

Somerset knew that at some point Stewart would take him back to the colonies in America where he'd remain enslaved for the rest of his life. So on 26 November 1771, he escaped Stewart's control and hid out on the streets of London. Somerset must have hoped that Stewart would give up on him and return home. But Stewart had no intention of sailing back across the Atlantic without his human 'property'.

Stewart hired slave-hunters to find Somerset and after a few weeks they caught him near Covent Garden market. The slave-hunters took Somerset to a ship on the River Thames that was soon heading to Jamaica. He was held below deck, destined to be sold to a sugar plantation owner for the worst kind of work that an enslaved person could suffer.

Somehow Somerset got a message to his church godparents, telling them that he had been captured and was to be sent to Jamaica. Those godparents, Elizabeth Cade, Thomas Walkin, and John Marlow, got the lord chief justice – Lord Mansfield – to have Somerset released while a court hearing was planned.

Somerset decided to use the law to win his freedom permanently. He needed help, and he turned to a man called Granville Sharp (see 17 April), an abolitionist who had been carefully studying the laws around slavery in England. Sharp had been looking for a case he could take to court that would force the judges to decide if slavery

was legal or illegal on English soil. Sharp decided he would take on Somerset's case and put together a team of lawyers.

Lord Mansfield began hearing the case in February 1772. The lawyers hired by Stewart used every argument they could think of. They said that if Somerset were set free all the enslaved people in Britain would have to be released. They claimed that there were around 14,000 or 15,000 enslaved people in the country and that freeing them would cost the slave owners £800,000. They also argued that slavery was so important to the British economy that anything that threatened it was against the interests of the country. It was not just Stewart who wanted James Somerset returned to slavery; the many slave-owners and the merchants who had grown wealthy from the trade in enslaved people were so concerned about this court case that they paid Stewart's legal bills.

The lawyers who had been hired by Granville Sharp to defend Somerset argued in court that under English law no man 'can be a slave in England'. They claimed that anyone who arrived in England was instantly made free and then protected by the law, whatever their race or religion.

In mid-May Lord Mansfield brought the court case to an end and returned to his mansion, Kenwood House, to consider his judgement. He shared his home with his wife and two young women: his orphaned niece and his illegitimate grand-niece, Dido Elizabeth Belle (see 20 November). She was the mixed-race daughter of Lord Mansfield's nephew, Captain Sir John Lindsay, and an enslaved African woman named Maria. Evidence suggests Lord Mansfield cared for Dido, and it was against this highly unusual (for the time) family backdrop that Lord Mansfield spent over a month deliberating on the status of the enslaved in England.

His judgement was finally given at Westminster Hall on 22 June 1772. It stated that slavery was so terrible that it could only be allowed in England if laws making it legal were passed by Parliament. As no such laws had ever been passed, he said '...the black must be discharged'. This meant Somerset was a free man, no longer enslaved.

Even after more than 200 years the exact meaning of Lord Mansfield's judgement is still unclear and there is disagreement about it. Many people at the time felt it granted freedom not just to James Somerset but to all Black people in Britain, although this is not what Mansfield said. Ultimately the exact terms of his judgement and intentions became less significant than the popular understanding, or misunderstanding, of it. Black people in Britain and their supporters were determined to take the decision as monumental and to regard its impact as far reaching, despite the technical narrowness of what Mansfield had actually ruled.

Many years after the Mansfield Judgement people continued to live under forms of slavery in England and advertisements for the sale or the recapture of escaped Black people still appeared in English newspapers (see 25 January). But the Mansfield Judgement was hugely important as it showed that the law could be used as a weapon against slavery.

22 JUNE - EMPIRE WINDRUSH

Late on the night of 21 June 1948, a passenger ship slipped into the River Thames and, in the darkness, anchored at Tilbury Docks. That ship, the HMT *Empire Windrush*, was completing a routine journey across the Atlantic Ocean. The next day, 22 June, the passengers on board the *Windrush*, including 802 people from the Caribbean, came ashore.

Reporters from the British newspapers and a Pathé News camera crew were waiting at the docks to record the moment. One of the people who was filmed and interviewed was a calypso singer from Trinidad called Aldwyn Roberts, whose stage name was Lord Kitchener. Roberts sang a new song he had written while crossing the ocean, called 'London Is the Place to Be'.

The *Windrush* was not the first ship to bring people from the Caribbean to Britain in the years after the Second World War, but there were two things that made the *Windrush* notable: firstly, its arrival was so well recorded by the media, and secondly it caused controversy within the government.

Although the newspapers celebrated the arrival of the *Windrush*, behind the scenes the government was unhappy at the prospect of fewer than a thousand Black people from the Caribbean starting new lives in Britain. The government had even considered trying to prevent the *Windrush* from docking, and the prime minister, Clement Attlee, had asked if these Caribbean people might instead be sent to East Africa where they could work on farms. One government official described the arrival as an 'invasion' of Britain. Some believed that if Black people came to live in Britain there would be tensions between them and white people. They also believed old stereotypes that suggested Black people didn't want to work, or would struggle to work in the cold climate of Britain.

But the passengers on board the *Windrush* were citizens of the British **Commonwealth**. They came from islands like Jamaica, which had been part of Britain's empire since the 17th century, and this meant they had every right to come to Britain, find work and build new lives. Many had served with the armed forces during the Second World War, most of them in the Royal Air Force. They had chosen to return to Britain in 1948 because there were so few jobs in the Caribbean.

Having disembarked at Tilbury Docks, the *Windrush* passengers headed off to find new jobs. Those with nowhere to stay were housed in an old air raid shelter at Clapham South in London, and they looked for work at an Employment Exchange in Brixton – an area that would later become a centre of London's Black population.

Within a month all but twelve of them had found jobs. This was because many British companies were very glad to have them. In 1948 Britain was in the midst of a serious labour shortage – during the war thousands of homes had been damaged by bombs, and factories, railways and roads had been neglected as all of the nation's attention and money had been focused on building tanks, guns and planes. Now the war was over there was a huge amount of work to do repairing and modernizing the country, but there were not enough people to do it. The people on the *Windrush* were eager to work, spoke English and had a legal right to be in the country and to work. Many of them also had very useful skills that British companies desperately needed. The passenger list for the *Windrush* tells us that among those on board were eighty-five mechanics, fifty-four carpenters, thirty-nine clerks, thirty-four tailors, twenty-three welders, twenty engineers, fifteen machinists, fourteen fitters, thirteen electricians, twelve civil servants, ten shoemakers, as well as two piano repairers,

EMPIRE WINDRUSH
LONDON

two hair-dressers, a hatter and, of course, the calypso singer Lord Kitchener.

Although the *Windrush* passengers had every right to be in Britain many of them experienced racism. Some struggled to find places to live, as the owners of some flats and houses did not want to rent them to Black people. As more ships brought more people from the Caribbean, Black people found they were denied access to some businesses and professions, a type of discrimination known as the **colour bar**.

While all of the *Windrush* passengers wanted to work, some only intended to stay for a few years to earn a bit of money and then go back to their families in the Caribbean. While some did return, others ended up settling down in Britain, getting married, having children and becoming part of a growing Black British community. Many years later Oswald Denniston, who had travelled on the *Windrush*, said, 'Many of us thought we would come here to get a better education and to stay for about five years ... but then some of us have ended staying for fifty.'

The arrival of the *Windrush* in June 1948 is often thought of as the symbolic start of the process that created the modern Black British community, although really it was a new chapter in the much longer story of Black people living in Britain.

23 JUNE - FANNY EATON

Born on 23 June 1835 in Jamaica, Fanny Eaton was brought to England as a child by her mother, a formerly enslaved woman. It is believed that Eaton's father was a soldier who died just a few days after Fanny's birth. Fanny worked as a domestic servant and married hansom-cab owner and driver James Eaton in 1857. They went on to have ten children.

Eaton began work as an artists' model when she was in her twenties and she soon became a favourite with a circle of artists known as the Pre-Raphaelites, appearing in many of their paintings. The first painting that she modelled for to be exhibited at the Royal Academy was Simeon Solomon's *The Mother of Moses* in 1860. Eaton also was among a group of women depicted in Dante Gabriel Rossetti's famous painting *The Beloved*, which is currently on display at Tate Britain in London.

At a time when images of beauty in the western world were represented by white people, Fanny Eaton made women of colour more visible, inspiring Victorian artists and offering an alternative model of beauty.

In later years, Eaton moved to the Isle of Wight where she worked as a cook and a seamstress. She spent her final years in London and died at the age of eighty-eight in 1924.

Princeton University Art Musem, Museum Purchase, Surdna Fund. Wikimedia Commons

Portrait drawing of Fanny Eaton by Walter Fryer Stocks, 1859.

24 JUNE - PATRICE LUMUMBA

The independence movement that swept through Africa in the 1960s (see 1 January) reached the Congo on 24 June 1960 when Patrice Lumumba became the country's first prime minister. His party, the Mouvement National Congolais (MNC), had not won outright in the elections and Lumumba was forced into coalition with his rival Joseph Kasa-Vubu of the Alliance des Bakongo (ABAKO), who became the president.

Harry Pot, Nationaal Archief, Netherlands

At the independence ceremony Lumumba's angry response to a speech by the Belgian King, in which he praised his **genocidal** predecessor King Leopold, gave rise to fears that he may not be as accommodating to the continued financial interests of the former **colonists** as other postcolonial government appointees. From the beginning Lumumba's government was beset with difficulties including a military revolt and a rebellion in the Katanga province. He replaced European military officers with African officers, installed Joseph Mobuto as chief of staff and increased army pay, but the unrest continued. Receiving only faint promises of help from the **UN**, Lumumba turned to the **Soviet Union**, a move which further dismayed the West and led to his dismissal as prime minister. In the subsequent chaos Mobutu staged a **coup** d'état and his takeover was then legitimized by the UN. Lumumba was arrested and was executed by firing squad on 17 January 1961. His body was desecrated.

Recent investigations have uncovered the involvement of the **CIA** and Belgian government in Lumumba's murder. In 2002 Belgium issued an official apology for the part that they played.

25 JUNE - JAMES MEREDITH

Born in Mississippi on 25 June 1933, James Meredith is a controversial figure of the American civil rights movement. Despite efforts to disassociate himself from the movement, his actions in the 1960s contributed greatly to the overall cause.

James Meredith walking on the campus of the University of Mississippi, accompanied by US marshals. October 1962

Meredith applied to the University of Mississippi in 1961. He was accepted, but once the University realized that he was Black they rescinded the offer. Meredith took his discrimination case to the **Supreme Court**, who, in the wake of the Brown vs. Topeka ruling (see 16 May), found in his favour. In September 1962 his attempt to register for class resulted in the erruption of violent riots on campus. When Meredith finally enrolled on 1 October he became the university's first Black student.

Meredith also orchestrated the March Against Fear, a solo walk across Tennessee and Mississippi to encourage African American voter registration. He began on 5 June 1966, but on only the second day he was attacked and shot several times. His wounds were not fatal but were too severe for him to continue. Instead the march was taken up by Dr Martin Luther King (see 10 January), Stokely Carmichael (see 4 June) and Floyd McKissick with the armed resistance group the Deacons for Defence and Justice (see 25 November) employed as security. By the time Meredith was fit to rejoin, more than 15,000 people were marching. The March Against Fear resulted in the registration of 4,000 new voters and, thanks to a rallying cry by Carmichael and activist Willie Ricks, it is remembered as the event that sparked the Black Power movement.

26 JUNE ~ OLIVE MORRIS

Olive Morris was born on 26 June 1952 in Jamaica and came to live in London aged nine. In 1969 Morris witnessed a Nigerian diplomat being beaten and arrested by the police for allegedly stealing his own car. She intervened and was herself arrested. Morris was badly beaten and was later given a suspended prison sentence for assaulting a police officer. She became a fully-fledged activist and a member of the youth section of the British Black Panther movement, fighting against racism, sexism and police brutality. In 1973 Morris co-founded the Brixton Black Women's Group.

In 1975 Morris enrolled in the University of Manchester to study for a degree in economics and social sciences. While there she became involved in community activism. She joined the Manchester Black Women's Collective and took part in a student exchange trip to China. After graduating in 1978, Morris returned to London and worked at the Brixton Community Law Centre. In 1978, critical of white feminism, she helped set up the Organization of Women of African and Asian Descent to bring African, Asian and Caribbean women together to discuss issues of race, social class and gender oppression.

Morris fell ill in 1978 and eventually was diagnosed with a type of blood cancer called non-Hodgkin lymphoma. The cancer did not respond to treatment and Morris died in 1979. She was only twenty-seven. The Remembering Olive Collective was formed in 2008 and a memorial award was set up in 2011 in her honour to help young activists. In 2023 a short film drama of her life entitled *The Ballad of Olive Morris* was nominated for a BAFTA.

27 JUNE - PAUL DUNBAR

The poet and author Paul Laurence Dunbar was born in Dayton, Ohio on 27 June 1872. His talent for writing was clear from childhood. He edited his high school paper, was president of the literary society, and had poems published in his local newspaper at the age of sixteen. Unable to afford university, he worked as an elevator operator, and continued writing in his spare time.

Kell, Library of Congress

Dunbar got the confidence to start publishing collections of his poems after his work was praised by established author James Newton Matthews in a letter that was printed in several newspapers. His first collection, *Oak and Ivy*, was published in 1893, with financial support from his childhood friend, the inventor Orville Wright, and his second, *Majors and Minors* in 1895. Dunbar started to give readings of his poems, some of which were written in an African American dialect, and he performed across the USA before touring England. While in England Dunbar met the composer Samual Coleridge-Taylor (see 15 August) and they collaborated on the operetta *Dream Lovers*.

Dunbar returned to America and a job as a clerk at the Library of Congress. He published a collection of short stories, *Folks from Dixie* (1898), in which he examined the lives of African Americans and their experiences of racism before and after emancipation. Dunbar's health began to deteriorate. He caught pneumonia in 1899 and again in 1903, and developed issues with alcohol. Despite this he continued to publish short stories and novels, often dealing with tales of racism and injustice. Dunbar died on 9 February 1906, aged only thirty-three.

28 JUNE - CHRIS HANI

Chris Hani was born Martin Thembisile Hani on 28 June 1942 in the town of Cofimvaba, in the Eastern Cape of South Africa. From childhood he was committed to resisting the apartheid regime of racial segregation in South Africa. At the age of fifteen he joined the Youth League of the African National Congress (ANC). Three years later, in 1960, the South African government banned the ANC.

After graduating from university, Hani joined uMkhonto we Sizwe, which was a group within the ANC that carried out armed attacks on government targets. He was eventually forced to leave South Africa and go into hiding in the neighbouring country of Lesotho, changing his name to Chris. Now the group's leader, Hani continued to organize attacks on the apartheid government in South Africa.

1990 saw the release of Nelson Mandela from prison and the ban on the ANC was lifted. The ANC called a stop to armed struggle and the actions of uMkhonto we Sizwe. Hani returned to South Africa and became the new leader of the South African Communist Party in 1991. On 10 April 1993, Hani was shot and killed outside his home. His killer was a Polish immigrant called Janusz Waluś. The investigation found that Waluś had been given the gun he used to assassinate Hani by a South African politician called Clive Derby-Lewis. He was a member of the South African Conservative Party who did not want the apartheid system to be taken apart. The men wanted Hani's death to interrupt the peace process, but instead it resulted in a new commitment to negotiate and a year later South Africa held its first fair, free and democratic elections in which people of all colours could vote (see 27 April).

29 JUNE - SAMUEL AJAYI CROWTHER

On 29 June 1864, Samuel Ajayi Crowther became the first African bishop of the Anglican Church.

Born into a Yoruba family in what is now modern-day Nigeria in around 1809, at the age of twelve he and family members were captured and sold to Portuguese slave traders. Put on a ship bound for Brazil, they were rescued when HMS *Myrmidon* of the British Navy's West Africa Squadron intercepted the ship  and took them to Freetown, Sierra Leone. Placed in the care of the Church Mission Society (CMS), he was given a new name, in honour of Samuel Crowther, one of the society's pioneers, and received a formal Christian education.

Crowther proved himself to be a talented linguist and was sent to Britain in 1826 to further his education. Returning to Sierra Leone in 1827, he became the first student at the CMS's Fourah Bay College. By the end of his studies he could speak English, Latin, Greek, Yoruba, Hausa, Ibo, Nupe and Temme and he went on to become a teacher at the school. In 1841 Crowther was chosen to join missionary expeditions and his success led to his ordination as a minister in the Anglican church in 1843.

Crowther continued his academic career, becoming doctor of divinity upon completion of a PhD at the University of Oxford, and became the first person to translate the Bible and the Book of Common Prayer into Yoruba. In October 1866 he co-founded the Academy in Lagos to promote literature, science and the arts. He died in Lagos in December 1891 aged eighty-two and was buried at Ajele Cemetery.

30 JUNE - THE PHILIPSBURG PROCLAMATION

The American War of Independence began in 1775. From the beginning both sides were aware of the role that enslaved Africans could play in the conflict. In 1775, the commander of the British forces, Governor John Murray, the Fourth Earl of Dunmore, issued a proclamation promising freedom to any enslaved Africans or indentured servants in Virginia who abandoned their plantations and came to join and fight with the British troops as Black Loyalists (see 7 November).

Four years later, on 30 June 1779, General Henry Clinton, Britain's commander-in-chief in North America, issued a new proclamation from his headquarters in the Philipsburg Manor House in Westchester County, New York, a proclamation that applied to the whole of the United States. He promised freedom to any enslaved person whose owner was an American Revolutionary, whether that enslaved person joined the British Army or not. As well as their freedom, he also promised them protection and land. Clinton had miscalculated and his proclamation was far more successful than he imagined and than he could cope with. Among the people who answered his call were enslaved people who had been owned by leaders of the revolutionary forces, including George Washington, James Madison, and Thomas Jefferson. So many people answered his call that Clinton tried to send many of them back.

After the war, the British negotiators broke the promises of the proclamation and agreed, in the Treaty of Paris of 1783, to return the formerly enslaved people back to their masters as their property. However, British Army commanders refused to do it. Instead compensation was paid to their former owners and the Black Loyalists were sent to free settlements in Nova Scotia, Canada. Others came to Britain before they were relocated to start new settlements in Sierra Leone on the west coast of Africa (see 15 May).

JULY

1 JULY – KWAME NKRUMAH

Kwame Nkrumah was born in September 1909 in the Gold Coast, then a British colony in West Africa. In 1935, his passion for politics led him to study in the USA. At university he developed interests in socialism, nationalism and Pan-Africanism, and the writings of W. E. B. Du Bois (see 23 February), Marcus Garvey (see 17 August) and others. He became a student activist, and established and became president of the African Students Association of America and Canada.

In 1945 Nkrumah moved to London. Here his studies took a back seat to his activism and he helped organize the fifth Pan-African Congress in Manchester (see 21 October), where delegates discussed strategies by which African nations might gain independence from colonial rule.

Returning home, Nkrumah formed the Convention People's Party in 1949, which campaigned for immediate independence. Nkrumah won the 1951 election and became prime minister. Years of negotiations with Britain followed, and in 1957 the Gold Coast became the independent state of Ghana (see 6 March), the first sub-Saharan African country to gain its independence from colonial rule. In 1960 Ghana voted to become a republic, and on 1 July Nkrumah was elected the country's first president.

In 1966 Nkrumah was overthrown in a military coup. He never returned to Ghana and lived in exile for the rest of his life. In 1972 he flew to Romania for treatment for cancer, but died there aged sixty-eight. Today Nkrumah's birthday is celebrated as a public holiday in Ghana.

2 JULY - THE CIVIL RIGHTS ACT OF 1964

At the end of the American Civil War, the people freed from enslavement were given full citizenship of the United States. This citizenship granted Black men, and from 1920 also Black women, the right to vote. However, in many American states, especially those in the south of the country, the authorities made it very difficult for Black people to register to vote. States set literacy tests and made people pay poll taxes before they could vote, and Black people were often threatened with violence for exercising their right to vote. In the 1950s the civil rights movement began to challenge this situation, as well as the Jim Crow laws that kept Black people segregated from white people.

By the early 1960s, after political pressure mounted thanks to years of civil rights campaigning, President, John F. Kennedy was willing to act and on 11 June 1963 he addressed the nation on television. In his speech he proposed new civil rights laws stating that the United States would 'not be fully free until all of its citizens are free'. On 22 November President Kennedy was assassinated, but his successor, President Lyndon B. Johnson, pushed on with the plans.

On 2 July 1964 president Johnson signed the 1964 Civil Rights Act into law. It banned discrimination on the basis of race, colour, religion, sex or national origin in the United States. The Act supported the rights of Black people to vote and ended the Jim Crow era and the legal segregation of schools and public spaces. The civil rights Act of 1964 was a landmark in the country's Civil Rights movement, and it would be strengthened by further Acts, including the Voting Rights Act of 1965 (see 7 March).

3 JULY - THE STONEWALL UPRISING

On Thursday 3 July 1969 the Stonewall Uprising in New York came to an end. This momentous event marked the beginning of the modern Pride movement with the very first Pride parade taking place a year later.

One of the best known faces of Stonewall and the subsequent Pride movement is that of Marsha P. Johnson. Born in 1945 and assigned male at birth, Johnson had never conformed to gender norms and was the victim of bullying all through childhood. As soon as she graduated from high school she left New Jersey for New York where she felt more able to live as herself. Although there has been some debate over whether Johnson was a trans woman, it is complicated by changes in the language used to describe trans people since the 1960s. She described herself as gay, a drag queen, transvestite and used female pronouns.

In 1960s America, LGBTQ+ people lived under oppressive laws and attitudes. Homosexuality had been categorized as a mental illness by the American Psychiatric Association and remained so until 1974. Gay people were deemed to be unsuitable federal employees and were purged from government agencies. They were often victims of harassment and persecution from authorities and there were many protests throughout the US against police brutality prior to the eruption at Stonewall. In the state of New York, homosexuality itself remained a criminal offence until 1980, in the 1960s the liquor laws banned bars from serving homosexuals, and old 'masquerade' laws, which were intended to target people disguising themselves to commit crime, were used to harass the gender nonconforming (these masquerade laws are still on the statute books and have been used to arrest masked protesters).

The Stonewall bar in Greenwich Village, New York, was often a target for police raids. On the evening of Friday, 27 July 1969 the bar was raided for the second time in a week. Several people were arrested and thrown into vans, from which an increasingly agitated crowd of bar patrons tried to free them. The disturbance attracted more and more people and by the early hours of Saturday 28 July the police were forced to barricade themselves inside the bar and call for reinforcements against hundreds of angry protesters. Urban legend has it that Johnson threw the first brick at the uprising, but she herself claimed only to have turned up when things were already well underway. She and her friend Sylvia Rivera joined the crowd and were heavily involved in the protests over the following days.

The Stonewall Uprising proved a turning point in the struggle for LGBTQ+ rights, inspiring a new wave of activisim. Johnson and Silvera went on to found Street Transvestite Action Revolutionaries (STAR), an organization to assist trans people, and set up STAR House which offered shelter to trans youths who had been thrown out of their family homes. Although Johnson died in 1992 at just forty-six years old, her name is carried on by the Marsha P. Johnson Institute, founded by Elle Moxely to advocate for the rights of the Black transgender community. In 2020 the Marsha P. Johnson State Park in Brooklyn, New York, became the first state park dedicated to an LGBTQ+ figure and a transgender woman of colour.

4 JULY - TINA TURNER

The singer, actor and songwriter Tina Turner was born Anna Mae Bullock on 26 November 1939 in Brownsville, Tennessee. After a difficult childhood, by her teens she was singing in nightclubs in St Louis, when she met the singer Ike Turner in 1957 and joined his band the Kings of Rhythm.

They married and became the Ike and Tina Turner Revue, a successful touring and recording group. In the 1960s and 70s they produced hit singles including 'River Deep – Mountain High', and 'Nutbush City Limits'. Behind the scenes, however, Ike was abusive and controlling, and locked Tina in hotel rooms when they were on the road. Eventually, on 1 July 1976, she escaped from a hotel in Dallas, with only thirty-six cents and a Mobil gas card, and filed for divorce later that month.

In the early 1980s, Turner's career as a solo artist started to grow. She was given a new contract and recorded her breakthrough solo album, *Private Dancer*. It went on to sell 10 million copies worldwide. The album's second single, 'What's Love Got to Do With It', reached number one in the US Billboard charts and won her the Grammy for Record of the Year. She continued to tour, released her memoir, *I, Tina* in 1986, and acted in the 1985 film *Mad Max: Beyond Thunderdome*.

Turner met her beloved second husband, German music executive Erwin Bach, in 1985. On 4 July 2013, they married on the banks of Lake Zurich in Kusnacht, Switzerland, where she lived until her death in 2023.

> **"** If you are unhappy with anything … whatever is bringing you down, get rid of it. Because you'll find that when you're free, your true creativity, your true self comes out. **"**

5 JULY ~ HENRY 'BLACK DEATH' JOHNSON

Henry 'Black Death' Johnson is now recognized as one of America's greatest First World War heroes. He was buried with military honours at Arlington National Cemetery on 5 July 1929, a veteran of the regiment known as the Harlem Hellfighters (see 25 September).

Records of the War Department General, National Archives Catalog

Born in July 1892 in North Carolina, when the First World War began he was a railroad baggage porter in New York. In June 1917 he enlisted and was posted to the front lines in France where his unit fought under the command of the French Army.

In May 1918 the Hellfighters were posted near the Argonne Forest. Privates Johnson and Needham Roberts were on night patrol when they both heard the noise of barbed wire being cut. The Germans were launching a surprise attack. While Roberts ran to raise the alarm, Johnson mounted a one-man defence, lobbing grenades and firing at the enemy. Roberts returned but then sustained a head injury in an explosion. Wounded and out of ammunition, Johnson defended himself and Roberts from the Germans who were now inside the dugout, using his rifle as a club and then finally his knife. He was shot twice and received over twenty wounds during the fight, but killed four and wounded more than ten enemy soldiers before the raid was abandoned. The men became the first of the Hellfighters to be awarded the Croix de Guerre medal by the French.

At the end of the war, Johnson's discharge papers failed to record his injuries and so he was denied a disability allowance and a Purple Heart. He died aged only thirty-six. Ninety-seven years later he was awarded a posthumous Medal of Honor by President Obama.

TIMELINE 6

6 JULY - VENUS AND SERENA WILLIAMS

The American sisters Venus and Serena Williams are two of the most successful tennis players of all time. They were trained by their parents from an early age and became professional tennis players in 1995. Together they dominated the world of women's tennis, with Venus winning seven Grand Slam singles titles and Serena

Elsa/Getty Images

winning twenty-three. Their strong sibling rivalry could be seen in the four consecutive Grand Slam finals they played against each other between 2002 and 2003, each of which Serena won. When Serena won her first ever Wimbledon Championship, on 6 July 2002, she beat the two-time defending champion, her sister Venus, and claimed the world number one ranking, which she would go on to hold for 319 weeks of her career. They are also both Olympic champions: Venus won gold in the women's singles at the 2000 Olympics, while Serena won it at the 2012 games. They won gold as a pair in the women's doubles at the 2000, 2008 and 2012 games.

Together, the Williams sisters have broken barriers in tennis, a game that has sometimes been criticized for its relative lack of diversity. In 2006, Venus took on the organizers of the French Open and Wimbledon tennis tournaments (the last remaining tournaments to pay women athletes less prize money than their male counterparts) in an essay she wrote for *The Times* newspaper. A year later both tournaments announced that they would award equal prize money in their future competitions.

7 JULY ~ SIMONE BILES

American athlete Simone Biles is renowned as being the greatest gymnast of all time and a powerful advocate for self-care for professional sportspeople.

Born on 14 March 1997, as a three-year-old she was adopted by her grandfather and step-grandmother when her mother was unable to care for her. She discovered a talent for gymnastics at the age of six, and as a teenager Biles was being home-schooled to make time for her daily training. She started competing nationally in 2011 and in 2013 she won her first two World Championship gold medals. Three years later, at the 2016 Olympics, she won three individual gold medals, in the all-around, vault and floor exercise categories, as well as a team gold.

By the time of the 2020 Olympics, Biles had won nineteen World Championship golds and the expectation was that she would retain her Olympic titles. However, during the competition Biles instead announced her decision to withdraw from her events. She had 'the twisties', a sudden loss of ability to carry out some of the complex gymnastic moves that she had previously been able to do safely. Rather than powering through, Biles decided to take some time out of competition. This decision brought some criticism, but generally gained her huge respect from the public and other athletes.

On 7 July 2022 twenty-five-year-old Biles became the youngest ever recipient of the **Presidential Medal of Freedom**. Biles returned to competitive gymnastics in 2023, appearing at the World Championships where she won gold and her sixth World all-around title. In 2024 Biles won her eighth Olympic medal – gold in the team competition – making her the most decorated American gymnast.

8 JULY - PHILLIS WHEATLEY

In July 1761 a ship called *Phillis* was making its way to Boston from West Africa with a cargo of seventy-four enslaved people. Among that number was an eight-year-old child bound for service with the Wheatley family, who would name her after the ship that delivered her.

Deemed too frail for the harsh work of the plantations, Phillis Wheatley was bought to be a household servant. The Wheatleys, who considered themselves progressive in their beliefs, decided to tutor her and were surprised to find her a gifted student. She displayed a particular talent for poetry and published her first poem at thirteen.

Her book of poetry, *Poems on Various Subjects, Religious and Moral*, was published in 1773. As Wheatley had been unable to find support in Boston, it was first published in London under the sponsorship of the abolitionist the Countess of Huntingdon, who also helped with the publication of the biography of James Gronniosaw (see 19 December). The book made Wheatley the first African American and the first enslaved person to publish a book of poems.

Wheatley was manumitted – freed from slavery – shortly before the death of Mrs Wheatley in 1774. However, the family had made no provision for her and Wheatley spent the rest of her short life in poverty, dying alone on 5 December 1784.

Although Wheatley's work has been criticized for a lack of commentary on slavery, scholars are now reinterpreting her work and unpacking her use of classical and biblical references to convey her views.

Engraver: Scipio Moorhead, Library of Congress

TIMELINE 4

9 JULY - THE ACT TO LIMIT SLAVERY IN UPPER CANADA

In March of 1793 an enslaved woman, Chloe Cooley, was tied up and forced into a boat by her owner. She screamed and resisted, but was taken from the British colony of Upper Canada across the Niagara River to the United States, and sold. A free Black Loyalist (see 23 November) called Peter Martin was among those who witnessed the event. Acting quickly, he reported it to the Executive Council of Upper Canada. John Graves Simcoe, the lieutenant governor, was spurred into action. He wanted to abolish slavery in the province, but slave-owning members of the Legislative Assembly that governed Upper Canada opposed him. In the end Simcoe reached a compromise and on 9 July 1793 the Act to Limit Slavery in Upper Canada was passed.

The Act was the first law passed in the British Empire that limited slavery. It did not free any enslaved people already in the colony, but did do two things: firstly, the Act made it illegal to import more enslaved people into Upper Canada, and secondly, from then on, any children born to enslaved women in the province would be freed when they reached the age of twenty-five. The Act remained in force until 1833 when the British government passed the Slavery Abolition Act (see 22 July).

An anti-slavery movement developed in Upper Canada after the Act was passed. It became a destination for people escaping enslavement in the United States in the 19th century via the Underground Railroad (see 18 September). Estimates suggest 30,000 people sought refuge from enslavement there.

DID YOU KNOW?

10 JULY ~ MARY MCLEOD BETHUNE

Mary McLeod Bethune was an educator, civil rights activist, feminist and philanthropist, who spent her life trying to improve the lives of African Americans. Born on 10 July 1875 in South Carolina, she started school at age ten and three years later won a scholarship to Scotia Seminary in North Carolina. When she finished her studies she became a teacher and moved to Florida in 1904, where she opened her own school for Black girls.

In 1920 American women gained the vote. McLeod Bethune helped establish the Federation of Women's Clubs to encourage Black women voters. She accompanied women to the polls, despite threats from terrorist groups like the Ku Klux Klan. She helped set up many more organizations, including the National Council of Negro Women in 1935 and the United Negro College Fund in 1944, which supported Black students across America. She was politically influential, and in 1936 she became the government's highest ranking African American woman when president Roosevelt appointed her director of negro affairs of the National Youth Administration. At the United Nations founding conference in 1945, she was the only woman of colour. McLeod Bethune died in 1955. In 1974 a memorial statue in Washington DC was erected dedicated to her as 'The First Lady of the Struggle'.

11 JULY - BLACK LIVES MATTER

On 26 February 2012 teenager Trayvon Martin left his family home to buy a snack. He never returned. A man named George Zimmerman, a Neighbourhood Watch officer, believed that Trayvon's presence in his neighbourhood was suspicious. Both the Watch handbook and the 911 dispatcher advised against direct contact with suspects, but a confrontation occurred in which Zimmerman shot Trayvon in the chest. At his trial in July 2013, he was found not guilty of Trayvon's murder.

The killing and the trial had been the focus of public outrage for months. The acquittal sparked a wave of protests across the country and began the Black Lives Matter movement.

#BlackLivesMatter first appeared in mid July 2013 when Alicia Garza posted on Facebook in response to the verdict. Along with activists Patrisse Cullors and Opal Tometi, she then co-founded the Black Lives Matter movement to highlight the violence suffered by the Black community. The murder of Mike Brown on 10 August 2014 in Ferguson, Missouri, further galvanized the movement. Brown's murder at the hands of a police officer led to an outbreak of unrest in Ferguson and St Louis, which was violently put down with curfews and a heavily militarized police force. In response, BLM organized Black Life Matters Ride to head to Ferguson and lend support to the protests. Their work in Ferguson inspired other organizers in other cities and the movement began to spread.

Sean Da Ros, Wikimedia Commons

The summer of 2020 brought the movement to mainstream

attention when the murder of George Floyd (see 25 May) lit the touch paper for weeks of global protests. BLM became the public face of the unrest. The website saw a 5000% increase in traffic and the global reach increased by 3370%. The issue of state violence against Black communities was flung to the front of media attention. Not all of the attention was positive and campaigns such as #Defundthepolice were misconstrued and used to ridicule the demands of the movement, delegitimize the protests and distract from the real and immediate threat of extreme violence that the Black community faces at the hands of the state. Since the hashtag first appeared there have been over three hundred fatal shootings of unarmed Black civilians by police officers in the USA.

Annette Bernhardt. Wikimedia Commons

Taking notes from the failures of previous Black liberation movements, BLM has from its inception made room for those people marginalized even within the already marginalized Black community, supporting the voices of women, disabled and LGBTQ+ people. Rather than a strict hierarchical structure, it has sought to encourage grassroots leaderships and network building in a truly intersectional way, believing that exclusion actually weakens the movement. Today BLM works globally with chapters in the UK and Canada and supports liberation movements worldwide.

12 JULY - BEATRIZ NASCIMENTO

Beatriz Nascimento was a Black Brazilian historian, writer and activist. Her work was primarily focused on the experiences and history of the African diaspora in Brazil, particularly those of Black women.

Born in the poor north of Brazil on 12 July 1942, Nascimento moved with her family to Rio de Janeiro at the age of seven. After finishing school, she moved on to the University of Rio de Janeiro where she studied history. During this time she became active in the Unified Black Movement of Brazil and went on to form and participate in several other organizations.

Nascimento was highly critical of traditional academia, arguing that its colonial and sexist structure excluded non-English speakers and women from debates in which they should be centred. Her most important theories around the 'quilombo' in Brazil saw them not only in their historical aspect of resistance hubs and settlements for those escaping enslavement, but also in their modern aspect where the descendants of those enslaved still live. She argued that the quilombo was not just a place but should be viewed as an idea, a way of life and a symbol for the struggle for equality for Black Brazilians. This idea of the quilombo was explored by Nascimento in her film *Ori*, released in 1989.

In 1995 Nascimento was shot dead. Her murder has not been solved.

13 JULY - WOLE SOYINKA

The novelist, poet and playwright, Wole Soyinka, was born on 13 July 1934 in Abeokuta, Nigeria. From childhood he was a gifted writer. He won prizes for his writing at school and went on to study literature, firstly at university in Nigeria and then in Leeds, England. He began writing plays as a student and also became involved in social activism and after he returned to live in Nigeria, Soyinka became an academic and writer. He was co-editor of the Nigerian literary magazine *Black Orpheus*. His play, *A Dance of the Forests*, was performed as part of the celebrations to mark Nigerian independence in 1960.

Soyinka's work was political and often critical of both **colonialism** and, after Nigeria gained its independence, of Nigerian politicians and political parties. During the Nigerian Civil War, in 1967, after Soyinka used his platform to call for peace he was arrested and put in solitary confinement for two years. He was released at the end of the war.

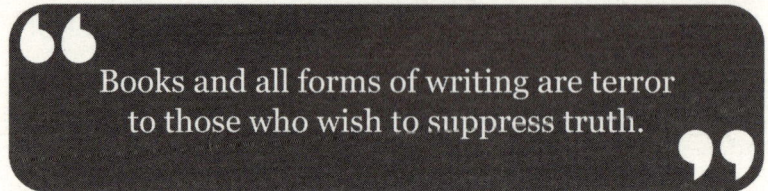

Books and all forms of writing are terror to those who wish to suppress truth.

In 1986 Soyinka's body of work was recognized when he was awarded the Nobel Prize for Literature, making him the first sub-Saharan African to win the prize. Soyinka dedicated his acceptance speech to Nelson Mandela and used it to call for the end of **apartheid**. Soyinka has spent a great deal of his adult life living in voluntary exile. He has been a prolific writer, producing plays, poems, novels and autobiographies, while working in Africa, Europe and America as an academic and political activist. He is considered to be one of the most important writers of the 20th century.

14 JULY - FIRST WORLD WAR VICTORY PARADES

The First World War (1914–18) has been largely remembered in Europe and America as a war between white Europeans fought on European soil. And yet it was the first truly global conflict; fought on four continents by soldiers from across the world. The first shots were fired in West Africa (see 7 August) and the last German forces surrendered in East Africa after the Armistice in Europe. Many of the nations who fought in the war had **colonies** and they recruited soldiers from those lands to fight for them. Africans found themselves fighting or labouring for Britain, France, Belgium or Germany. Most fought in Africa, but France and Britain also brought men from their African and Caribbean colonies to the battlefields in Europe. Over a million Black people – from Africa, the Caribbean, Europe and later from the United States – were drawn into the First World War, working behind the front lines or fighting in Africa, Europe or the Middle East, and yet in the 20th century their contributions were all but forgotten.

One reason why Black people have been missing from this history is that they were also missing from many of the victory parades that took place in 1919. Less than a month after the signing of the Treaty of Versailles, on 14 July 1919, the French held their victory parade in Paris. Having lost 1.3 million men, and with France having been devastated by years of conflict, this parade was intended to celebrate the end of the war and celebrate the soldiers who had sacrificed so much.

Mounted on horseback, Marshall Foch, commander of the Allied Armies, led 25,000 troops through Paris. The black and white film of the parade shows white French soldiers, cavalrymen and sailors, trooping through the Arc de Triomphe. France had relied heavily on its African colonial soldiers during the war and their North African cavalry regiments stood out from the white French soldiers streaming under the

Arc, on their Arabian horses with flowing headdresses. Black African infantrymen known as Tirailleurs Senegelais (mostly) from West Africa, 135,000 of whom had fought for France, marched too.

All of the Allies who had fought alongside France sent troops to take part in this spectacular event. There were soldiers from Greece, Italy, Serbia and Siam – the country we today call Thailand. The British brought 1,500 troops to the Paris parade, soldiers from the UK, Canada, Australia and New Zealand. But none of the Black Africans or West Indians, not even those who had served on the Western Front, were deemed to be suitable representatives of the British Empire at this moment of celebration.

The American general John J. Pershing led a large contingent of the American Expeditionary Force to represent the United States, which had joined the fight in 1917. But the US government was determined that none of the 380,000 African Americans who had served in the First World War would attend the parade. Even the men of the 369th Infantry Regiment – the famous Harlem Hellfighters (see 25 September) – were excluded, despite having spent longer in the trenches of the Western Front than any other US regiment, despite having suffered more than 1,300 casualties and despite having been awarded France's highest military honour – the Croix de Guerre.

Five days later the British held their Peace Parade in London. The city was decorated with bunting and the flags of the Allied nations. Military bands played and 15,000 troops marched through the streets to celebrate the end of the war and the memory of their fallen comrades. Within the British columns were white men from Canada, Australia, South Africa and New Zealand. There were also Indian troops who were there to represent the 1.5 million men from India who had served. Yet none of the 15,000 Black men who had served in the British West Indies was permitted to march. Neither were any Black African units.

Right from the start of the conflict there had been a view in Britain and among the white dominions (Australia, Canada, New Zealand, and especially South Africa) that the war would be a 'white man's war'. Unlike the French, who recruited and armed Black African troops to fight white European enemies, the British sought to avoid the scenario in which people of colour from their colonies were given the licence to kill white people. The exception to this rule would be the Indian Army. When asked to explain why the Nigeria Regiment, which had fought against German forces in the East African campaign, had not been invited to take part in any of the official victory celebrations, the Colonial Office suggested that it would be 'impolitic to bring [to England] coloured detachments to participate in the peace processions'. Later they said it was because of the cost of transportation, despite the fact that Indian troops had been shipped to London specifically to take part in the celebrations. Whatever the reason, the effect of excluding Black people who had served with the British from the parade was to edit them out of popular memory.

The Peace Parades were the first stage in the process of whitewashing the First World War. The role of Black people in the conflict was not simply forgotten; in some cases it was intentionally wiped from the public record, even before memories faded. This helped forge the myth of a 'white man's war'.

15 JULY - THE BATTLE OF PARK STREET

Between 1942 and 1945, one and a half million American troops (known as GIs) were stationed in Britain. 130,000 of them were Black. The US Army was divided by race and Black GIs were kept together in Black units, although they were led by white officers. These tended to be labour units, responsible for constructing army bases and supplying fighter units with food, resources and weaponry. White military police (MPs) enforced military laws, including segregation that kept Black troops separate from white troops on military bases and from civilians when they were out in public. While segregation was common in the southern states of America, it was not part of life in Britain. The British government allowed the US Army to enforce segregation in US military bases, but not when the troops were away from their bases visiting villages, towns and cities. This angered some white US troops, especially when they saw Black US troops talking and dancing with white British women, and sometimes fights broke out.

On 15 July 1944, a fight between groups of GIs broke out in Park Street in Bristol after Black GIs were barred from going to local pubs by some white GIs. The white military police came to the scene and told the 400 Black GIs gathered there to go back to their camps. The Black GIs refused and more military police arrived, parking buses across the road to close Park Street. The sympathy of the people of Bristol was with the Black GIs and they cheered them on. The situation became more violent, and turned into a riot. One military policeman was stabbed and several Black GIs were shot in the legs. The Black GIs were eventually bussed back to their camp and a curfew was imposed on them for a few days. One of the Black GIs later died of his injuries.

16 JULY ~ DR JOHN ALCINDOR

Born in Trinidad in 1873, John Alcindor won a scholarship to study medicine at Edinburgh University. Alcindor graduated in 1899 and moved to London, where he worked at several hospitals before setting up his own practice in the Paddington area.

Wikimedia Commons

When the First World War started in 1914, Alcindor applied to join the Royal Army Medical Corps. Although he was an experienced doctor, Alcindor was rejected outright on account of his 'colonial origin'. Determined to help, Alcindor volunteered for the British Red Cross, treating wounded soldiers returning from battle at London railway stations throughout the war. He was later awarded a Red Cross medal for his life-saving work.

In 1921 Alcindor became senior district medical officer and worked for the Paddington Poor Law Guardians, giving free treatment to those in need. His pioneering research into diseases like tuberculosis helped prove the relationship between poverty, diet and poor health.

The so-called 'Black Doctor of Paddington' died in 1924, having spent his life helping others. On 16 July 2014, on the one-hundred-year anniversary of the war, a plaque was erected in Dr John Alcindor's honour in Paddington.

17 JULY ~ JOHN LEWIS

Civil rights leader and politician John Lewis was born on 21 February 1940 in rural Alabama. As he grew up and started to visit the local city of Troy, he experienced racism and the segregation of the Jim Crow laws.

He studied religion and philosophy at college and became a student activist, committed to non-violent action. In 1961 Lewis was one of the first Freedom Riders to travel to bus terminals in the South to challenge their segregated facilities (see 4 May). He was arrested and beaten during these protests, as he would be on many other occasions in his life. In 1963 Lewis was elected chairman of the **Student Non-Violent Co-ordinating Committee (SNCC)**, and was one of the 'big six' civil rights leaders who helped organize and who spoke at the historic March on Washington for Jobs and Freedom (see 28 August). Two years later he led a peaceful civil rights demonstration of around 600 people through Selma, Alabama. The police inflicted brutal beatings on many of the demonstrators and Lewis's skull was fractured (see 7 March).

In 1981 Lewis was elected to the Atlanta City Council and he was later elected to the US House of Representatives in 1986 and served seventeen terms. He was awarded the **Presidential Medal of Freedom** by president Barack Obama in 2011.

John Lewis died on 17 July 2020. On the day of his funeral the *New York Times* published his essay, in which he declared his solidarity with activists and the Black Lives Matter movement.

18 JULY - NELSON MANDELA DAY

18 July is the birthday of the South African anti-apartheid activist and eventual South African president, Nelson Mandela (see 5 August). It is now also Nelson Mandela Day; an annual event to honour his work and legacy. It is celebrated around the world, encouraging people to volunteer and take part in community service.

MONUSCO Photos. Wikimedia Commons

TIMELINE 8

Mandela Day was established in South Africa in 2009, on the day of Mandela's ninety-first birthday, by the Nelson Mandela Foundation. A year later it became recognized by the United Nations as a global event. Following Mandela's death in 2013, the UN General Assembly set up the UN Nelson Rolihlahla Mandela Prize. Every five years, two prizes are given to two laureates, one man and one woman, from different parts of the world. The first laureates, Dr Helena Ndume of Namibia and Jorge Fernando Branco Sampaio of Portugal, received their awards in 2015. Dr Ndume was recognized for her work as an ophthalmologist, pioneering the treatment of blindness and eye-related conditions in Namibia and beyond, Mr Sampaio for his work as a lawyer and political leader in the struggle for the restoration of democracy in Portugal. The prize recognizes their service to humanity and commitment to the principles of peace, reconciliation and community.

19 JULY - DAVID LAMMY

British politician David Lammy was born in London on 19 July 1972 to Guyanese parents. As a child he was awarded a choral scholarship to attend the King's School, Peterborough. Lammy went on to study law at the University of London's School of Oriental and African Studies and became the first Black British student at Harvard Law School.

Lammy embarked on a legal career, working in London and California before entering politics. In 2000 he was elected to the London Assembly. Later that same year he was elected as the MP for Tottenham. He was only twenty-seven years old and, at the time, the youngest Member of Parliament. Between 2002 and 2010, Lammy served in the Labour government in a series of posts, and from 2020–2024 he was a minister in the Shadow Cabinet.

Lammy has championed issues of race and social justice, including the Windrush Scandal (see 29 April) and the Grenfell Tower tragedy in which his friend Khadija Saye died (see 14 June). In 2019 he presented a documentary exposing the racist treatment of the remains of soldiers from Africa, India and the middle East who died in Africa while fighting for Britain in the First World War. This prompted an investigation by the Commonwealth War Graves Commission and, in 2021, a public apology by the secretary of state for defence in the House of Commons. In 2022 Lammy co-founded the Black Equity Organization, an independent, British Black civil rights organization which aims to tackle systemic racism and improve the lives of Black people.

In July 2024, Lammy was appointed the UK's Secretary of State for Foreign, Commonwealth and Development Affairs. In a speech outlining his plans for the role he said, 'I will take the responsibility of being the first foreign secretary descended from the slave trade incredibly seriously.'

20 JULY ~ **FRANTZ FANON**

Born on 20 July 1925 on Martinique (then a French colony), Frantz Fanon was a political philosopher and psychotherapist, known for his work on colonialism and racism.

After serving in the Free French Army during the Second World War, Fanon studied medicine and psychiatry at university in France. He qualified as a psychiatrist in 1951. His first book, *Black Skin, White Masks* (1952) examined the impact of colonization and racism on the psychology of colonized people. In 1953 he became head of psychiatry at a hospital in Algeria. In 1954 the Algerian war of independence against French colonial rule began. Fanon supported the Algerian cause in secret for two years and in 1956 resigned from his job to work with the Algerian liberation movement. Due to his political activism, Fanon was eventually expelled from Algeria. He moved to Tunisia and became editor of the newspaper *Freedom Fighter*.

Fanon's books established him as a revolutionary anticolonialist thinker. His final book, *The Wretched of the Earth*, was read and cited by many civil rights leaders, including Stokely Carmichael (see 4 June) and Bobby Seale (see 21 January). It is a powerful study of the dehumanizing effects of colonial rule and decolonization, which ends with a call for a revolution.

Fanon became ill with leukemia and travelled to America for treatment where he died in hospital on 6 December 1961. His body was returned to Tunisia to lie in state before being taken to Algeria to be buried. His work remains an inspiration for many.

21 JULY - ANDREA AGUYAR

The Uruguayan Civil War of the 1800s had the unintended side effect of abolishing slavery in the country. With both armies desperate for more fighters, the enslaved were liberated and enlisted. This was likely how Andrea Aguyar came to be defending Montevideo with 5,000 other freed men, and where he met the Italian revolutionary Giuseppe Garibaldi.

In 1848 the First Italian War of Independence broke out and Garibaldi returned home. Aguyar, who had become his most trusted companion and who had also proved himself an excellent fighter, joined him as his lieutenant. Italy's bid for independence was being slowly crushed by the weight of the Austrian Empire. Garibaldi took his army to assist Rome; and it was here that Aguyar became something of a sensation. As the only Black soldier he was easily visible on the battlefield, but his stature and flamboyant dress, his bravery (he is said to have saved Garibaldi's life) and his use of a lasso to bring

down enemy horsemen made him a magnetic and exciting figure to the international press covering the war. On 21 July 1849 the *Illustrated London News* reported that Aguyar had died in battle on 30 June as the Roman Republic finally fell.

Image of Aguyar with Garibaldi, published with the report of Aguyar's death

Illustration by George Housman Thomas. The Illustrated London News 1849. Wikimedia Commons

Aguyar's place in Italian history has been neglected until relatively recently. A campaign to have his bust installed alongside other heroes of the Risorgimento (Unification of Italy) on the Janiculum hill is ongoing, with permission being granted but no funds as yet attached.

22 JULY - THE SLAVERY ABOLITION ACT OF 1833

In Great Britain, Parliament voted to end slavery on 22 July 1833. An 1807 act had already banned the trading of slaves in British **colonies**, but it did not protect those people already enslaved. The Slavery Abolition Act of 1833 made it illegal to own, buy or sell humans as property in most of the British Empire. On 28 August 1833, the Act was given Royal Assent and it came into force on 1 August 1834 (see 1 August). However, there was no immediate end to slavery. All enslaved people over the age of six were made to participate in an 'apprentice' scheme, which saw them working on the plantations in the same conditions as before. These 'apprenticeships' did not end until 1 August 1838. In order to get the Act through Parliament, the government agreed to pay British slave owners compensation for losing what was viewed as their property. Those who had suffered enslavement received nothing.

The monetary value of each enslaved man, woman and child was calculated by the Slave Compensation Commission, taking into account their age, gender, the types of work they had been trained to do and their skill levels, plus how profitable their work was, which varied across the different British colonies. Twenty million pounds (probably equivalent to around 20 billion pounds today) was paid out to around 46,000 slave owners. While some claimants owned hundreds of enslaved people, many claimants were widows, single women and clergymen who had never left Britain, but had inherited small numbers of enslaved people as property, and made money from selling their labour to plantations in the colonies.

DID YOU KNOW? The amount borrowed by the British Government in the 1830s to pay the slave owners was so huge that it was not paid off until 2015.

TIMELINE 5

23 JULY – THE MAU MAU REBELLION

There had been a British presence in Kenya since the 1840s and in 1895 Britain declared it the East Africa **Protectorate**, in order to prevent other European powers from trying to claim influence in the region. Around the same time the British began work on a railway that ran all the way from the coast to Lake Victoria – 600 miles inland (see 29 September). The cost of the railway was enormous and to help make Kenya profitable the British began to seize land that belonged to the local African people and sell it to new white settlers. In 1920 Britain made Kenya a **colony** and more and more land was sold to white settlers who turned it into large farms. The local people were either expelled or they were made to pay taxes. To get the money for the taxes many had no choice but to work as low-paid labourers on the farms of the white settlers.

There had been armed resistance and rebellions throughout colonial rule but after the Second World War, when even more British settlers arrived and more land was sold to them, organized resistance to British rule increased. In the 1940s a new political party, the Kenya African Union, was formed, but the British ignored their attempts to negotiate better rights for the African majority. Out of this failure a new group, the Kenya Land and Freedom Army – also referred to as the Mau Mau – was eventually formed.

In 1952 the Mau Mau assassinated Senior Chief Waruhui, a Kenyan leader who was loyal to the British. This was the start of a guerrilla war. Assured of their own military superiority, the British had previously dismissed the threat of a major uprising. Now alarmed, Governor Evelyn Baring declared a state of emergency and began a violent crackdown, starting with mass arrests. However, the rebels retreated to the forests and continued their war, killing both British settlers and Kenyans who supported British rule. In 1953 the British government finally realized the severity of the situation and sent General George Erskine to quash the rebellion. In 1954 he began Operation Anvil, a sweep of the whole of the capital city Nairobi in which all native Kenyans were rounded up and questioned for Mau Mau sympathies. In a further move to cut off support for the Mau Mau, Erskine began a 'villagization' programme which imprisoned thousands of Kikuyu people. These 'villages' were billed as places where people would be safe and where they could be rehabilitated, but in reality they were detention camps. The Kenya Human Rights Commission estimates that around 160,000 people were detained and 90,000 people were subjected to torture, maiming and summary executions.

By 1956, with their supporters imprisoned, the Mau Mau uprising was effectively over. Thirty-two white settlers, 2,000 Kenyan civilians and over 10,000 Mau Mau fighters had been killed. Independence finally came to Kenya in 1963 following the collapse of colonialism across much of Africa (see 1 January).

© IWM (BF 10956)

In 2011 three Kenyan victims of the detention camps brought a court case against the British Government. In what became known as the 'Hanslope Disclosure' it was discovered during the trial that the British authorities had removed or destroyed thousands of documents relating to the violence they had committed against the Kenyan people. In the documents that had survived were details of torture techniques that had been approved for use against the detainees. With this concrete evidence, the Kenyans won their case and the British government was forced to pay compensation to 5,228 victims.

24 JULY - GARRETT MORGAN

African American inventor Garrett Morgan was born in Kentucky on 4 March 1877. His mother was of Native American and African descent, and his father had formally been enslaved. Morgan did not finish high school and by the age of fourteen he had left home, moving away to find work, first in Cincinnati and then in Cleveland where he lived for the rest of his life. It was when he started working in sewing machine factories that Morgan began inventing things and applying for patents for a wide range of ideas. He invented ways to improve how sewing machines work, and once accidentally invented a bestselling hair-straightening treatment, when he was attempting to invent a way of making material run more smoothly through machines when it was being sewn.

On 25 March 1911, Morgan learned about a fire in a clothing factory that killed 146 female workers. He realized that if the firefighters had had proper breathing devices the death toll might have been less. He drew up successful designs and his device even became adapted during the First World War to protect soldiers from toxic gas attacks. He took his breathing devices to trade shows across America, but found that many fire departments were not prepared to buy equipment from a Black inventor. So Morgan employed a white actor to pretend to be the inventor at these events while he wore the apparatus to demonstrate how it worked. Morgan also used his breathing device on 24 July 1916 when there was an explosion in a tunnel under Lake Erie. He and his brother rescued eight trapped men, but were not given public recognition at the time.

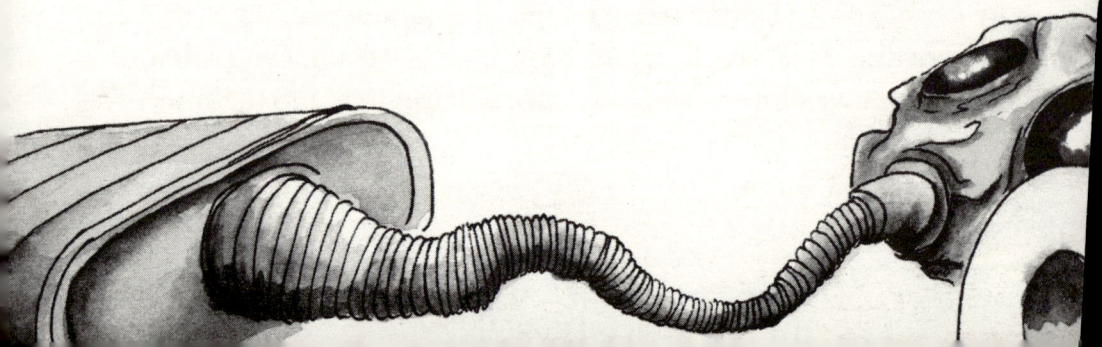

In 1923, having witnessed a bad crash between a car and a horse-drawn carriage at the intersection between two roads, Morgan invented a three-way traffic signal. Instead of just having 'stop' and 'go' it also had a 'warning' position to let drivers know that the signal was about to turn to 'stop'. He patented his idea in America, Canada and Britain and was able to sell the rights for $40,000, which is just under $7 million dollars today.

Morgan used his wealth to support other African Americans and established a weekly African American newspaper called the *Cleveland Call*. He was an early member of the NAACP. He bought 250 acres of land and opened a country club for African Americans and he gave money to many colleges and universities that offered higher education for African Americans.

Morgan did eventually receive public recognition for his role in the Cleveland Tunnel rescue. He also won prizes for his invention of breathing devices. Morgan died in 1963, aged eighty-seven, survived by his second wife and three children. Just after he died he was honoured for his traffic light invention at a national event to celebrate a century since the Emancipation Declaration (see 31 December) that announced the end of slavery.

25 JULY - EMMETT TILL

Born on 25 July 1941, Emmett Till lived in Chicago. In 1955, at the age of fourteen, he went to stay with his uncle in the town of Money, Mississippi. Till went into the local store on 24 August. Accounts of what happened vary, but the white woman who worked there, Carolyn Bryant, later accused Till of flirting with her. Till returned to his uncle's house without mentioning any kind of incident.

Four days later, Bryant's husband and his half-brother J. W. Milam kidnapped Till and drove him to the river. There they savagely beat Till, gouged one of his eyes out, shot him in the head, tied him up with barbed wire and threw him into the river. When found, Till's body could only be identified from a ring he had been wearing.

Till's body was returned to Chicago for the funeral. His distraught mother decided to have her son displayed in an open casket, to show the world what had been done to him. Thousands of mourners came and a photograph of Till's body was printed in *Jet*, an African American magazine. The shocking photo was picked up by newspapers, and it became an international story. In September, Bryant and Milam were found not guilty of murder by an all-white jury, on the grounds that the state had failed to prove the identity of the body.

In 2022 Till was posthumously awarded the Congressional Gold Medal and the Emmett Till Antilynching Act was passed. On 25 July 2023 a presidential order establishing the Emmett Till and Mamie Till-Mobley National Monument was signed.

26 JULY - EXECUTIVE ORDER 9981

On 26 July 1948 President Harry S. Truman signed Executive Order 9981, ending racial **segregation** in the US Armed Forces. The order was made in response

Library of Congress Prints and Photographs Division

to pressure that had grown during and after the Second World War, in which 1.2 million Black troops had served.

While progress had been made, such as the training of Black airmen at Tuskegee, Black troops had not received equal treatment. They waited longer for training, were given support roles rather than front-line roles, and received racist, sometimes violent, treatment by some peers and officers (see 26 April). During the war, southern African American soldiers stationed in Europe had experienced living away from the **Jim Crow** laws (see 15 July), and came back unwilling to accept the indignity and restrictions placed on them by their own country.

In 1946 Black soldier Isaac Woodard Jr was attacked by South Carolina police while still in uniform, and left permanently blinded. Lobbied by the **NAACP**, President Truman ordered a federal inquiry. When no one was convicted for the attack, Truman established the President's Committee on Civil Rights, which reported in December 1947. More pressure came when civil rights activists A. Philip Randolph and Grant Reynolds formed the Committee Against Jim Crow in Military Service and Training and called for Black communities to refuse to enlist in the armed forces. Truman acted on the Commission's report, sending a civil rights bill to Congress in February 1948, and finally signing Executive Orders 9980 and 9981, **desegregating** the federal workforce and the armed forces.

TIMELINE 6

27 JULY - MARIELLE FRANCO

Marielle Franco was a Brazilian politician known for her human rights activism.

Born 27 July 1979, Franco was raised in the favelas of Rio de Janeiro. The favelas are home to the poorest Brazilians, the housing is makeshift and the areas lack utilities like energy and sanitation. Also regarded as a haven for criminals, the police have

Midia Ninja. Wikimedia Commons

used brutal military tactics against the inhabitants, engaging in battles with disregard for civilian casualties. It was this environment that shaped Franco's career.

After losing a friend in the crossfire of a police incursion, Franco joined activist Marcelo Freixo's campaign to become state deputy in 2005. Freixo campaigned on a platform of human rights and when he won, he asked for her help to create the Committee for the Defence of Human Rights and Citizenship. She continued to work with Freixo until 2016 when she stood for election to the Rio City Council. Her bid was successful and she became one of only two Black women councillors. Franco used her position to improve the lives of those in the favelas, proposing laws to combat corruption, to provide childcare and to help people escape domestic violence.

On 14 March 2018 Franco was murdered. She had spent much of her career investigating police brutality and corruption and many people called for an investigation as it was widely suspected that her killing had been politically motivated. The investigation stalled but the newly elected Da Silva government promised to reinvigorate it, and in July 2023 new arrests were made.

28 JULY - CATHAY WILLIAMS

After the American Civil War, Congress created six new regiments made up of African Americans. These regiments of 'Buffalo Soldiers' were deployed on the frontiers in America, building roads and forts and defending settlers. They developed a reputation for skill and bravery and in 1992 Congress finally honoured their contribution, designating 28 July as Buffalo Soldiers Day.

One of the soldiers who enlisted was William Cathay. On 15 November 1866 Cathay joined the 38th US Infantry Regiment. In order to be deemed fit for duty each recruit had to pass a basic medical examination. If the examination had been a little more thorough, it might have been noticed that William Cathay was actually a woman.

Born into slavery in Missouri in 1844, Cathay Williams was captured by Union forces in 1861. Many of those previously enslaved were pressed into service for the army and Williams worked as cook and laundress before enlisting. Her deployment was delayed after she caught smallpox, but once recovered she took up her position in New Mexico. Unfortunately the disease had weakened her and she spent the next two years in and out of hospital until a doctor finally uncovered her secret and she was honourably discharged in 1868.

Williams died in 1893. She had become ill and had tried to claim a disability pension from her military service but her request was denied and she died soon afterwards. As the first known African American woman in the military and the only female Buffalo Soldier, a memorial to Williams was finally erected at Forth Leavenworth, Kansas in 2016.

29 JULY ~ THE BATTLE OF MOLESWORTH STREET

On 29 July 1981 anti-apartheid protestors in Aotearoa New Zealand marched up Molesworth Street in the city of Wellington. They were protesting against a rugby tour by the South African Springboks. Heading for the South African Consul building, they were met by police who, for the first time in the country's history, used batons to violently beat back the protestors.

Since the late 1960s South Africa's apartheid regime had resulted in growing sanctions from the United Nations that included a boycott on sports matches with South Africa. Rugby is popular in Aotearoa New Zealand and their national team, the All Blacks, attracted players and supporters of Māori heritage. There was a long rivalry between the two teams, but when the All Blacks visited South Africa in the 1950s and 60s, officials excluded Māori players rather than challenge the racist apartheid regime. Ignoring international sanctions, the All Blacks toured South Africa in 1976 but the tour was dogged with protests. Despite public and international pressure prime minister Robert Muldoon gave permission for a return tour by the Springboks in 1981. However, people opposing the tour organized a national protest group, Halt All Racist Tours (HALT), led by John Minto. Their goal wasn't just to protest the tour, they aimed to stop it altogether.

On 25 July, a pitch invasion by 350 protestors caused the second match, in Hamilton, to be called off. As some angry spectators threw bottles at them, the protestors chanted 'The whole world's watching'. The protests were indeed reported all over the world and, years later, John Minto was told that the news had even reached Nelson Mandela in his prison cell in South Africa. Four days after the Hamilton match, the violence of what became known as the Battle of Molesworth Street shocked the country. After that the size of the protests for the rest of the tour grew, and protestors began to wear helmets to protect against police batons. The final match, in Auckland, was disrupted when a small plane dropped flour bombs on the pitch and protestors switched off local television transmitters.

Despite the violence and disruption of the tour, in 1985 the New Zealand Rugby Football Union (NZRFU) proposed an All Blacks tour of South Africa. Aghast at this proposal, members of the Auckland University Rugby Football Club and the Teachers Rugby Football Club took the NZRFU to court and successfully sued them on the grounds  that a tour would be in breach of the country's constitution. The two countries did not play against each other again until 1992, after the end of apartheid. In 1996, prime minister Jim Bolger visited Cape Town and issued a formal apology to the people of South Africa from Aotearoa New Zealand for the 1981 tour.

Associated Press / Alamy

30 JULY - LEARIE CONSTANTINE

Born in Trinidad in 1901, cricketer Learie Constantine moved to England in 1929 to play for Lancashire club Nelson. On 30 July 1943 he arrived in London to play in a charity cricket match at Lord's cricket ground. He had booked four nights at the Imperial Hotel in Russell Square for himself and his family, but upon arrival the manager informed him that he could  only stay for one night as their presence would offend the American guests who were used to segregation. Constantine insisted that they honour his booking and in the subsequent argument manageress Margaret O'Sullivan resorted to language that a judge later referred to as 'grossly insulting'. Constantine eventually accepted a booking at another hotel but later took London Imperial Hotels to court for failing in their duty to provide accommodation. In June 1944 Constantine's complaint was upheld. As Britain had no discrimination laws, his damages were limited to only five guineas, but the case made headlines and raised the issue of racial discrimination in the public conscious and in parliament.

Constantine decided to pursue his own legal career and passed the bar in 1954. His post-war years were filled with activism, as chairman of the League of Coloured Peoples and as a member of an advisory committee at the Colonial Office. He also intervened with the government on behalf of Seretse Khama (see 3 March). In 1962 he was knighted and used his profile to support the Bristol Bus Boycott (see 17 September) the following year. His 1969 appointment to the House of Lords made him Britain's first Black peer. He died two years later and was hounoured with a state funeral in Trinidad and Tobago.

31 JULY - THE ZULU KINGDOM

The Zulu are the largest ethnic group in South Africa today. The origins of their kingdom go back thousands of years to when their ancestors, the Nguni people, migrated southwards from central Africa towards the east coast, where they established settlements.

During the 17th century the Zulu emerged as an independent force and Zulu clans, led by chiefs, began to form. In the early 1800s Zulu chief Shaka came to power and began conquering the peoples of Zululand. He eventually created an army of 40,000 warriors and established a powerful empire, ruling from 1816 until his assassination in 1828. Shaka Zulu became legendary, and his barefoot warriors renowned for their courage and military tactics.

In 1872 Cetshwayo, Shaka Zulu's half-nephew, became ruler of the Zulus. The British saw the Zulu empire as a threat to their plans to create a federation of states in South Africa and they invaded on 22 January 1879, fighting the Zulus at the Battle of Isandlwana. However, they underestimated the Zulus' numbers, strength and skill. The British army lost more than a thousand soldiers, marking the first time they had been defeated by an African army using African tactics. Later that day a smaller British force defeated a Zulu regiment at Rorke's Drift.

In July, the British returned with a larger force and defeated the Zulus at the Battle of Ulundi, destroying their capital. King Cetshwayo was captured and exiled to Cape Town while Zululand was broken up into autonomous areas. In 1887 Zululand was declared British territory.

1 AUGUST - EMANCIPATION DAY

Slavery in the British Empire came to an end gradually. The Act of Parliament that ended slavery was passed in the summer of 1833 (see 22 July). Britain's 46,000 slave owners were paid £20 million between them to compensate for the loss of the human 'property' – namely the 800,000 enslaved people working on plantations in British colonies. The slave-owners got another concession too: the enslaved were not freed immediately. Instead the enslaved were forced to serve what was called an 'apprenticeship', which meant they had to continue working without pay, on the same plantations, for the same masters, for a period of up to six years. Notionally this 'apprenticeship' was meant to prepare the enslaved for working lives as free people. Effectively they were paying for some of the cost of their 'manumission' – their release from slavery. Understandably, enslaved people were extremely unhappy with the apprenticeship system and those who refused to work were often severely punished. Abolitionists sent investigators to the West Indies to monitor the apprenticeship system and their reports soon revealed that apprenticeships were little more than slavery by another name (see 11 August). A government commission of enquiry confirmed the injustices of the apprenticeship system and this pressure, combined with campaigning by abolitionists, ensured the apprenticeship system was scrapped after only four years, and the date for the final emancipation of the enslaved was brought forward to 1 August 1838.

It is said that on the evening of 31 July 1838, the night before Emancipation Day, enslaved people in Jamaica climbed the hilltops to watch the dawning of the first day of freedom. One of the best accounts describing what happened on that first emancipation day was written by a white missionary called William Knibb, who ran a small chapel for poor Black people in the port town of Falmouth, on the northern coast of Jamaica. On the evening of 31 July 1838, the congregation came to the chapel to pray and celebrate the end of slavery. Over the entrance to the chapel yard a banner had been placed carrying a single word – 'FREEDOM'. As midnight approached, Knibb theatrically pointed to the clock on the chapel wall and spoke. 'The hour is at hand, the monster is dying.' As the bell struck the first chime of midnight he continued, 'The clock is striking. The monster is dead: the negro is free.'

To the Friends of Negro Emancipation. Engraving by David Lucas after a painting by Alexander Rippingille, 1834

© National Maritime Museum, Greenwich, London.

In the early morning of Emancipation Day one of the most unusual funerals in British history took place. In the grounds of a school near the chapel a grave had been dug. A coffin was carried forward into which were placed the instruments of slavery: a pair of shackles, a chain, a whip and an iron collar. A crowd assembled and, in the dawn light, the coffin was lowered into the earth, just as the bodies of around a million enslaved people had been buried over the previous three centuries. The congregation sang their hymns and gave their cheers and the flag of freedom, with the union flag set into its corner, was flown. A headstone placed above the grave read, 'Colonial Slavery died 31 July 1838, Age 276 years'.

It was not just the enslaved people of the British Empire who celebrated the first emancipation day. In the United States of America around 2 million Black people lived under slavery in

1838. The night before Emancipation Day free Black people in Cincinatti, Ohio, held a vigil in a church to celebrate the end of slavery in the West Indies. A quarter of an hour before midnight the congregation was hushed to silence. Only when the clock struck midnight did they burst into cheers and song.

Courtesy Windsor Star

Moses Brantford Jr leading an Emancipation Day parade down Dalhousie Street, Amherstburg, Ontario 1894

Through the 1840s and 50s Britain's Emancipation Day continued to be celebrated in parts of the USA, among free Black people in the northern states who dreamed that emancipation would one day arrive in their own nation, freeing the millions of their brothers and sisters who lived in chains in the southern states where slavery was still legal.

2 AUGUST - JAMES BALDWIN

In Harlem, on 2 August 1924, one of the 20th-century's most significant writers was born. James Baldwin was a gay Black man and his plays and novels were often semi-autobiographical, addressing issues of race, racism, social class and sexuality. Baldwin was close friends with other Black artists, including Nina Simone (see 10 September), Langston Hughes (see 1 February) and Toni Morrison (see 31 March).

Sjakkelien Vollebregt, Nationaal Archief, CCO/ Fotocollectie Anefo, The Netherlands

Wanting to escape from the virulent racism of Jim Crow-era America, Baldwin chose to live in Paris for much of his adult life. Nevertheless, he played an active role in the civil rights struggle in the 1960s, and attended 1963's March on Washington (see 28 August). Baldwin died in 1987, but his writing continues to be influential today. His unfinished manuscript, *Remember This House*, was the basis for the 2016 documentary *I Am Not Your Negro*, which was nominated for an Oscar (see 9 September). His novel *If Beale Street Could Talk* became an Oscar-winning film in 2018.

TIMELINE 11

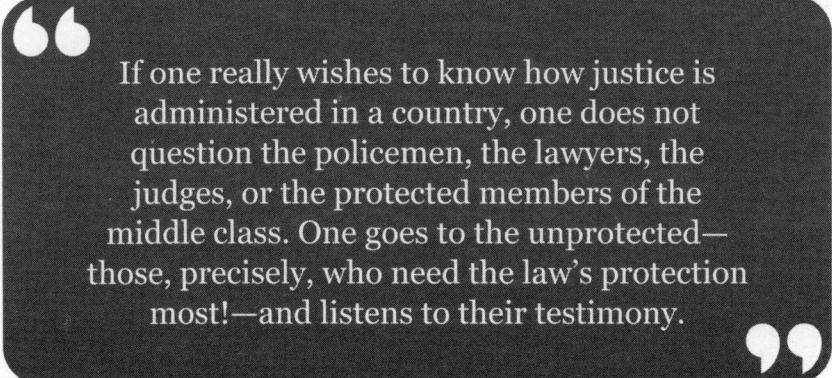

> If one really wishes to know how justice is administered in a country, one does not question the policemen, the lawyers, the judges, or the protected members of the middle class. One goes to the unprotected—those, precisely, who need the law's protection most!—and listens to their testimony.

3 AUGUST - JESSE OWENS

In 1931, Berlin, Germany, was selected to host the 1936 Olympic Games. Adolf Hitler rose to power in Germany in 1933 and by 1936 the Nazi regime was in control and had transformed Germany into a state in which some Germans were regarded as members of the allegedly superior Aryan race. The Olympics would have been an ideal opportunity to prove their idea of Aryan superiority had it not been for one man in particular.

Library of Congress

Jesse Owens and several other Black athletes were selected to compete for the US Olympic Team in Berlin. The NAACP was unwilling to be part of sports-washing a regime that was targeting minority groups for imprisonment, expulsion and violence, and called for a boycott, but the American Olympic Committee would not be swayed. The games opened on 1 August and, as expected, Germany dominated the medals. But on 3 August Jesse Owens took to the track and blasted his way to victory in the 100m race (fellow African American Ralph Metcalfe took silver). Over the next few days he also took gold in the 200m (fellow African American Mack Robinson took silver), the long jump and the 4x100m relay.

Despite the fame and adulation these victories brought to Owens, he returned to a country in which he was not allowed to use the front doors of the hotel hosting the victory reception. Segregation laws controlled everything from his choice of home to his choice of bus seat. Owen's outstanding performance remained unacknowledged by the White House until 1976 when he finally received the Presidential Medal of Freedom.

4 AUGUST - EDWARD ENNINFUL

At the beginning of August 2017 Edward Enninful became the first man and the first Black editor of prestigious fashion magazine *Vogue*.

Born in Ghana in 1972 but raised in England, Enninful's talent and love for fashion were shaped by his seamstress mother. At sixteen years old he was spotted by a stylist and began his fashion career as a model. Enninful soon realized that he preferred to work on the other side of the lens and at eighteen became the youngest ever fashion editor at British fashion magazine *i-D*. He later moved on to become a contributing editor at Italian and American *Vogue* before his appointment at the British publication.

Enninful has made it a mission to increase racial diversity throughout the fashion industry. At *Vogue Italia* he worked on the 'Black Issue' in 2008 (see 3 September) which featured only Black models and was a huge success. His first issue for British *Vogue* featured mixed-race model Adwoa Aboah on the cover, the Duchess of Sussex was invited to be guest editor of the September 2019 issue, and Enninful's hire of photographer Misan Harriman made him the first Black male photographer to shoot a *Vogue* front cover. Changes were also made to promote diversity in *Vogue's* employees.

In 2016 Enninful received an **OBE** for his diversity work in the fashion industry. In 2023 he moved on from British *Vogue* to become global creative and cultural advisor for the publication.

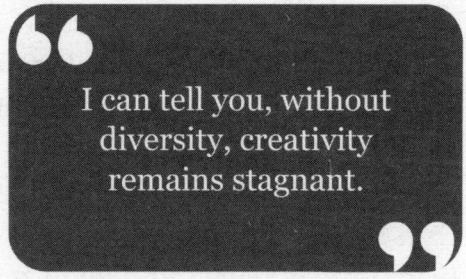

I can tell you, without diversity, creativity remains stagnant.

5 AUGUST ~ NELSON MANDELA

Nelson Rolihlahla Mandela was born on 18 July 1918 in the South African village of Mvezo. His family were of the Xhosa people and part of the Thembu royal family. As a young man he studied law, and moved to Johannesburg where he worked in a law office. In 1948 he joined the African National Congress (ANC), a political party that campaigned against racial discrimination and the apartheid system of racial segregation that existed in South Africa, and denied many civil rights to Black people. Mandela became an activist and helped to establish the ANC's Youth League, organizing boycotts, strikes and non-violent protests. By 1961, after years of peaceful action, Mandela helped to co-found uMkhonto we Sizwe. This part of the ANC began to conduct a campaign of more direct and sometimes violent sabotage against government targets.

Oistein Thomassen/Alamy

On 5 August 1962 Mandela and fellow activist Cecil Williams were arrested near the town of Howick in South Africa's KwaZulu-Natal Province. Mandela was charged and found guilty of leaving the country illegally and organizing workers' strikes, and sentenced to five years in prison. A year later, more charges of state sabotage were brought against Mandela and others at a trial at Rivonia in Johannesburg. On 12 June 1964, Mandela and seven others were sentenced to life imprisonment. All of them remained in prison for decades, with Mandela serving the longest sentence. He spent a total of twenty-seven years and eight months in prison, before he was finally released by order of the South African prime minister F. W. de Klerk on 11 February 1990. Mandela took his place as the leader of the ANC, and worked with de Klerk to bring a peaceful end to apartheid. In 1993 they were both awarded the Nobel Peace Prize to recognize this achievement.

In 1994, after the country's first truly democratic elections (see 27 April), Mandela, the ex-political prisoner, became the president of South Africa. His government created the Truth and Reconciliation Commission to investigate the violent crimes of the apartheid years and he appointed Archbishop Desmond Tutu to lead it (see 5 October).

Mandela retired after one term as president and he devoted the rest of his life to campaigning against poverty and raising funds and awareness of the HIV/AIDS crisis in Africa. He died at the age of ninety-five on 5 December 2013. He is remembered in South Africa as 'Madiba', the Father of the Nation.

> I had no epiphany, no singular revelation, no moment of truth, but a steady accumulation of a thousand slights, a thousand indignities and a thousand unremembered moments produced in me an anger, a rebelliousness, a desire to fight the system that imprisoned my people. There was no particular day on which I said, 'Henceforth I will devote myself to the liberation of my people'; instead, I simply found myself doing so, and could not do otherwise.

6 AUGUST - THE LONDON RIOTS

On 4 August 2011, in Tottenham Hale, London, Black British man Mark Duggan was stopped by police officers as part of Operation Trident, an initiative targeting gun crime. While attempting arrest, the police shot and killed him. At first police reports seemed to indicate that Duggan had shot at the police during the arrest, but later evidence proved that this was not true. Duggan's death was later ruled to be a lawful killing.

Two days later, on 6 August, a protest was organized by Duggan's friends and family. Protestors marched from Broadwater Farm to Tottenham Police Station. Initially the protest was peaceful. After a few hours outside the police station the mood became angry, and that evening looting and rioting broke out. The following night the riots spread to other parts of London, and by 8 August it had spread to other cities in Britain. Between the 8 and 11 August unrest spread to cities including Birmingham, Bristol, Liverpool and Nottingham.

An estimated 20,000 people were involved in the riots. The levels of looting and criminal activity that unfolded over the five days of rioting, plus the deployment of additional policing, brought the total cost of the riots to an estimated £500 million. There were 5,000 arrests, five people died, and at least sixteen people were injured. The looted areas were left badly damaged.

Later research into the riots found that while the initial confrontation outside Tottenham Police Station had been the spark for the riots, the areas where rioting occurred were also characterized by high levels of economic deprivation and unemployment, and much lower levels of trust in the police than non-rioting areas. Long-term and widespread use of police stop and search powers was also a feature of the rioting areas, leading the researchers to question whether the practice of stop and search was a problem rather than a solution.

7 AUGUST ~ ALHAJI GRUNSHI

The first shot fired by a soldier in the British Army in the First World War was fired in East Africa. The soldier was called Lance Corporal Alhaji Grunshi, and he served in the Gold Coast Regiment (the Gold Coast is now known as Ghana – see 6 March).

Wikimedia Commons

At the start of the war in 1914, the Gold Coast Regiment was sent to fight in Togoland, which was then a German colony, and it was here that Grunshi took that first shot of the war. Eventually they were sent to France where, although the regiment was highly trained and experienced in warfare, they were not allowed to fight. Instead they, and the other 1 million Africans who took part in the First World War, worked to support white soldiers by building roads, digging trenches and transporting supplies to and from the front lines.

Grunshi survived the war and was eventually promoted to the rank of sergeant. In 1919 he was awarded the Military Medal for his bravery and actions during the East African Campaign.

8 AUGUST ~ MATTHEW HENSON

The African American explorer Matthew Henson was born on 8 August 1866 in Nanjemoy, Maryland. He was twelve when he began his life of travel, working as a cabin boy on a merchant ship. At the age of twenty-one, Henson met Commander Robert E. Peary, and joined his team for an expedition to Nicaragua. Henson and Peary went on to undertake seven expeditions to the Arctic over the next twenty years.

During their expedition to Greenland in 1908–09, Peary claimed that he, Henson and their four Inuit guides, Ootah, Seeglo, Egingwah, and Ooqueah, reached the North Pole. This claim was disputed, and it is possible that, due to navigation errors, they were some miles short of the pole. However, the National Geographical Society and the US House of Representatives both accepted the claim. Henson published a memoir, *A Negro Explorer at the North Pole*, in 1912. He wrote that he had been the first to reach the pole, had overshot it and had to retrace his steps in the snow before planting the American flag.

In 1937 Henson became the first African American to be given life membership of the Explorers Club, and in 1944 the US Congress awarded the six men the Peary Polar Expedition Medal.

Henson died in 1955 and in 1988 his remains, along with those of his wife, were moved to rest at Arlington National Cemetery. In 2000, the Geographical Society posthumously awarded Henson the Hubbard Medal for distinction in exploration, discovery and research.

9 AUGUST ~ NATIONAL WOMEN'S DAY IN SOUTH AFRICA

National Women's Day has been celebrated as a public holiday in South Africa since 1995. It marks the anniversary of the Women's March of 9 August 1956, when members of the Federation of South African Women rallied against the apartheid government. Twenty thousand women marched to the Union buildings in Pretoria to express their anger at planned amendments to the Urban Areas Act of 1950, which aimed to further restrict the lives of Black women by the use of passbooks, the documents that limited Black South Africans' freedom under apartheid.

The women delivered a petition containing more than 100,000 signatures, then stood for thirty minutes in silent protest. A song specially composed for the march was then sung: 'Wathint'Abafazi Wathint'imbokodo!', which in English means, 'You strike a woman, you strike rock'.

Today National Women's Day calls attention to issues facing women such as domestic violence, access to schooling and to fair pay, and it celebrates the contribution of women to South African society and honours their courage, strength and resilience.

K.Kendall. Wikimedia Commons

10 AUGUST - IVORY BANGLE LADY

In August 1901, on Sycamore Terrace in the British city of York, a stone coffin was unearthed during an archaeological dig. Inside was the skeleton of a woman, adorned with jewellery and buried with a collection of luxury items. On her wrists were black bangles, made of jet from the nearby coastal town of Whitby, and white bangles of ivory that gave rise to her name: Ivory Bangle Lady. Archaeologists discovered that she lived in Roman York and died in the 4th century CE.

In 2010 her remains were studied further using craniometric analysis – the study of bones and skulls, and isotope analysis – the study of chemicals left in teeth and bones of people by the things they ate and drank during childhood. Ivory Bangle Lady was aged between eighteen and twenty-three when she died. From studying her skull, archaeologists think that she is likely to have been of North African descent. Chemical traces in her teeth indicate that she probably spent her childhood in a warm coastal area in Western Europe or the Mediterranean, and migrated to York in later life.

Her manner of burial, and the valuable objects buried with her, show that Ivory Bangle Lady was wealthy and of high social status. York was known as Eboracum in Roman times, and was one of the most important cities in Roman Britain. Like most Roman cities it had a diverse population, which included visitors and citizens from Africa. Archaeologists have found that a significant number of the citizens of Eboracum had African ancestors.

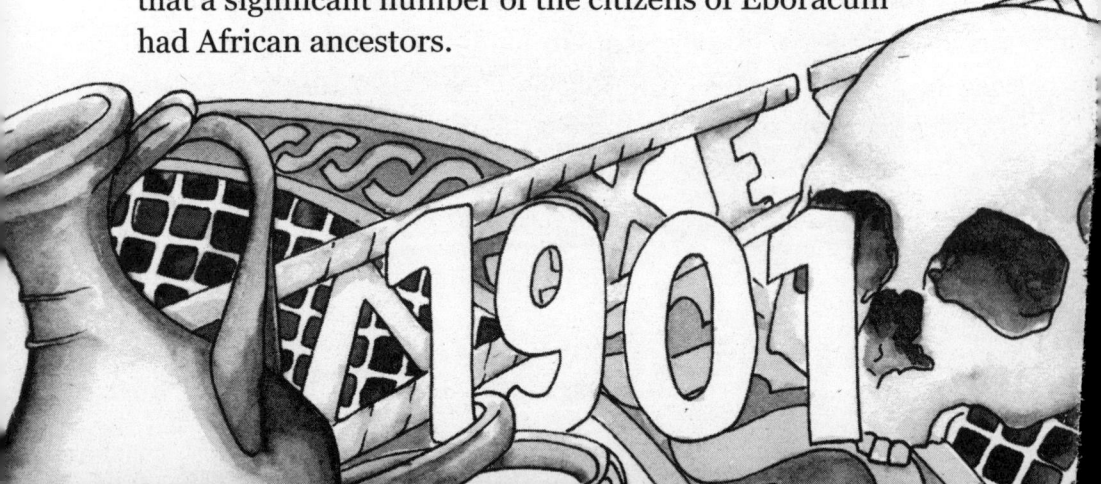

11 AUGUST - APPRENTICESHIP ABOLISHED

The 1833 Slavery Abolition Act came into force in 1834, yet instead of freeing enslaved people in the British Empire straightaway, the act set up the apprenticeship system. This required them to continue working for their former owners for the next six years, without being paid. This decision caused outrage among many abolitionist campaigners.

The Quaker activist Joseph Sturge led a campaign against the apprenticeship system. In 1834 he went to Jamaica to study the system in action, and met with apprentices and their former owners. On his return to England he published a twenty-four-page pamphlet, *Narrative of Events since the First of August 1834*. The book presented a statement he had obtained from a Jamaican apprentice. His name was given as 'James Williams', a pseudonym used to protect his identity. In the statement Williams described in his own words how the same kinds of treatment that had been inflicted on him when he was enslaved continued to be inflicted on him as an apprentice. He said he feared dying from these brutal punishments before the apprenticeship system ended. In the book's introduction, Sturge stated that two freed Black men and six apprentices from the island all signed a document confirming Williams as being truthful and of good character.

Sturge helped buy Williams out of his apprenticeship and brought him to England. Sturge then returned to the Caribbean again, this time visiting Antigua, Montserrat, Dominica, St Lucia, Barbados and Jamaica. On his return he published *The West Indies*, in 1837. Both books called public attention to the injustice of apprenticeship and Sturge's campaign put so much pressure on the British government that they eventually agreed to end the apprenticeship system early, on 1 August 1838, which became known as 'Emancipation Day' (see 1 August).

TIMELINE 4

12 AUGUST - KAMALA HARRIS

Kamala Devi Harris was born on 20 October 1964 in Oakland, California to an Indian-born mother and a Jamaican-American father. From childhood she was a keen student and went on to study law at university. She worked as a lawyer from 1990, before beginning her high-profile career in politics.

Harris was elected to the role of district attorney of San Francisco in 2003. In 2005 she was awarded the Thurgood Marshall Award in recognition of her long-term contribution to the advancement of civil rights, civil liberties and human rights. In 2010 Harris became attorney general of California, and in 2016 she became an elected senator, which made her the first South Asian American and the second African American woman to serve in the US Senate.

Harris put herself forward as a candidate for the 2020 Democratic Party presidential nominations, although she withdrew just before the primaries. On 12 August 2020 she was named as Joe Biden's running mate. The pair defeated Donald Trump and Mike Pence in the 2020 election. On 20 January 2021 Harris was inaugurated as the first female, first African American and first Asian American vice-president of the United States of America and the highest ranking woman official in US history. In July 2024 Harris became the official Democratic nominee for the US Presidential election, following the withdrawal of President Biden from the campaign.

During her career, Harris has fought for better protections for immigrants and refugees, for healthcare reform, women's rights and for voters' rights. As a senator she sponsored the anti-lynching bill introduced by Bobby Rush in 2019. She has also supported legislation to protect and preserve America's HBCUs, which was passed in 2020.

13 AUGUST - KING CETSHWAYO

Cetshwayo kaMpande was King of the Zulus from 1872 to 1879. Following the British defeat of the Zulus at Ulundi in 1879 he was exiled to Cape Town, where he campaigned vigorously for his return to the throne. The British Parliament debated and eventually the King was invited to London.

Photographed by Alex Bassano, 25 old Bond Street

Cetshwayo arrived by ship in August 1882. His visit caused a big impact. The story was widely reported in the press and crowds gathered to get a glimpse of the Zulu King. Indeed, a letter written by Lady Wolseley on 13 August confirmed that the crowds were so big that police had to be called to escort him out of the studio of portrait photographer Alexander Bassano.

On 14 August he was granted an audience with Queen Victoria at her house on the Isle of Wight. The Queen was impressed, later writing that the King was a 'very fine man', and she arranged to have his portrait painted. King Cetshwayo's dignity and charm also impressed the prime minister, William Gladstone, and it was decided that the British government would support the King's return to the throne. King Cetshwayo returned to Zululand to be reinstated as King, but the divisions in his country were now so deep that he was not able to prevent civil war breaking out. King Cetshwayo died in February 1884 and he is now remembered as being the last king of an independent Zulu nation. His memorable London visit is commemorated with a blue plaque at the house where he stayed in Holland Park.

14 AUGUST - HALLE BERRY

In 2002 Halle Berry became the first Black woman to win the award for Best Actress at the Academy Awards. Berry was born on 14 August 1966 in Cleveland, Ohio to a white mother and an African American father. As a teenager Berry started entering beauty contests and in 1986 she became the first African American contestant in the Miss World competition.

Berry decided to become an actor and moved to New York and then to Los Angeles. Her first film role was in director Spike Lee's film *Jungle Fever* in 1991, and soon she was developing an interesting career, starring in serious roles as well as comedies and action films.

> **DID YOU KNOW?**
>
> In 1999 Berry starred in the film *Introducing Dorothy Dandridge*. The real Dorothy Dandridge was an actress, singer and dancer in the 1950s and 60s. In 1954 Dandridge became the first African American woman to be nominated for a Best Actress Oscar. Berry won a Golden Globe for her portrayal of Dandridge.

In 2001 Berry starred in the film *Monster's Ball*, playing a woman who had been married to a man executed for murder. For her performance in the role Berry became the second African American woman to be nominated for the Best Actress Oscar. On 23 March 2002 she became the first African American woman to win it.

Berry is also a committed activist, campaigning on environmental issues and women's rights. In 2013, testimony from Berry and from the actress Jennifer Garner helped to change the law in California to protect the children of celebrities from being harassed by photographers.

15 AUGUST - SAMUEL COLERIDGE-TAYLOR

Samuel Coleridge-Taylor was born in London on 15 August 1875 to an English mother and Sierra Leonean father. He inherited his musical ability from his mother's family, and at fifteen he enrolled at the Royal College of Music, studying the violin and then composition. On graduation he became a professor at the Crystal Palace School of Music.

By the late 1890s Coleridge-Taylor was becoming recognized as a talented composer. Inspired by the 1855 epic poem, *The Song of Hiawatha*, in 1898 he composed a choral work entitled *Hiawatha's Wedding Feast*. Its premiere took place on 11 November 1898. The piece was instantly declared to be a work of genius, and two sequel pieces, *The Death of Minnehaha* (1899) and *Hiawatha's Departure* (1900) were commissioned.

Throughout his career, *Hiawatha's Wedding Feast* remained Coleridge-Taylor's most successful and widely performed piece. It brought him fame beyond Britain, including three tours conducting the work in concert halls in the United States. In 1904 he even had an audience with President Theodore Roosevelt at the White House.

Tragically, Coleridge-Taylor died of pneumonia in 1912, aged only thirty-seven. Despite the huge success of *Hiawatha's Wedding Feast*, he and his family received no royalties from its success, as he had sold the rights to the piece soon after writing it. In 1914, partly inspired by his case, a group of music publishers established the Performing Rights Society to protect the rights of composers, songwriters and publishers to gain royalties from performance of their works as well as from their publication and distribution.

16 AUGUST - TREVOR McDONALD

Born on 16 August 1939 in San Fernando, Trinidad, Trevor McDonald became one of the most respected and popular television journalists in the United Kingdom.

He began his career working for Trinidadian newspapers and radio in the 1960s. In 1969 McDonald moved to London to become a producer for the World Service's Caribbean section. In 1973 he became the first Black reporter for ITN (Independent Television News). McDonald was promoted to presenter of ITV's *News at Ten* in 1992 and he continued his news career for more than thirty years, presenting *Tonight with Trevor McDonald* from 1999–2007 alongside ITV's *Evening News*. He also made acclaimed documentaries such as *Inside Death Row* in 2013.

McDonald has interviewed many prominent figures during his long career and was the first journalist to interview Nelson Mandela in 1990 on his release from prison. He is also an author, and has written biographies of the legendary West Indian cricketers Viv Richards and Clive Lloyd.

Trevor McDonald has won more awards than any other news broadcaster in the UK, including Newscaster of the Year three times. In 1999 he was made a knight for his services to journalism, and in 2011 he received a BAFTA fellowship in recognition of his long and groundbreaking career.

17 AUGUST – MARCUS GARVEY

Born on 17 August 1887 in Jamaica, Marcus Garvey was a passionate activist and pan-Africanist leader. He left school at fourteen to work as an apprentice in a print shop. He quickly learned the trade and by 1907, at the age of just twenty, he had become a master printer. He also became a union activist, rising through the ranks of the Printmakers' Union. His involvement in organizing a strike in 1908 led to him being sacked. Unable to find other print work, Garvey

became more involved in politics. He became a public speaker and began to communicate his ideas of pan-Africanism, starting a short-lived newspaper, *Garvey's Watchman*, in Jamaica and the bilingual newspaper, *Nation/La Nación* in Costa Rica, where he had moved for work. In 1912, Garvey moved to London. There he studied philosophy and law and worked as a writer for the *African Times* and *Orient Review*. On his return to Jamaica in 1914 Garvey founded the Universal Negro Improvement Association (UNIA) to seek empowerment for Black people through economic self-reliance and racial pride.

In 1916 Garvey moved to New York and set up a branch of the UNIA. Over 20,000 people attended Garvey's first convention in 1920, and heard his inspiring 'Declaration of Negro Rights' speech. The speech described the global issues of discrimination, violence and colonialism faced by Black people and listed a fifty-four-point declaration of Negro rights. By the mid-1920s, the UNIA had millions of worldwide members. Garvey believed in the power of organization and economic strength. He founded *Negro World* newspaper and other businesses. He was later targeted by the US Bureau of Investigation (the precursor to the FBI), and prosecuted, convicted and imprisoned for mail fraud in 1923, although he maintained his prosecution was politically motivated. Released in 1927, Garvey was deported to Jamaica.

Often controversial, Garvey clashed with other civil rights leaders. Garvey advocated racial separatism. He believed that Black people should live separately from whites, free from racial discrimination, and attempted to establish a nation on Africa's west coast for African Americans. Marcus Garvey died on 10 June 1940. In 1964 he was named Jamaica's first national hero.

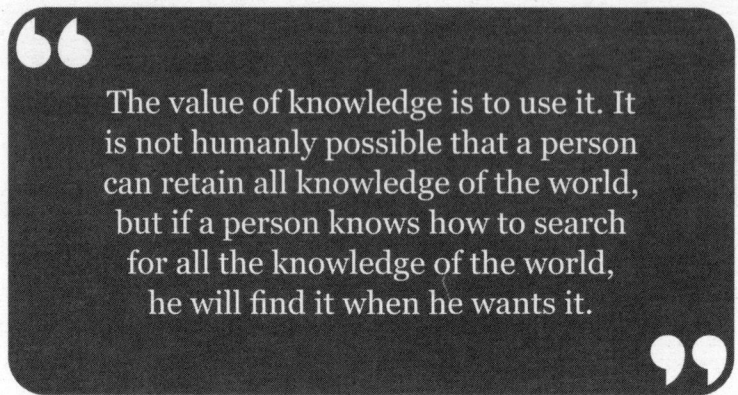

The value of knowledge is to use it. It is not humanly possible that a person can retain all knowledge of the world, but if a person knows how to search for all the knowledge of the world, he will find it when he wants it.

18 AUGUST ~ THE AURELIAN MOORS

In Roman times, Britain marked the northernmost edge of the Roman Empire. Emperor Hadrian's seventy-three-mile-long wall was built from coast to coast across the north of what is now England, so that the Roman Army could control trade and the movement of people. The wall held a fortress called Aballava, which is where the Cumbrian village of Burgh by Sands is today.

A section of Hadrian's Wall, near Housesteads Fort, Northumberland National Park, UK

In 1934 a building stone in a cottage near Burgh by Sands was identified as a mid-3rd-century Roman altar stone that had been repurposed. Roman altar stones carry carved inscriptions of words and sometimes images. The Latin inscription on this stone was a dedication to the Roman god Jupiter, from a man called Caelius Vibianus. He was the commander of the 'Numerus Maurorum Aurelianorum' – the Unit of Aurelian Moors. They were a unit of Roman soldiers originally from the province of Mauretania in North Africa, which lay at the southernmost edge of the Roman Empire. The unit's name was likely a tribute to Emperor Marcus Aurelius. Wherever Roman soldiers were posted, their families lived too. So outside Aballava fort there would have been a settlement (called a vicus) where the wives and children of the soldiers lived, alongside craftsmen and traders. This Roman unit of Aurelian Moors, with their families and associates, are the first recorded community of African people living in Britain.

19 AUGUST - BARONESS PATRICIA SCOTLAND

Baroness Patricia Scotland is a barrister, politician and diplomat. Born on 19 August 1955 in St Joseph, Dominica, Scotland came to the UK as a young child and was brought up in east London, one of twelve children.

As a young woman she chose to study law at the University of London. Warned by a lecturer that she might never succeed in the legal profession as a Black woman, Scotland in fact excelled, and was called to the bar in England in 1977 and in Dominica in 1978. In 1991 she became the first Black woman to be appointed a Queen's Counsel (QC).

In 1997 Scotland was made a life peer by the Labour party. She became Baroness Scotland of Asthal and joined the House of Lords. Ten years later she was appointed attorney general of the UK, the first woman to hold the post since it was founded in 1315. Scotland has always been committed to ending violence against women and in 2003 she achieved a major reform of the criminal justice system when she introduced the Domestic Violence Crime and Victims Act. She founded the Eliminate Domestic Violence Global Foundation in 2011 and is the patron of Children and Families Across Borders, a charity that reunites children who have been separated from their families. In 2015 Scotland was nominated by Dominica for the position of Commonwealth secretary-general. She won that election, and became the sixth secretary-general and the first Black person to hold the position. She was re-elected in 2022.

20 AUGUST - TWENTY ENSLAVED AFRICANS DELIVERED TO THE ENGLISH COLONY OF VIRGINIA

On 20 August 1619, twenty enslaved Africans were delivered to the English colony of Virginia, the first English settlement in North America. The enslaved people had been brought to Jamestown, Virginia on board the Dutch warship the *White Lion*. This was a privateer (or pirate) ship and its crew had seized the Africans from a Portuguese slave ship called the *San Juan Bautista*.

> About the latter end of August, a Dutch man of Warr of the burden of a 160 tunnes arrived at Point-Comfort, the Comandors name Capt Jope, his Pilott for the West Indies one Mr Marmaduke an Englishman. They mett with the Treasurer in the West Indyes, and determined to hold consort shipp hetherward, but in their passage lost one the other. He brought not any thing but 20. and odd Negroes, which the Governor and Cape Marchant bought for victualls (whereof he was in greate need as he pretended) at the best and easyest rates they could. He hadd a lardge and ample Commyssion from his Excellency to range and to take purchase in the West Indyes.
>
> Excerpt from a letter from John Rolfe to Sir Edwin Sandys (1619/20)

The arrival of these twenty people marked the beginning of the brutal enslavement of Africans in North America for the next 244 years.

21 AUGUST - THE TIMBUKTU MANUSCRIPTS

In 2012 Mali descended into war. Timbuktu was occupied by the Ansar Dine group who, seeking to impose their own version of Islam, set about destroying the internationally important heritage of the city that they deemed blasphemous.

Timbuktu was the centre of the 14th-century Malian Empire and a hub of learning and scholarship in the medieval world. Its libraries held thousands of manuscripts, covering religion, astronomy, medicine and more, some of which were over 800 years old. There had previously been attempts to digitize the collections, but events in 2012 brought new urgency to the matter and in August 2013 the Dutch government stepped in with funding for a new project in Bamako, Mali's Capital. Not only would this keep the valuable contents safe from future damage, but would also allow global access to them.

However, the project would not have been possible without the courage and determination of Abdel Kader Haidara, a Malian scholar and archivist. During the Ansar Dine occupation of the city, he and his brave colleagues and other volunteers, under cover of night, loaded lockers of manuscripts onto donkeys and moved them to safety. Over a period of eight months they smuggled over 350,000 documents out of Timbuktu and, through a network of couriers and safe houses, southwards to safe storage in Bamako. Although they were unable to save everything, it appears that only 4,000 of the 400,000 manuscripts of Timbuktu were destroyed. Within a year the Hill Museum and Manuscript Library along with SAVAMA-DCI (Sauvegarde et Valorisation des Manuscrits pour la Défense de la Culture Islamique) had digitized over 250,000 of the manuscripts and they are now available to view online.

22 AUGUST - THE HAITIAN REVOLUTION

On 22 August 1791, in the French colony of Saint-Domingue, on the Caribbean island of Hispaniola, enslaved people began a long and hard-fought rebellion against the white colonial authorities and plantation owners. They liberated themselves from slavery and, alongside free Black and mixed-race people on the island, they began to take control of the plantations, and eventually the main towns. Toussaint L'Ouverture (see 20 May), a formerly enslaved man, became the most important military leader of the revolutionary forces, leading the military campaign against the white plantation owners and the French army.

On 1 January 1804, one of the leaders of the revolution, Jean-Jacques Dessalines, declared Saint-Domingue's independence, and announced its new name – Haiti. It was the first independent state in the Caribbean, the first to make slavery illegal and the first to be governed by non-white political leaders. The success of the Haitian Revolution sent shockwaves through the world, particularly to those countries whose economies benefited from the labour of enslaved people. Over 200,000 Haitians had been killed during the revolution, and the land and economy were devastated. However, to enslaved people elsewhere the Haitian Revolution was an inspiration, showing that uprisings could be successful and that slavery could be abolished.

TIMELINE 3

23 AUGUST - THE NOTTINGHAM RIOTS

In Britain in the summer of 1958 the city of Nottingham became the scene of a race riot. In the late 1940s and early 1950s Britain had had a shortage of workers, and so many people had come from the West Indies to live in Britain and fill those job vacancies. By 1958, however, Britain's economy was struggling and there was a shortage of jobs instead of workers. Some white people began to blame Black people for this and to express prejudice against interracial relationships.

On 23 August, an interracial couple became the target of a racist attack in a bar in the St Ann's area of Nottingham. The couple, a Black man and a white woman, had walked into the bar together. Some of the white men in the bar attacked the man and soon a large crowd of over one thousand people had gathered in the area. Over the next few hours there were violent clashes between groups from both communities. Many men and women were injured, including one man who had to have thirty-seven stitches after he was stabbed in the throat.

Police finally managed to stop the riot and for the next week they patrolled the area in greater numbers. However, a week later, violence errupted again as another crowd of white people gathered. Intent on inciting further violence, but finding no Black people on the streets, the mob turned on itself.

The Nottingham Riots were reported in newspapers all over Britain and around the world. Less than a week later, a similar riot broke out in the Notting Hill area of London (see 29 August). Together these riots would bring government attention to the issue of race relations in Britain.

24 AUGUST ~ NEIL KENLOCK

In August 2018 Neil Kenlock launched the exhibition *Expectations: The untold story of Black community leaders.* Running through August and September of that year, the exhibition pulled images from Kenlock's extensive back catalogue of photography from the 1960s and 1970s.

Born in Jamaica in 1950, Kenlock came to Brixton in London in 1963 to join his parents, who had emigrated to the UK in the late 1950s. He developed a keen interest in photography and set out to capture a more full and accurate representation of his community, exploring the culture and the sometimes painful experiences of being Black in Britain. Along with the images of family and community, as

© Neil KKenlock, 1972

official photographer of the British Black Panther movement, Kenlock also photographed many of the movement's important figures and other leaders in the Black community, collecting an invaluable archive of the political landscape of the era.

Expectations was put together to mark the seventieth anniversary of the arrival of the *Empire Windrush* at Tilbury Docks (see 22 June). Curated by his daughter, the exhibition centred the themes of 'Challenge', 'Collaboration' and 'Change' and aimed to inspire a new generation.

Kenlock's cultural contributions also included founding Black magazine *Root* and Choice FM, a radio station aimed at a Black audience. For his services to media he was awarded an MBE in 2022.

25 AUGUST - FRANKIE KNUCKLES

In Chicago, Illinois, 25 August has been Frankie Knuckles Day since 2004. To honour the man known as the Godfather of house music, the city also renamed a street where the Warehouse nightclub, Knuckles' DJ residence, used to stand as Honorary Frankie Knuckles Way.

Knuckles was born in the Bronx in 1955 and began his DJ career in the clubs of New York. He moved to Chicago in 1977, taking a residency at the Warehouse club while disco music was at its most popular. Knuckles introduced his own style, adding edits to tracks and mixing beats, and established himself as a trailblazer. His status brought producers flocking to him to get their new dance music on his playlist, a music that became known as house after the Warehouse club that nurtured it.

In 1988 Knuckles eventually entered the world of production, joining the Def Mix production company. As house music spread across the Atlantic demand for his talents followed. He continued to DJ and to work as producer throughout the 1990s, releasing dance remixes that launched several tracks to the top of the charts and won him the first Grammy Award for Remixer of the Year in 1997.

Diagnosed with diabetes in the mid-2000s, his health declined and he died in March 2014. Knuckles was honoured by the City of Chicago not just for his contributions to music and culture but also for his extensive work for education, poverty and AIDS charities.

26 AUGUST - SPIKE LEE

On 26 August 1986, Spike Lee released his first feature film *She's Gotta Have It*. Set in a Black community in Brooklyn and shot in just twelve days, the film instantly earned him his place as one of America's most distinctive and original film-makers. His 1989 film *Do the Right Thing* is widely considered a classic of Black cinema, the screenplay for which won Lee his first Oscar nomination.

Angela George. Wikimedia Commons

Lee set up his own production company and his films have helped launch the careers of generations of actors, including Denzel Washington, Rosie Perez, Laurence Fishburne, Samuel L. Jackson, and John David Washington. His films explore themes of racism, crime, politics and the history of the civil rights movement. In 1992 Denzel Washington starred in Lee's film *Malcolm X*, based on the autobiography of the civil rights leader (see 12 and 21 February), and was nominated for an Oscar for his performance. Lee's 1997 documentary *4 Little Girls* examined the 1963 bombing of the 16th Street Baptist Church in Birmingham Alabama. The Library of Congress has selected all four of these films for inclusion in America's National Film Registry.

Lee was awarded an Academy honorary award in 2015, in recognition of his contribution to film. In 2019 he was finally nominated in the Best Picture and Best Director categories for his 1970s true-crime drama *BlackkKlansman*, and won the Oscar for Best Adapted Screenplay. As well as continuing to direct in film and television, Lee is a tenured professor at New York University's Tisch School of the Arts.

27 AUGUST - PERCY LAVON JULIAN

Born on 11 April 1899 in Montgomery, Alabama, Percy Lavon Julian was a brilliant chemist whose work developing steroid medicines has helped save many lives.

Black students could not attend high school in Montgomery, so Julian had to complete his high school and college education at the same time. DePauw University in Indiana admitted Julian but would not allow him to stay in a college dormitory because of his colour. Julian excelled at his studies and won a scholarship to Harvard University, where, in 1920, he became the first African American student to complete a **master's degree** in organic chemistry. He got his **doctorate** from the University of Vienna in 1931 and returned to DePauw as an academic.

Over the following years, Julian's work on medicinal compounds from plant sources was groundbreaking. In 1935, he and Josef Pikl developed a treatment for the eye disease glaucoma, derived from Calabar beans. Even though their work was recognized as a National Chemical Landmark, the university refused to appoint Julian to a permanent faculty position because of his race. He left to work in industry, but the Dupont chemical company declined his job application for the same reason. Julian then got a job at the Glidden company, where he researched uses for chemicals derived from soybeans and developed steroid medicines to treat arthritis. In 1953 Julian set up his own company, which he sold for more than $2 million in 1961.

Percy Lavon Julian died in 1975, having won numerous awards for his pioneering work. Many places now bear his name, but the most unusual must be asteroid 5622 – which was named *Percyjulian* in his honour on 27 August 2019.

28 AUGUST ~ THE MARCH ON WASHINGTON

The March on Washington Movement (MOWM) had been started in 1941 by civil rights activist A. Philip Randolph with support from Bayard Rustin, who later organized the Freedom Rides (see 4 May). They wanted to apply pressure on the then president, Franklin D. Roosevelt to tackle employment discrimination against African Americans and to desegregate the US Army. They achieved some success with the first, but desegregation of the US Army did not come until 1948 (see 26 July).

Philip Randolph, organizer of the demonstration, veteran labour leader

On 28 August 1963, a new march, the March on Washington for Jobs and Freedom, took place in Washington DC. It had taken Randolph and Rustin and the leaders of civil rights groups just under three months to organize. Black communities from across America travelled to the capital by cars, buses, trains and planes. Black, white and Latino celebrities also attended, including Harry Belafonte, Sidney Poitier, James Baldwin, Eartha Kitt, Josephine Baker, Sammy Davis Jr (see 1 March, 24 March, 2 August, 19 January, 3 June, 6 June), Tony Curtis, James Garner, Paul Newman, Rita Moreno and Marlon Brando. The singers Mahalia Jackson, Joan Baez and Bob Dylan were among those who performed.

That afternoon a crowd of over 250,000 people gathered in the National Mall to listen to speeches delivered from the steps of the Lincoln Memorial. The march and speeches received global

TIMELINE 7

interest. The speeches were translated into different languages and parts of the event were televised live across the world. Dr Martin Luther King was the final speaker and his speech that day was historical. He argued that despite the Emancipation Proclamation of 1863 (see 31 December), which had declared

Crowd attending Martin Luther King's speech at the Lincoln Memorial, 1963

the freedom of the millions of enslaved people in America, one hundred years later their descendants were still not truly free. Towards the end of his speech, he spoke movingly and in detail of his dream of an end to racism. It is this part of the speech Patrice that has become the most famous, and it is still often quoted decades later.

Following the march, the speakers were invited to the White House to meet with president John F. Kennedy. The legacy of the March on Washington, and the tendency afterwards for attention to focus only on Dr King's speech, are still contested. In recent years more attention has been paid to the roles of others, such as Randolph and Rustin, and to the contributions of women including Dorothy Height (see 20 April) and Daisy Bates (see 4 September).

29 AUGUST - THE NOTTING HILL RIOTS

In late August 1958, just under a week after the first of the Nottingham Riots (see 23 August), a race riot took place on the streets of Notting Hill in London. Notting Hill was home to many migrants from the Caribbean. The area was poor, with a shortage of housing. Leaders of small racist political groups used the conditions to target the white working-class population with the message to 'Keep Britain White'. That summer some white men in the area had started to carry weapons and to attack Black people on the streets.

On 29 August 1958, the violence became an actual riot when a crowd of 400 young, white men began attacking Black people, both on the streets and in their homes. Many of the white crowd were not actually from the area but had travelled from other parts of London to join the five consecutive nights of violence. Black men from the community, some of whom had fought for Britain in the Second World War, came together to defend their community. They were also joined by some of their white neighbours.

After the riots, the police tried to argue that the riots were not about race. This caused lasting distrust between the Black community and the Metropolitan Police. Many newspapers and politicians, however, tried to place the blame for the riots on the Black population. In response to the riots the writer and political activist Claudia Jones decided to organize Britain's first ever Caribbean carnival to celebrate Caribbean culture and to raise the community's spirits (see 30 January).

30 AUGUST - BERYL GILROY

Beryl Answick was born on 30 August 1924 in British Guiana, and became Beryl Gilroy when she married in 1954. She was a pioneering educator, writer and psychotherapist.

Gilroy trained as a teacher then came to London in 1952 to study Child Development. Even with her qualifications, Gilroy found it impossible to get a teaching job and was forced to work as a maid and a filing clerk until 1954, when she finally became a primary school teacher. Gilroy wrote about her experiences in her 1976 memoir *Black Teacher*, describing the everyday discrimination that she faced in school and in life. In 1969 she became one of the first Black headteachers in London.

In the 1970s Gilroy wrote stories that reflected life for working-class Black and white children for a groundbreaking children's book series called *Nippers*. Her novel for adults, *Frangipani House*, was published in 1986 and won the GLC Black Literature Award. More novels followed and also a collection of poetry called *Echoes and Voices*.

Gilroy studied all her life, and gained master's degrees in Psychology and in Education and a PhD in Counselling Psychology. She served on the Race Relations Board in the 1960s and became an honorary fellow at the Institute of Education.

Beryl Gilroy died in 2001. She is remembered as one of the most important documenters of the post-war Caribbean experience in England and her archive is held at the British Library.

> **DID YOU KNOW?**
> In 2004 the outfit Gilroy wore when she arrived in the UK (an orange skirt suit) was included in the Black British Style exhibition at the Victoria and Albert Museum.

31 AUGUST - NOTTING HILL CARNIVAL

The Notting Hill Carnival is a three-day street festival held during August bank holiday weekend in London that celebrates Afro-Caribbean culture and heritage.

David Sedlecký, Wikimedia Commons

In the 1950s, Notting Hill was home to one of the UK's largest communities of Caribbean immigrants and the scene of the Notting Hill race riots of 1958 (see 29 August). The original event was the idea of Claudia Jones, a Trinidadian activist (see 30 January). In 1966 the first outdoor carnival was set up by community activists Rhaune Laslett and Andre Shervington. Trinidadian musician Russell Henderson played steel pans and steel bands have been part of the carnival ever since.

The festival grew into a major national event, with live bands and colourful carnival parades. In 1973, Leslie 'Teacher' Palmer became director of the carnival, and sound systems became a feature when Duke Vin brought his to the event. The Notting Hill Carnival is now one of London's biggest annual celebrations, enjoyed by more than two million people every year.

SEPTEMBER

1 SEPTEMBER - COLIN KAEPERNICK

On 1 September 2016, quarterback for the San Francisco 49ers, Colin Kaepernick, sparked an international movement when he knelt during the pre-game playing of the US national anthem.

The summer of 2016 had seen a spate of shootings by the police against Black civilians. Kaepernick chose to protest initially by remaining seated during the anthem, but after a conversation with a military veteran, he decided that kneeling would honour the military who had fought for their country yet still make his point. The silent protest proved highly controversial. American football fans boycotted games, Kaepernick received death threats and even the president weighed in demanding that protesting players be sacked. Still the gesture took hold and Kaepernick was joined by teammates Eric Reid and Eli Harold as it spread throughout the NFL (National Football League) and outside the world of football and around the world.

Despite settling an employment grievance against the NFL

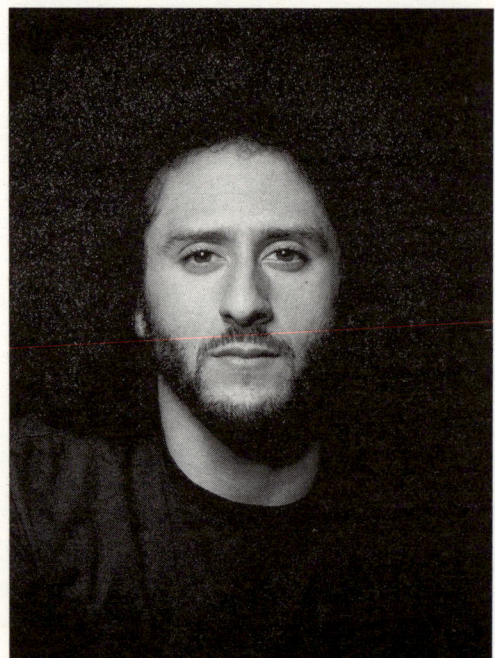

in 2019, Kaepernick has not played professional football since he was let go from the 49ers at the end of the 2016 season. His activism and the reaction to it effectively ended his career. Undeterred, he has continued to campaign for Black liberation and the abolition of the police and prison systems through his Know Your Rights organization.

2 SEPTEMBER - JAMES FORTEN

James Forten was born in Philadelphia on 2 September 1766, to free Black parents descended from enslaved grandparents. He left school aged eight, joining his father to work for sailmaker Robert Bridges. A year later he became the family's main earner when his father died in a tragic accident. During the War of Independence, aged fourteen, Forten volunteered to join the Revolutionary forces. He served aboard the ship the *Royal Louis* as a powder boy, carrying gunpowder from the ship's powder room to the cannons. During his service the ship was captured by the British, which put Forten at risk of becoming enslaved. Instead he became a prisoner of war aboard the British ship the HMS *Jersey* and was taken to London before being released in a prisoner exchange in 1782. Forten then worked in the London docks to earn the money to return to Philadelphia, where he went back to his job as a sailmaker. When his employer retired Forten took charge, and by the age of thirty-five he had saved enough money to buy the business.

Forten was an innovator. He invented new tools and sails that made ships faster and more agile, and he became Philadelphia's leading and most prosperous sailmaker. He used his wealth for the abolitionist cause, civil rights for Black people and voting rights for women. He campaigned against the American Colonization Society which sought to send free Black Americans to Africa instead of recognizing their right to live as free people in America. In 1831 he funded and wrote for the newspaper *The Liberator* which was later cited as a huge influence by the anti-slavery campaigner Frederick Douglass (see 14 February).

3 SEPTEMBER - BETHANN HARDISON

At the beginning of September 2013, the Diversity Coalition sent a letter to the world's foremost fashion houses in New York, London, Paris and Milan criticizing the lack of racial diversity in the world of fashion. Models Naomi Campbell and Iman joined the campaign launched by veteran model and activist Bethann Hardison to demand that this imbalance be addressed.

Hardison began her modelling career in the late 1960s when she was discovered by designer Willi Smith. She soon graced the catwalk for major designers and appeared in top fashion magazines. Her 1973 appearance at the Battle of Versailles – a fashion face-off between the best American and French designers – cemented her reputation at the top of the industry and helped to open it up to more Black models.

In the 1980s Hardison, determined to push the industry away from its narrow vision, started her own model agency. She also founded the Black Girls Coalition with Iman which took on the work of monitoring diversity and of raising awareness of industry colour bias. In 2008 she worked on *Vogue Italia*'s 'Black Issue', which featured all Black models (see 4 August), but despite the edition's success it did not result in any significant change. Frustrated by the lack of progress, the Diversity Coalition penned its open letter. Since then diversity in the fashion industry is now more closely monitored and statistics are made public, holding fashion houses accountable for their choices.

In recognition of her work Hardison has received multiple awards. She continues her activism in the industry, campaigning for diversity both on the catwalk and among designers.

4 SEPTEMBER - THE LITTLE ROCK NINE

After the Supreme Court ruling in the Brown vs. Board of Education of Topeka case (see 16 May), American states that still kept Black and white children in separate schools were forced to begin desegregation. In Little Rock, Arkansas, the school board drew up plans to begin desegregation of its high schools in September 1957. The local NAACP group selected and registered nine Black students – Minnijean Brown, Elizabeth Eckford, Ernest Green, Thelma Mothershed, Melba Pattillo, Gloria Ray, Terrence Roberts, Jefferson Thomas and Carlotta Walls – to attend Little Rock Central High School. However, local governor Orval Faubus opposed the plans, announcing on 2 September that he was calling in the Arkansas National Guard to stop the students entering the school. But on the 3 September, Federal Judge Ronald Davies ruled that the desegregation would proceed as planned.

US Library of Congress's Prints and Photographs division under the digital ID cph.3c25125

New York City Mayor Robert Wagner greeting the teenagers who integrated Central High School, Little Rock, Arkansas.
Pictured, front row, left to right: Minnijean Brown, Elizabeth Eckford, Carlotta Walls, Mayor Wagner, Thelma Mothershed, Gloria Ray; back row, left to right: Terrence Roberts, Ernest Green, Melba Pattillo, Jefferson Thomas

On 4 September 1957, the Little Rock Nine arrived for their first day at Little Rock Central High School. Eight were driven to the school together, but the ninth, Elizabeth Eckford, arrived separately and had to walk alone through an angry mob of white school students and adults screaming at her. The Arkansas National Guard obeyed their orders and none of the Black students was able to enter the school. On 20 September, Judge Davies ordered the Guard to stand down. On 23 September the Little Rock Police Department escorted the Little Rock Nine through the mob and into the school, but removed them again after the mob began rioting. President Eisenhower then sent 1,200 US Army troops and put them in charge of the Arkansas National Guard. On 25 September, the Little Rock Nine were finally able to attend their first day of classes.

In 1999 the Little Rock Nine were invited to the White House where president Clinton presented them each with a Congressional Gold Medal, America's highest civilian honour.

> **DID YOU KNOW?**
>
> The person who provided daily support and mentoring to the Little Rock Nine, putting herself at risk as she walked with them as they tried to gain entry to the school, was Daisy Bates. president of the Arkansas Conference of Branches of the NAACP. Bates was also a journalist and the co-founder of the civil rights newspaper, the *Arkansas State Press*. Today, on the third Monday of every February, Little Rock celebrates Daisy Gatson Bates Day as a state holiday, shared with the birthday of George Washington.

5 SEPTEMBER ~ WILLARD WIGAN

Throughout his education in 1960s Wolverhampton, Willard Wigan was bullied and belittled by teachers for his difficulties with reading. Cruelly informed that he would never achieve anything in life, Wigan is now a world-renowned artist and holder of an MBE, an honorary doctorate from Warwick University and of several world records for his astonishing miniature sculptural work.

Failed by an education system that did not care to recognize the undiagnosed autism and dyslexia that impacted his learning, Wigan in turn rejected education and turned his attention to art. His first micro sculpture was an ant-house, which he carved as compensation for the ant colony his dog had dug up. Encouraged by his mother, Zita, Wigan continued to carve and continued to shrink his pieces.

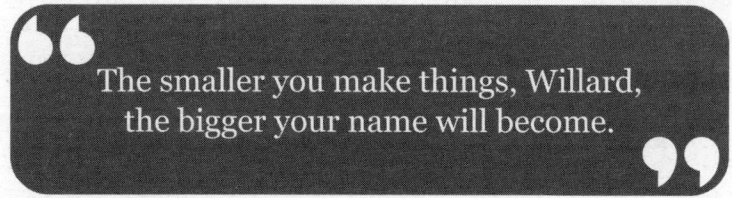

> The smaller you make things, Willard, the bigger your name will become.

Taking his mother's advice to heart, Willard is now famous for his sculptures set within the eye of a needle or on the head of a pin. His works are only visible with the aid of a microscope.

Wigan's art reflects his belief that the small things in life can often have big impacts. His Small Things Matter project is centred around helping people to understand the power of small individual changes that can combine into something huge, particularly in relation to environmental issues and attitudes around neurodiversity.

6 SEPTEMBER - DAPO ADEOLA

Dapo Adeola is an award-winning British picture-book illustrator and author, known for creating characters and illustrations that defy expectations and stereotypes around gender and race.

© Tim Lane Penguin Books

Adeola was born in London to Nigerian parents and from an early age he was interested in drawing. After school he studied graphic design but found that illustration was where his interests really lay. He began working with the actor Nathan Bryon and together they co-created the picture-book *Look Up*. The book introduced the character Rocket, a female astronaut who Adeola based on one of his nieces. In March of 2020 the book was shortlisted for the Waterstones Children's Book Prize in the Illustrated Book category and was declared the winner that June. There is now a series of books focused on Rocket and her brother Jamal, and Adeola has gone on to work with other authors, including Malorie Blackman (see 14 January).

As a high-profile illustrator and writer, Adeola has used his position to advocate for representation and to challenge gender and racial stereotypes. He has also championed the work of Black British illustrators, creating a supportive community around the use of the hashtag #BlackBritishIllustrators on Twitter. Adeola also runs creative illustration and design workshops for children and events to encourage Black people and under-represented groups into careers in the creative industries. On 6 September 2021, Adeola was appointed the Writer-Illustrator in Residence for BookTrust, which is the UK's largest children's reading charity.

7 SEPTEMBER - JOB MASEKO

Job Maseko was born in the town of Springs near Johannesburg, South Africa on 7 September 1915. Until the outbreak of the Second World War, Maseko worked in the gold mines, but in 1940 he, along with around 80,000 other Black South Africans, signed up to the Native Military Corps. These soldiers were not permitted to fight alongside white soldiers, but were used as labourers, cooks and stretcher bearers and were not issued with firearms. However, the lack of a weapon did not stop Maseko from blowing up a German ship.

After the fall of Tobruk to German forces in 1942, Maseko was captured as a prisoner of war. POWs were segregated by race and the Black and Indian prisoners found themselves in a camp with brutal conditions where they were given starvation rations, were subject to random violence, and endured forced labour on the docks. It was during a shift on the docks that Maseko took the opportunity to strike back. He made a small bomb from a tin and some gunpowder he took from bullets, and placed it strategically near fuel stored in the hold of a German freight ship. As he took the last load from the ship, Maseko lit the fuse.

Maseko was awarded the Military Medal for his ingenuity and courage in destroying the German ship, but many believe he should have been awarded the higher honour of the Victoria Cross. The sacrifice of Black soldiers was not rewarded in the same way as that of their white counterparts. After the war, white South Africans were given new homes and Black veterans received a pair of boots or a bicycle, war graves were segregated and the names of many soldiers had been carelessly recorded making commemoration of their deaths impossible.

Maseko died in poverty in 1952 after an accident.

8 SEPTEMBER - OPRAH WINFREY

On 8 September 1986, the first episode of *The Oprah Winfrey Show* aired nationwide across America. What had started as a morning talk show, hosted by former news anchor Oprah Winfrey and broadcast only in Chicago, became a national and international

Shutterstock/Joe Seer

phenomenon. By the time the show ended in 2011, Winfrey was a billionaire and one of the most influential people in America.

Winfrey was born on 29 January 1954 in Mississippi and was a bright child, already reading by the age of three. During her childhood she was repeatedly moved to live with different relatives, and was the victim of sexual assault. After some difficult years she went to live with her father as a teenager and became a high achiever at school. She was awarded a scholarship to attend university after winning a public speaking contest, and she chose to study communication.

Winfrey began working in local radio and television, and moved to Chicago where she took over the morning programme that would launch her as a national talk show host. Winfrey also pursued opportunities to produce and act. She co-starred in the 1985 film *The Color Purple*, based on the novel by Alice Walker (see 18 April) and was nominated for a Best Supporting Actress Academy Award.

Winfrey has become a media icon, she has established an influential book club, a magazine, her own production company and charity. She has won twenty Emmys, a Tony award, and a Peabody award. In 2013 she was awarded the Presidential Medal of Freedom by President Obama.

9 SEPTEMBER ~ RAOUL PECK

Born 9 September 1953 in Haiti, film-maker Raoul Peck was eight when his family fled from the Duvalier dictatorship to the newly independent Democratic Republic of Congo.

Peck received an international education, attending institutions in Kinshasa, New York, France and Berlin, but Haiti remained an important touchstone for him. His first feature length film, *Haitian Corner*, was released in 1987 and was the start of a series of films focused on his birth country which included *The Man by the Shore*, which was nominated for a **Palme d'Or**. Peck is also known for his documentary films. In 1991 he produced *Lumumba, Death of a Prophet*, which explored Patrice Lumumba's place in the history of the DRC and the anti-**colonial** movement (see 24 June), a subject he revisited nine years later as a feature film, *Lumumba*. His 2016 documentary film *I Am Not Your Negro*, based on the work of James Baldwin (see 2 August) received an **Oscar** nomination for Best Documentary Feature. In the film, Peck uses his signature collage style to tell the story of the African American struggle through archive film footage with narration by Samuel L. Jackson.

Aside from his film accolades, he has received recognition for his activism, including the Human Rights Watch Irene Diamond Lifetime Achievement Award in 2001. Peck continues to explore the subjects of colonialism, race and class through his work with the intention of offering new perspectives and provoking discussion.

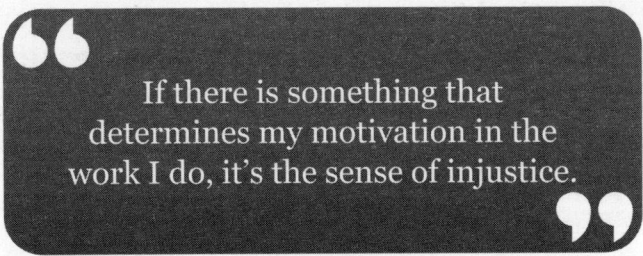

> If there is something that determines my motivation in the work I do, it's the sense of injustice.

10 SEPTEMBER - NINA SIMONE

On 15 September 1963 the 16th Street Baptist church in Alabama was bombed. Four Black children were killed in the attack. In response, musician Nina Simone wrote 'Mississippi Goddam'.

2.24.01.03, Component number: 918-5601,
Nationaal Archief, Netherlands.

Simone had not previously made her work political, but her friend Lorraine Hansberry (see 11 March) had insisted that whether she liked it or not, she was part of the civil rights movement. The song, written in an hour of focused rage, was a furious attack on the violence of the bombing and on the continued oppression of African Americans. Many record stations in the south banned the song and some returned the promotional copies snapped in half to the record company. A year later, on 10 September 1964, Simone was invited on to *The Steve Allen Show* to perform and discuss the song before a national audience. She told Allen:

> First you get depressed and then you get mad. And when these kids got bombed, I sat down and wrote this song. And it's a very moving, violent song 'cause that's how I feel about the whole thing.

Simone often changed the lyrics of the song to reflect current events in the civil rights movement. She sang for Selma after the violence at Edmund Pettus Bridge (see 7 March), and for Memphis after the murder of Dr King (see 10 January). 'Mississippi Goddam' became an anthem for the movement and in 2018 was added to the Library of Congress National Recording Registry for its cultural significance.

11 SEPTEMBER ~ JOHN WARE

Born into slavery in around 1845 in Tennessee, John Ware defied prejudice and stereotypes to become a cowboy. Following his emancipation at the end of the Civil War, as a young man he moved to Texas and was soon moving thousands of cattle on huge journeys across the state.

Ware left Texas for Montana in 1879 where he stayed for some years, until, in 1882, he was hired by an agent from the North West Cattle Company to drive cattle to the District of Alberta in Canada where a new ranch, the Bar U, was being set up. Once there he decided to stay on, working at the Bar U and then the Quorn Ranch on the Sheep River.

In 1888 he established his own cattle ranch near Calgary. At a time when cattle ranching was white-dominated and increasingly being controlled by corporations, being a Black cowboy running an independent ranch earned Ware respect. In 1902, now married to his wife Mildred, Ware moved his family again, establishing another new ranch near the town of Brooks, Alberta. Sadly, in 1905 Mildred died of pneumonia at the age of just thirty-five. Ware died a few months after, on 11 September 1905, when his horse landed on him after stepping in a hole. Ware's funeral was well attended and he and his family are still remembered in the area. Today several local landmarks and buildings are named after him. In 2022 the Canadian government designated John Ware, Canada's Black cowboy, as a person of National Historic Significance.

John Ware, rancher, with wife Mildred and children Robert and Nettie in southern Alberta, (ca. 1896)

12 SEPTEMBER – STEVE BIKO

Bantu Stephen Biko was born on 18 December 1946 and raised in poverty in a township in the Eastern Cape. He studied medicine at Natal University and co-founded the South African Students' Organization (SASO) in 1968, and served as its first president. Influenced by the work of philosopher Frantz Fanon (see 20 July) and the Black Panther movement in America, Biko placed Black Consciousness at the heart of

Everett Collection Historical/ Alamy

the SASO's approach, writing about it in the SASO Newsletter where he used the pseudonym 'Frank Talk'. He soon became an influential anti-apartheid leader. He used the slogan 'black is beautiful' to emphasize the need for Black South Africans to empower themselves.

The apartheid government saw him as a threat and in 1973 they put a banning order on Biko, ensuring that he could not leave his hometown or make public speeches. Biko was monitored closely by the state until his 1977 arrest.

Biko was arrested by the authorities on 18 August when he broke a travel ban by visiting Cape Town. He was taken into custody and over the next few days transferred to the security police headquarters in Port Elizabeth. On 6 September he was interrogated for twenty-two hours, and at some point during his imprisonment he was brutally beaten by police officers. Despite his injuries he was shackled, standing, to a metal grille and left for two days. On 11 September, after being seen by three different doctors, Biko was thrown in the back of a van for a 700-mile journey to a prison hospital. He died as the result of injuries sustained in police custody on 12 September 1977.

The minister of police stated that Biko's death was due to a hunger strike, but an inquest showed that it was caused by traumatic brain injuries. Biko's killing caused an outcry across the world and 15,000 people came to mourn at his funeral. Ten years later, in 1987, a biography of him by his friend Donald Woods was adapted into the award-winning film *Cry Freedom*.

South Africa's post-apartheid Truth and Reconcillation Commission sought answers about his death and in 1997 heard testimonies from the five officers accused of Biko's murder. The policemen maintained that they had acted lawfully, and that Biko's injuries had occured accidentally during a 'scuffle'. The Commission was unconvinced by their version of events and concluded that they had failed to tell the full truth. However, despite this finding, and an admission by Medical Association of South Africa of its role in covering up torture and murder by the police, in October 2003 South African Justice Ministry officials announced that the policemen would not be prosecuted because of insufficient evidence.

13 SEPTEMBER - YORK (AND LEWIS AND CLARK)

The explorer York was born in Virginia in around 1770, the enslaved property of John Clark. From an early age he was the body servant of Clark's son William.

After the Louisiana Purchase of 1803, William Clark, now a captain in the US Army, was commissioned alongside Captain Merriweather Lewis to lead an expedition to map the new territory. President Thomas Jefferson was keen to establish the most practical river routes for trade and movement across the new land to the west coast of America. The expedition's secondary purpose was to study the flora, fauna and geography of the new territory and to establish trade with the Native American tribes living there.

As Clark's body servant, York took part in the expedition. He was a skilled frontiersman, able to hunt and find resources. As the only African American on the team, however, he was not paid. The expedition records show that he played an active role in the expedition, hunting with his rifle, helping to navigate and having his opinions recorded when decisions were being made.

When the expedition ended he had become the first African American to cross the North American continent and the first to see the Pacific Ocean. York was also reportedly angry and disappointed at being made to return to his previous life as an enslaved man rather than being formally freed by Clark. The last mention of York appears in letters from Clark in 1815, where instead of freeing York, Clark appears to have hired him out to work as a waggoner. In 2001 York was posthumously given the rank of honorary sergeant in the US Army by President Bill Clinton.

14 SEPTEMBER ~ SARAH REMOND

American anti-slavery campaigner Sarah Remond was born in 1826 into a free Black family in Massachusetts. As a child she was expelled from her local high school because of her colour. At sixteen she gave her first public speech and was soon travelling the north-east of America, giving lectures at abolitionist events. In 1858 Remond travelled to England, Scotland and Ireland, where she toured for three years raising money for the anti-slavery cause. On 14 September 1859 in a speech at the Manchester Athenaeum, she explained to the crowd how the labour of the enslaved in America was linked to Britain:

> When I walk through the streets of Manchester and meet load after load of cotton, I think of those 80,000 cotton plantations on which was grown the $125m worth of cotton which supply your market, and I remember that not one cent of that money ever reached the hands of the labourers.

Remond became the first Black student at Bedford College and trained as a nurse at University College London. In 1867 she moved to Florence, Italy. She trained and then worked as a doctor for over twenty years and died in Rome in December 1894. In 2019 University College London established the Sarah Parker Remond Centre for the Study of Racism & Racialisation, named in her honour.

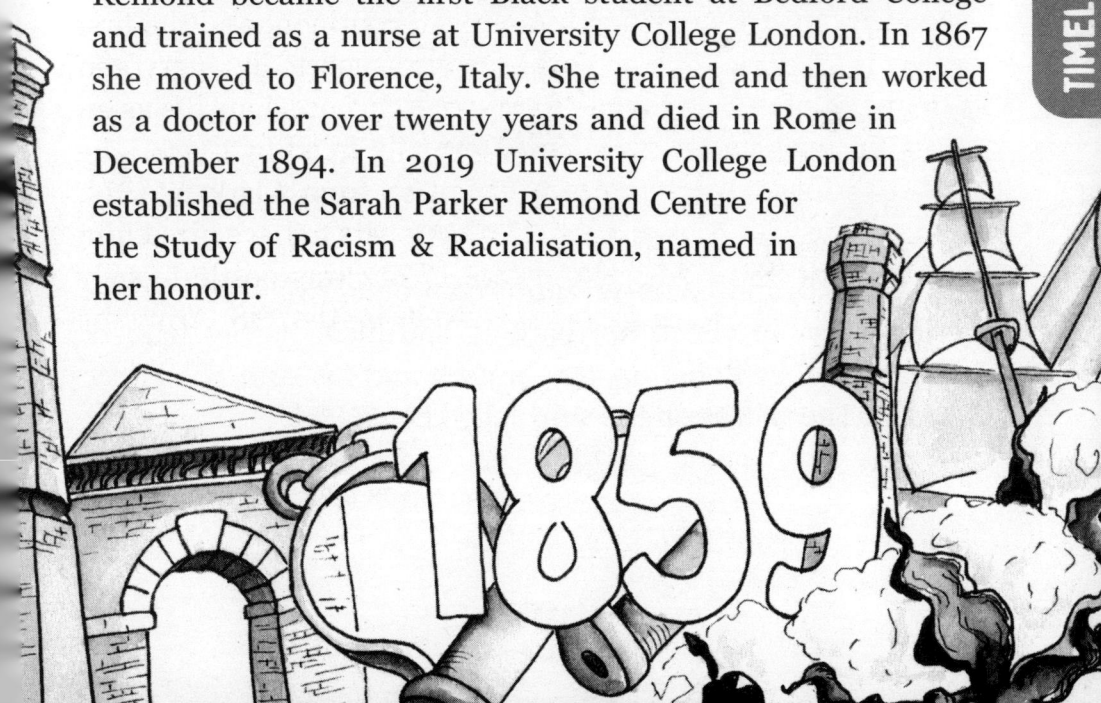

15 SEPTEMBER ~ SARA FORBES BONETTA

In May 1850, an officer in the British Navy, Captain Frederick Forbes, visited the court of King Ghezo of Dahomey in West Africa. Forbes' mission was to persuade King Ghezo to abandon the trade in enslaved people, even though earlier attempts with similar objectives had failed. Forbes brought letters to King Ghezo that detailed Britain's opposition to the slave trade, including a personal letter of opposition from Queen Victoria, who also sent gifts of silks and cloths.

King Ghezo refused to abandon the slave trade, reminding Forbes that the British had in the past traded in enslaved people. As was the custom, the King also gave Forbes gifts to give to Queen Victoria, and Forbes listed the gifts in his diary: they included expensive cloth, a footstool, cowrie shells (which were valuable in Africa) and a barrel of rum. There was also what Forbes described in his diary as 'a captive girl'. The girl, who was probably seven or eight,

was enslaved, and had been captured around two years earlier during a war in which her parents had died. Forbes named her Sara Forbes Bonetta, after himself and his ship, the HMS *Bonetta*. The sailors on the ship called her 'Sally'.

When the HMS *Bonetta* arrived back in Britain, Forbes contacted Queen Victoria and the Queen agreed to pay for Sara to go to school and to make sure she was cared for. Queen Victoria also requested that 'Sally' be brought to Windsor Castle to meet her. So, on 9 November 1850, the little girl made her first appearance at court, and her first entry in the Queen's journal.

> "
>
> We came home, found Albert still there, waiting for Capt. Forbes and a poor little negro, girl, whom he brought back from the King of Dahomey, her parents and all her relatives having been sacrificed. Capt. Forbes saved her life, by asking for her as a present...She is seven years old, sharp and intelligent, and speaks English. She was dressed as any other girl.
>
> "

Sara Forbes Bonetta's life was transformed by the Queen's willingness to draw her into the extended circle of her court and provide her with an excellent education. But as a Black child, formerly enslaved, thrust into the heart of Victorian Britain's elite, her life story was also buffeted and shaped by the profound contradictions and confusion about race that the Queen and most of her subjects shared in the middle decades of the 19th century. One idea that was common in Britain at the time was that the cold British climate was dangerous to the health of Black people, and so in January 1851 Sara was sent to live in Sierra Leone, then a British colony, for her own safety.

After a few years Sara returned to England, and in December 1855 again appeared in Queen Victoria's diary.

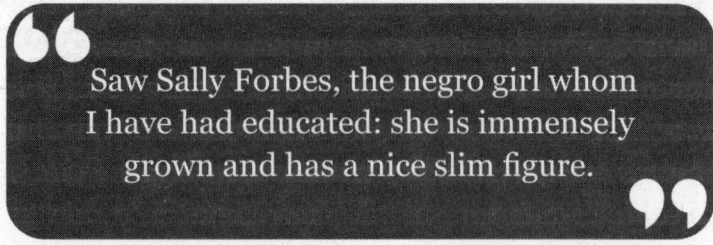

> Saw Sally Forbes, the negro girl whom I have had educated: she is immensely grown and has a nice slim figure.

Three years later Sara was invited to be a guest at the wedding of the Queen's eldest daughter, who was also called Victoria.

In 1862 Sara was living in Brighton under the care of Miss Sophia Welsh, when a thirty-three-year-old West African businessman, named James Pinson Labulo Davies took an interest in her. He was from Sierra Leone and they had been introduced there some years before, when Sara was a child. He came to visit Sara in Brighton and declared a wish to marry her. Aged nineteen, Sara seems not to have been enthusiastic about this plan, but Queen Victoria approved of Mr Davies and in August they were married. When she signed her marriage certificate she gave her name as Sara but also included the African name given by her parents – Ina.

Their wedding was a lavish affair and became a big story in the newspapers. Hundreds of people came out onto the streets of Brighton on the day to cheer, and reports of their wedding appeared in hundreds of newspapers in Britain and all over the British Empire.

On 15 September 1862, shortly after their wedding, Sara and James attended the photographic studio of Camille Silvy, who was famous for taking expensive photographs of the rich and famous. The photographer captured Sara and James, in fine clothes, posed like other high society Victorians of the day.

Not long after, the couple travelled back to West Africa where, in 1863, their first child was born. They named her Victoria, after the Queen, who became her godmother. Sara took her daughter to Britain and introduced her to the Queen on 9 December 1867. In her diary Queen Victoria described Sara's daughter as 'aged four, a lively intelligent child, with big melancholy eyes'. When little Victoria was christened the Queen sent her new goddaughter a gold cup on which was inscribed these words:

Camille Silvy, WikiCommons

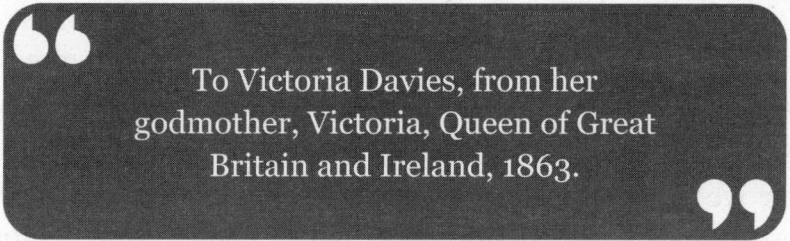

> To Victoria Davies, from her godmother, Victoria, Queen of Great Britain and Ireland, 1863.

In the 1870s Sara and James had two more children; Arthur, who was born in 1871 and Stella, born in 1873. In 1880 Sara caught tuberculosis and died, aged just thirty-seven. Queen Victoria continued to support her goddaughter Victoria and paid for her to go to school at Cheltenham Ladies' College. Today, the descendants of Sara Forbes Bonetta live in Britain, Nigeria and Sierra Leone.

16 SEPTEMBER ~ THE BARBADOS SLAVE CODE 1661

The island of Barbados became an English colony in 1625. The English settlers who arrived in 1627 established profitable plantations that produced expensive cash crops that they sent across the Atlantic for sale. By the 1640s business was booming and the plantation owners began to rely on the labour of enslaved African people. Within a few years the enslaved Black population far outnumbered the white settlers.

In 1661 the Barbados Assembly, the island's colonial government whose members were white landowners, created the Barbados Slave Code. The new code claimed to help protect enslaved people, but was actually designed to protect the landowners and to keep the enslaved population under control. It divided the population into two legal groups – the free white European population and the enslaved Black population. The enslaved Black population were to be treated as chattel instead of as people.

The Code established a shockingly brutal set of rules that governed how enslaved men, women and children were to be treated, what they were and were not allowed to do, and what punishments could be applied to them if these rules were not obeyed. Enslaved people were not allowed to be away from their plantations without written permission. They were not allowed to carry a weapon. Any child born to an enslaved woman was enslaved too. Punishments for enslaved people were extremely severe and white plantation owners and their white staff could have them whipped, slit their nostrils, brand their faces with hot irons and even kill them.

Barbados was the first English colony to introduce a slave code and other colonies soon copied the idea, creating new versions across the Caribbean and in the southern states of America.

17 SEPTEMBER - THE BRISTOL BUS BOYCOTT

In Bristol, England in 1963, a four-month-long civil rights protest took place against racial discrimination in employment. Despite labour shortages the government-owned Bristol Omnibus Company operated a colour bar; Black and Asian applicants were refused bus driver and conductor roles, and given less well-paid support roles instead.

In response, Roy Hackett, Owen Henry, Audley Evans and Prince Brown formed the West Indian Development Council. Paul Stephenson, a local youth worker of West African descent, became their spokesman. Inspired by the 1955 Montgomery Bus Boycott (see 1 December), on 29 April they announced a boycott of the company's buses. West Indian and Asian customers stopped taking the buses, and soon they were joined by many white customers. Two days later, on 1 May, a student protest march was held. The bus company blamed Transport and General Workers' Union (TGWU) members who had voted for the colour bar, despite also passing resolutions opposing apartheid in South Africa.

The local press ran many stories and were inundated with letters from readers. Ex-cricketer Learie Constantine (see 30 July), then high commissioner for Trinidad and Tobago, supported the boycott, and local MP Tony Benn informed the Labour party leader Harold Wilson, who spoke in support of the boycott at an anti-apartheid rally in London.

Eventually, on the day of the March on Washington in America (see 28 August), the company announced the end of the colour bar. On 17 September, Raghbir Singh became Bristol's first bus conductor of colour, joined two days later by Jamaican-born Norman Samuels and Norris Edwards, and Pakistani-born Mohammed Raschid and Abbas Ali.

18 SEPTEMBER – THE UNDERGROUND RAILROAD

The Underground Railroad was the route to freedom for enslaved people from the slave-owning states of America. It began in the late 1700s and continued until the mid-1800s. The railroad was

'A bold stroke for freedom'

actually a series of safe houses, guides and secret escape routes created and run by Black and white people who were trying to bring an end to slavery in the USA. Those using it and running it faced great danger, but it offered a way for enslaved people to escape to the free northern states and to Canada, Mexico and some Caribbean islands where slavery was not legal. By 1850, it is thought that around 100,000 enslaved people had escaped to freedom via the Underground Railroad, with the help of guides like Harriet Tubman (see 10 March) who risked their lives repeatedly to help others escape.

On 18 September 1850, President Millard Fillmore signed the Fugitive Slave Act. Tensions had been rising between the slave-owning southern states and the northern free states and the new law was supposed to be a compromise between the two sides. It stated that if enslaved people who had escaped to freedom were caught, all US citizens had a legal duty to cooperate in returning them to their owner. Dogs were used to track down escaping people, and the Act became known as the Bloodhound Bill. Instead of easing tensions, the Act further aggravated them, pushing both sides towards an increasingly inevitable confrontation.

19 SEPTEMBER - MAUD SULTER

Maud Sulter was born in Glasgow on 19 September 1960 to a Ghanaian father and Scottish mother. As an artist, photographer, writer, historian, teacher and curator, Sulter, like many children of the diaspora and of mixed heritage, focused much of her work on exploring the historically difficult relationship between Europe and Africa. In particular she sought to highlight the roles of Black women in art, both as the subject and in institutional spaces.

> I'm very interested in absence and presence in the way that particularly black women's experience and black women's contribution to culture is so often erased and marginalized.

The 19th-century Haitian actress Jeanne Duval often provided a conduit for Sulter to explore these themes. Of French and West African mixed heritage, Duval had been the 'exotic' inspiration for several French artists during her lifetime. In 1989 she provided the visual inspiration for Calliope in Sulter's photographic work *Zabat*. In the early 2000s, Sulter curated an international exhibition on Duval, and in 2002 produced *Les Bijoux*, a series of nine self portraits in which she featured herself as Duval. Sulter was also known for her poetry and in her final work *Sekhmet*, she used both poetry and photography to explore her family and the connections between Scotland and Ghana.

After a long illness, Sulter died in 2008 at only forty-seven years old. Her award-winning work can still be seen in museums throughout the UK.

20 SEPTEMBER - MAE C. JEMISON

On 20 September 1992, Mae Jemison's 190 hours, 30 minutes and 23 seconds in space aboard the fiftieth space shuttle mission came to an end. She had become the first African American woman in space.

Born in October 1956 in Alabama, from childhood Jemison was interested in a career in science. After studying chemical engineering and medicine at university, she joined the Peace Corps and worked in Liberia and Sierra Leone. On her return to America, she applied to the astronaut programme at NASA. Her application was successful, and in 1987 she became a mission specialist, tasked with designing scientific experiments.

In 1992 her chance to experience space flight came on the Space Shuttle *Endeavour*. The flight was a joint mission involving the USA and Japan, and Jemison worked alongside Japanese astronaut Mamoru Mohri on a series of physiological experiments. During her time in space Jemison began all of her communications with the phrase 'Hailing frequencies open', a quote from the *Star Trek* character Lieutenant Uhura played by Nichelle Nichols who had inspired her as a child (see 28 December).

Jemison retired from NASA in 1993. Bringing together her interest in technology and its impact on society, she founded the Jemison Group and the medical technology company BioSentient Corp. She also established the Dorothy Jemison Foundation for Excellence, named after her mother.
In 1993, she guest starred in an episode of *Star Trek: The Next Generation*, following in the footsteps of her childhood hero.

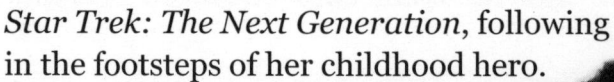

21 SEPTEMBER ~ CHRISTIANA CARTEAUX BANNISTER

Christiana Carteaux Bannister was an entrepreneur and social activist. She was born Christiana Babcock in around 1820 in Rhode Island and was of African American and Narragansett Indian heritage.

She moved to Boston as a young woman and married her first husband, Desiline Carteaux. She opened several successful hair salons over the years, establishing herself as 'Madame Carteaux, Women's Hairdresser and Wigmaker'. Once her marriage ended she moved to Providence, Rhode Island. There, in 1857, she met her second husband, artist Edward Bannister, and her financial success helped to support him as he established his career.

The couple lodged with Black abolitionists Lewis and Harriet Bell Hayden and together they helped enslaved people escaping from the South via the Underground Railroad (see 18 September). They sheltered approximately one hundred formerly enslaved people, and Carteaux Bannister's hair salons were used as meeting places for activists. Carteaux Bannister also campaigned for equal pay for Black soldiers during the Civil War years and financially supported the 54th Massachusetts Infantry Regiment, a Black military unit.

After the Civil War the couple moved to Rhode Island, where Carteaux Bannister founded a Home for Aged Colored Women in 1890, to help retired Black women who found themselves homeless in old age. In her final months she herself was admitted there on 21 September 1902, and was later transferred to the Howard Asylum, where she died on 29 December 1902. In 2003 Carteaux Bannister was inducted into the Rhode Island Heritage Hall of Fame in recognition of her contribution to Black history.

22 SEPTEMBER - KING SUNNY ADÉ

Chief Sunday Adeniyi Adegeye performs under the stage name of King Sunny Adé. He is an award-winning Nigerian musician, singer and songwriter, famous for bringing African music to a global audience.

Adé was born on 22 September 1946 in Osogbo, Nigeria to a Yoruba royal family. He moved to Lagos as a young man and started his long musical career playing Nigerian highlife music with Moses Olaiya's Federal Rhythm Dandies. He began to play juju music, and in 1967 established his own band, at first named the Green Spots, then changing to African Beats in 1972 and finally the Golden Mercury of Africa in 1985. Adé developed a distinctive sound that blends traditional instruments, Yoruba lyrics, Western instruments and modern elements like synthesizers. He established his own record label in Nigeria in 1974 and became known for his rich live performances.

In the 1980s Adé signed to the Jamaican record label Island Records and his 1982 album *Juju Music* became an international hit. He became the first Nigerian artist to be nominated for a Grammy award when his next album, *Synchro System* (1983), was nominated in the Ethnic/Traditional Folk Recording category. He received a second Grammy nomination for his 1998 album *Odu,* in which he presented his interpretations of traditional Yoruba songs. Adé has also collaborated with other artists, including Stevie Wonder (see 21 May). Outside of music Adé runs several other businesses, is president of the Musical Copyright Society of Nigeria and runs the charitable King Sunny Adé Foundation.

23 SEPTEMBER – JUDY W. REED

Judy Woodford Reed is thought to be the first African American woman to receive a patent in the United States. Not much is known about Reed's life except that she worked as a seamstress in Virginia, USA, and was married with five children. She moved to Washington DC between 1880 and 1885, following her husband's death.

In January 1884 Reed applied for a 'Dough Kneader and Roller' patent. She had come up with an improved design for a machine with rollers that kneaded dough much more evenly than previous devices. The patent was granted on 23 September 1884, giving Reed legal ownership of her invention.

Her patent certificate was signed with an 'X', which tells us that Reed was unable to sign her name. This was not unusual at the time. It is estimated that in 1880 only 20 per cent of the Black population in the USA was able to read and write; a legacy from the days of slavery when it was a crime for an enslaved person to learn these skills.

Though we know so little about Judy W. Reed, it seems clear that she was an innovative person; a woman who recognized the value of her work and rightly wanted it acknowledged.

> **DID YOU KNOW?**
>
> The National Inventors Hall of Fame has over 600 inductees. The first two Black women to be inducted were Patricia Bath (see 18 December) and Marian Croak, the inventor of Voice Over Internet Protocol (VOIP) and holder of 200 patents.

24 SEPTEMBER - OTTOBAH CUGOANO

Ottobah Cugoano was a Black Georgian anti-slavery campaigner who wrote one of the most important early books for the abolitionist cause. He was born free in the late 1750s on the Gold Coast (in what is now Ghana) in West Africa. At the age of thirteen he was kidnapped by slave traders and transported in a slave ship across the Atlantic, where he was sold into slavery on the island of Grenada in the West Indies. At first he worked on sugar plantations but eventually he was sold to an owner who brought him to England in 1772.

1772 was also the year that the case of James Somerset was heard, and Lord Mansfield issued his ruling on whether it was lawful on British soil for a person to be enslaved (see 21 June). Inspired by the case, Cugoano decided to leave his owner. He was baptized as a Christian and began his life as a free man, working for the painter Richard Cosway. During this time Cugoano learned to read and write and began to get to know other members of the Black population in Georgian London. He became good friends with Olaudah Equiano (see 6 April) and, with his support, Cugoano wrote a book about his life called *The Thoughts and Sentiments on the Evil of Slavery and Commerce of the Human Species*. In the book he told the story of his capture and his treatment as an enslaved person, and he called for an end to the slave trade and to slavery. The book was published in 1787. That same year he also became a founding member of the abolitionist group, the Sons of Africa (see 31 January). In 1791 he supported the scheme to establish a colony in Sierra Leone for former enslaved men who had fought for the British during the American War of Independence (see 15 May). After this Cugoano disappears from the historical record.

25 SEPTEMBER - THE HARLEM HELLFIGHTERS

Originally formed in 1916 as the 15th New York (Colored) Regiment, the 369th Infantry Regiment was one of the US Army's first Black regiments. Around 70 per cent of the men came from Harlem in New York, the rest from surrounding areas including Brooklyn, New Jersey, Connecticut, and Pennsylvania. The regimental band was headed by jazz bandleader (and lieutenant) James Reese Europe.

In 1917 the unit left to join the First World War in France. Before leaving, however, they were refused permission to join the farewell parade with the rest of New York's National Guard.

International Film Service, National Archives Catalog

The unit arrived in France on 1 January 1918, and the regimental band greeted their French hosts by playing a jazz rendition of 'La Marseillaise', the country's national anthem. There, the unit was renamed and became the 369th Infantry Regiment. Initially, like most Black units in the US Army in both world wars, they were restricted to supply and support roles such as digging latrines, loading and unloading supplies. But when the French asked the US government for American reinforcements, they sent the 369th to join the 16th Division of the French Army, and kept white units under US command. On 15 April 1918, after three weeks of training with the 16th, the 369th joined the front line, a month before the American Expeditionary Forces under General Pershing saw their first battle of the war. They fought in the trenches, facing heavy bombardment from the Germans, and distinguished themselves in combat (see 5 July). At some point they became known as the Harlem Hellfighters, though it is not clear where this name came from.

On 25 September 1918, the unit took part in the Meuse–Argonne Offensive, attacking German lines. The unit captured the important village of Séchault, but 144 of the men were killed and almost 1,000 wounded. The French government awarded the prestigious Croix de Guerre medal to 171 members of the regiment, and a Croix de Guerre citation to the unit as a whole. During the war, some of the men also received military awards from the US government, including the Distinguished Service Cross.

The Harlem Hellfighters were the first combat unit to return to New York after the war. They were given the parade in victory that had been denied them when they left to join the war. On 17 February 1919, the men marched up Manhattan's Fifth Avenue, to the music of their regimental jazz band.

26 SEPTEMBER - BESSIE SMITH

Elizabeth 'Bessie' Smith was born in Chattanooga, Tennessee, on 15 April 1894. She grew up in poverty. An orphan by the age of eight, Smith used her impressive voice to survive, making money by singing in the street with her brother accompanying on guitar. At the age of seventeen she joined a show, touring the Chitlin' Circuit in the southern states. Hired as a dancer, she worked her way to the chorus and then was given her own act, singing the blues.

Library of Congress, Prints & Photographs Division, Carl Van Vechten Collection, (LC-USZ62-54231)

Smith caught the attention of Columbia Records and signed a contract with them in 1923. Her first recording for them, the song 'Downhearted Blues', was a massive hit, selling over 2 million copies. Smith's popularity grew and she became the highest paid Black entertainer of her time, even appearing in one of the first ever movies with sound – 1929's *St Louis Blues*. She made hundreds of recordings, working with some of the leading musicians of her time, including Louis Armstrong.

From the late 1920s, jazz music rose in popularity and Smith's career began to decline. She cut back on touring and led a quieter life. On 26 September 1937, Smith died after a car accident in Mississippi. Thousands came to file past her coffin in the week before her burial. Her grave remained unmarked until 1970 when the singer Janis Joplin and Jaunita Green, president of the North Philadelphia chapter of the NAACP, paid for a headstone, with the epitaph 'The Greatest Blues Singer in the World Will Never Stop Singing'. In 1989, Smith, the 'Empress of the Blues', was inducted into the Rock & Roll Hall of Fame.

27 SEPTEMBER - THE ROYAL AFRICAN COMPANY

TIMELINE 1

The Royal African Company (RAC) was a trading company set up in England in 1660 by James, Duke of York (who became King James II) and a group of London merchants. It began as the Company of Royal Adventurers Trading into Africa and its initial purpose was to secure a share of the gold trade, but the trade in enslaved people proved far more lucrative. King Charles II awarded the company exclusive trading rights in Africa, giving it an effective monopoly of the slave trade, which was enforced by the Royal Navy's protection of the RAC's ships.

Over the next ninety-two years the RAC established the country's transatlantic trade in enslaved people and the luxury crops grown using their labour in the plantations of the English (and from 1707 British) American and Caribbean colonies. The company built slave castles on the West African coast, filled them with African people they bought or captured, and used hot metal to brand their skin with the initial RAC or DoY (for Duke of York). From the slave castles, the enslaved were herded onto the slave ships for the dangerous journey across the Atlantic Ocean. They were packed into the lower decks of the ships, chained together. Many became ill; around 20 per cent did not survive the crossing and their bodies were tossed into the sea. Those who did survive were taken to the colonial slave markets and sold to plantation owners.

By the time it finished trading in 1752, it is estimated that the RAC had transported around 150,000 men, women and children into slavery. From 1712 other companies were allowed to trade in enslaved people, further growing the British slave trade that the RAC had established, and making Britain extremely rich, until the Act for the Abolition of the Slave Trade in 1807 finally made the trade illegal (see 1 May). By that time it is estimated that British companies had enslaved and transported over three million African people.

28 SEPTEMBER – ALTHEA GIBSON

Born on 25 August 1927 in South Carolina and raised in Harlem, New York, Althea Gibson began playing paddleball at the age of ten as part of a programme for deprived children. She became a local champion and was encouraged to switch her talent to tennis. Again she excelled and won a string of championship titles. At this time Gibson was only allowed to play for the American Tennis Association, an African American organization, but she later became one of the first Black athletes to break the colour line in international tennis.

In 1944 and 1945 Gibson won the ATA Junior Championships and in 1949 she won a place at university on a tennis scholarship. During the 1950s Gibson was a champion player, winning fifty-six singles and doubles titles. In 1956 she became the first African American to win the French Open and in 1957 the first to win Wimbledon. She won eleven **Grand Slams** altogether – five singles titles, five doubles and one mixed doubles – including the US Open twice. In 1957 and 1958, Gibson was voted Female Athlete of the Year, the first African American to receive the honour. She was inducted into the International Tennis Hall of Fame in 1971.

Althea Gibson retired from tennis in 1958 and took up golf. In 1963 she became the first Black competitor on the Women's Professional Golf Tour, but racial discrimination meant that she was refused entry to some clubhouse facilities and sometimes was not even allowed to play. She died on 28 September 2003. Her statue now stands at the Althea Gibson Tennis Centre in New Jersey.

29 SEPTEMBER – THE BECHUANALAND KINGS VISIT BRITAIN

The imperialist ambitions of Cecil Rhodes, owner of the British South Africa Company, included building a railway running the length of Africa. Unfortunately the British Protectorate of Bechuanaland, over which he had no control, lay in the way. When news of Rhodes' plans to gain control of their country reached Bechuanaland, Kings Khama, Sebele and Bathoen left for Britain to petition the government directly.

They arrived in September 1895 and, after a brief meeting with the Colonial Office, embarked on a publicity tour of Britain, hoping to gain public support and strengthen their case. With help from the London Missionary Society, they spent three months touring Britain, holding meetings and attending events and dinners, and soon became national celebrities. The groundswell of support and public sympathy for their cause was reflected in and multiplied by a surprisingly helpful press, and when they met with the Colonial Office again, with the weight of public opinion behind them, they were finally granted the protections they sought from Rhodes' plans. The Kings went on to meet Queen Victoria on 20 November. The meeting of these heads of state provoked much press interest and cemented affection, and therefore protection, for Bechuanaland.

The Kings returned as national heroes. The country remained a protectorate until it gained independence in 1966 (see 3 March) and became Botswana. On 29 September 2005 a monument to the Three Dikgosi (Kings), was unveiled in Gaborone.

KHAMA III   SEBELE I   BATHOEN I

Jota @ BRAZIL, CC BY-SA 4.0, via Wikimedia Commons

30 SEPTEMBER ~ EDWARD BOUCHET

Born on 15 September 1852, in New Haven, Connecticut, Edward Bouchet was a physicist who gave many young Black people the opportunity to learn about science.

As a child Bouchet attended one of the few local schools that would accept Black students. He did so well that at the age of fourteen he got into Hopkins School, which helped prepare pupils for the renowned Yale University. Philanthropist Alfred Cope heard about this talented student and offered to pay his college fees. Bouchet graduated from Yale in 1874, coming sixth out of a class of 124, and in 1876, he completed his PhD in Geometrical Optics, becoming the first African American to gain a PhD from an American university.

Despite his qualifications, Bouchet could not get a university job because of his colour. He moved to Philadelphia where he worked at the Institute for Colored Youth, teaching chemistry and physics for twenty-six years. In 1902 the board changed the school's focus to industrial education, part of a controversial policy to steer young Black people away from academic subjects. Bouchet lost his job, but he continued teaching at other institutions.

Bouchet died in 1918 and his achievements are at last being commemorated. The American Physical Society now awards an Edward A. Bouchet Award for outstanding contribution to physics. On 30 September 1988, the Edward Bouchet Abdus Salam Institute (EBASI) was founded. It is a scientific organization with the aim of promoting collaboration between African and American physicists and encouraging the training of physicists from the African continent.

1 OCTOBER - MICHAELA COEL

Michaela Coel is an acclaimed British writer and actor. She was born Michaela Ewuraba Boakye-Collinson on 1 October 1987 in London, to Ghanaian parents, who brought her up in a religious Pentecostal household.

Coel began her writing career as Michaela the Poet in 2006, performing at open mic nights. She started a degree in English literature and theology at the University of Birmingham, then transferred to a degree in acting at the prestigious Guildhall School of Music and Drama, where her talent earned her a Laurence Olivier Bursary. For her final year graduation project she wrote the play *Chewing Gum Dreams*. After graduation Coel took on leading roles at the National Theatre. She developed and performed her play as a theatre show, and then as the sitcom *Chewing Gum* for television, for which she won the BAFTA for Best Female Comedy Performance and the BAFTA for Breakthrough Talent for her writing.

Coel has gained international acclaim as a writer and as a film and television actor. In 2020 she created, wrote, co-directed, starred in and produced the comedy-drama *I May Destroy You*, informed by her own experience of sexual assault, which went on to win five BAFTAs and two Emmy Awards. Her win for Outstanding Writing for a Limited Series, Movie or Dramatic Special made her the first Black woman to be awarded an Emmy in that category.

Coel has had film roles in *Star Wars: The Last Jedi* and *Black Panther: Wakanda Forever*. In 2022 she was elected a fellow of the Royal Society of Literature.

2 OCTOBER - GIORGIO MARINCOLA

Born in Somalia in 1923, Giorgio Marincola was an Afro-Italian anti-fascist hero of the Second World War. The children of an Italian colonial officer and a Somali woman, Marincola and his younger sister Isabella were, in an extremely unusual move, fully acknowledged by their father and sent to Italy to be raised by relatives in Calabria.

After their father returned to Italy, the children moved to Rome to live with him, his new wife and their half siblings. Initially attracted to a career in medicine, Marincola's path changed when he encountered the partisan group Partito d'Azione through philosophy professor Pilo Albertelli, who was a founding member. In 1943 he joined their armed wing and executed raids and sabotage missions against the occupying Nazi forces. Taken prisoner by the SS in 1945, Marincola's captors tried to force him to speak against the partisans on the radio, but instead he spoke for freedom. Sounds of the beating he received could be heard on the broadcast.

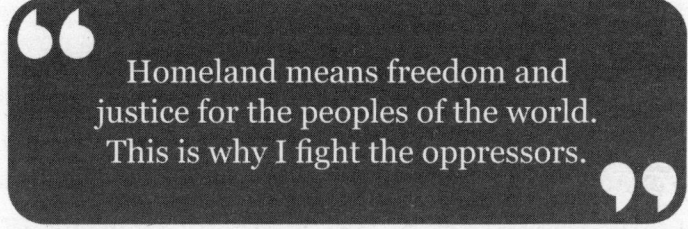

Homeland means freedom and justice for the peoples of the world. This is why I fight the oppressors.

In April 1945 the Nazis in Italy were defeated and Marincola was freed. He chose to continue to fight and headed north with the partisans to free the last few occupied cities. On 4 May 1945 Marincola was killed along with twenty-five others at a Nazi checkpoint.

Marincola was posthumously awarded the Medaglia d'Oro al Valor Militare, Italy's highest military honour, on 2 October 1952. Following the BLM protests in 2020, a motion to have a new metro station in Rome named in his honour was passed.

TIMELINE 6

3 OCTOBER - THE AKSUMITE EMPIRE

The ancient Kingdom of Aksum lay in what is now northern Ethiopia between around 100CE and 940CE. It was an important trading nation and controlled trade routes that linked Africa with Rome, Arabia, Mesopotamia and India.

In around 270CE the Aksumites began minting their own coins, making them the earliest African nation to do so. The kingdom also became the first Christian state in the world and the sign of the cross appeared on its coins. They spoke a language called Ge'ez which they wrote using a modified form of Arabic writing. This writing appears on carved stone obelisks they erected as gravestones to mark the tombs of kings and nobles.

As the kingdom grew in wealth and power it expanded north into Nubia and east across the Red Sea and into southern Arabia, creating the Aksumite Empire and making them the rivals of the Romans and the Persians, who were the other major powers at the time. The kings of Aksum saw themselves as protectors of Christianity but are also remembered in Islam as protectors of the early Muslim community. Aksum was weakened by war with Persia during the late 500s. The rise of Islam in 610 transformed the region around Aksum and largely cut it off from the medieval Christian world. However, the Ethiopian Orthodox Tewahedo Church persisted and still exists today. Furthermore, the kings of Ethiopia, until its monarchy was abolished in 1975, all took the Aksumite title of Atse (Emperor).

4 OCTOBER - ULRIC CROSS

The Royal Air Force navigator, legal scholar and diplomat, Ulric Cross, was born on the Caribbean island of Trinidad on 1 May 1917. In 1941, during the Second World War, he travelled to Britain and joined the Royal Air Force, where he trained to be a navigator. Once he completed his training, he was posted to the 139 Jamaica Squadron where his navigation skills shone. He was promoted to the rank of squadron leader and was invited to join the RAF's Pathfinder Force, an elite unit that took part in dangerous night missions to identify potential enemy bombing sites and mark them with flares to guide the following bombers.

Imperial War Museum, London (HU58315)

Cross received many commendations for his efforts. He was awarded the Distinguished Flying Cross in 1944 and the Distinguished Service Order in 1945 in recognition of his skill and commitment as an officer.

After the war, Cross stayed in Britain to study law. He then returned to Trinidad and began his career as an important legal writer and scholar, in demand in the Caribbean and in Africa. He became a judge and in 1990 was appointed as Trinidad and Tobago's ambassador to Britain. He died on 4 October 2013 at the age of ninety-six.

TIMELINE 6

5 OCTOBER ~ DESMOND TUTU

Library of Congress Prints and Photographs Division

Desmond Tutu was a South African peace, human rights and anti-apartheid campaigner. He was also the first Black African person to become Bishop of Johannesburg and Archbishop of Cape Town.

Tutu was born on 7 October 1931 in Klerksdorp, South Africa. During his childhood he became ill with the polio virus, which left him with permanent damage to his right hand. His father was a school principal and education was important to the family. They were also a religious family and Tutu became involved in the Church. When he left school Tutu trained as a teacher, but in the mid-1950s decided to leave teaching and trained to become a priest in the country's Anglican Church instead. In 1962, the Church sent Tutu to England to train as a future leader. When he returned to Africa in 1966 he became a lecturer, working at religious colleges and universities in South Africa and then in Botswana. He enjoyed working in organizations that brought different religious groups together to cooperate and campaign for human rights. By the 1970s he was becoming the leader he had trained to be, and was becoming known internationally for his work campaigning for the end of the apartheid system of racial segregation in South Africa.

On 5 October 1984 it was announced that Tutu was being awarded the Nobel Peace Prize for his work campaigning

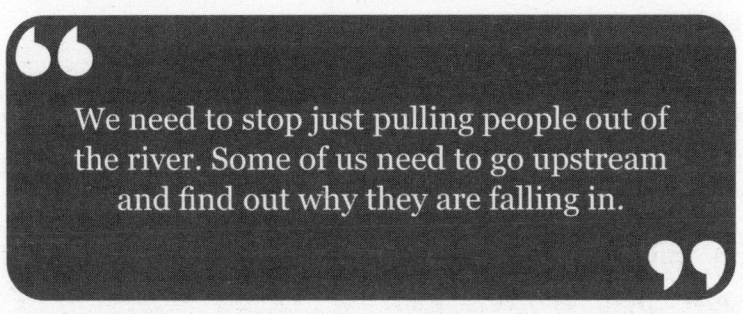

> 66
> We need to stop just pulling people out of the river. Some of us need to go upstream and find out why they are falling in.
> 99

against apartheid. A year later, in 1985, Tutu became Bishop of Johannesburg and, the year after, became the Archbishop of Cape Town and the most senior leader in the Anglican Church in South Africa. In 1990, the South African president F. W. de Klerk ordered the release of the anti-apartheid leader Nelson Mandela (see 5 August), who had been kept imprisoned by the government for twenty-seven years. Mandela and Tutu then worked together, leading the negotiations that would eventually see the end of apartheid and the first truly democratic elections in South Africa in 1994, in which adult citizens, regardless of their colour, had the right to vote. Mandela was elected as the new president and he appointed Tutu to lead the country's Truth and Reconciliation Commission, investigating the violence and killings by the authorities and different political groups that had happened during the decades under apartheid (see 12 September). Tutu retired in 2010 and died on 26 December 2021 at the age of ninety.

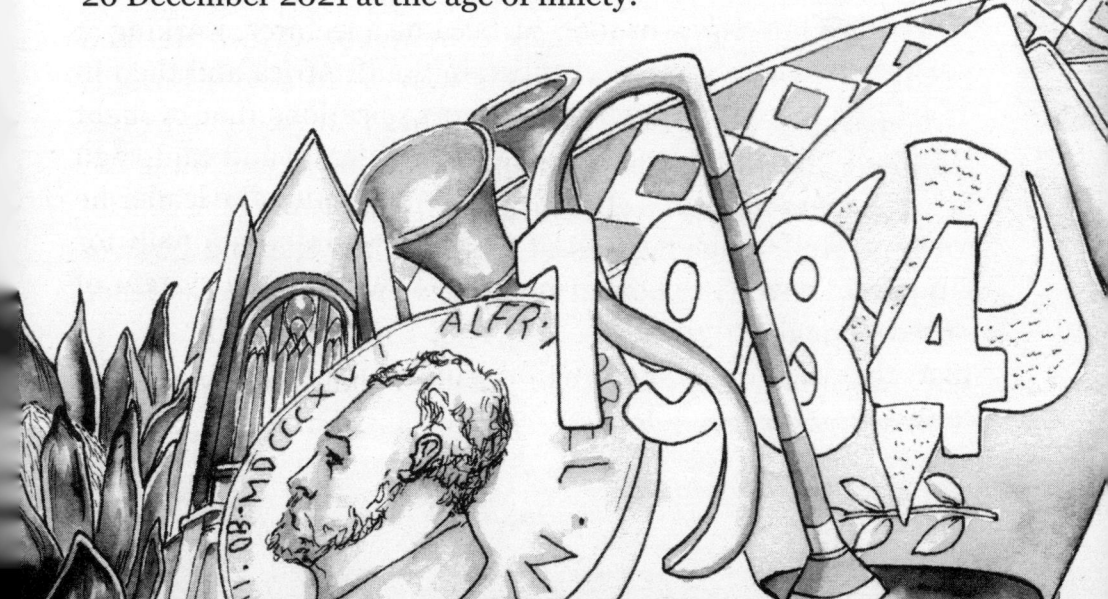

6 OCTOBER - THE FISK JUBILEE SINGERS

On 6 October 1871 a group of African American students from Fisk University, Nashville, Tenessee, began a tour which would, over the next seven years, take them all over the world.

Despite having a number of generous benefactors, Fisk University could not afford to offer education to the numbers of recently freed Black people, and was in danger of closure. The fundraising tour was the idea of the university's music teacher. The choir – the Fisk Jubilee Singers – held performances along the route

(American Missionary Association, 1872
James Wallace Black, Library of Congress)

Studio portrait of the original Fisk Jubilee Singers: Isaac P Dickerson, Georgia Gordon, Benjamin Holmes, Jennie Jackson, Julia Jackson, Mabel Lewis, Maggie L. Porter, Thomas Rutling, Ella Shepard, Minnie Tate and Edmund Watkins

of the Underground Railroad (see 18 September) and worked their way north. After a difficult start, their popularity grew and in 1872 they sang for president Grant at the White House. This success led to an invitation to tour Europe.

Shortly after their arrival in Britain in 1873, they sang for Queen Victoria. White experience of Black musical performance had previously been limited to minstrelsy (see 19 March) but the Jubilee Singers chose to perform spiritual songs, rarely performed outside of the Black community. Critics warmed to this new music and the singers were feted across Europe. Although they performed for several heads of state and royal families many of their performances were small and intimate, held for community and church groups. One event in the coastal town of Hull, England was at a school for training boys of families in poverty to be mariners. This tiny and poor audience raised enough to gift a book to Fisk University's library. By 1878 this kind of small donation from the general public had raised $150,000 and ensured Fisk University's future.

7 OCTOBER - EVELYN DOVE

Evelyn Mary Dove was born in London on 11 January 1902 to an English mother and Sierra Leonean father. Her father was a barrister, and Evelyn had a comfortable childhood and a good education. She attended the prestigious Royal Academy of Music, where she studied piano, singing and elocution. She began her career working in all-Black orchestras and revue shows, touring Britain, Europe, India and America.

By the late 1930s Dove was also appearing on the radio, and she became the first ever Black singer to feature on BBC Radio. She starred with singer Edric Connor in over fifty episodes of the musical variety radio show *Serenade in Sepia*. During the Second World War her radio performances would entertain the troops, and she became even more popular and well known.

After the war Dove became one of the first Black people to appear on British television when she performed in a television special featuring Black entertainers. The show, *Variety in Sepia*, was broadcast on 7 October 1947, live from the RadiOlympia Theatre at Alexandra Palace in London.

Evelyn's older brother Frank Dove was a decorated First World War veteran and an Oxford-educated barrister, who represented Britain in boxing at the 1920 Olympics in Antwerp, Belgium. Her younger half-sister, Mabel Dove Danquah, was a pioneering Ghanaian author, journalist and politician, whose work was included in anthologies of African writing edited by Langston Hughes (see 1 February) and Margaret Busby (see 9 May).

DID YOU KNOW?

8 OCTOBER ~ WANGARI MUTA MAATHAI

On 8 October 2004, the Nobel Committee announced that Kenyan environmental activist Wangari Muta Maathai had won the Nobel Peace Prize. She was the first African woman recipient and the first environmental activist to receive the prize.

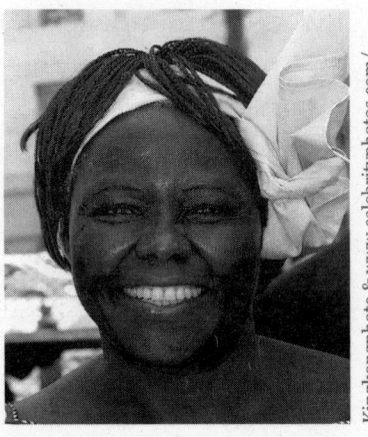

Kingkongphoto & www.celebrityphotos.com/ Wikimedia Commons

Born Wangari Muta in April 1940 in the Kenyan village of Ihithe, she started school aged eight. She excelled at learning and, at the age of twenty, was selected as one of the 300 students for the Kennedy Airlift programme to study in America. There she studied biology and environmental science and learned about work to tackle pollution and environmental damage. She went on to study for a doctorate, firstly in Germany and then at the University of Nairobi, Kenya. There, in 1971, she became the first woman in East and Central Africa to be awarded a PhD, and started her career as an academic.

Now married, Muta Maathai became the first woman in East and Central Africa to become the head of a university department and to become an assistant professor. She joined the National Council of Women of Kenya, and in 1976 began the work that would win her the Nobel Prize. She founded the Green Belt Movement in 1977, which brought women in Kenya together to plant trees. Since then over 51 million trees have been planted and over 30,000 women trained in sustainable trades. In 1998 she founded the Jubilee 2000 Coalition to campaign for poorer African countries to be given debt cancellation.

Muta Maathai died in September 2011, aged seventy-one, having won many prizes for her pioneering work.

9 OCTOBER ~ BENJAMIN BANNEKER

Benjamin Banneker was born in 1731 in Baltimore, Maryland to freed parents. He was taught to read and write by his grandmother, who had come from England to America as an indentured servant, and he had some education at a small nearby school. But it was his own drive for knowledge that led him to design and construct a clock, and his fascination with mathematics and astronomy that led him to write his almanacs and also garnered him a position as assistant surveyor on the project to construct Washington DC in 1791.

Although the abolitionist movement was gathering momentum, the view that Black people were intellectually inferior was still firmly in place. Banneker found himself increasingly angered by the way in which his work was seen through the lens of race.

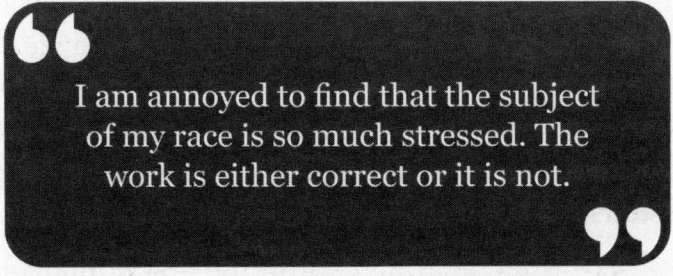

> I am annoyed to find that the subject of my race is so much stressed. The work is either correct or it is not.

He sent a copy of his first almanac to then secretary of state, Thomas Jefferson, along with a letter outlining Jefferson's hypocrisy as an owner of enslaved people, and his erroneous views on Black inferiority. The exchange had little impact on Jefferson's actions, but in his next almanac Banneker published the letters and the subject of abolition was pushed back into the spotlight. However, as a free man in a state where slavery was still legal, Banneker was aware of his vulnerability and his later publications omitted further discussion of abolition.

Banneker published his last almanac in 1797 and sold his farm to fund his retirement. He died on 9 October 1806.

10 OCTOBER - HIMMLER'S NEGRO REGISTRATION ORDER

In the years following the First World War, Black Germans experienced an increase in racism. Many had settled in Germany from its African colonies, many had been born in Germany, in particular in the Rhineland area where a number of French Colonial troops had been stationed during the war, but the growth and influence of the Nazi Party became an existential threat.

Although the Jewish population were the primary targets of the Nazi ideology, the scope of Nazi policy widened to include other minority groups. Whether born in Germany or not, Black Germans, along with Sinti and Roma people, found that their identity papers suddenly labelled them 'racial aliens' and that they were now subject to the regime's ambition of racial purification. To prevent further increase of the Black German population, the Nuremberg Race Laws were extended in 1935 to outlaw interracial relationships between Africans and white Germans. In 1937 the Ministry of the Interior sterilized 385 of the Black youths of the Rhineland to ensure that they would not reproduce.

On 10 October 1942, Heinrich Himmler, chief of police, issued his Order for the Registration of all Negroes. In 1938 a similar registration order had been made for Sinti and Roma people, most of whom were then sent to the death camps. While Himmler did not follow through the Registration Order with systematic extermination in this case, Black Germans were still imprisoned in camps, subjected to sterilization and increasing violence and persecution. Those that could, left, and others went into hiding.

11 OCTOBER - THE MORANT BAY REBELLION

The Morant Bay Rebellion took place in October 1865 in Jamaica. Tensions had been rising between the island's Black population and the white authorities. Black people began to protest their poor living conditions, and the lack of democracy on the island – the local government, the Jamaican Assembly, was dominated by white planters and Black people were not allowed to vote.

The rebellion was sparked when a poor Black man was accused in court of trespassing on a plantation. A series of protests at the man's unfair treatment led to fighting between locals and police and, on 11 October, a local preacher called Paul Bogle led hundreds of protestors to the courthouse demanding justice. The militia opened fire and uproar broke out. The courthouse was set on fire and eighteen militia and seven protestors were killed.

The island's governor, Edward John Eyre, retaliated brutally. He declared martial law on 13 October and sent in troops who killed hundreds of Black people, including women and children. More than four hundred people were shot dead or hanged, and their bodies strung up to warn off others. Hundreds more were arrested and later executed, including Bogle, who was hanged on 24 October.

A Royal Commission inquiry after the event was critical of Governor Eyre and he was dismissed from his post. The Jamaican Assembly was abolished, and Jamaica became a Crown Colony, directly ruled by Britain until it gained its independence in 1962. In 1969 Jamaica officially named Paul Bogle a national hero.

12 OCTOBER - OLA HUDSON

Ola Oliver was born on 12 October 1946. Raised in California, she started her career as a dancer and studied in Los Angeles, Switzerland and then London, where she married and became Ola Hudson. She moved away from dance and into modelling which, fortuitously, introduced her to the world of fashion, where her talent flourished.

Hudson moved back to Los Angeles in the early 1970s and opened her own shop, Skitzo, on the Sunset Strip. Her reputation as a designer grew and she began producing work for many famous musicians, including the Pointer Sisters and John Lennon. It is her work with David Bowie that she is most remembered for. After Bowie famously 'killed off' his Ziggy Stardust persona he collaborated with Hudson on reinventing himself. The sharp 1940s tailoring imbued with a 1970s feel that characterized Bowie's new persona, the Thin White Duke, was Hudson's creation. The look was showcased in the film *The Man Who Fell to Earth* and was translated to the stage for Bowie's live tours. Some of Hudson's designs from this period are held at MoMA in New York.

Hudson died in 2009 after battling lung cancer.

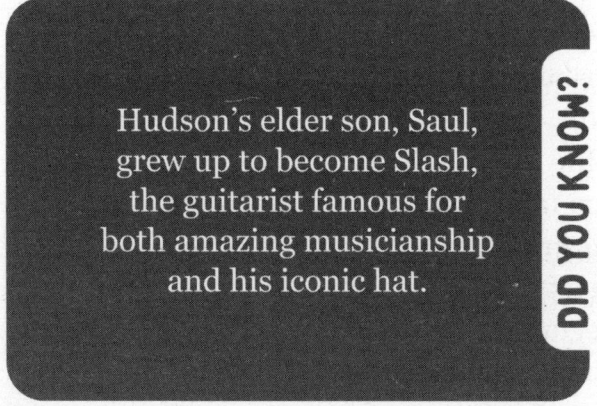

Hudson's elder son, Saul, grew up to become Slash, the guitarist famous for both amazing musicianship and his iconic hat.

DID YOU KNOW?

13 OCTOBER ~ ANGELA DAVIS

In 1970, writer and scholar Angela Davis was on Wanted posters all across America, the third woman ever to appear on the FBI's Top Ten Most Wanted Fugitives list. Guns she owned had been used by a young Black student who held a California courtroom at gunpoint on 7 August 1970. In the incident he and three others were killed. Although she had not been present, a warrant for her arrest was issued in relation to charges of aggravated kidnapping and conspiracy to murder.

© Bernard Gotfryd, Library of Congress

Davis went into hiding, but was captured by the FBI on 13 October 1970 in New York, and was imprisoned for over a year. She maintained her innocence and, outside of the prison walls, a nationwide campaign, Black People in Defense of Angela Davis, was set up to free her. When she was found innocent and freed in June 1972, Davis continued her work as an activist and academic.

Born in Birmingham, Alabama, in 1944, one of Davis's first experiences of activism was protesting against racial segregation. She also personally knew the four Black girls killed in the 16th Street Baptist Church bombing in 1963. Growing up in this atmosphere, Davis was drawn to Marxism and Communism. She attended university in the USA, France and Germany and continued her political education. By 1969 she had begun her academic career and her work as an author. She continues to write about Black and Queer liberation, Marxism and her opposition to the death penalty and the prison–industrial complex.

14 OCTOBER - ANTON WILHELM AMO

Dutch missionaries in Axim (Ghana) often sent children to Europe to receive a Christian education, and this is probably how Anton Wilhelm Amo, 18th-century philosopher and lecturer, ended up in Germany. Born in Axim in 1703, Amo was gifted to the household of the Duke of Braunschweig-Wolfenbüttel. In 1708 he was adopted and baptized and 1721 church records name him as Anthon Wilhelm Rudolph Mohre.

Amo undertook and excelled in his Christian education. He studied philosophy at Halle University and went on to Wittenberg University, where he graduated as magister of philosophy (PhD) in 1734, the first African to gain a doctorate from a European university. He returned to Halle as a lecturer and in 1738 published his *Treatise on the Art of Studying Philosophy with Sobriety and Exactitude*. Unfortunately Amo fell foul of the university authorities when he held lectures discussing the work of banned political philosopher Christian Wolff. Under pressure, he left for a post at the University of Jena and some time later returned to Ghana.

Amo was generally well liked and respected by peers and students, but as the first and only African philosopher at that time he was also isolated and vulnerable. His African heritage was clearly important to him: the first dissertation he submitted at Halle argued on the illegality of the European slave trade, and he often signed his correspondance as 'Anton Wilhelm Amo, African'. His critics heaped praise upon him while his actions reflected well on his noble adoptive family, but his misstep resulted in personal attack and public ridicule.

His work has mostly been lost, sadly including his work on the slave trade, and Amo himself largely forgotten. In 1975 Halle University finally installed a commemorative plaque for him and in 1994 began offering a prize in his name.

15 OCTOBER ~ THOMAS SANKARA

Thomas Sankara was an African revolutionary who came to power in what was Upper Volta in 1983. Fellow revolutionary Blaise Compaoré led the August Revolution to remove the government and allow Sankara to take the presidency. One of Sankara's first acts was to change the country's name to Burkina Faso, which translates as 'Land of the Upright People'. The country had seen a series of dictators decided by military coups d'état since it became a self-governing colony in 1958 and gained independence in 1960, and many of these regimes had been corrupt.

Sankara's Pan-African and Marxist philosophies shaped the direction of his reforms. He demanded both transparency and accountability from government to combat corruption. An environmentalist ahead of his time, he began a tree planting programme (10.5 million trees in fifteen months) to halt the spread of the encroaching desert. He outlawed forced marriages, polygamy and FGM and placed many women in positions of power. His targeted social reform programme raised literacy rates from 13% to 73% in just four years and cut the child mortality rate in half. Determined to grant Burkina Faso a true independence, Sankara cut the last ties with France and took a stance against the IMF. This move was not received well.

On 15 October 1987 Sankara was murdered. Compaoré took power and ruled for twenty-seven years until being deposed. In 2022 a trial found him guilty of Sankara's murder. President Macron of France promised to declassify documents about Sankara in 2017 to aid investigation but, as yet, they have not been released.

16 OCTOBER ~ JOHN CARLOS AND TOMMIE SMITH

At the Summer Olympics in Mexico City, on 16 October 1968, two Black American athletes walked to the Olympic podium to receive their medals. Twenty-four-year-old Tommie Smith had won the gold medal in the men's 200m race, setting an Olympic record time of 19.8 seconds which stood until the 1984 games. His teammate, twenty-three-year-old John Carlos, had won bronze. What happened next would change their lives and would produce one of the most iconic images in sporting history.

Smith and Carlos were Olympic teammates, but before that they had been students together at San José State University. In 1967, a Black sociology professor at San José, Dr Harry Edwards, had set up the Olympic Project for Human Rights (OPHR) which Smith and Carlos joined. The aim of the OPHR was to protest and draw attention to racial discrimination in sport and to campaign for civil rights in America and around the world. As the 1968 Olympics drew closer, the OPHR tried to persuade Black American athletes to boycott the games. Eventually it was decided that they would attend but that they would each try to make some sort of civil rights protest to draw attention to their cause.

Smith and Carlos were both selected for the US Olympic team and earned their medals. As they waited in the changing rooms to go out for the podium ceremony, Smith and Carlos prepared to seize their chance while the world's cameras were watching them. Both men wore the badge of the OPHR on their tracksuit tops. They removed their shoes and wore black socks to symbolize the poverty in which Black communities were made to live. To symbolize Black pride Smith wore a black scarf around his neck. Carlos wore beads around his neck to symbolize the many Black lives taken during slavery and in lynchings, where Black people were killed by racist mobs.

To symbolize solidarity with working-class people, Carlos also unzipped his tracksuit top. The final items they had both planned to wear were black gloves but Carlos soon realized that he had forgotten his. With them in the changing room was the silver medal winner, Australian sprinter Peter Norman. Norman supported the cause of the OPHR and asked to borrow an OPHR badge to wear in solidarity. It was Norman who then suggested that Smith and Carlos should split the gloves and wear one each.

Bettmann/Getty Images

That evening, the athletes made their way to the podium, Smith and Carlos carrying their shoes. The ceremony began and the three men took their places on the podium where each was awarded his medal. As the national anthem of the United States began to play, Smith and Carlos each raised a black gloved hand towards the sky, while bending their heads towards the ground. This type of silent gesture was widely known as the 'Black Power Salute', a political symbol of Black protest against racism. Its appearance on the winners podium at the Olympics shocked and even outraged many people, and Smith and Carlos were booed as they left the arena.

Their image was on newspaper front pages all over the world the next day, and for both men the response to the protest was severe. Many people argued that politics should be kept out of sport and that Smith and Carlos had been disrespectful. Others argued that politics and racism were already part of sport. For example, it was due to pressure from the OPHR and political organizations such as the **African National Congress** (ANC) that South Africa had recently been banned from the Olympics because of its **apartheid** system of racial **segregation**. The chairman of the International Olympic Committee threatened to send the United States team home unless they suspended Smith and Carlos, and he banned them from the Olympic Village. When they returned home it was to anger and even death threats. Although they both stayed in athletics, eventually becoming coaches, both men lost out on jobs and opportunities for years to come, until attitudes to their protest began to change.

The image of their protest is now one of the most famous of all time. Indeed, in 2021 *Life* magazine named it as one of the top 100 photographs that changed the world. In 2005, *Victory Salute*, a statue in their honour, was erected at San José State University. Its inscription reads:

> At the Mexico City 1968 Olympic Games, San José Student-Athletes Tommie Smith and John Carlos stood for justice, dignity, equality and peace. Hereby the university and associated students commemorate their legacy.

17 OCTOBER - BILL RICHMOND

Bill Richmond, sometimes called the world's first Black sportstar, was born enslaved in Staten Island, New York in 1763. During the American Revolutionary War, he liberated himself. Escaping to join the British, he enlisted under the command of General Hugh Percy to serve as a stablehand. After witnessing Richmond win a fight against an officer and two soldiers who had racially abused  him, Percy made Richmond his valet and had him fight as entertainment for his guests. When Percy returned to England, he took Richmond with him.

Percy arranged an apprenticeship for Richmond with a Yorkshire cabinetmaker and ensured that he was taught to read and write. After his apprenticeship, Richmond, now married to his English wife Mary, moved to London where he worked in the household of Thomas Pitt, Second **Baron** Camelford. Pitt was interested in boxing and the two attended fights together. At one fight Richmond challenged the boxer George Maddox to a fight; Maddox won but it took him nine rounds to do so.

When Pitt died in 1804, Richmond, now in his forties, embarked on a career as a Georgian bare-knuckle boxer. He soon became known as one of England's most formidable boxers and won seventeen of his nineteen professional fights. Soon after his loss in an epic battle with Tom Cribb in October 1805 he retired. He forged a career outside of the ring, opening his own boxing academy. Among others, he trained writers Lord Byron and William Hazlitt, and the Black boxer Tom Molineaux.

18 OCTOBER - TOM MORELLO

Tom Morello is a musician and activist. His American mother, Mary Morello, met his Kenyan father, Ngethe Njoroge (a cousin of Kenya's first democratically elected president, Jomo Kenyatta), in Kenya in 1963. Their son was born in Harlem, New York in 1964. As a teen Morello discovered his passion for music and politics. After graduating with a degree in political science from Harvard University, he worked to become a professional musician.

Morello has been a guitarist, a singer and a songwriter in many influential rock bands. In 1991 he, singer Zack de la Rocha, bassist Tim Commerford and drummer Brad Wilk formed the group Rage Against the Machine (RATM); a band for whom music was a form of political activism and protest. On 18 October 2000, just before the release of their fourth album, RATM split when de la Rocha announced his departure from the band. Morello, Commerford and Wilk went on to form the group Audioslave with singer Chris Cornell between 2001 and 2007. Morello also formed the supergroup Street Sweeper Social Club with the rapper Boots Riley and has pursued a solo career under the name of the Nightwatchman.

Morello continues to campaign for workers' rights and against racism and fascism. In 2002, after seeing racist symbols at the music festival Ozzfest, he and fellow musician Serj Tankian, of the rock group System of a Down, set up the non-profit, social justice organization, Axis of Justice. It aims to bring music fans, musicians and grassroots activism together to promote social justice, anti-racist and anti-fascist causes.

19 OCTOBER - IDIA, BENIN WARRIOR QUEEN

Queen Idia was the wife of Oba Ozolua, who reigned over the Benin Empire, in what is now Nigeria, from 1483–1514. When Ozolua died their two sons, Esigie and Arhuaran, fought each other for control of the empire. Civil war broke out and the neighbouring Igala people saw an opportunity to take Benin's northern territories, sending their warriors across the Benue River.

The Michael C. Rockefeller Memorial Collection, Gift of Nelson A. Rockefeller, 1972, WikiCommons

Bone and ivory mask of Queen Idia, 16th century

Queen Idia chose to support Esigie in his bid to become Oba, and she was instrumental in his success. She raised an army, advised him on military and political strategies and even led warriors into battle, gaining a reputation as a fearless warrior queen. Idia was thought to have magical powers and she used her knowledge of medicine to help her son. With her support, Esigie defeated the Igala warriors to regain Benin's land and won a victory over his brother to become the sixteenth Oba of the Benin Empire.

Oba Esigie rewarded his mother by creating a new position of Queen Mother, called the 'iyoba'. Intricate masks and heads, made of ivory, iron, copper and brass were made in Idia's honour. In February 1897 they were among thousands of statues looted from Benin City by the British Army (see 9 February). The Benin Ivory Masks, a set of four miniatures of Idia, and three of the larger brass heads, are currently held in museums in Britain, the USA and Germany. An international campaign continues for their return to Nigeria.

20 OCTOBER - MARY PRINCE

Mary Prince was an abolitionist campaigner whose autobiography, *The History of Mary Prince, A West Indian Slave. As Related by Herself*, became a bestselling book in Victorian Britain.

Born into slavery in 1788 on the island of Bermuda in the Caribbean, Prince was bought and sold by a number of different slave owners across the West Indies during her childhood. In 1828, when her owner was planning on travelling to Britain, Prince asked to come too.

On arrival in England Prince left her household and was allowed to stay at the Moravian church in Hatton Garden, London. There she met the abolitionist Thomas Pringle, who was secretary of the Anti-Slavery Society. He encouraged her to tell the story of her life, and so Prince began dictating her life story to fellow abolitionist, Susanna Stickland. Pringle became the book's editor.

Real-life stories like Prince's were known as slave narratives, and they were an important part of the work of the abolitionist movement to help educate the public about the realities of slavery. When the book came out in 1831, Prince became the first Black woman to have a slave narrative published in Britain. The book was an instant success and helped to gather more public support for the anti-slavery movement in Britain. In 2007 a plaque in her honour was put up on a building in Bloomsbury, London where Prince had once lived.

21 OCTOBER ~ THE 1945 PAN-AFRICAN CONGRESS

The fifth Pan-African Congress took place from 15–21 October 1945, in Manchester, England. The Congresses were a series of meetings held to promote unity between African people and those of African descent around the world. In total eight congresses have been held between 1919 and 2014.

The fifth Congress came at the end of the Second World War and was probably the most important. This was a crucial time for colonial powers and colonized peoples. The Allies had fought the war supposedly in the name of freedom. Yet for millions of people living under colonial rule, freedom of their countries for self-rule and self-determination was still to be fought for.

The congress brought together a hugely influential group of people who laid the foundations for independence for many African countries. Among the ninety delegates were future leaders like Jomo Kenyatta, who became the first president of Kenya in 1964, and Kwame Nkrumah, later the president of Ghana in 1957 (see 1 July), who had helped to organize the congress. They debated the end of colonization with intellectuals and civil rights activists such as W. E. B. Du Bois (see 23 February) and Amy Ashwood Garvey (see 11 May). A statement issued by the congress read:

> We are determined to be free. We want education. We want the right to earn a decent living; the right to express our thoughts and emotions, to adopt and create forms of beauty.

A red plaque now marks the occasion at Chorlton Town Hall in Manchester.

22 OCTOBER ~ STORMZY

British grime rapper Michael Ebenezer Kwadjo Omari Owuo Jr., known by the stage name Stormzy, was still an unsigned act when he won Best Grime Act at the MOBO Awards (see 18 November) on 22 October 2014. A year later he performed 'Shut Up' at the Anthony Joshua vs. Dillian Whyte boxing match and the track shot up the charts, giving Stormzy his first hit and propelling him into fame.

Raph_PH, Wikimedia Commons

Stormzy has used his platform to uplift his community and is renowned for his outspoken views as much as his music. He has talked of the narrow perception of Black British culture and of how it is often swamped by Black American culture, and so he took the opportunity to highlight the breadth and distinctiveness of Black British art in 2019 when he headlined at the Glastonbury music festival. Wearing a Union Jack stab vest by artist Banksy, he appeared on a stage designed to reflect the architecture of his home town, Croydon. The show included ballet dancers, a gospel choir, fellow musicians and words from author Malorie Blackman (see 14 January) and MP David Lammy (see 19 July).

Stormzy continues to champion Black excellence. He founded the Stormzy Scholarship to fund Black students at Cambridge University, and in 2018 launched his publishing imprint #Merky Books to encourage new voices into the publishing industry.

23 OCTOBER ~ ABRAM PETROVICH HANNIBAL

In 18th-century Europe a Black child was considered the 'must have' fashion accessory among the nobility. Taken from his home at seven years old and gifted to Czar Peter the Great of Russia, Abram Petrovich Hannibal grew up to become an internationally celebrated military general and engineer.

Adopted and baptized by the Czar in 1705, Hannibal took on his name, 'Petrovich'. He spent his childhood travelling Europe with his adoptive father and in 1716 was sent to school in Paris to study engineering. When war broke out across Europe Hannibal joined the French forces, entering the military academy at La Fère in 1720. He gained both the rank of captain and the name of Hannibal, after the great Carthaginian general, and was referred to as 'the dark star of the Enlightenment'.

He returned to Moscow in 1723 and became an engineer and teacher, but when the Czar died two years later, he found himself out of favour and exiled to Siberia. With the ascension of Czarina Elizabeth to the Russian throne in 1741, Hannibal was back in favour and was given military command of Tallinn in Estonia. He completed a string of engineering projects across the empire and rose to the rank of general before retiring in 1762 to his farm estate in northern Russia.

Hannibal's extraordinary life was immortalized in *The Negro of Peter the Great* by his great-grandson, Russian novelist Alexander Pushkin. However, this incomplete and semi-fictional account still leaves many mysteries about his origins. Ethiopia and Eritrea have both claimed him as theirs, but recent research has named his birthplace as Cameroon. It was Cameroon's ambassador who, along with French, Russian and Estonian dignitaries, on 23 October 2010 attended the unveiling of a plaque to Hannibal at the site of the military academy at La Fère, each country staking a claim to this extraordinary historical figure.

24 OCTOBER - JOHN HAWKINS

In October of 1562, the Englishman John Hawkins (a cousin of Sir Francis Drake) set sail on the first of three journeys to the west coast of Africa. He was an experienced sailor and trader, but on this journey he would become the first Englishman to make a fortune by trading in enslaved African people. On the way he engaged in privateering, attacking Portuguese ships and stealing their cargoes – the Portuguese had been trading in enslaved people for some time, supplying the Spanish colonies in the Caribbean and South America. Hawkins plundered their ships, and took the enslaved people as well as their treasure and other cargo. At the Sierra Leone River in Africa, he traded for goods and added to his human cargo by seizing African people by force and dealing with slave traders. Hawkins then set sail for the island of Hispaniola (which is now modern-day Haiti and the Dominican Republic).

Hawkins came back to England in September 1563. The profits he had from trading in enslaved people and his other cargo had made him a rich man. He had shown that the English could join in the trade in enslaved people and make huge fortunes from it. This drew the attention of London's richest merchants and of Queen Elizabeth I herself. They invested money on his second extremely profitable journey in 1564, and the Queen provided two of her ships. Hawkins' third and final slave journey in 1567, however, ended in disaster. Of the five ships that set out, only two made it back to England after a fierce battle against Spanish ships off the coast of Mexico. After that, for the next century, instead of trading in enslaved people, English captains stuck to privateering, raiding foreign ships for their treasure and non-human cargo.

25 OCTOBER - THE YOUTH MARCH

In 1954 the US Supreme Court ruled against continued racial segregation in schools at the conclusion of the landmark Brown vs. Topeka case (see 16 May). Despite this ruling, many schools, particularly in the southern states, continued to educate Black children separately and attempts at integration were often met with violent protest from white students and their parents (see 4 September). To force the implementation of desegregation forward, A. Philip Randolf, organizer of the 1963 March on Washington (see 28 August), planned a Youth March for Integrated Schools, believing that a march led by the actual children being denied their rights might gain more support from the public. Letters of recruitment were sent to schools with the intention of mobilizing around 1,000 children.

US National Archives

On 25 October 1958, 10,000 children and adults marched to the Lincoln Memorial in Washington DC. Coretta Scott King delivered a speech prepared by her husband, Dr Martin Luther King, as he was recovering from a stab wound and unable to attend. Harry Belafonte (see 1 March) led a small delegation of children to the White House, but their request for an audience with President Eisenhower was denied. The marchers vowed to return.

> Keep marching and show the pessimists and the weak of spirit that they are wrong. Keep marching and don't let them silence you. Keep marching and resist injustice with the firm, non-violent spirit you demonstrated today.
>
> The future belongs, not to those who slumber or sleep, but to those who cannot rest while the evil of injustice thrives in the bosom of America. The future belongs to those who march toward freedom.
>
> Dr Martin Luther King Jr

A second march on 18 April 1959 rallied 26,000 participants. Another delegation managed to have an audience with the president's deputy assistant, who assured them that the president was anxious to see an end to discrimination. However anxious he may have been, when the opportunity was presented, the president and Congress failed to enhance laws that would have aided the process of integration.

Even without specific results the marches were important to the movement. Not only did they provide practice runs for the larger marches that followed in the 1960s, they also galvanized a youth wing within the SCLC, and in 1960 the Student Nonviolent Coordinating Committee (SNCC) was formed.

26 OCTOBER ~ THE BRITISH WEST INDIES REGIMENT

Three weeks after the start of the First World War, Britain's Colonial Office contacted the War Office. The Colonial Office had received many requests from people in the islands of the Caribbean who were keen to come to Britain's aid and join the war effort. Despite the fact that Britain desperately needed troops, the War Office rejected the idea of creating a West Indian regiment and they instructed the Colonial Office to discourage West Indian people from travelling

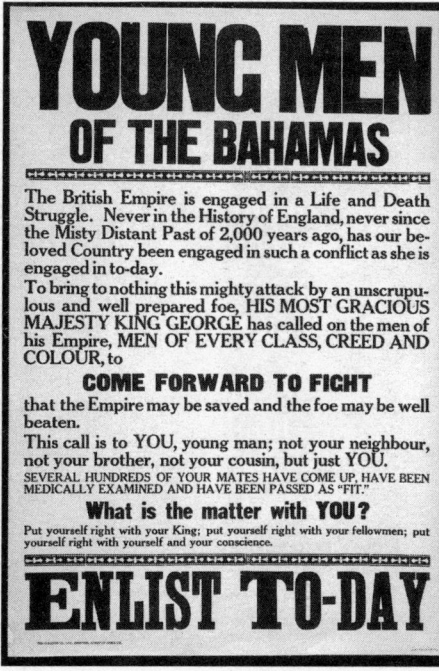

YOUNG MEN OF THE BAHAMAS

The British Empire is engaged in a Life and Death Struggle. Never in the History of England, never since the Misty Distant Past of 2,000 years ago, has our beloved Country been engaged in such a conflict as she is engaged in to-day.

To bring to nothing this mighty attack by an unscrupulous and well prepared foe, HIS MOST GRACIOUS MAJESTY KING GEORGE has called on the men of his Empire, MEN OF EVERY CLASS, CREED AND COLOUR, to

COME FORWARD TO FIGHT

that the Empire may be saved and the foe may be well beaten.

This call is to YOU, young man; not your neighbour, not your brother, not your cousin, but just YOU. SEVERAL HUNDREDS OF YOUR MATES HAVE COME UP, HAVE BEEN MEDICALLY EXAMINED AND HAVE BEEN PASSED AS "FIT."

What is the matter with YOU?

Put yourself right with your King; put yourself right with your fellowmen; put yourself right with yourself and your conscience.

ENLIST TO-DAY

Library of Congress Prints and Photographs Division, Wikimedia Commons

to Britain to join the armed forces. In the end, however, under pressure from King George V, on 19 May approval was finally given to create a West Indian regiment.

The very same day, a group of nine West Indian men, who had stowed away on a ship to reach Britain, landed at London's East End docks. They were arrested and taken to court, where they explained that they had come to Britain to volunteer for the British Army. They were brought back to court a week later, and although they were found guilty of being stowaways, they were freed and advised by the court clerk that a 'coloured regiment' was being formed in Cardiff that they could join. This turned out to be false, but on 26 October 1915 it was announced that the army would have a new unit where Black men from the West Indies could serve, led by white officers. It was called the British West Indies Regiment (BWIR) and on 31 October an appeal from King George V was read out in church services in the West Indies, calling for men to join it.

In action: West Indian troops stacking eight-inch shells at a dump on the Gordon Road, Ypres, October 1917

Over the course of the war a total of twelve battalions of the BWIR were raised, consisting of 397 officers and 15,204 men. The BWIR fought in Egypt and the Middle East. However, when some of their battalions were deployed in Europe their role was limited to that of a labour unit, carrying out important and often dangerous support roles, rather than joining their white counterparts fighting at the front line.

After the war the BWIR was sent with other battalions to Taranto, Italy, to await demobilization. It was during this post-combat period that the continued ill treatment by the British Army led the men to breaking point, and the Taranto Mutiny of 1918 began (see 6 December).

27 OCTOBER ~ OLIVER TAMBO

The lawyer and anti-apartheid campaigner Oliver Tambo was born on 27 October 1917 in Bizana, South Africa. As a university student, he was involved in organizing strikes and protests to fight for student rights. In 1944, with Nelson Madela and Walter Sisulu, he co-founded the Youth League of the ANC. Together they proposed a new 'Programme of Action', organizing strikes, boycotts and acts of civil disobedience.

In the early 1950s, Tambo partnered with Nelson Mandela to set up Mandela and Tambo, South Africa's first Black law firm. They became known for challenging apartheid laws and working pro bono when they represented poor clients in court. Tambo became deputy president of the ANC in 1958, and in 1960, after the Sharpeville Massacre (see 21 March) when the ANC was banned by the South African government, he went into exile. For thirty years he lived abroad, mainly spending his time in England. He became president of the ANC in 1969 and continued to run the party in exile, campaigning internationally for governments and organizations to put pressure on the South African government to end apartheid.

In 1990 the ban on the ANC was lifted and Tambo returned to South Africa. By then his health was deteriorating and in 1991 he stepped down as ANC president and was succeeded by Nelson Mandela. He died on 24 April 1993, just a year before the ANC won the country's first democratic elections and Mandela became president. In 2006, Johannesburg International Airport was renamed O. R. Tambo International Airport.

Rob C. Croes, , CCO/Fotocollectie Anefo, Nationaal Archief, The Netherlands

28 OCTOBER - CLEO LAINE

British singer and actress Cleo Laine was born on 28 October 1927 as Clementine Dinah Hitching to an English mother and Jamaican father. She was raised in London and as a child had singing and dancing lessons, but during her teenage years she meandered through a series of unfulfilling jobs before joining the the Johnny Dankworth  Seven jazz group in 1951. She and Dankworth married in 1958, becoming a high-profile interracial couple at a time of intense racial unrest.

After the Notting Hill Riots (see 29 August), the music newspaper *Melody Maker* issued an appeal for music audiences to speak out in opposition to racism. This sparked Laine, Dankworth and a host of musicians, actors and activists to form SCIF – The Stars Campaign for Interracial Friendship. They wrote and distributed papers and set up interracial clubs in defiance of the colour bar, and received support from Paul Robeson and Frank Sinatra. As an interracial couple, Laine and Dankworth became the faces of the campaign to defeat Notting Hill's White Defence League. Recognizing the power of celebrity endorsement and the reach of celebrity voices, SCIF aimed to combat prejudice and promote harmony, and provided a template for many future campaigns and organizations.

Laine's international singing and acting career has continued over seven decades, as has her activism. She has received many awards and accolades and in 1997 she was made Dame Commander of the Order of the British Empire.

29 OCTOBER - HENDRIK WITBOOI

At the Berlin conference (see 15 November), Germany awarded itself control and exploitation rights to South West Africa. There was already a small German settlement but 1889 saw the arrival of a colonial army and heralded the beginning of a period of extreme violence, during which over 130,000 of the Indigenous Nama, Herero and San people were murdered.

Hendrik Witbooi was one of the leaders of the Nama people. The Nama had been in conflict with the Herero people, but he recognized the greater threat that the colonists represented and proposed a plan for unity. This would have been disastrous for the colonists and so they offered the Nama a treaty, but Witbooi rejected it. His refusal was not received well and in April 1893 his people were massacred in a night-time attack. Witbooi retreated to the mountains and waged guerrilla warfare against the Germans until forced into a treaty a year later.

That treaty lasted until 1904 when Witbooi received news of an uprising by the Herero people and of their vicious slaughter at the hands of the Germans. The genocidal intent of the colonizers finally made clear, Witbooi started the Nama uprising. Knowing that they could not match the firepower of the Germans, the Nama used their knowledge of their country to mount ambushes and then melt away into the surrounding area. With a force of just 2,000 the Nama brought the 15,000-strong colonizing forces to the brink of defeat, but on 29 October 1905 Witbooi was fatally wounded during a raid. He died a few days later, and without his leadership the Nama forces splintered. During the following years the Nama and Herero were either shot on sight or forced into concentration camps where they died from exhaustion and disease. South West Africa remained a colony until control was handed over to South Africa in 1919. It was finally liberated and renamed Namibia in 1990.

30 OCTOBER - MARIE VAN BRITTAN BROWN

Born on 30 October 1922 in Queens, New York, Marie Van Brittan Brown invented an innovative security system in 1966. Her 'Home Security System Utilizing Television Surveillance' was granted a patent in 1969 and is now recognized as the first closed-circuit television security system (CCTV).

Because Brown was a nurse who worked different shifts from her husband, she often found herself alone in the house. Their neighbourhood had a high crime rate and Brown wanted to be able to see who was at her front door before she opened it. With support from her husband, who was an electrician, she devised a system with peepholes and a sliding camera that could capture an image of the person outside on television monitors. The system also included a two-way microphone, which allowed her to speak with them without opening the door.

Within just four days of having the patent granted, there was media and business interest in the invention. Brown continued to develop the system, adding an alarm button for contacting the police and a remote control feature for opening the door when the emergency services arrived. In recognition of the success of the invention, she received an award from the National Science Committee.

Marie Van Brittan Brown died in 1999 at the age of seventy-six. Her invention revolutionized home security systems and her surveillance features can be seen in the modern security systems used in many homes and businesses today.

31 OCTOBER ~ UK BLACK HISTORY MONTH

In October 1987 the first Black History Month was launched in the UK, led by Akyaaba Addai-Sebo, a special projects officer at the Greater London Council. Born in Ghana in 1950, in his youth, as part of Kwame Nkrumah's (see 1 July) Young Pioneers Movement, Addai-Sebo had travelled to study in America. While he was there he encountered and was inspired by 'Negro History Week', which had been celebrated in America every February since the 1920s.

In 1984, Addai-Sebo moved to the UK. He started working on the idea of creating an opportunity for Black British children to learn about their history and to give them a sense of pride and identity. Addai-Sebo thought that October would be the best month as it would be near the start of the academic year and children would not have any exams to do.

The first schools that celebrated Black History Month were in London, but soon other cities followed their lead. Black History Month is now celebrated all over the country with events happening in schools, libraries, museums and other public places. It gives everyone an opportunity to reflect upon the history and culture of Black British people and to mark their contribution to society. Black History Month continues, after nearly forty years, and increasingly Black history is being integrated by schools into their curricula all year round rather than being restricted to a single month every year.

TIMELINE 10

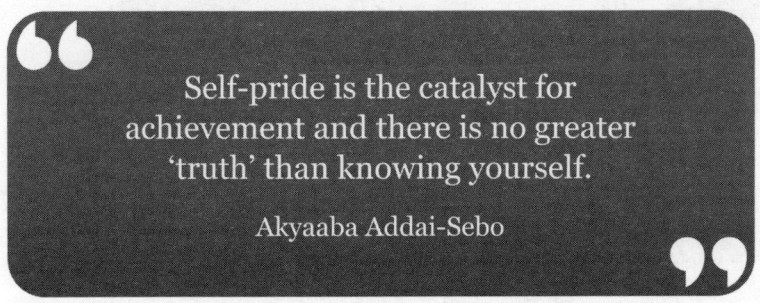

> Self-pride is the catalyst for achievement and there is no greater 'truth' than knowing yourself.
>
> Akyaaba Addai-Sebo

1 NOVEMBER - SARAH ROBERTS

On 1 November 1849, over one hundred years before the Supreme Court ruled that racial segregation in schools was unconstitutional (see 16 May), the Massachusetts Supreme Judicial Court heard the case of Sarah Roberts.

Having initially agreed on the idea of separate and safe educational provision for their children, Boston's African American residents changed their minds when the reality of the underfunding and neglect of those schools became obvious. They launched several petitions to the Boston Primary School Committee calling for desegregation, but their demands were ignored.

In 1849 Benjamin Roberts brought a case against the school committee after his five-year-old daughter, Sarah, had been excluded from her nearest school, the white-only Otis School, on the grounds of her race, and removed from the premises by a police officer. He was informed that she must attend the Black school that was both much further away and in a state of neglect. Roberts hired one of the first Black lawyers in the USA, Robert Morris, to represent his daughter. Morris and his co-counsel Charles Sumner argued that Massachusetts' own constitution made educational segregation unlawful, but Judge Lemuel Shaw ruled that equality did not have to be applied equally and that the school committee could do as they saw fit. This ruling was used to dismiss many later attempts to bring cases against segregation in schools.

The Boston parents, however, would not be defeated. They continued their protest and after an eleven-year boycott of the Black schools, Massachusetts finally desegregated education in 1855.

2 NOVEMBER - MAGGIE LENA WALKER

On 2 November 1903, the St Luke Penny Savings Bank opened for business, under Maggie Lena Walker, the very first African American woman to be president of a bank.

As a teenager, Walker joined the Independent Order of St Luke, an organization set up to provide aid and benefits to the African American community in Baltimore. Her keen organizational skills and business sense saw her progress through the ranks to become Right Worthy Grand Secretary in 1899. At this time African Americans were both dependent on and excluded from white financial and commercial institutions. In her new position Walker declared her intentions to free African Americans from that dependence by creating a set of Black-owned and Black-operated institutions.

> " Let us put our moneys together; let us use our moneys; let us put our money out at usury among ourselves, and reap the benefit ourselves. "

Within five years she had established her vision. She founded the *St Luke Herald* newspaper which she used to spread financial advice and discuss Black women's suffrage. She opened the St Luke Emporium department store which employed Black women as salespeople. The opening of the bank brought the promised financial independence to the community, offering mortgages and business loans.

Walker continued to work for her community right up until her death in 1934. Her Richmond home became a National Historic Site in 1979 and a statue was placed in the newly dedicated Maggie L. Walker Memorial Plaza in 2017.

3 NOVEMBER ~ PHIL LYNOTT

Harry Potts, CC BY-SA 2.0 via Wikimedia Commons

On 3 November 1972 a little known Irish rock band released a single that would mark the beginning of an international career. Thin Lizzy released 'Whiskey in the Jar', a rock reinterpretation of a traditional Irish folk ballad. Originally intended as a B-side, the record company reversed it and the song was a massive hit in Ireland and the UK. Over the following years the band released many hit albums and toured extensively, culminating in the recording of their legendary live album *Live and Dangerous* in 1978.

As one of very few Black musicians in the rock world at that time, singer, bassist and songwriter Phil Lynott naturally became the iconic face of the band. Born in England to an Irish mother and Guyanese father, Lynott was sent to Dublin to live with his grandparents from the age of four. Despite being a very visible minority, Lynott reported very little experience of direct racism and was vocally proud of his mixed heritage.

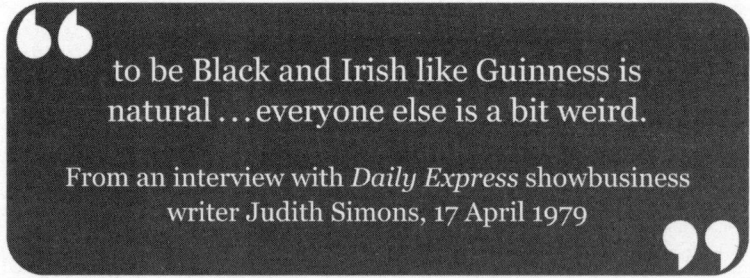

to be Black and Irish like Guinness is natural ... everyone else is a bit weird.

From an interview with *Daily Express* showbusiness writer Judith Simons, 17 April 1979

Lynott collapsed and died on 4 January 1986 at only thirty-six years of age. To commemorate his contribution to Irish culture, in 2005 a statue of him was erected in Dublin city centre.

4 NOVEMBER ~ BARACK OBAMA

On 4 November 2008, Barack Obama was elected the 44th president of the United States. He was the first African American president and first mixed-race president, and he went on to be re-elected, serving until 2017.

Barack Hussein Obama was born on 4 August 1961 on the island of Honolulu in the American state of Hawaii. His white American mother, Ann Dunham, had met his Black Kenyan father, Barack Obama Sr, the year before at a language class at the University of Hawaii at Mānoa. Obama Sr had come to America to study on a scholarship from the African American Students Foundation, a charitable programme set up by actors Sidney Poitier (see 24 March) and Harry Belafonte (see 1 March) and sportsman Jackie Robinson (see 26 March).

Between the ages of six and ten, Obama lived in Indonesia with his mother and stepfather, before he returned to Honolulu to live with his maternal grandparents. Obama gained a degree in political science with international relations from Columbia University, and then a law degree from Harvard, where he became the first Black president of the *Harvard Law Review*. During his summer vacations from Harvard, Obama worked at the Chicago law firm Sidley Austin and it was there, in June 1989, that he met Michelle Robinson, his future wife (see 17 January).

From 1993 Obama was a civil rights lawyer and academic, and he published his first bestselling book, *Dreams from My Father*, in 1995. In 1996 his political career began when he was elected to the Illinois Senate. Eight years later he ran for a seat in the US Senate and won, becoming the Senator for Illinois. Four years after that he won the 2008 election, and became America's 44th president. He was the country's first Black president and his wife was its first Black First Lady.

Since leaving office, having served two terms, Obama has established the charitable Obama Foundation. Its projects include the building of his presidential library in Chicago, a scholarship programme for public policy students and the My Brother's Keeper Alliance, which provides mentoring and opportunities for men and boys of colour. He and his wife Michelle have set up a production company, Higher Ground Productions, which makes documentary film and television content. Its first film, *American Factory*, won the 2020 Academy Award for Best Documentary Feature.

5 NOVEMBER - LONNIE JOHNSON

Lonnie Johnson is an American inventor and engineer. While his name may not be as well known, one of his inventions – the Super Soaker water gun – is famous to children all over the world.

Johnson was born on 6 October 1949 in the city of Mobile, Alabama. From childhood he was interested in science and how things around him worked. When he was a teenager, he represented his high school in an engineering competition, and was the only African American student in the contest. He won first place in the competition with a robot called Linex that he had built from found and recycled material.

After graduating from high school he attended Tuskegee University, before going on to join the United States Air Force as an engineer. From there he went on to join NASA, and during his time there he won many awards for his work designing the systems that power spacecraft. Johnson was also interested in designing toys, and he had the idea for his most successful invention when, in 1982, the heat pump design he was trying to improve sprung a leak, shooting water right across the room. Realizing that this had the makings of a really great squirt gun, Johnson worked for years to refine his design, finally patenting the toy in 1986. In 1989 he set up his own engineering firm and licensed the squirt gun design to the company Laramie. They relaunched it as the Super Soaker water gun and within two years it was the biggest-selling toy in America. Johnson continued to run his engineering company and is one of America's most successful inventors. On 5 November 2015 the Super Soaker was inducted into America's National Toy Hall of Fame, and in 2022 Johnson was inducted into America's National Inventors Hall of Fame.

TIMELINE 12

6 NOVEMBER ~ THE CREOLE

The Creole Rebellion of 1841 was the largest successful uprising on a slave ship in US history. Enslaved people on board a ship called *The Creole*, which was bound for the slave markets of New Orleans, seized control of the vessel from its white crew, and sailed to the British Bahamas islands where slavery had recently been abolished.

The Creole departed from Richmond, Virginia, on Monday 25 October 1841. On board were Captain Robert Ensor, his ten crew members, eight Black servants, several white passengers (including three slave traders), and 103 enslaved people. Although the Transatlantic Slave Trade had been been abolished by the United States in 1808, the sale of enslaved people within US territory was still legal. *The Creole* was set to take a well-worn 'domestic slave trade route' down the south-eastern coast, along the Gulf coast to New Orleans. The ship stopped on the way, collecting more enslaved people, so that a week into the journey there was a 'cargo' of 135 enslaved.

Twenty-six of the enslaved were the property of a Virginian slave trader, Thomas McCargo, who was on board himself. His business was buying enslaved people in Virginia and selling them in New Orleans, which had the largest slave markets in the US. One man owned by McCargo was Madison Washington, who had been born into slavery then escaped to Canada, only to be recaptured when he returned to Virginia to find his wife. Another enslaved man from Virginia on board was twenty-one-year-old Elijah Morris.

On 7 November, 130 miles north-east of the coast of Abacos, Bahamas, Madison Washington, Elijah Morris, Ben Blacksmith and Doc Ruffin led a band of nineteen enslaved people and took control of the ship. Captain Ensor was wounded but there were only two fatalities – one slave trader and one enslaved person.

The rebels' plan was to sail to territory controlled by the British, who had abolished slavery in 1838, where they knew they could become free people. Ben Blacksmith proposed heading to the British West Indies because he knew that enslaved Americans had escaped there successfully the

Révolte sur un bâtiment négrier.

year before. Two days later they arrived at the British port of Nassau, in the Bahamas, where the nineteen ringleaders were arrested by British officials and imprisoned.

The US Consul in the Bahamas put together a plan to re-capture *The Creole* and sail it back into US waters before the British could free the enslaved. But the Consul's efforts were carefully and deliberately thwarted by 'free' Black Bahamians, who showed solidarity with the enslaved, surrounding *The Creole* in their boats, ensuring the safe passage of the enslaved to the shore and freedom. Five people – three women and two children – decided to stay aboard *The Creole* and sailed with the ship to New Orleans, returning to slavery.

Five months later, in April 1842, a British court decided the ringleaders were not guilty of manslaughter or piracy because they had been illegally held in slavery, and their use of force to effect their freedom was justified. To the fury of the American slave owners, the ringleaders were released by the court and emancipated. Little is known about what became of the 128 people who achieved their freedom in the Creole Rebellion. Some settled in Jamaica, some stayed in the Bahamas. But records show that by 1879 Elijah Morris owned his own farm, in Gambier Village, Bahamas. His descendants still live in the area today.

The Creole Rebellion took place at a time of strained relations between the United States and Britain in the 1840s, when the two nations were arguing over the border between the US and Canada (then British territory), as well as being out of step on the issue of slavery. The British had let the ringleaders of the rebellion go free but they had not pressured the Americans to abolish slavery. The priority for the British following the rebellion was to avoid a deterioration in its relationship with the US, not least because much of Britain's northern textile industry was reliant on a supply of cheap, slave-produced American cotton. Years later the British ended up contributing to compensation payments to the American slave owners who had lost their human 'property' in the Creole Rebellion.

This was not the first enslaved uprising on a ship, nor the last, but it was successful in liberating so many enslaved people and served as an inspiration to abolitionists, on both sides of the Atlantic, wishing to end slavery in the United States.

In 1852 Frederick Douglass (see 14 February) published a novella entitled *The Heroic Slave, a Heartwarming Narrative of the Adventures of Madison Washington, in Pursuit of Liberty*. This was Douglass' only work of fiction but was based on the facts of the Creole Rebellion and its hero.

DID YOU KNOW?

7 NOVEMBER ~ DUNMORE'S PROCLAMATION

In the 1770s tensions began to rise between the British government and Britain's colonies in North America, which ultimately led to the start of the American War of Independence in 1775. American settlers who supported British rule became known as Loyalists and those who fought for American independence became known as American Patriots. The commander of the British forces was Governor John Murray, the Fourth Earl of Dunmore. On 7 November 1775, Dumnore issued a public announcement that became known as Dunmore's Proclamation.

The proclamation was printed and sent out to the people of Virginia. In it Dunmore promised freedom to enslaved men whose owners had joined the American Patriots. To gain this freedom they had to escape from their plantations, make their way to the ships of British forces and agree to join the Loyalist forces.

Within two weeks escaped men began arriving on the British ships at the James River. Dunmore created a new unit for them, Dunmore's Royal Ethiopian Regiment. They were armed with guns and given uniforms and badges with the words 'Liberty to Slaves' sewn on. By the end of 1775 around 300 men had joined the regiment.

In 1776 Dunmore was defeated, the American Patriots declared their independence from Britain and the Royal Ethiopian regiment was disbanded. British forces continued to fight for another seven years and many of the soldiers from the unit went on to join a new regiment, the Black Pioneers. It is estimated that between 800 and 2,000 men responded to Dunmore's proclamation and escaped enslavement, serving as soldiers, labourers and spies in the Loyalist forces.

TIMELINE 2

8 NOVEMBER - CY GRANT

RAF veteran, lawyer, actor, singer, writer, poet and activist Cyril 'Cy' Grant was born on 8 November 1919 in Guyana (then British Guiana). Following a recruitment drive in the colonies, Grant joined the RAF (Royal Air Force) in 1941 as one of only a handful of Black officers. On the way back from a mission, Grant's Lancaster was shot down over the Netherlands. He survived the crash but was captured and imprisoned in the Stalag Luft III camp, which became famous for two attempted breakouts, one of which inspired the film *The Great Escape*.

After the war Grant returned to the UK and trained as a lawyer, but was unable to find work. He moved into acting and singing instead, a decision that proved to be very successful for him. He recorded several folk albums and had his own television series in the 1950s. Grant also had a slot on the *Tonight* show on the BBC, producing improvised Calypso versions of news items, making him a household name as the first Black person to make regular televison appearances. Yet despite his popularity he still expressed despair at the difficulty in securing good roles as a Black actor.

Grant channelled his frustration into founding the Drum Arts Centre in 1974 to foster Black talent, a move that saw him accused of separatism by the theatre establishment. Unconcerned by what he saw as ignorant criticism, he went on to produce and tour a show based on a poem by Aimé Césaire, a writer and politican from the Caribbean island of Martinique and founder of the Negritude movement, whom he cited as a huge influence in his life.

Grant continued to write and campaign up until his death in 2010. His last project was the creation of an archive of Second World War Caribbean RAF crews, to ensure that their heroic contributions were not forgotten.

9 NOVEMBER ~ JACKIE KAY

Scottish poet Jackie Kay was born on 9 November 1961, in Edinburgh, to a Scottish mother and Nigerian father. She and her siblings were then adopted by a white couple in Glasgow. Encouraged to become a poet by the writer and artist Alasdair Gray, Kay studied English at university. Her identity as an adopted, mixed-race, lesbian woman influences her work. Kay's first book of poems, in 1991, was *The Adoption Papers*, which examines the fictional perspectives of an adopted woman, her birth mother and adopted mother. Kay writes for adults and children and has published novels and stage plays, dealing with issues including race and racism, gender and sexuality. Kay is professor of creative writing at Newcastle University and her poem 'Welcome Wee One' is included in the Baby Box given to babies born in Scotland.

> O ma darlin wee one
> At last you are here in the wurld
> And wi' aa your wisdom
> Your een bricht as the stars,
> You've filled this hoose with licht,
> Yer trusty wee haun, your globe o' a heid,
> My cherished yin, my hert's ain!
>
> O ma darlin wee one
> The hale wurld welcomes ye:
> The mune glowes; the hearth wairms.
> Let your life have luck, health, charm,
> Ye are my bonny blessed bairn,
> My small miraculous gift.
> I never kent luve like this.
>
> Jackie Kay, 'Welcome Wee One'

10 NOVEMBER ~ ALVIN AILEY

Groundbreaking dancer and choreographer Alvin Ailey was born in segregated rural Texas in 1931. His early experiences of poverty and violent racism shaped his career and were the source of his artistic expression.

Ailey's relationship with dance began when he moved to Los Angeles. He trained with Lester Horton, a dancer known for his mix of Indigenous and Western dance traditions, and eventually joined his company as both dancer and teacher. When Horton died suddenly in 1953 Ailey took over the company and began choreographing work.

Demand for Ailey as a dancer grew, and he made several Broadway appearances before moving to New York and founding the Alvin Ailey American Dance Theatre in 1958. As a Black dancer work was hard to find and he wanted to provide a place that could give both real support and a voice to the hidden African American experience. His 1960s production *Revelations* was a groundbreaking work of modern dance with a soundtrack of spirituals and gospel music that referenced Ailey's own rural Texan childhood. It is widely regarded as his masterpiece.

Ailey died in 1989. The dance company continues his work to provide opportunities and to encourage the arts in excluded communities. On 10 November 2014 the Obama administration announced that he was posthumously awarded the Presidential Medal of Freedom.

11 NOVEMBER ~ AHMET ALI ÇELIKTEN

Ahmet Ali Çelikten was one of the very few Black military pilots who flew during the First World War. American Eugene J. Bullard is often credited with being the very first, but Çelikten's graduation on 11 November 1916 beat Bullard's by six months. Çelikten's own graduation was preceded in February 1914 by that of Italian-Eritrean pilot Domenico Mondelli, now acknowledged as the very first Black military aviator.

Born in Turkey, accounts of Çelikten's heritage are muddled, but he is thought to have been born to a Nigerian mother and a father of mixed Turkish and Somalian parentage. Originally a naval graduate, Çelikten retrained as a pilot in 1914 when the Ottoman Empire found itself facing the First World War. Little is known about his service during the war other than that he held the rank of captain and his codename: Black Eagle of Steel.

Çelikten is more well known for his role in the Turkish War of Independence that followed, where he provided air support and intelligence for the navy. Following the successful war and the establishment of the republic, Çelikten was decorated for his services and given the position of air undersecretary. He retired in 1949 after reaching the rank of colonel, but his legacy carried on through his wife, sister, sons, daughters and niece and nephew, who all became pilots.

NA, Public domain, Wikimedia Commons

TIMELINE 6

12 NOVEMBER - HEZEKIAH MOSCOW

Born around 1862 in the West Indies, Hezekiah Moscow was a boxer who lived in Victorian London. Boxing was very popular, and boxing gymnasiums sprang up under London's railway arches, in clubs and back rooms of pubs, where fights took place in front of enthusiastic crowds.

The UK National Archives (COPY 1/392/58)

In the 1880s, Hezekiah Moscow was a regular fighter on the east London circuit, and he boxed successfully for a decade under the name of 'Ching Ghook'. Moscow had other talents, too. He entertained audiences with comic sketches, performing in music halls around the country. He even had a short-lived career as a lion tamer at a menagerie called the East London Aquarium.

What is known about Moscow's life in Britain largely comes from surviving newspaper stories and advertisements about his various public appearances. For example, we know from an advertisement in the *Manchester Courier* and *Lancashire General Advertiser* from Saturday 12 November 1887 that the previous week Moscow had been sharing the bill with the Bohee Brothers (see 19 March) at an evening of music, boxing competitions and gymnastic displays at St James Hall in London.

Moscow married in Whitechapel in 1890 and when the 1891 census was taken he was living in Spitalfields with his wife and daughter. However, in 1892, he completely disappeared. Mary Moscow placed a notice in a newspaper asking if anyone knew the whereabouts of her missing husband, but the mystery was never solved. Hezekiah Moscow was never heard of again.

13 NOVEMBER ~ SEYDOU KEÏTA

Born in Mali in the early 1920s, Seydou Keïta had been set to follow his father into carpentry before an uncle gave him a Kodak Brownie camera and opened up a new career path to him. Keïta was largely self-taught, honing his skills on images of friends and family, until 1948 when he began professional photography and opened a small outdoor studio. The rudimentary nature of the studio forged Keïta's signature style. Only ever taking one shot and using natural light, Keïta's images were renowned for their clarity, composition and flattering outcomes.

> " It's easy to take a photo, but what really made a difference was that I always knew how to find the right position, and I was never wrong. "

Keïta's business flourished and his reputation grew. He was approached in 1962 by the new independent government who offered him regular work. His studio continued operating under his brother and son until 1977 when all of the equipment was stolen, prompting Keïta to close the doors for good.

It was not until the 1990s that Keïta's work came to the attention of a wider audience. Some of his images had been displayed unascribed at a New York exhibition, prompting two French photographers to track down the artist. His photography career unexpectedly revived, Keïta found himself in demand internationally for magazine work and exhibitions until his death in Paris in 2001. Now largely credited as the father of African photography, with his masterful portraiture placing him among the greats, Keïta's work is held in collections around the world.

14 NOVEMBER - RUBY BRIDGES

On 14 November 1960, six-year-old Ruby Bridges arrived for her first day at William Frantz elementary school in New Orleans. The Brown vs. Topeka Board of Education judgement had been made in 1954 (see 16 May), a few months before Bridges was born. The judgement stated that racially **segregated** schools in the south of the USA must **desegregate**. Despite a ruling the following year to desegregate 'with all deliberate speed', progress was slow thanks to resistance from white leaders.

US Marshals escorting Ruby Bridges from William Frantz Elementary School, New Orleans, 1960

US Department of Justice, Wikicommons

On the day she arrived, Bridges was escorted by four federal marshals through a crowd of reporters and angry white protestors, which included white parents and children from the school. They shouted racist names at her, chanted and waved signs with racist slogans. One woman held up a Black doll inside a small coffin.

TIMELINE 7

White parents refused to send their children to the school and the staff refused to teach her, except for a teacher from Boston called Barbara Henry, and for the next year she taught Bridges alone in a classroom.

Although the protests outside the school continued, gradually some white children started returning to the school. However, for her own safety Bridges was not allowed to play in the playground and she brought her own food to school. A child psychiatrist called Robert Coles volunteered to meet with her every week to support her mental health through this traumatic time, and Bridges later found out that his family had donated the clothes she wore to school in those first days.

Photographs of Bridges being marched under the protection of federal marshals through an angry mob, just to get to her classroom, were seen all across America and the world, and became important images of the civil rights movement. In 1964 the American artist Norman Rockwell reproduced the scene in his painting *The Problem We All Live With*.

In 1999 Bridges founded the Ruby Bridges Foundation, to continue the fight against racism. In 2001 President Clinton awarded Bridges with the Presidential Citizens Medal.

15 NOVEMBER ~ THE BERLIN CONFERENCE

On Saturday 15 November 1884, the Berlin Conference began. It was an international conference that lasted three months, during which representatives from fourteen European nations met to discuss how they could colonize the continent of Africa. Two representatives of the United States of America also attended to monitor the talks and report back to the American government, but no representatives from any African state were invited.

For centuries, European nations had made money from the enslavement of African people, taking them from Africa to grow cash crops like sugar and cotton in colonies in the Americas and West Indies. Europeans had carried out this trade with African rulers and had built a network of forts on the coast of Africa, but they had not been able to take control of land in the centre of the African continent. By the 1880s new weapons and better medicines meant that for the first time European armies were able to invade African kingdoms inland, far away from the coast.

At the Berlin Conference the powerful nations of Europe met to agree which parts of Africa they were each to attempt to conquer. The conference was an important moment in what became known as the 'Scramble for Africa'. Before the scramble, in 1870, 90% of African land was controlled by Africans. By the end of the scramble in 1900 that figure was only 10%. Just two African nations, Liberia and Ethiopia, remained independent. Millions of people and 9 million square miles of African territory had been brought under European control, meaning that European empires controlled one-fifth of the land area of the world.

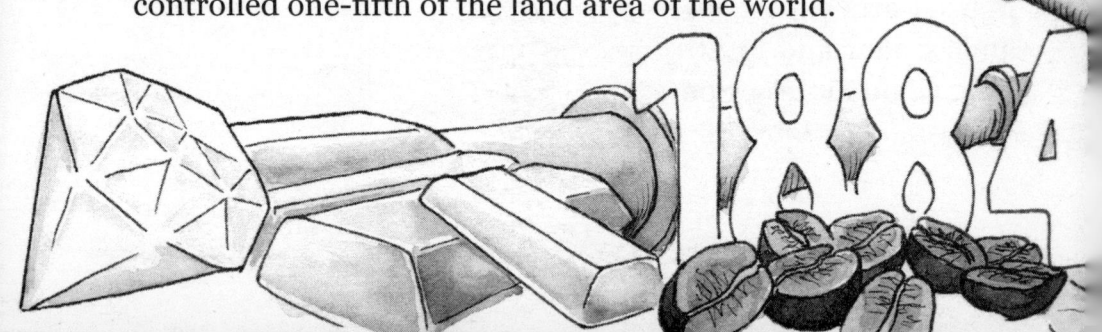

On 16 November 2016, Kareem Abdul-Jabbar was awarded the **Presidential Medal of Freedom** by Barack Obama. Born in Harlem, New York in April 1947, he began playing basketball as a child and won a basketball scholarship to attend UCLA. When he made the varsity team he scored fifty-six points in his first match, and the team won the national championship undefeated. A committed civil rights activist, he attended the Cleveland Summit of Black athletes in support of the boxer Muhammad Ali after he refused to fight in the Vietnam War (see 20 June). In 1968 he converted to Islam, took on the name Kareem Abdul-Jabbar and refused to try out for the US Men's Olympic Basketball team in a protest for Black civil rights in America.

> **DID YOU KNOW?**
>
> Abdul-Jabbar was named Ferdinand Lewis Alcindor at birth. He is the great grand-nephew Dr John Alcindor (see 16 July).

Abdul-Jabbar turned professional in 1969 and was named NBA (National Basketball Association) Rookie of the Year. He played professional basketball for twenty seasons for the Milwaukee Bucks and the LA Lakers. Named the NBA Most Valuable Player a record-breaking six times, both teams retired his number thirty-three shirt. When he retired in 1989, he had played more games than any other player in history and held the record for points scored, a record held until 2023 (see 30 December).

Outside of basketball, Abdul-Jabbar is an actor, author and martial arts expert. In 2012 he became a US global cultural ambassador and in 2017 he was appointed to the President's Council on Fitness, Sports and Nutrition by Barack Obama.

17 NOVEMBER - OBA EWUARE THE GREAT

Oba Ewuare the Great was once the ruler of the Benin Empire, in what is now Nigeria. According to legend, Ogun (Ewuare's birth name) was the rightful heir to the kingdom, but his brother took the throne. Ogun marched into Benin in 1440 to seize power and much of the city was destroyed. He defeated his brother and took control of the Kingdom of Benin. Ogun then changed his name to Ewuare, meaning 'the trouble has ceased'.

Oba Ewuare the Great ruled Benin from 1440 to 1473 and is now known for transforming its fortunes. He rebuilt the city, constructing huge walls to secure it. He expanded the empire by conquering other towns and cities. The economy grew strong because Oba Ewuare began doing business with European and Asian traders, establishing contact with Portuguese traders who came for gold, ivory, pepper and Benin's renowned bronze artworks. Trade with the Portuguese would go on to involve the Benin Empire in the Transatlantic slave trade.

Benin was invaded by the British in 1897, who annexed the region and plundered it for precious goods (see 9 February). Thousands of artefacts are now in the collections of European museums, the British Museum among them. In November 2022, the Horniman Museum in London returned ownership of its Benin Bronzes to Nigeria.

Stephencdickson, Wikimedia Commons

Bronze relief of Oba Ewuare the Great

18 NOVEMBER - KANYA KING

Kanya King is an entrepreneur, the founder and CEO of the International MOBO (Music of Black Origin) Awards.

King was born in 1969 in Kilburn, London, to a Ghanaian father and Irish mother. She dropped out of school at sixteen when she got pregnant, but later worked her way back into education and studied English literature at Goldsmith's College. After completing her degree King got a job as a TV researcher, and it was here that she saw the lack of mainstream inclusion for music of Black origin. None of the large televised music awards ceremonies were focused on this genre. The achievements of Black artists in the music scene remained largely uncelebrated and unrewarded and so King took matters into her own hands and devised the MOBO Awards.

Lack of mainstream interest forced her to re-mortgage her house to fund the TV production of the event and King worked hard to persuade Carlton TV to broadcast it. The first MOBO ceremony took place on 18 November 1996 in London, and its success paved the way for a number of urban artists to break into the mainstream.

Since its humble beginnings MOBO has expanded to become a champion of diversity in the arts and a facilitator of social change. The organization supports new talent and celebrates achievement across the cultural spectrum. In 2016 King set up the MOBO Trust which provides opportunities in the music industry for young people from diverse backgrounds, and in 2018 was awarded a CBE.

The Kingdom of Da'amat was located in the Horn of Africa, in what is now parts of Ethiopia and Eritrea. It was the region's oldest kingdom, and began using ploughs to improve its crops in the second millennium BCE. Producing bigger crops helped Da'amat to become an important trading nation, and the kingdom also traded in iron tools and weapons, precious metals, and luxury goods such as ivory and tortoise shells. Its access to the coast allowed Da'amat to establish important trading links with neighbours across the Red Sea in southern Arabia.

A. Davey, Wikimedia Commons

Ancient stone slabs with Sabaean inscriptions found at Yeha, Ethiopia

The decorations and inscriptions left by the people of Da'amat on temples and in their art tell us that they worshipped gods based on animals from nature, and that they spoke a language called Ge'ez. Da'amat's capital is thought to have been Yeha, which survives as a town in modern Ethiopia. The great Temple of Yeha, built circa 700BCE, is the oldest standing structure to have survived in the Horn of Africa. Da'amat was succeeded by the Aksumite Kingdom (see 3 October).

20 NOVEMBER - DIDO ELIZABETH BELLE

Dido Elizabeth Belle was born in the West Indies in 1761. She was born enslaved, the daughter of Maria Belle, an enslaved African woman, and Sir John Lindsay, a white British naval officer. When Lindsay returned to Britain he took Belle with him and we know that Belle was baptized, at the age of five, in St George's Church in Bloomsbury on 20 November

Wikmedia iCommons

1766. When Lindsay went back to sea he sent Belle to live with his uncle William Murray, First Earl of Mansfield, and his aunt, Elizabeth, Countess of Mansfield, in their home Kenwood House, just outside of London. Belle was living with Mansfield in 1772 when he was the judge in the Somerset case about whether slavery was legal in England (see 21 June).

The Mansfields already had their great-niece, Belle's second cousin, Lady Elizabeth Murray living with them. Thanks to a portrait by the Scottish artist David Martin, of Belle with her cousin Elizabeth Murray, Belle is one of very few Black Georgians for whom we have a name and know what she looked like.

Belle received an education and affection from her new family. She became a companion for her second cousin and learned to help her great uncle by writing up notes he dictated to her. However, she was not treated as an equal, probably because she was illegitimate and maybe also because she was of mixed race. Mansfield did leave her money in his will and made sure that her status as a free woman was recognized legally. After Mansfield's death Belle married a Frenchman called John Davinier, and they went on to have a family together before her death in July 1804.

21 NOVEMBER ~ LOPE MARTIN

Over 200 years before Captain Cook's *Endeavour* set sail, Afro-Portugese navigator Lope Martin crossed uncharted waters to establish a trading route across the Pacific.

Martin was a descendant of West Africans enslaved by the Portuguese in 1444. He spent his youth working on the docks of southern Portugal, and from contemporary descriptions it is likely that he was of mixed heritage, which he later used to his advantage to pass as a Spanish native. After moving to Spain he trained as a ship's navigator, a highly skilled position that demanded a knowledge of mathematics, astronomy and cartography. Martin gained his licence and a reputation as an outstanding navigator, which eventually led to a commission from the Spanish king, Philip II, to join a fleet attempting to open up a trans-Pacific trade route.

The fleet set sail from Mexico on 21 November 1564 but after only ten days a storm hit and the *San Lucas*, on which Martin was navigator, was separated from the other ships. The *San Lucas* continued on to the Philippines to find the others, but after waiting for a month they decided to risk the return voyage alone and arrived back in Mexico on 9 August 1565. At first their achievement was celebrated, but then the other ships returned and the captains accused Martin of glory hunting and treachery. As a man with no connections Martin was vulnerable. Rather than bother with a trial, he was sent on another voyage by government officials, with instructions that he be executed upon arrival at his destination. However, Martin suspected a plot and staged a mutiny. A further mutiny left him stranded on an island, but what happened to him after that remains a mystery.

Martin's seafaring contribution had a huge impact on the following 200 years of Spanish trade, but his name has been largely forgotten.

22 NOVEMBER - THE UK RACE RELATIONS ACTS

After the Second World War, post-war immigration from some of its former colonies in the Commonwealth helped Britain to fill jobs. In the 1950s and 60s, Black migrant workers were also producing a second generation, their children, born in the UK. Although Britain had needed these workers to help build the economy after the war, and staff the new National Health Service, not all of Britain had been welcoming to Black immigrants. Many of them faced discrimination and found that they were denied jobs and refused housing because of their race.

One notable case of racial discrimination demonstrated the pressing need for political action. In 1963 a bus company in Bristol was found to be operating its own 'colour bar' by unofficially refusing to employ Black and Asian workers. In response, youth worker Paul Stephenson organized the Bristol Bus Boycott (see 17 September), inspired by Rosa Parks and the Montgomery bus boycott in the USA (see 1 December). The leader of the Labour party, Harold Wilson, spoke out in support of the Bristol Bus Boycott and promised that the law would change if the Labour party came to power. Labour won the 1964 general election, and Wilson kept his word. Indeed, over the next decade his administrations would introduce bills for what became the three Race Relations Acts of 1965, 1968 and 1976.

The first Race Relations Act was given Royal Assent on 8 November 1965 and became effective from 8 December. The Act outlawed discrimination 'on grounds of colour, race, or ethnic or national origins' in public places. It also established the Race Relations Board to help deal with discrimination complaints.

In 1968, the government introduced a new Race Relations Bill to extend protection against racial discrimination to include employment, housing and service provision. Building on the 1965 Race Relations Act, the Bill proposed to make it illegal for people to discriminate and refuse housing, employment or public services to people because of their colour, race, ethnicity or national background. The Bill faced months of opposition inside and outside of parliament, including the infamous 'Rivers of Blood' speech made by the Conservative MP, Enoch Powell, but finally the Race Relations Act was passed on 25 October 1968.

By the 1970s it had become clear that more legislation was needed, and a Select Committee on Race Relations was set up to make recommendations. In February of 1975, a new Race Relations Bill was introduced which expanded the definition of 'discrimination' to include 'indirect discrimination' – meaning any practice that disadvantaged a particular racial group. The subsequent 1976 Race Relations Act was given Royal assent on 22 November 1976 and was effective from 1 September 1977. Complaints of discrimination could now be taken to court or to an industrial tribunal. The Race Relations Board was replaced with the Commission for Racial Equality, which was given greater powers to enforce the law.

23 NOVEMBER - THE EVACUATION OF BLACK LOYALISTS FROM NEW YORK

In 1783, the British government accepted that the American War of Independence was over. British ships came to the ports of Savannah, Georgia, Charleston, South Carolina, and New York and began the withdrawal of British forces from America. This included the withdrawal of the Black Loyalists. These were enslaved people who had escaped from their owners to join the Loyalist forces in exchange for their freedom, in response to Dunmore's proclamation of 1775 (see 7 November) and the Philipsburg Proclamation of 1779 (see 30 June). They knew that if they remained in America, they would be sent back into slavery.

On 25 November 1783, George Washington marched his Patriot army into New York. At one o'clock in the afternoon a cannon was fired, signalling that the last of the British troops had left on the final ship out of New York Harbour. Among them was Harry Washington, a Black Loyalist who had been owned by George Washington, but who had escaped to join the British and get his freedom. Most of the Black Loyalists, including Harry Washington, were sent to Nova Scotia in the British-controlled part of Canada, and some came to Britain, where they became known as the Black Poor (see 15 May). Years later, Harry Washington and many other Black Loyalists from London and Nova Scotia would be relocated to Sierra Leone in Africa and battle through terrible conditions to establish new settlements there (see 15 May).

24 NOVEMBER ~ JAMES BERRY

James Berry was a Jamaican poet and part of the Windrush Generation. Born in Portland, Jamaica in 1924, Berry was eager to leave the restrictions of rural Jamaica and improve his prospects. First he tried America. He signed up to work as a farm labourer during the Second World War, but his experience of segregation and racism there soon confirmed that it was not the place for him. After the war British companies began to recruit workers from the colonies to come to Britain and help to rebuild, and Berry jumped at the opportunity, making it onto the SS *Orbita*, the ship that followed the *Windrush* (see 22 June) in 1948.

London suited him well and he found employment as a telegraph operator to sustain him while he worked on writing stories, plays and poetry. In 1977 he won a fellowship that allowed him to work full-time as a writer and in 1979 he published his first volume of poetry, *Fractured Circles*. Two years later he became the first West Indian to win the National Poetry Competition. Berry continued to write poetry, becoming known for the use of Jamaican patois in his work, and also wrote many successful books for children. In 1990 he received an OBE for his services to poetry and the Royal Society of Literature made him an honorary fellow in 2007.

Later in life Berry was diagnosed with Alzheimer's disease and his last book, *A Story I Am In*, was published on 24 November 2011. He died in 2017 at ninety-two years old.

25 NOVEMBER - DEACONS FOR DEFENSE AND JUSTICE

While the civil rights movement of the 1950s and 60s is largely remembered for the non-violent tactics of Dr King's SCLC, Black liberation in the south of the US was, by necessity, often quite different.

The Ku Klux Klan waged a war of terror against the Black population in the southern states. Often with the cooperation of local law enforcement (some of whom were Klan members), they would take part in 'nightrides' where they would randomly attack homes in Black neighbourhoods, firebombing properties and shooting people as they attempted to escape. With no help from the law, Black communities set up their own armed patrols to protect their homes and families.

Warren K. Leffler, Library of Congress

It was a summer-long effort of protecting the non-violent activists of SNCC and CORE that led to the formation of the Deacons for Defense and Justice. The Freedom Summer campaign of 1964 was a project to register Black voters in the South. Jim Crow legislation and violent intimidation had thrown up legal and practical barriers to Black voters and few of those who could vote were actually registered. The campaign recruited largely from the student campuses of big northern cities and 1,000 volunteers, 90 per cent of whom were white, joined up to work alongside the Black campaigners on the ground. They were unprepared for the level of violence with which they would be met.

Earnest 'Chilly Willy' Thomas was a Korean War veteran from Jonesboro, Louisiana. While in broad agreement with CORE, he found their rigid stance on non-violence to be naive at best. He and a handful of other armed activists took up guard at the Freedom House that CORE had established as a base for their activities in Jonesboro. He respected the activists' right to their non-violent policy, but Jonesboro was a Klan town and the police would offer no protection should the activists be attacked. When the chief of police in Jonesboro provided an escort for a Klan drive through the Black district, distributing leaflets that warned the community to stay away from CORE, the situation escalated, and Thomas's armed self-defence group formalized its organization. With the backing of this new group, CORE, at the request of Jonesboro activists, stepped outside of the original goal of voter registration and began a push for the desegregation recently signed into federal law (see 2 July).

Eventually the summer protesters returned to their homes, but Thomas' group remained. In November of 1964, at a meeting in a local church hall, the group finally named itself the Deacons for Defense and Justice. Still facing violence from the Klan, the Deacons' armed resistance movement began to spread, with chapters springing up across the south, the most notable of which was the Bogalusa chapter under Robert Hicks. Although the civil rights movement still maintained a stance of non-violence, the Deacons often provided protection for voters and activists and were the security for the 1966 March Against Fear after its creator James Meredith (see 25 June) was shot. It was the later rise of the Black Panther Party that led to the end of the Deacons, when the idea of armed resistance became a central part of the Black liberation movement.

AmaechiPerformance, Wikimedia Commons

John Amaechi is a British-American psychologist, leadership consultant, author and basketball player. He was born in Boston, USA on 26 November 1970 to a white English mother and a Black Nigerian father. Raised in Stockport, England by his mother, by the age of seventeen, when he was six foot and nine inches tall, the suggestion was made that he should take up playing basketball. Soon afterwards he won a basketball scholarship in America and graduated with a degree in psychology. In the mid-1990s he achieved his goal of becoming the first Briton to play in America's National Basketball Association (NBA). After playing for teams in the United States and in Europe, he retired in 2003, but came out of retirement to play for England in the 2006 Commonwealth Games, where the team won a bronze medal.

Away from basketball, Amaechi studied for a doctorate and qualified as a professional psychologist. He became a leadership coach, mentor and a writer. In his autobiography, *Man in the Middle*, published in 2007, Amaechi made history by becoming the first National Basketball Association player to come out as gay. He was applauded by many commentators and LGBTQ+ activists for this pioneering move, but was also subjected to homophobic comments, including from some fellow basketball players. Amaechi now runs his own company where he supports people and organizations to develop teamwork and communication, and to value diversity. Amaechi has been awarded many honours, including Humanist of the Year 2015 from Harvard University. In 2011 he was awarded an OBE by Queen Elizabeth II.

27 NOVEMBER ~ JIMI HENDRIX

The American guitarist Jimi Hendrix was born on 27 November 1942 in Seattle, Washington. He grew up in poverty, in an unstable home due to his parents' problems with alcohol.

Hannu Lindroos / Lehtikuva, Wikimedia Commons

His interest in music started early, but he did not get his first guitar until he was fifteen. He quickly taught himself to play from listening to the work of blues stars such as Muddy Waters (see 14 March). He formed his first band, the Velvetones, but soon realized that he needed to get an electric guitar. The electric guitar sound that he would go on to develop, involving feedback and intense sound distortion, would eventually make him one of the most celebrated guitarists of all time.

After a short time in the US Army, Hendrix began working as a professional guitarist for acts including the Isley Brothers and Little Richard (See 23 May). In 1966 he moved to Britain when Chas Chandler, the bassist with the band the Animals, became his manager. This transformed Hendrix's career and within months his songs 'Hey Joe', 'Purple Haze' and 'The Wind Cries Mary', had all been top ten UK hits. An appearance at the Monterey Pop Festival in California in 1967 ensured that he became just as famous in the USA. Hendrix went on to headline at the Woodstock Festival in 1969 and the Isle of Wight Festival a year later. He died accidentally in September 1970, from the effects of a drug overdose. He was just twenty-seven years old.

28 NOVEMBER - BERRY GORDY

Motown Record Corporation was responsible for the careers of many of the 20th-century's most iconic musicians. Its founder, Berry Gordy, was born on 28 November 1929 in Detroit, Michigan. An early successful career as a boxer was ended when, in 1950, he was drafted into the Korean War. Drawn to music, he spent some of his tour as an organist for a military chaplain, and after his return to the US opened a record store and began writing songs. It was the song 'Reet Petite', written by him and his sister and performed by Jackie Wilson, that gave Gordy his break. He began working as a producer and talent scout and, with a loan of $800 from his family, began building what would become Motown Records in 1960.

Gordy's songwriting and his eye for talent combined to devastating effect and Motown dominated the R&B scene. The acts were carefully managed through his Artist Development Department, teaching them the art of performance and crafting a suitable public image offstage too. He cultivated a collection of artists that defined the genre, such as the Supremes, the Jackson 5 and Stevie Wonder (see 21 May) whose names still resonate decades later. Motown moved into film production in the 1970s and kept on producing hit records, but not at the frantic pace of the 1960s, and in 1988 Gordy sold up and moved on.

For a career littered with hit after hit, Gordy has been honoured many times by the music industry: 1988 saw his Rock & Roll Hall of Fame induction; 2013 brought the Songwriters Hall of Fame Pioneer Award; and in 2016 President Obama awarded him the National Medal of Arts in recognition of his extraordinary contribution to the nation's culture.

29 NOVEMBER ~ BETTY CAMPBELL

The pioneering Black teacher Betty Campbell was born Rachel Elizabeth Johnson in Cardiff, Wales on 6 November 1934 to parents of Barbadian and Jamaican heritage. After her father was killed during the Second World War, she spent her childhood in poverty. At school she excelled, and she won a scholarship to attend high school. When she became pregnant at seventeen, she left school and went on to marry her husband, Rupert Campbell.

In 1960 Campbell decided to return to education. She was one of only six female students when she enrolled in a teacher training course at college, after which she became a primary school teacher. Her second teaching post was at Mount Stuart Primary School in the area in which she had herself grown up. She was to stay there for the next twenty-eight years, eventually becoming the first Black headteacher, not only at the school but in the whole of Wales.

An inspirational trip to America motivated Campbell to develop her school's curriculum to include and celebrate Black history and culture. She became a Cardiff City councillor and a member of the UK's Commission for Racial Equality. When Nelson Mandela visited Wales in 1998, Campbell was invited to meet him.

Campbell died in October 2017, aged eighty-two. In 2019 a vote was held to decide which Welsh woman to dedicate a new statue to, and Campbell won the vote. In September 2021 her statue was unveiled. The statue proved popular and in late November 2022 it went on to win the public vote at the Public Statues and Sculpture Association Awards.

30 NOVEMBER - STEVE MCQUEEN

Steve McQueen is an award-winning British artist, writer, producer and director. He was born in London in 1969, and his parents were originally from the Caribbean islands of Grenada and Trinidad. In 1999 he won Britain's Turner Prize for visual art, which is one of the most prestigious awards an artist can win.

April Lamb, WikimediaCommons

He then moved into the film industry, where he won a Caméra d'Or Award at the Cannes Film Festival for his debut movie, *Hunger*. His film *12 Years a Slave*, based on the true story of Solomon Northup (see 10 December), was released in the UK on 10 January 2014. The film won the Oscar for Best Picture at the 2014 Academy Awards, the first film with a Black director or producer to win that award.

In 2020 McQueen made an anthology of five films for television called *Small Axe*. They tell five different stories about the lives of the West Indian community in London from the 1960s to the 1980s. The final film in the anthology, *Education*, was based on the experiences McQueen and many others had in the 1970s and 80s, of schools who had low expectations of Black children.

Two of the films from *Small Axe*, *Mangrove* and *Lovers Rock*, were selected to be shown at the 2020 Cannes Film Festival. McQueen would have been the first director to have two films in the competition in the same year, but the festival was cancelled due to the Covid pandemic. In 2020, McQueen was made a knight by Queen Elizabeth II for services to film.

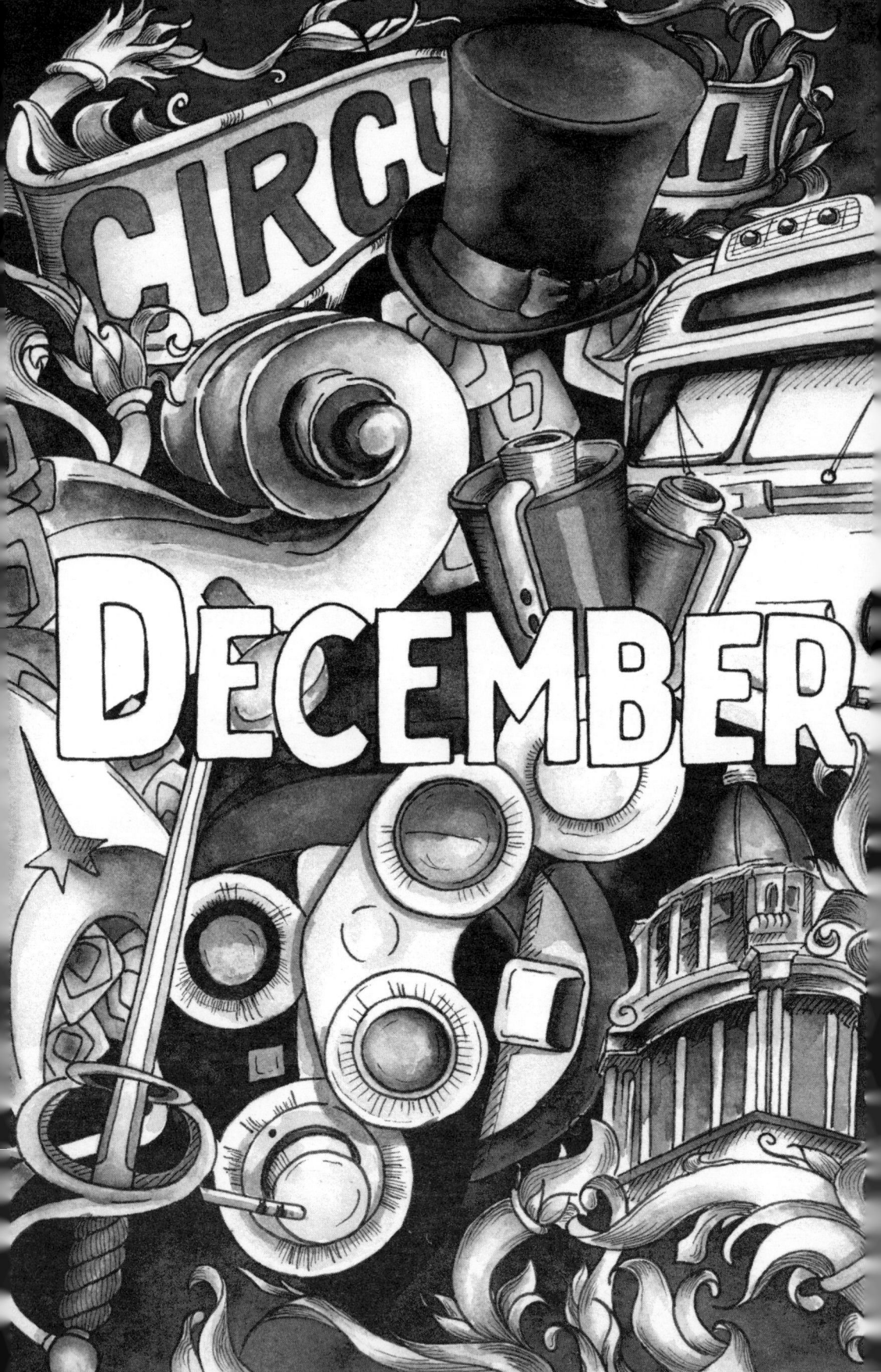

DECEMBER

1 DECEMBER - ROSA PARKS

Rosa Parks was an American civil rights activist and organizer, famous for her role in the Montgomery Bus Boycott of 1955. She was born Rosa Louise McCauley on 14 February 1913 in Tuskegee, Alabama. From a young age she encountered racism and racial segregation. When she was nineteen she married a fellow activist called Raymond Parks and moved to Montgomery, and it was there, in 1948, that Parks became a member of the NAACP.

Rosa Parks at the March on Washington, 1963

Warren K. Leffler, Library of Congress

On 1 December 1955, when travelling home from work by bus, Parks was one of four Black passengers instructed by the bus conductor to get up from their seats and move to the back of the bus to make room for white passengers. Parks was the only one of the four to refuse. The conductor called for the police, who arrested Parks and took her to be charged at the police station.

Parks was not the first Black person to refuse to give up a seat on a Montgomery bus; a number of activists had done so in the months before her arrest. This time, however, the Montgomery chapter of the NAACP and a group called the Women's Political Council (WPC) came together to support and build on the stand that Parks had taken. Three days later, on 4 December, they announced plans for a one-day boycott of buses in Montgomery, scheduled for the next day, 5 December, the day of Parks's trial. 90 per cent of Montgomery's Black citizens complied with the day's boycott, largely due to the planning of the WPC who organized car pooling to ensure people could still get to their jobs. Following its success the decision was made to extend the boycott. The Montgomery Improvement Association (MIA) was formed and a young minister who had recently moved to Montgomery was elected as the group's president. His name was Dr Martin Luther King Jr. The boycott went on to last 381 days. In the end, following a legal ruling that found racial segregation on buses to be unconstitutional, the city of Montgomery was forced to desegregate its buses.

Parks was awarded the Presidential Medal of Freedom in 1996. She died on 24 October 2005 aged ninety-two and her casket was taken to the US Capitol building in Washington DC to lie in state.

> The legal ruling that racial segregation on buses was unconstitutional came in the case of Browder vs. Gayle. The case was brought by the NAACP on behalf of four teenagers and women who had been arrested, charged and fined during 1955, before Rosa Parks had been, for refusing to give up their seats on Montgomery buses – Claudette Colvin (March 1955), Aurelia Browder (April 1955) Susie McDonald and Mary Louise Smith (both October 1955). The city of Montgomery and state of Alabama appealed the decision and on 13 November 1956 the US Supreme Court upheld the ruling and ordered city and state to desegregate their buses.

DID YOU KNOW?

2 DECEMBER ~ THE ZONG MASSACRE

In 1783, people in Britain began to read reports in their newspapers, and hear rumours on the streets, about horrific events that had happened two years earlier on a slave ship called the *Zong*, which was owned by a group of merchants from Liverpool.

The *Zong* had set sail in August 1781 from the coast of West Africa, bound for Jamaica. With 442 enslaved Africans and seventeen crew on board, it was significantly overloaded. The Africans were packed tightly together, chained to the lower decks of the ship. Disease regularly broke out on slave ships and overcrowding increased the risk that large numbers of the captive Africans would become sick and die.

The *Zong*'s journey took longer than usual as the crew had miscalculated their position and sailed hundreds of miles past Jamaica, before realizing their mistake and turning around. By then disease – probably typhus – had broken out among the Africans held on the slave decks. Around sixty of them, and seven crew members, had already died. Many more were unwell.

The captain of the *Zong*, Luke Collingwood, told the crew that the merchants who owned the *Zong* would lose money if the sick Africans died of disease. However, if the sick Africans were thrown into the sea, the owners of the *Zong* could claim that they had been killed in order to save the ship and slow the spread of disease. Under those circumstances, Collingwood explained, the owners could claim financial compensation for the loss of the people thrown overboard from the company that had insured the voyage.

After some discussion, the crew of the *Zong* agreed to Collingwood's plan and embarked upon one of the most terrible crimes in the history of the Transatlantic Slave Trade. Over the course of three days they selected 133 of the most sick enslaved Africans and threw them into the sea, where they drowned. When the *Zong* arrived in Jamaica three weeks later only 208 of the 442 Africans on board had survived.

The ship's owners demanded that the insurance company pay them £3,960 – £30 for each of the people thrown overboard. The insurance company refused, and so the merchants who owned the *Zong* took them to court.

Even though the crew of the *Zong* admitted to throwing 133 people to their deaths they were not charged with murder. The jury were asked to decide just one question – whether the value of the people killed by the crew was covered by the *Zong*'s insurance policy. In court the owners and crew claimed that they had thrown the Africans overboard not just to reduce the spread of disease, but also because the ship was running out of fresh water. The crew argued that by throwing the sick to their deaths they had saved the lives of those who were not yet unwell. After hearing the evidence, the jury decided that the insurance company did have to pay the owners of the *Zong* compensation for the value of the enslaved people thrown overboard.

But again the insurance company refused to pay. They appealed the decision and two new judges were brought in to hear new evidence. It was discovered, during this appeal, that the crew had lied about the fresh water running out on the ship. The judges decided that the insurance company did not have to pay the owners of the *Zong*.

No documents survive to tell us exactly what happened after the court case, but we do know that the *Zong* case had a very big impact on the story of the Transatlantic Slave Trade. Before the *Zong* case most people in Britain did not know very much about the trade in enslaved people. The numbers of people who died of disease on slave ships, or who were killed if they tried to rebel against the crew and fight for their freedom, were well-kept secrets. But because court cases are held in public, many people heard the evidence that was given in court and were deeply appalled. Lord Mansfield (see 21 June), the judge in both the trial and appeal, admitted that the case was one that 'shocks one very much'. Some of those who had heard the evidence in court wrote letters about it for newspapers, informing yet more people about the *Zong*. The case shone a light on some of the darkest secrets of the slave trade. Never before had the details of such a terrible crime been brought to the attention of so many people.

This encouraged more people in Britain to oppose the slave trade. One of the people who read newspaper reports of the *Zong* court case was Olaudah Equiano (see 6 April). Equiano was so shocked at what he had read that he visited the home of another campaigner against slavery, Granville Sharp, and told him about the terrible crime.

Although the crew of the *Zong* were never charged with the murder or punished for the terrible crimes they committed, the atrocity motivated some people in Britain to start a campaign to abolish the slave trade.

3 DECEMBER ~ HORACE OVÉ

In 1975 Horace Ové released his film *Pressure*, making him the UK's first Black director of a feature film.

Born on 3 December 1936 in Belmont, Trinidad, Ové moved to the UK in 1960 and enrolled in film school in London in 1965. He established his career with documentary-making, finding it hard to get funding for more experimental works. Even with his film *Pressure* he found support lacking when the British Film Institute (BFI) withheld the release of the film for three years, apparently uncomfortable with its depiction of police brutality.

Ové was also well known as a photographer, particularly for his imagery chronicling the Black diaspora and the Windrush Generation. At the time of his arrival in the country, Britain was a hub of political and creative thought. Ové was ideally placed to capture the growing international liberation movement and its protagonists, including James Baldwin (see 2 August), Stokely Carmichael (see 4 June) and Michael X, founder of the UK's Black Power Movement. His images have been the subject of many international exhibitions.

In 2022 he received a knighthood. Hailed as a pioneer of Black British cinema, Ové publicly expressed his frustration at the film industry and at its constraints on Black film-makers.

> I believe that film is an art and I'm interested in experimenting and taking it further, but I know that's a problem because we live in a society where they don't associate that sort of creativity with Black people.

Ové died in September 2023 at the age of eighty-six.

4 DECEMBER - FRED HAMPTON

At 4.30 a.m. on 4 December 1969, fourteen armed police officers drove up to an apartment in Chicago. Inside were members of the Black Panther Party, including twenty-one-year-old Fred Hampton, their deputy chairman. The police had been given the address by an FBI spy, who drugged Hampton so that he wouldn't wake up. The police kicked down the door and started shooting. They fired more than ninety times, killing twenty-two-year-old Mark Clark and injuring several others. Then they shot Hampton in his bed.

Hampton's assassination had been ordered by Edward Hanrahan, the Cook County state's attorney. He later claimed that his officers were attacked by the Black Panthers and that Hampton himself had fired at the police. All his claims were false.

The Black Panthers were an African American revolutionary organization founded by students in 1966 in response to police brutality. They became an influential Black Power group, calling for social change. Fred Hampton had joined them in 1968.

Hampton was a brilliant student and an activist from a young age. At high school, he organized walkouts and campaigned to get more Black teachers hired. After graduating, he worked hard to help poor Black communities. His strong leadership concerned the authorities and Hampton was secretly placed on an FBI Key Agitator list. It was later revealed that FBI director, J. Edgar Hoover, believed that the Black Panthers were the 'greatest threat to the internal security of the country.'

The plot to kill Hampton was not the end of the Black Panthers, however, as they continued their activism into the 1980s. Fred Hampton's story is told in the 2021 film *Judas and the Black Messiah*.

5 DECEMBER – ALEXANDRE DUMAS

Alexandre Dumas was born in France in 1802, grandson of enslaved Haitian woman Marie-Cessette Dumas and a minor French noble, and son of Thomas-Alexandre Dumas, a general in Napoleon's army. Although General Dumas had been held in high regard, he was left to languish in the captivity of the Holy Faith Army in Napoli for two years  in which he experienced torture that left him disabled. When he was finally released he was refused a military pension and died two years later in 1806, leaving his wife scrabbling for work to ensure her son received an education.

As a teenager Dumas found a job with a notary, and by 1822 he had moved to Paris where his connection to nobility got him employment as a scribe for the Duke of Orléans. This exposure to the literary world in Paris inspired him to write, and he debuted his first play *Henry III and his Court* in 1829. It proved a success and spurred Dumas to try writing across many genres, but it was with the novel that Dumas achieved popularity and longevity, if not immediate critical acclaim.

In 1844 he wrote the first of his d'Artagnan Romances, *The Three Musketeers*, which was originally released as a serial in the newspaper *Le Siècle*. A work of semi-fiction, Dumas was careful to research the historical figures it was based on and their roles in the Musketeers (King's Guards). According to the records at Marseille library, Dumas borrowed *Les Memoires d'Artagnan*, the first-hand account of the titular musketeer, but never returned it. The work was wildly popular and he completed two sequels and *The Count of Monte Cristo* over the next three years. Dumas penned hundreds of works over his lifetime and his successful career funded an extravagant lifestyle that saw him travel extensively and eventually exile himself from France for a while to avoid people to whom he owed money.

Despite his apparent social acceptance, Dumas was still subject to racism and was aware of his family's origins in slavery. The plot of his novella *Georges*, written in 1843, appears a somewhat veiled account of his own experiences. Set on the island of Mauritius, Dumas' mixed-heritage protagonist Georges experiences racism from a particular white plantation owning family on the island, and is sent away to France by his father for protection and to be educated. His lighter complexion allows him to pass as white and he forms friendships among French high society. However, upon his return to Mauritius to exact revenge against his tormentors, these relationships become complicated and strained and devolve into violence.

Dumas eventually returned to France. He moved in with his son, also a successful writer, and died on 5 December 1870. In 2002 he was granted the honour of being reinterred at the Pantheon in Paris in recognition of his contribution to French and world literature.

6 DECEMBER ~ THE TARANTO MUTINY

When the First World War started, the British War Office strongly opposed the recruitment of men from the British West Indian colonies. In 1915, after huge losses on the battlefields, they changed their policy. Thousands of West Indian men volunteered to fight, and the British West Indies Regiment (BWIR) was formed (see 26 October). However, the regiment's twelve battalions were mostly not allowed to actively fight on the front lines. Instead, they were assigned to support tasks as labourers, digging trenches, building and working in ammunition depots. It was critical work but not what they had been trained to do. Despite this unequal treatment, men of the BWIR went on to be mentioned in dispatches forty-nine times and to win eighty-one medals for bravery.

When the war came to an end, BWIR battalions were sent to Taranto, Italy, to wait to be demobilized. Here, they were put into racially segregated accommodation and denied access to some of the facilities, including the soldiers' hospital and the cinema. The men were assigned the same sorts of support work – loading and unloading supplies, digging and building. However, they were also ordered to clean latrines for the white British soldiers and Italian civilian labourers, cook their meals and wash their laundry. At the same time, the white troops received a pay rise that the Black troops were denied.

After four years of poor treatment by the British Army, on 6 December 1918, the men of the BWIR 9th Battalion mutinied and refused to obey orders. One hundred and eighty Black sergeants in the BWIR signed a petition in which they demanded the same pay increase that had recently been given to the rest of the British Army. The mutiny lasted four days and on 9 December the men of the 10th Battalion of the BWIR joined the protest, downing tools and refusing to work.

Troops from the Worcestershire Regiment were sent in to restore order, and they disarmed all of the BWIR troops. Between fifty and sixty BWIR soldiers were later tried in court. The leaders were sentenced to imprisonment, the longest sentence being twenty-one years. One man was executed by firing squad. Eventually, in February 1919, the BWIR were awarded the pay rise in line with white regiments. The BWIR was completely disbanded in 1921.

Imperial War Museum, London (Q1202)

Troops of the British West Indies Regiment in camp on the Albert-Amiens road, September 1916, photographed by Lieutenant Ernest Brooks

The experience led a group of BWIR officers to form the Caribbean League on 17 December 1918, a group that promoted self-determination for the islands of the Caribbean. Although the league soon disbanded, several BWIR veterans went on to play important roles in Marcus Garvey's Universal Negro Improvements Association (see 17 August), furthering the cause of **Pan-Africanism** and the end of colonial rule.

7 DECEMBER - JAMES VAN DER ZEE

The African American photographer and musician James Van Der Zee was born in Lenox, Massachusetts, on 29 June 1886. From an early age he developed passions for music and photography. He played piano and violin and bought his first camera at the age of sixteen, setting up a darkroom in his parents' house to develop his own photographs.

In 1906 he moved to New York. At first he worked as a waiter and an elevator operator, but soon he was earning money from his music as one of the founding members of the Harlem Orchestra. In 1916 he opened the Guarantee Photo Studio on West 125th Street in Harlem with his second wife, Gaynella Greenlee. It became a huge success, particularly in the 1920s and 30s. Van Der Zee became the most important photographer of the Harlem Renaissance, taking portrait photographs of the movement's writers, artists, actors and musicians. His portfolio of work also included portraits of men, women and children of the Black middle class that was developing in Harlem at the time. He also documented more serious subjects, such as funerals and the victory parade of the 369th Infantry Regiment – known as the 'Harlem Hellfighters' – when they returned to New York in 1919 from the First World War (see 25 September).

Van Der Zee's work began to get more recognition in the art world from the 1960s onwards. He died on 15 May 1983 and a year later was inducted into the International Photography Hall of Fame and Museum. On 7 December 2021, the James Van Der Zee Archive was established at the Metropolitan Museum of Art to look after and research his collection of photographs and preserve it for future generations.

TIMELINE 11

8 DECEMBER ~ DAVID HAREWOOD

The British actor, director, author and mental health activist David Harewood was born in Birmingham, England on 8 December 1965, to Barbadian parents. In his teens he developed an interest in acting, and won a place at the prestigious Royal Academy of Dramatic Art in London.

Harewood soon began his acting career, both on the stage and in a host of British television shows and films. In 1997 he became the first Black actor to play the role of Othello at the National Theatre in London. Harewood's career took him to America, where he starred in two seasons of the drama series *Homeland*, and in the series *Supergirl*. Harewood has also presented television documentaries. In his 2019 documentary *Psychosis and Me*, Harewood investigated his experience of being hospitalized because of a psychotic breakdown at the age of twenty-three, brought on in part by the pressures of racism. It was a theme he went on to discuss further in his 2021 autobiography, *Maybe I Don't Belong Here*.

Harewood has become a campaigner for mental health and also for formal reparations for slavery. His surname is a legacy of slavery and the historical ownership of his ancestors by Henry Lascelles, the second Earl of Harewood. In 2023 a portrait of Harewood, commissioned by David Lascelles, the 8th Earl of Harewood, went on display at Harewood House in West Yorkshire, alongside an exhibition examining how their families are linked by the British Slave Trade. In 2023 Harewood was given an **OBE** for services to drama.

9 DECEMBER ~ ROY DeCARAVA

Roy DeCarava remains one of the most important photographers of the 20th century, not only for the rare content of his archive, but for the artistry with which he approached his craft. Born in Harlem on 9 December 1919, DeCarava started out as an artist, studying painting and sculpture at the Cooper Union Institute, to which he later returned as a teacher. He made the shift into photography in the 1940s, and by 1950 had begun to exhibit his work. His inaugural show caught the attention of the director of MoMA and just two years later DeCarava became the first African American photographer to win a Guggenheim Fellowship.

DeCarava had expressed his frustration with the shallow depiction of African American life in photography and set out to portray the depth and breadth of his subjects' lives through his imagery, using his signature style of moody lighting and high contrast.

His long-running project *The Sound I Saw* traced the New York jazz scene and featured images of John Coltrane and Billie Holiday. DeCarava also collaborated with poet Langston Hughes (see 1 February) on the book *The Sweet Flypaper of Life*.

DeCarava died in 2009, leaving an extensive body of work which is held in museums and galleries all over the world.

10 DECEMBER ~ SOLOMON NORTHUP

Author and anti-slavery campaigner Solomon Northup was born free in New York in around 1807. His mother was freeborn and his father, a farmer, had been freed from enslavement on the death of his owner. At first Northup too was a farmer before he became a professional musician. He married and started a family, earning a living playing his violin while his wife worked as a cook.

In 1841 Northup was approached by two men, Merrill Brown and Abram Hamilton, who offered him a job as a travelling musician. They took him to New York to perform and then persuaded him to travel with them to Washington DC for more work. Once there, Merrill and Brown drugged Northup and sold him to a slave trader, telling him that Northup was a fugitive who had escaped enslavement.

Northup spent the next twelve years enslaved by various owners and received violent treatment. Finally, a carpenter from Canada, who had been doing some work for his final owner, befriended Northup and agreed to carry secret letters to friends and relatives in New York so that they could find him and return him to freedom. With the help of the son of his father's former owner, and the governor of New York, Northup was finally freed in 1853.

On his return home, Northup spent three months writing a book, *Twelve Years a Slave*, with support from the lawyer and writer David Wilson. He went on a tour to promote the book and it became an important anti-slavery text in the years leading up to the American Civil War. Northup campaigned against slavery until his death in 1863 or 1864. In 2013 *Twelve Years a Slave* became an award-winning film by the director Steve McQueen (see 30 November).

11 DECEMBER - ADVERTISEMENTS FOR ENSLAVED CHILDREN FOR SALE

In recent years, historians have been learning more about the presence of Black people in 18th-century Britain as newspapers from the Georgian era have been digitally scanned and placed in online archives. Some of these newspapers contain advertisements for the sale of Black children, even though it was not clear at the time whether slavery was legal on British soil.

Broadside announcing the sale of an enslaved man named Dick and an enslaved girl named Lydia, Cross Plains, Tennessee, 18th June 1857

As people made their fortunes owning plantations on the British colonies and the enslaved people who worked on them, they would often return to Britain, bringing enslaved children and adults with them. Additionally, captains of slave ships, after they sold the rest of their human cargo in the colonies, would bring one or two enslaved children back with them to Britain to be sold. Among the upper classes it became fashionable to have a Black child, most often a boy, to act as a house servant. They were given new names by their owners and were referred to as 'Negro' children. Once they reached their later teen years, however, they were often sold or returned to the colonies to work in the harsh conditions of the plantations.

12 DECEMBER - JOHN EDMONSTONE

John Edmonstone was born into slavery in British Guiana (now Guyana) in the 1790s. Plantation owner Charles Edmonstone often received guests at his estate, including naturalist Charles Waterton. It was from Waterton that Edmonstone learned the skill of taxidermy, although he later claimed that Edmonstone was slow and difficult to teach.

The Edmonstone family returned to Scotland in 1817, taking a handful of enslaved people with them. However, as Scotland had declared slavery illegal in 1778 (see 15 January), Edmonstone found himself a free man. He left his previous owner, moved to Edinburgh and took a job as a servant for a Dr Duncan at the university. He began to build his taxidermy business and by 1823 had opened a shop on Lothian Street where he met and fell in love with his neighbour, Mary Kerr. Their marriage on 12 December 1824 provides one of the few definite records for Edmonstone's life, although there is a possible inclusion on an 1841 census of the couple and their three children.

As well as selling specimens to museums and private collectors, Edmonstone offered lessons in taxidermy at one guinea an hour to students from the university. Bored teenage medical student Charles Darwin wrote to his sister of his decision to take lessons with Edmonstone as they were a cheap way to pass time. As a bonus he also got to hear tales of his naturalist hero Waterton. Darwin clearly found no issue with Edmonstone's skills and, after finally meeting Waterton, described his former hero as 'the strangest mixture of extreme kindness, harshness & bigotry, that I ever saw'.

Edmonstone's business continued to grow and his shop moved to bigger and more prestigious addresses, ending up on Princes Street in 1843. After that records for him and his family disappear and nothing further is known.

13 DECEMBER - FRANCIS BARBER

In around 1740 a child called Quashey was born on a Jamaican plantation. At age ten he was brought to Britain, baptized as Francis Barber, and sent to school. His owner was Colonel Richard Bathurst, who may have been his father.

Painting, thought to be of Francis Barber, in the style of Joshua Reynolds, 18th Century

Tate Collection, Wikimedia Commons

The colonel's son, also named Richard Bathurst, was a friend of the writer Samuel Johnson, author of the famous *A Dictionary of the English Language*. In 1752 Johnson's wife suddenly died and Bathurst sent Barber to work for Johnson as his valet. When Colonel Bathurst died two years later, he freed Barber in his will. Barber left Johnson's service for a time, and found work as an apothecary's assistant before he joined the navy. He served two years aboard HMS *Stag* until Johnson secured his release. Barber returned to London and became Johnson's butler. Johnson then paid for Barber to receive a grammar school education for five years, after which he became Johnson's secretary and surrogate son.

On 13 December 1784, Samuel Johnson died. The contents of his will caused a sensation in the press. Johnson had left Barber £70 per year in income (roughly £9,000 today), all his books and papers and a gold watch. He wanted Barber and his family to move to the city of Johnson's birth, Lichfield. Barber duly did, and for a time opened a school in the city. He died in Stafford in January 1801. A portrait from the 1770s, called *A Young Black*, thought by some historians to be of Barber, is now in the collection of the Tate Museum.

14 DECEMBER - IGNATIUS SANCHO

Writer, composer and abolitionist Ignatius Sancho was born around 1729 on board a slave ship. He was brought to England as a young child and worked in the house of three sisters in Greenwich, who gave him the surname Sancho (a reference to the squire Sancho Panze from the novel *Don Quixote*). In around 1740 he was befriended by John Montagu, Second Duke of Montagu. Impressed by Sancho's intelligence, Montagu helped him to educate himself and Sancho left to work for the duke.

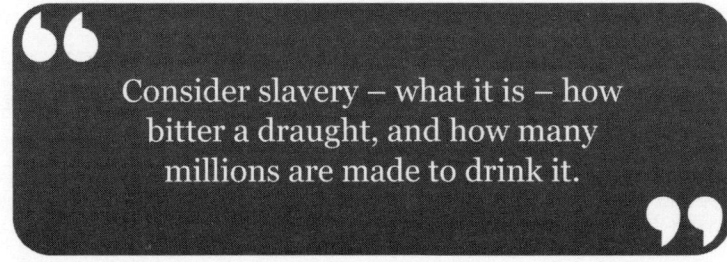

National Gallery of Canada, Wikimedia Commons

In 1773, Sancho used an inheritance from the Duchess of Montagu to open a grocery store in Westminster. He was now well known in society and the shop became a meeting place for his friends: writers, artists and politicians. Sancho was a composer and writer whose letters contained fascinating observations on 18th-century culture and politics. He told people about his experiences of the slave trade, and his writings were later used as evidence to support the abolitionist movement. Being a male property-owner, Sancho was eligible to vote and in 1774 he became the first known Black man to vote in Britain. When he died on 14 December 1780 he was the first Black person to have an obituary printed in the British press. Two years later, his letters were published in a bestselling book, *Letters of the Late Ignatius Sancho*.

> 66
> Consider slavery – what it is – how bitter a draught, and how many millions are made to drink it.
> 99

15 DECEMBER ~ bell hooks

On 15 December 2021, the acclaimed author, poet, educator and academic bell hooks died at the age of sixty-nine. She was born Gloria Jean Watkins in September 1952 in the then racially segregated town of Hopkinsville, Kentucky. In her childhood she developed a love of poetry, performing readings of poets such as Langston Hughes (see 1 February) and Gwendolyn Brooks.

She began her education in segregated schools and finished it at an integrated school. This experience would influence her later work, and her interest in education for social justice. She went on to gain a degree in education from Stanford University. For her PhD, at the University of Southern California, she completed a dissertation on the writer Toni Morrison (see 31 March) and became a professor there. Her first major book, *Ain't I a Woman? Black Women and Feminism*, was published in 1981. The book launched her literary career and is still a highly influential work. She chose to use the pseudonym bell hooks, her much admired great-grandmother's name, and wrote in it in lower case to emphasize that the reader should focus on the work rather than the author.

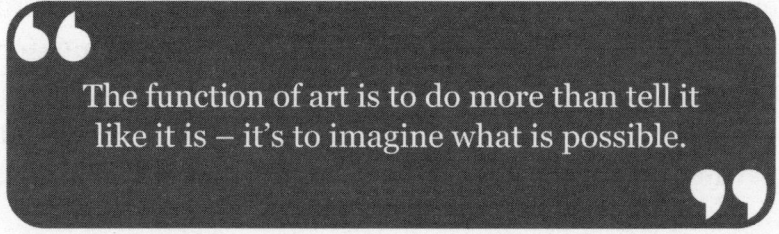

> The function of art is to do more than tell it like it is – it's to imagine what is possible.

hooks went on to publish over thirty books, tackling issues of race, gender, social class, feminism, masculinity, intersectionality and education, and she wrote for children as well as adults. Many of her books went on to win literary prizes and poetry awards. hooks identified in part as Buddhist and queer, and her most famous book is aptly titled *All About Love*.

16 DECEMBER – THE MANGROVE NINE

The National Archives (MEPO 31-21-5)

16 December 1971 was the first time that it was officially acknowledged, by a judge in a British court, that there was racism in London's Metropolitan Police. That was because this was the date that the Mangrove Nine were declared innocent of the charges brought against them of inciting a riot.

The Mangrove was an all-night restaurant in Notting Hill, run by Frank Crichlow, a community activist from Trinidad. Popular among the local Black community for its Caribbean food, it even attracted celebrity customers like Bob Marley (see 6 February) and Jimi Hendrix (see 27 November). The restaurant was targeted by the Metropolitan Police who said they suspected that drugs were being sold there. Between January 1969 and July 1970 they raided it twelve times, and each time failed to find evidence of drugs and criminal activity. Despite this, in December 1969, the local council withdrew Crichlow's licence to run the Mangrove as an all-night cafe, as they said that it was being used at night by people with criminal records. Crichlow saw this new restriction to the cafe's opening hours as yet more unfair discrimination, and soon a community-led movement called the Action Committee for the Defence of the Mangrove started, with the aim of saving the cafe.

On 9 August 1970, 150 protestors marched to a local police station. Violence broke out between the police and the protestors and several people, later dubbed the Mangrove Nine, were arrested and falsely blamed for inciting a riot. Their case was initially dismissed, but the director of public prosecutions sent it back to court and their trial began in 1971. Two of the accused, Black Power activists Altheia Jones LeCointe (see 9 January) and Darcus Howe, made the important decision to defend themselves in court. They argued that the jury should be Black so, in accordance, they said, with the laws of Magna Carta, they could be tried in front of a jury of their peers. The argument for an all-Black jury did not succeed. Each potential juror was asked what they understood the term 'Black Power' to mean. They rejected sixty-three potential jurors. The final jury of twelve included two Black jurors.

The trial lasted fifty-five days. By the end of it the defendants were all cleared of the main charge of inciting a riot. Instead the trial had shone a spotlight on the racism and harassment carried out by the Metropolitan Police.

The trial of the Mangrove Nine was an important watershed for Black activists in Britain, inspiring others to stand up to racist institutions. In 2020 the Mangrove Nine were the subject of one of the films in Steve McQueen's *Small Axe* television series (see 30 November).

Condoleezza Rice was born in 1954 and raised in the southern state of Alabama in the USA which, during her childhood, was still racially segregated. In 1963 her local church, the Birmingham Sixteenth Street Baptist Church, was bombed and her friend Denise McNair was killed, along with three other children, Carole Robertson, Addie Mae Collins and Cynthia Wesley.

Rice studied political science at university, before gaining a **PhD** in international studies. She worked as a political advisor during the 1980s and then began an academic career at Stanford University in the 1990s.

In the 2000s she served under President George W. Bush, firstly as the national security advisor from January 2001, and then as secretary of state from January 2005 until January 2009. In both roles she made history – as the first woman to serve as national security advisor, and then as the first female African American secretary of state.

As secretary of state in April 2008, Rice petitioned Congress to finally lift the travel ban on South African officials. As members of the ANC they had been categorized as terrorists during their anti-**apartheid** struggle. Rice said, 'It is frankly a rather embarrassing matter that I still have to waive in my own counterparts – the foreign minister of South Africa, not to mention the great leader, Nelson Mandela.' Three months later the ban was lifted.

DID YOU KNOW?

18 DECEMBER - PATRICIA BATH

On 18 December 1986 ophthalmologist and laser scientist Patricia Bath applied for a patent for her invention, the laserphaco probe. When the patent was granted in 1988 it made her the first African American female doctor to receive a medical patent.

Born in 1942 in Harlem, New York, Bath decided on a medical career as a child. She studied medicine at Howard University and moved on to a fellowship in ophthalmology at Columbia University and an internship at Harlem Hospital. It was through working in these two differing environments that she noticed a difference between the occurrences of blindness in Black and white populations. Following more research, she documented that African Americans were twice as likely to suffer from blindness and that it was the result of a lack of access to ophthalmic care. Bath set out to bring eye care to deprived communities with an outreach programme of screening for eye disease. In 1977 she co-founded the American Institute for the Prevention of Blindness to 'protect, preserve, and restore the gift of sight'.

Bath had a particular interest in treating cataracts and in 1981 she began work on what would become her laserphaco probe. It was designed to replace the damaged cornea with an artificial prosthetic (keratoprosthesis) in a quicker, easier and less painful operation. It took five years for the technology to catch up with her idea but she finally completed her invention in 1986. Since then it has gone into worldwide use, restoring sight to thousands of people.

Two years after her death in 2019 Bath became one of the first African American women to be inducted into the National Inventors Hall of Fame.

19 DECEMBER ~ JAMES GRONNIOSAW

James Albert Ukawsaw Gronniosaw was born into a royal family in what is now Nigeria. As a teenager he was captured, enslaved and shipped across the Atlantic to the island of Barbados. There he was bought and taken to New York, where he was sold once again. He was now the property of Theodorus Jacobus Frelinghuysen, a religious minister who taught Gronniosaw to read and converted him to Christianity. When Frelinghuysen died, he freed Gronniosaw in his will. Gronniosaw stayed with Frelinghuysen's widow and children for four years. After they all died he decided to travel to England, a place where he thought he would meet other people with his strong religious faith.

Gronniosaw travelled first to the Caribbean, where he served in the British Army for a while. Once he left the army he set sail for Britain, arriving in Portsmouth before moving to London where he met a young widow called Elizabeth. They married and started a family, however Gronniosaw had a difficult time securing work. He and his family had to move around the country a great deal in search of employment. He often struggled to house and feed his family, though he did sometimes get support from fellow Christians. Gronniosaw told his life story to an Englishman called Walter Shirley, who wrote it down, and in 1772 his autobiography *Narrative of the Most Remarkable Particulars in the Life of James Albert Ukawsaw Gronniosaw, an African Prince, as Related by Himself* was published. He was the first Black African person to have a book published in Britain and his was the first of what became known as 'slave narratives'.

Gronniosaw died in Chester, England in 1775 and the death notice published in the *Chester Chronicle* gave his age as seventy and described him as 'an African Prince of Zaara'.

20 DECEMBER - FANNIE LOU HAMER

Born the twentieth child of sharecroppers in Mississippi in 1917, Fannie Lou Townsend Hamer was raised in poverty and was picking cotton from the age of six. Her involvement in the civil rights movement began with an attempt by herself and a group of volunteers to register to vote. Unsurprisingly denied, the group were also harassed by police and Hamer was fired from her plantation job and evicted from her home. This marked the beginning of a lifetime dedicated to Black liberation.

She sustained lifelong injuries in 1963 after an arrest and beating for sitting in a whites-only restaurant. In 1964 she co-founded the Mississippi Freedom Democratic Party and made an unsuccessful run for Mississippi Congress. Hamer also understood the need for economic freedom and founded the Freedom Farm Cooperative in 1969, a project to help rural Black families with food security, housing and education. Her last big project was the founding of the National Women's Political Caucus to support women entering politics. Suffering from nervous exhaustion and deteriorating health, Hamer had a number of hospital spells in the early 1970s before she was diagnosed with breast cancer. She died on 14 March 1977.

Hamer is most remembered for her powerful speeches. It was on 20 December 1964 in Harlem that she delivered her most famous speech, a line from which is inscribed on her headstone:

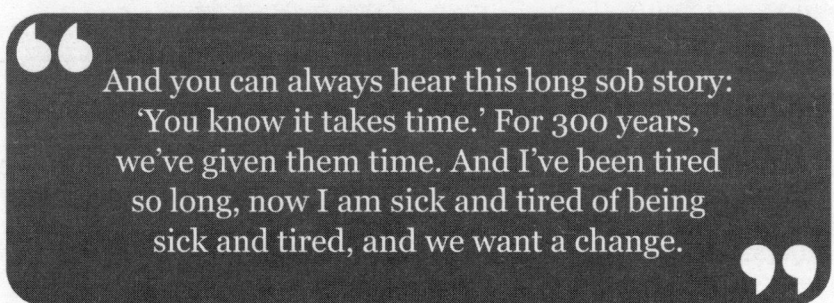

> And you can always hear this long sob story:
> 'You know it takes time.' For 300 years,
> we've given them time. And I've been tired
> so long, now I am sick and tired of being
> sick and tired, and we want a change.

21 DECEMBER ~ SCIPIO AFRICANUS

In St Mary's churchyard, in Bristol, England, lies the grave of Scipio Africanus. Born in around 1702, he died aged eighteen on 21 December 1720. Decorated with Black cherubs and flowers, the inscription on his gravestone reads, 'I who was Born a PAGAN and a SLAVE Now Sweetly Sleep a CHRISTIAN in my Grave'.

Little is known of Africanus' life, but by the early 1700s he was working for Charles William Howard, the 7th Earl of Suffolk. It is unclear whether he was treated as an enslaved person, or as a paid servant, and he died before the ruling on the legality of slavery on British soil in 1772 (see 21 June). He was given the name Scipio Africanus, probably by Howard, after a Roman general who had freed people he had enslaved – this might indicate that Africanus was free.

Historians estimate that around 10,000 Black people worked as servants or as enslaved people in Georgian Britain. What makes Africanus unusual is that he was given an individual grave marked with a decorated headstone and footstone, both costly items.

In June 2020, his grave was vandalized and smashed. A chalked message on nearby flagstones read 'Put Colston's statue back or things will really heat up'. This referred to the toppling of a statue of slave trader Edward Colston during a Black Lives Matter protest following the murder of George Floyd (see 7 June, 11 July and 25 May). The stones have been repaired and remain in the churchyard, a rare memorial to an enslaved person.

William Avery, Wikimedia Commons

22 DECEMBER - JEAN-MICHEL BASQUIAT

Jean-Michel Basquiat was born on 22 December 1960 in Brooklyn, New York. His father was Haitian, and his mother was of Puerto Rican heritage.

As a child, Basquiat loved to draw and his mother always encouraged his interest in art. He met his friend, Al Diaz, at high school and the pair began spray-painting graffiti around downtown New York. Basquiat loved cartoons and he created his own character called SAMO, who became the pair's 'tag'.

Basquiat left home at seventeen and lived with other artists and musicians in New York, selling hand-painted postcards and T-shirts to make a living. He began developing his own unique and distinctive artistic style, mixing images of skulls, body parts and crowns with 'graffitied' references to African American historical figures, pop culture and politics.

In the 1980s Basquiat's work gained critical and commercial success. He had his first solo exhibition in Italy in 1981 and he became the youngest artist to exhibit at the Whitney Museum of American Art at the age of twenty-two.

In 1988, Jean-Michel Basquiat died of a drug overdose. He was twenty-seven years old. Despite his short career, he is now one of the few African American artists to have broken into the international art scene. In 2017 a Japanese billionaire bought his skull painting, *Untitled, 1982*, for £85.2 million, the highest price paid at auction for the work of an American artist.

23 DECEMBER ~ HILARIUS GILGES

Hilarius Gilges was a dancer and actor and committed Anti-Nazi activist born in Dusseldorf, Germany in 1909, to a European mother and African father. Although there had been a Black presence in Europe for many years, Gilges was still subject to verbal and physical abuse because of his race. As a teenager he joined the Young Communist League and through them the Nordwest Ran, a travelling theatre group that used entertainment to spread ideas of socialism and to combat the growing influence of the Nazi Party.

Gilges engaged in many protests and demonstrations along with his fellow communists against the Nazi threat, and in 1931 was arrested and sentenced to a year in jail for his part in a fight. Once released he continued to spread the word about the dangers of Nazism, until 1933 when Adolf Hitler became chancellor and then swept away any remaining opposition, particularly that of the communists.

Being both Black and a known communist made Gilges an easily identifiable target for the Nazis. The Gestapo and SS came for him on the night of 20 June 1933, tearing him from his wife and two children. The following day his body was found floating in the River Rhine. He had been tortured, stabbed multiple times and then shot in the head.

On 23 December 2003 Dusseldorf officially named a square in the city Hilarius Gilges Platz to honour his memory and his fight against Nazism.

TIMELINE 6

24 DECEMBER - IDA B. WELLS

Wikimedia Commons

On 24 December 1884 Ida B. Wells successfully sued the Chesapeake and Ohio Railroad. Wells had been forcibly removed from the train after the conductor decided that she should not be in the first-class car despite having a ticket. However, her victory was later overturned on appeal and she turned to journalism to express her frustration. She wrote pieces for many Black newspapers under the pen name 'Iola' and eventually became editor and part owner of the *Memphis Free Speech and Headlight* newspaper.

While Jim Crow was taking hold across the American South, Wells had plenty to write about, but her work found its focus when a friend, Thomas Moss, was lynched in 1892. Many lynchings were carried out under the pretext that the mostly Black male victims had attacked white women, but Wells was sceptical and set out to investigate the practice. In a series of increasingly incendiary pieces, Wells exposed the acts of white mob violence and proposed the likelihood of the lynched victims actually having been in consensual romantic relationships with the women they were alleged to have attacked. The response was immediate and violent; her offices were set alight and her family threatened. Wells, in New York at the time, elected to remain in exile and moved to Chicago, where she continued her anti-lynching campaigning until her death in 1931.

One hundred and thirty years after the murders of Thomas Moss and more than 6,500 other victims, the USA finally made lynching a federal crime. On 29 March 2022 the Emmett Till Anti-lynching Act was signed into law in a ceremony attended by relatives of both Wells and Till (see 25 July).

25 DECEMBER - CHEVALIER DE SAINT-GEORGES

Born in Guadeloupe in the French West Indies on 25 December 1745, Joseph Bologne was the son of a plantation owner and an enslaved Senegalese woman. At seven years old his father sent him away to school in France.

Bologne attended prestigious schools for fencing and horsemanship, and his speed and skill with the blade was renowned. As a student he defeated fencing Master Alexandre Picard in a grudge match, enhancing his standing among his aristocratic peers. Once graduated, Bologne became a knight (or chevalier), known as Chevalier de Saint-Georges, but after this his military career took a back seat to his music.

An immensely gifted violinist, Saint-Georges also received a musical education. He began to compose his own music in the 1770s while also performing as a violin soloist, conducting an orchestra and directing the private theatre of Madame de Montesson, the wife of the Duke of Orléans. Unfortunately the death of the duke in 1785 left Saint-Georges unemployed, destitute and homeless, and he left for London.

In 1790 he returned to France. Looking for a place in the new post-revolution landscape, he resumed his military career. In 1792 the National Assembly agreed to form legions from the colonies and Saint-Georges was given command of what became known as the Legion Saint-Georges, made up entirely of free Black men. However, his previous connections to the aristocracy came back to haunt him and in 1793 he was accused of non-revolutionary activities and imprisoned. Upon his release he attempted to rejoin the army but was rejected. He returned to music for his last few years until his death in 1799.

26 DECEMBER ~ PABLO FANQUE

The inspiration for the 1967 song 'Being for the Benefit of Mr Kite!', by the Beatles, was a Victorian poster one of the band members, John Lennon, bought in the 1960s. It advertised a show by Pablo Fanque's Circus held on 14 February 1843 in Rochdale, England. Lennon used phrases from the poster in the lyrics of the song.

Wikimedia Commons

Pablo Fanque was born in Norwich, England, likely in the year 1810. Britain in the Georgian period had a sizeable Black population because of the regular movement of people between Britain and its colonies. As a child Pablo Fanque became a circus apprentice, doing stunts on horseback and performing tricks with ropes. His first known stage appearance took place on 26 December 1821, when he was around eleven years old. Eventually he became the owner of his own circus. For thirty years Pablo Fanque's Circus Royal travelled the country performing, including once playing for the royal family in Brighton. He married twice and had children who also became performers in his circus.

The poster that John Lennon bought was advertising a 'benefit' show that had taken place to raise money for a retiring performer, Mr Kite. During his career Pablo Fanque held many benefit shows to raise funds for injured or retired performers, and for organizations that supported people in need. Fanque died on 4 May 1871 and is buried at St George's Field at the University of Leeds. In 2010 a blue plaque was installed in Norwich near the site of his birth, commemorating his life.

27 DECEMBER - SAM SHARPE'S REBELLION

On 25 December 1831 enslaved people on the Caribbean island of Jamaica began a general strike in protest at their terrible treatment, under the leadership of a man called Sam Sharpe. He was born on the island in 1801 and, unlike most enslaved people at the time, had received some education, learning to read and write. By 1831 Sharpe was a Baptist preacher in Montego Bay.

Sharpe and his followers refused to go back to work after Christmas unless the slave owners agreed to hear their grievances. They hoped that the strike, held at a crucial harvesting time, would be enough to make the slave owners meet their demands, but the peaceful protest quickly turned violent. Sharpe's Rebellion began on 27 December when the slave owners went on the attack and the strikers began burning the expensive sugarcane crops. For ten days at least 20,000 (and maybe as many as 60,000) enslaved people fought for their freedom against the local British Army troops, setting fire to crops and plantation houses.

It took three months to completely put down the rebellion. During the fighting over 300 rebels were killed, and 340 of them, including Sam Sharpe, were caught and executed. One hundred and forty of the surviving rebels were shipped to Australia as convicts. The cost to the plantation owners and colonial government was huge, estimated at over a million pounds. Although it did not succeed, its scale and cost, and the likelihood of a second, bigger rebellion, meant that the authorities in Jamaica and in Britain began to recognize that change was inevitable. Sharpe was acknowledged in 1975 as a National Hero of Jamaica and today his image can be found on the Jamaican $50 note.

28 DECEMBER ~ NICHELLE NICHOLS

The character of Lieutenant Nyota Uhura in the 1960s sci-fi television show *Star Trek* proved to be more important to the movements for social change than could possibly have been foreseen. The role itself was revolutionary, and it was actor Nichelle Nichols who brought Uhura to life and provided inspiration for generations to come.

Born on 28 December 1932, Nichols began her career as a singer and dancer. She was cast as Uhura in 1966 but, after the first season of *Star Trek*, was keen to return to stage work, until a meeting with Dr Martin Luther King changed her mind. He impressed upon her the importance of her weekly presence on screens across the country as a Black person in a position of trust and competence and as a role model. So, Nichols stayed in her role as Lieutenant Uhura and continued to break new ground. In season two an on-screen interracial kiss between Nichols and William Shatner (Captain Kirk) proved to be an iconic moment in television history.

After *Star Trek*, Nichols worked with NASA on a recruitment drive for female and Black personnel. Astronaut Mae Jemison (see 20 September) attributes her career choice to Nichols' influence. Nichols died in 2022 at the age of eighty-nine.

29 DECEMBER - DR MILES V. LYNK

Despite being widowed early, Miles Vandahurst Lynk's mother insisted that her six-year-old son stay at school and get a decent education, even though she needed his help to run their farm. Her insistence paid off when, in 1891, Lynk graduated from Meharry Medical College, Nashville at just nineteen years old.

Miles Vandahurst Lynk, Library of Congress

Lynk moved to Jackson, Tennessee and became the first Black physician practising in the city. While this was an achievement, it was also isolating, and Lynk recognized a need for some community between the few African Americans in the medical world. In December 1892 he published the first edition of the *Medical and Surgical Observer*, by and for Black health workers. The white-dominated sector excluded Black practitioners from journals and societies, limiting their opportunities for learning, research and contribution and compounding a lack of confidence in their abilities from even their Black patients. Lynk started his 'journal of our own' to change this.

The journal published its last edition in 1894 but by that time Lynk was already working on plans for a Black medical society. In late 1895 he, along with several other Black physicians, founded the National Medical Association, which is still advocating for Black professionals and patients today.

Lynk also went on to found his own medical school in 1900, the University of West Tennessee. It offered degrees in medicine, dentistry, pharmacy, nursing and law to African American students.

Dr Lynk died on 29 December 1956 at eighty-six years of age after a lifetime of advocacy and action.

30 DECEMBER - LeBRON JAMES

LeBron James is widely regarded as one of the greatest basketball players of all time. Since he entered the NBA (National Basketball Association) in 2003 he has set and smashed records, been awarded multiple MVPs (Most Valuable Player), won Olympic medals and taken teams to success at championships over and over again. His sporting legacy is assured, but James has also worked to ensure a legacy outside of basketball.

James was born in Akron, Ohio on 30 December 1984 and has, from the very beginning of his career, chosen to give back to the place that raised him.

In 2004 he founded the LeBron James Family Foundation, intending to offer real assistance and change to disadvantaged families, much like his own had been. It began with fundraising and community events, but in 2011 James initiated his 'I Promise' programme, centred on providing not only education opportunities, but the pastoral support for families that would allow children to access the opportunities on offer. The programme has so far supported more than 1,100 students and their families and, with the opening of the 'I Promise' School, a further 343 students are being helped. James continues to expand the programme, offering students support into higher education and accommodation support for families in distress.

31 DECEMBER - THE WATCH NIGHT MEETINGS

On the evening of 31 December 1862, across the United States of America, African American people gathered to spend the final hours of the year together. These gatherings were called Watch Night Meetings and the people who attended them were waiting for the clocks to strike midnight.

At midnight on 1 January 1863, the Emancipation Proclamation that had been issued by president Abraham Lincoln on 22 September 1862 would come into effect, and 31 December 1862 became known as Freedom's Eve. However, some of these Watch Night meetings had to take place in secret as, although the Emancipation Proclamation freed the majority of America's enslaved people, it did not yet free them all. The Civil War was not yet over, with many areas still under Confederate control. So the fight for an end to slavery for all continued until the fall of the last Confederate holdout to the Union army (see 19 June).

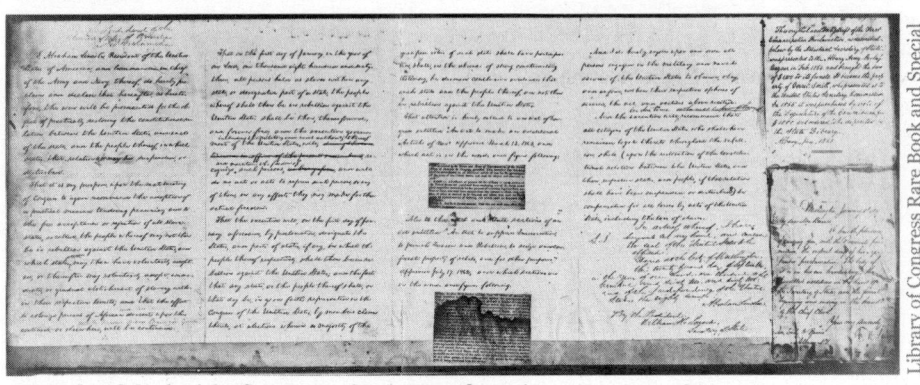

Original and draft of the first Emancipation Proclamation, 4 January, 1864

The Watch Night meetings were commemorated in an 1863 painting by the artist William Tolman Carlton that was given as a gift to President Lincoln. It shows a group of enslaved Black men, women and children inside a wooden cabin. Among them, holding a Black baby, is a white woman. Some of the people are kneeling in prayer, and one man stands in the doorway holding the United States flag in his arms. Another man, wearing a slave collar, is holding a flaming torch above his head, shining a light on the clock being held by a man in the centre of the painting, that is ticking its way towards midnight and freedom.

Ent'd according to Act of Congress, A. D. 1863, by W. T. Carlton, in the Clerk's Office of the District Court of the District of Mass.

Watch Night Meeting, 31 December 1862, 'Waiting for the Hour'

Wikimedia Commons

TIMELINES

TIMELINE 1 ~ ESTABLISHMENT OF THE ENGLISH TRADE IN ENSLAVED AFRICANS

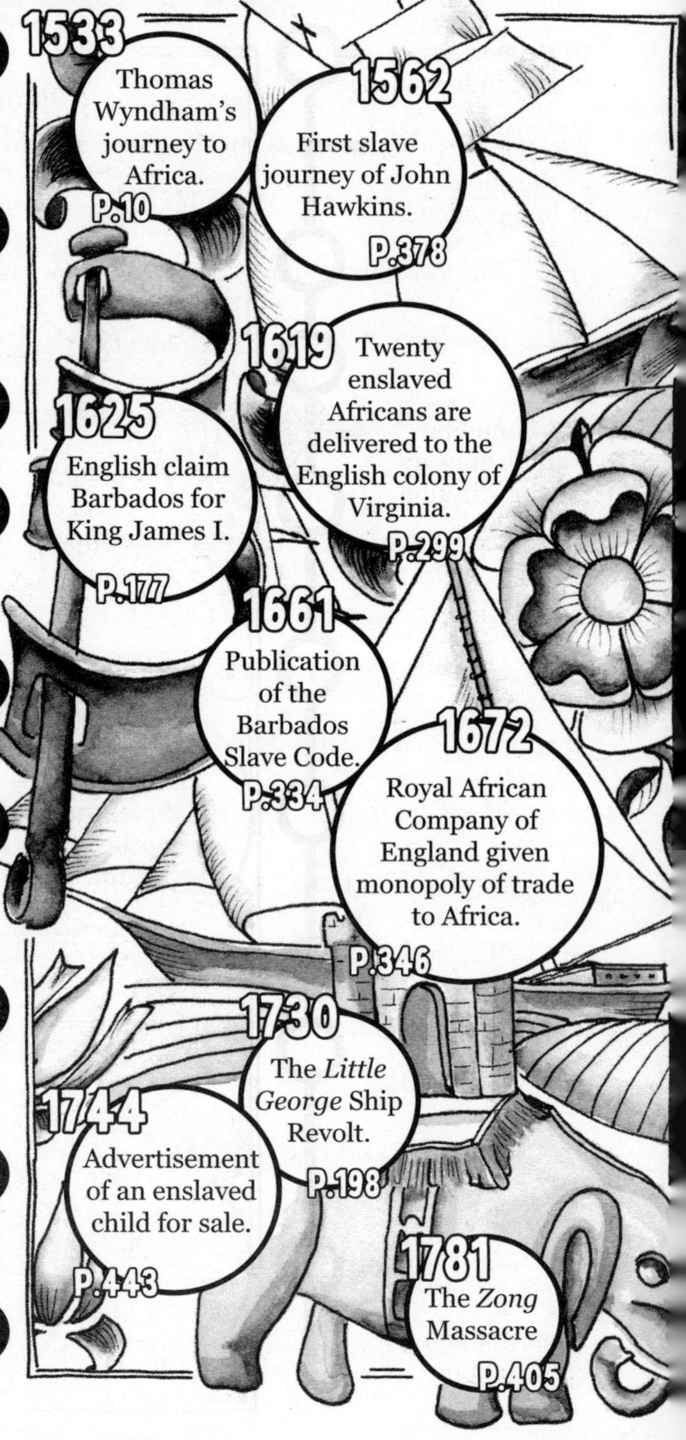

1558: Elizabeth I becomes Queen of England

1606: King James I establishes Virginia as an English colony

1666: The Great Fire of London

1727: George II becomes King

1760: George III becomes King

1533 Thomas Wyndham's journey to Africa. P.10

1562 First slave journey of John Hawkins. P.378

1619 Twenty enslaved Africans are delivered to the English colony of Virginia. P.299

1625 English claim Barbados for King James I. P.177

1661 Publication of the Barbados Slave Code. P.334

1672 Royal African Company of England given monopoly of trade to Africa. P.346

1730 The *Little George* Ship Revolt. P.198

1744 Advertisement of an enslaved child for sale. P.443

1781 The *Zong* Massacre P.405

TIMELINES

TIMELINE 2 – BLACK RESISTANCE TO SLAVERY IN NORTH AMERICA

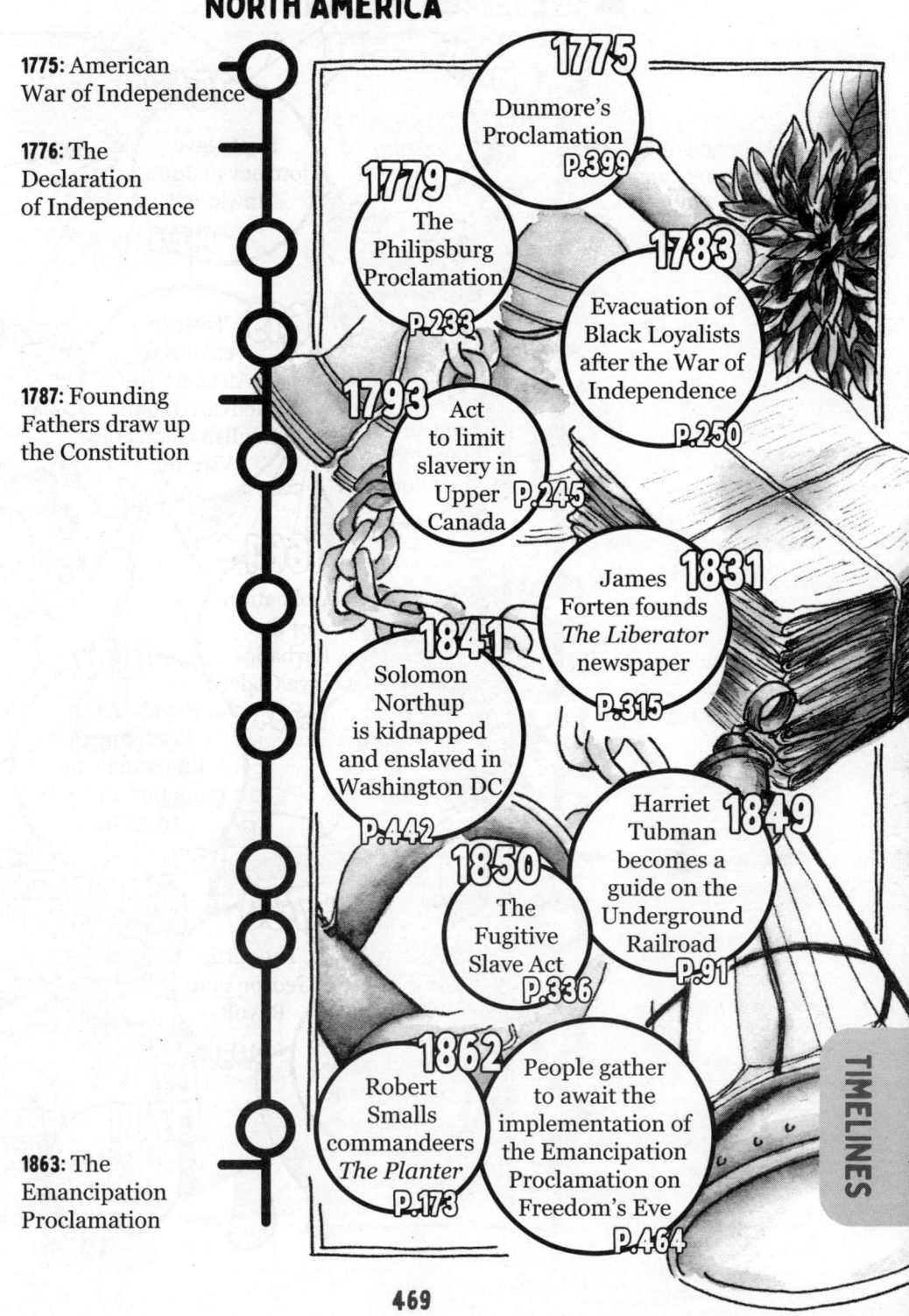

1775: American War of Independence

1776: The Declaration of Independence

1787: Founding Fathers draw up the Constitution

1863: The Emancipation Proclamation

1775 Dunmore's Proclamation P.399

1779 The Philipsburg Proclamation P.233

1783 Evacuation of Black Loyalists after the War of Independence P.250

1793 Act to limit slavery in Upper Canada P.245

1831 James Forten founds *The Liberator* newspaper P.315

1841 Solomon Northup is kidnapped and enslaved in Washington DC P.442

1849 Harriet Tubman becomes a guide on the Underground Railroad P.91

1850 The Fugitive Slave Act P.336

1862 Robert Smalls commandeers *The Planter* P.173

People gather to await the implementation of the Emancipation Proclamation on Freedom's Eve P.464

TIMELINES

469

TIMELINE 3 – BLACK RESISTANCE TO SLAVERY IN THE CARIBBEAN

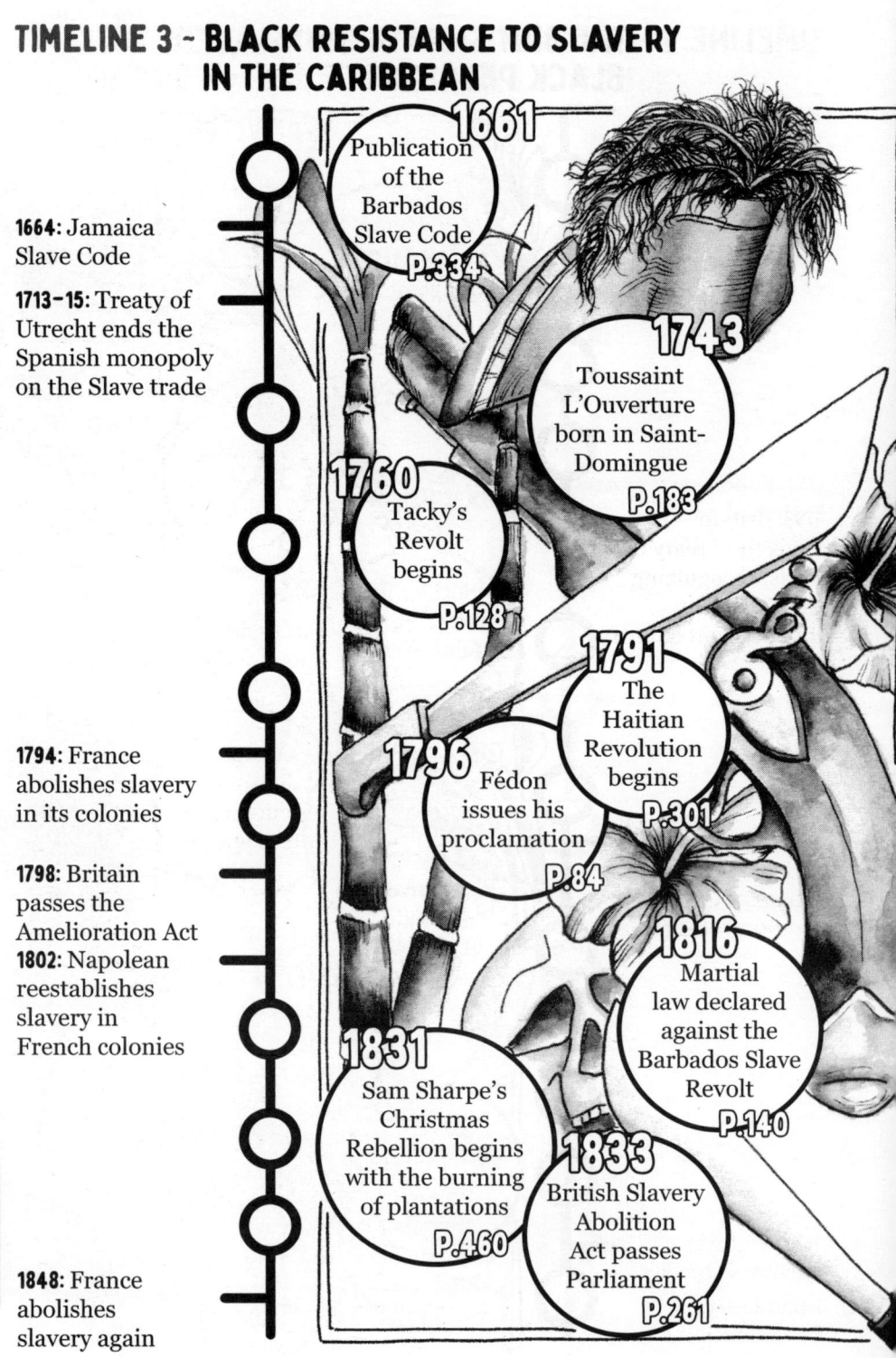

1664: Jamaica Slave Code

1713-15: Treaty of Utrecht ends the Spanish monopoly on the Slave trade

1794: France abolishes slavery in its colonies

1798: Britain passes the Amelioration Act

1802: Napolean reestablishes slavery in French colonies

1848: France abolishes slavery again

1661 Publication of the Barbados Slave Code **P.334**

1743 Toussaint L'Ouverture born in Saint-Domingue **P.183**

1760 Tacky's Revolt begins **P.128**

1791 The Haitian Revolution begins **P.301**

1796 Fédon issues his proclamation **P.84**

1816 Martial law declared against the Barbados Slave Revolt **P.140**

1831 Sam Sharpe's Christmas Rebellion begins with the burning of plantations **P.460**

1833 British Slavery Abolition Act passes Parliament **P.261**

TIMELINE 4 ~ THE BRITISH ABOLITIONIST MOVEMENT & BLACK PEOPLE IN GEORGIAN BRITAIN

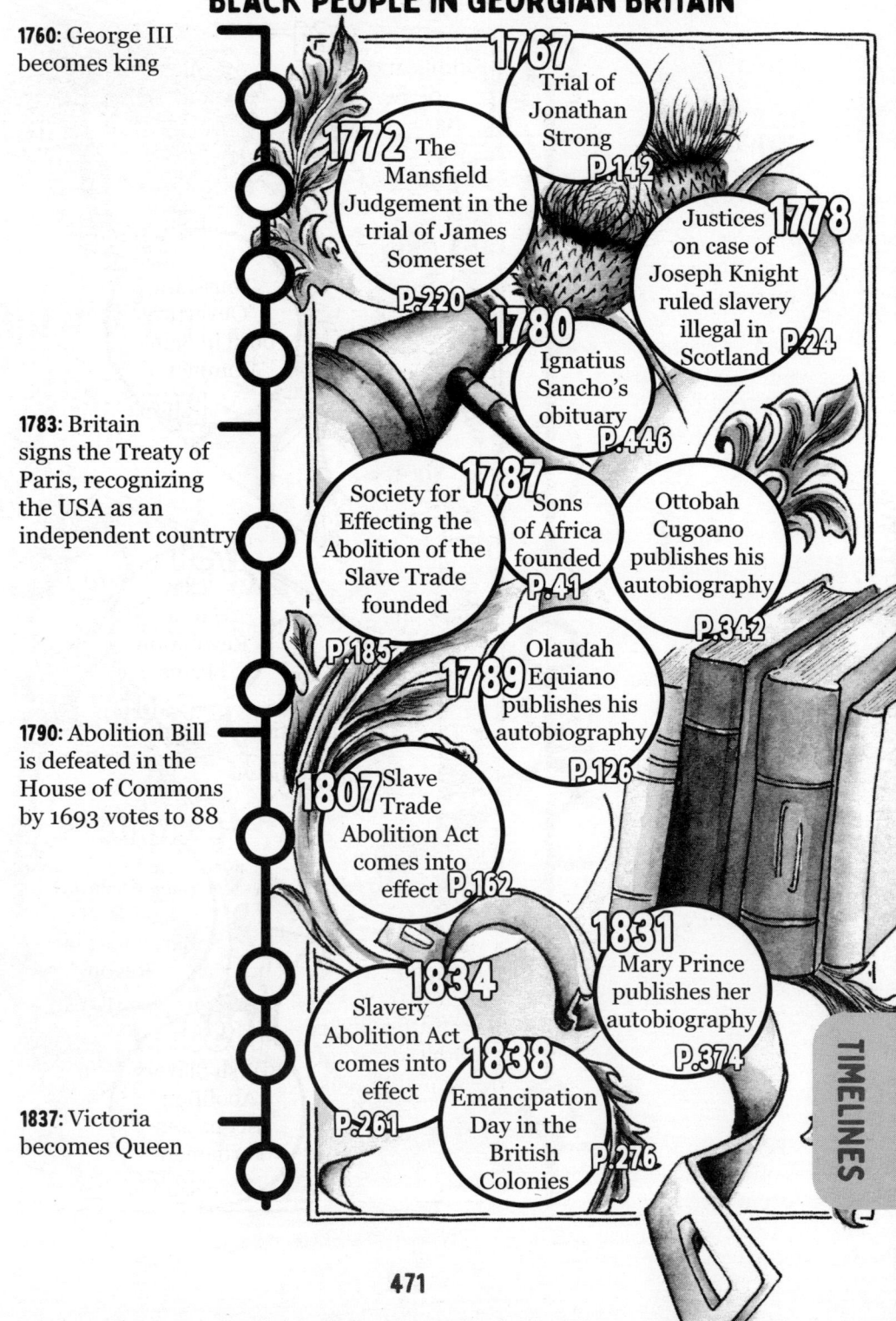

1760: George III becomes king

1767 Trial of Jonathan Strong P.142

1772 The Mansfield Judgement in the trial of James Somerset P.220

1778 Justices on case of Joseph Knight ruled slavery illegal in Scotland P.24

1780 Ignatius Sancho's obituary P.446

1783: Britain signs the Treaty of Paris, recognizing the USA as an independent country

1787 Society for Effecting the Abolition of the Slave Trade founded P.185

1787 Sons of Africa founded P.41

Ottobah Cugoano publishes his autobiography P.342

1789 Olaudah Equiano publishes his autobiography P.126

1790: Abolition Bill is defeated in the House of Commons by 1693 votes to 88

1807 Slave Trade Abolition Act comes into effect P.162

1831 Mary Prince publishes her autobiography P.374

1834 Slavery Abolition Act comes into effect P.261

1838 Emancipation Day in the British Colonies P.276

1837: Victoria becomes Queen

TIMELINES

471

TIMELINE 5 ~ VICTORIAN ANTI-SLAVERY MOVEMENT

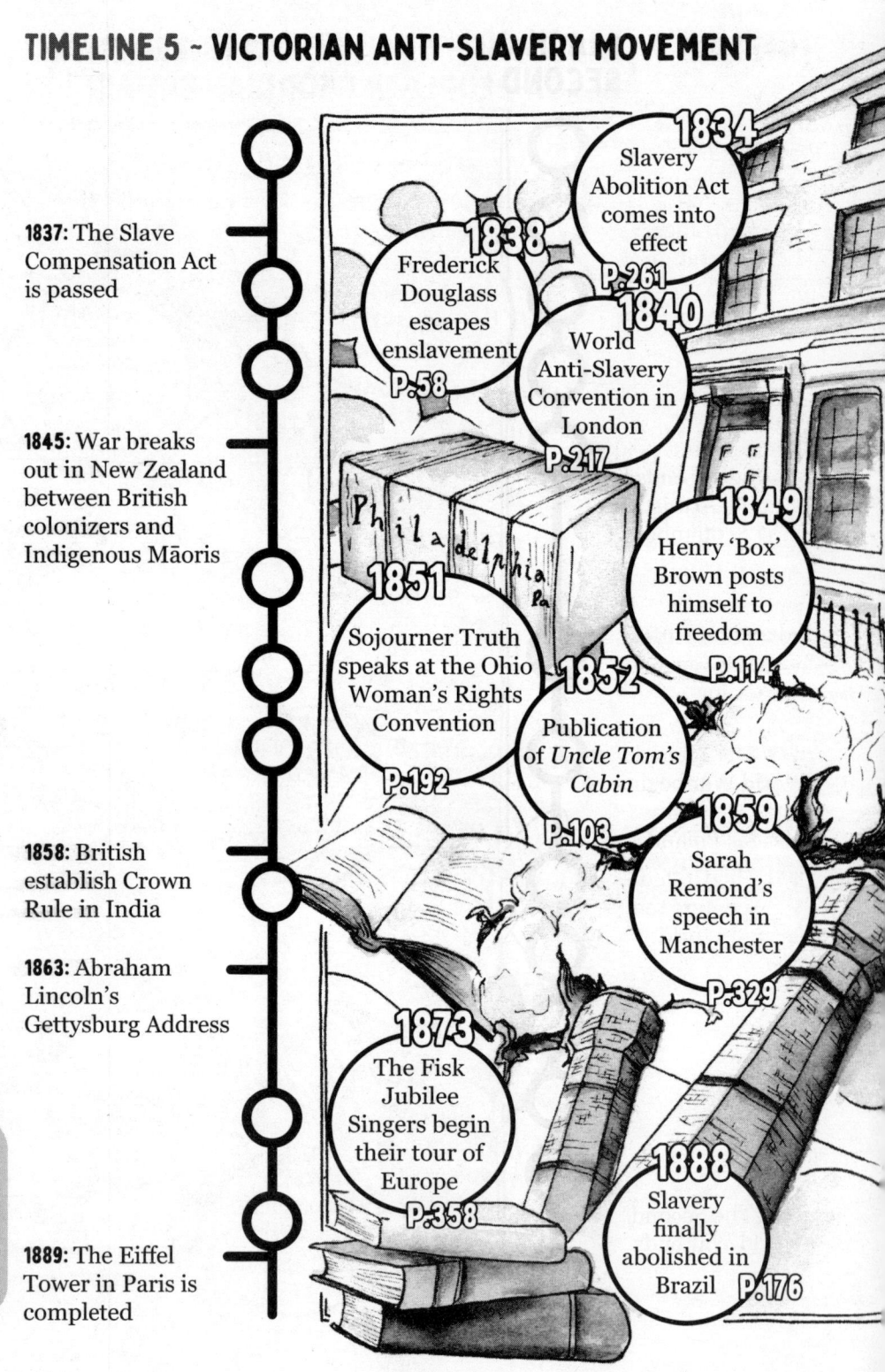

1837: The Slave Compensation Act is passed

1845: War breaks out in New Zealand between British colonizers and Indigenous Māoris

1858: British establish Crown Rule in India

1863: Abraham Lincoln's Gettysburg Address

1889: The Eiffel Tower in Paris is completed

1834 Slavery Abolition Act comes into effect P.261

1838 Frederick Douglass escapes enslavement P.58

1840 World Anti-Slavery Convention in London P.217

1849 Henry 'Box' Brown posts himself to freedom P.114

1851 Sojourner Truth speaks at the Ohio Woman's Rights Convention P.192

1852 Publication of *Uncle Tom's Cabin* P.103

1859 Sarah Remond's speech in Manchester P.329

1873 The Fisk Jubilee Singers begin their tour of Europe P.358

1888 Slavery finally abolished in Brazil P.176

TIMELINE 6 ~ BLACK CONTRIBUTION TO THE FIRST AND SECOND WORLD WARS

1914: The First World War begins when Austria-Hungary declares war on Serbia

1918: The First World War ends with the Armistice on 11 September

1933: Adolf Hitler becomes German chancellor

1939: The Second World War begins when Germany invades Poland

1941: The United States enters the Second World War

1945: The Second World War ends

1914 Alhaji Grunshi is the first British soldier to fire a shot P.285

1915 BWIR formed P.437

1916 Ahmet Ali Çelikten becomes one of the first Black pilots. P.403

1917 Walter Tull is promoted to second lieutenant P.108

1918 The Harlem Hellfighters fight alongside France P.343

1939 Lilian Bader excluded from military training P.113

1941 Black pilots begin training at Tuskegee P.152

1942 Job Maseko destroys a German ship P.321

1943 Giorgio Marincola joins the Italian Partisans P.353

1944 Battle of Park Street, Bristol P.254

1945 Ulric Cross is decorated for his distinguished service P.355

1948 Executive Order 9981 P.343

473

TIMELINE 7 ~ US CIVIL RIGHTS MOVEMENT OF THE 1950S/60S

1955: The Vietnam War begins

1960: John F. Kennedy becomes president

1963: President Kennedy is assassinated

1967: The Biafran War begins

1969: First episode of *Sesame Street* airs

1954 Supreme Court desegregates education P.179

1955 Rosa Parks refuses to give up her bus seat P.428

1957 Dr Martin Luther King Jr founds SCLC P.16

1960 The Greensboro Four lunch counter protest P.45

1961 The Freedom Riders P.165

1963 The March Against Fear P.228

1963 250,000 attend the March on Washington P.31

1963 The Birmingham Children's Crusade P.163

1964 The Civil Rights Act P.237

1965 Selma to Montgomery march P.87

1965 The murder of Malcolm X P.67

1968 The murder of Dr Martin Luther King Jr P.16

1969 The Black Panthers' Breakfast Program P.31

1969 Fred Hampton murdered by police P.434

TIMELINES

474

TIMELINE 8 - THE CAMPAIGN AGAINST APARTHEID

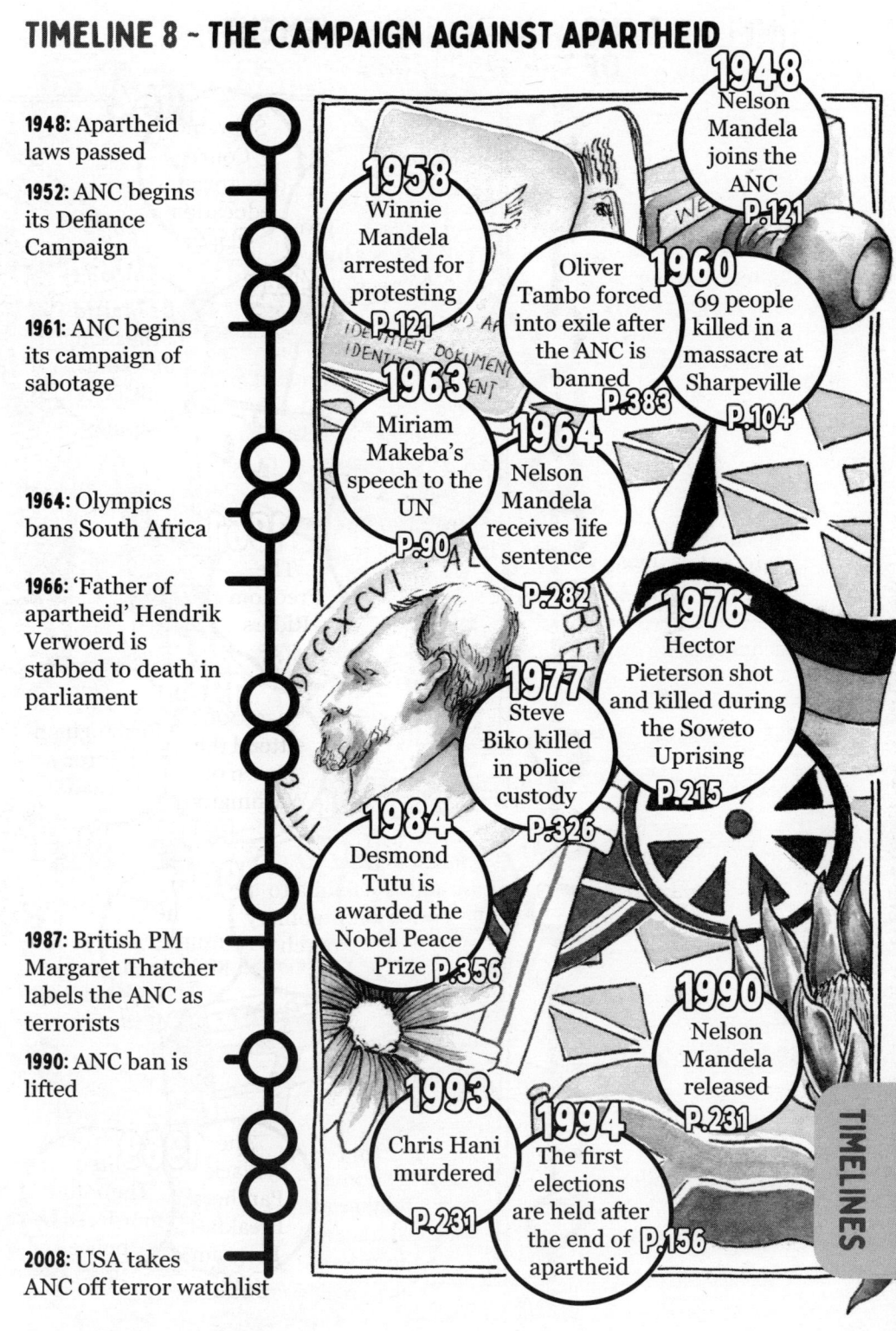

1948: Apartheid laws passed

1952: ANC begins its Defiance Campaign

1961: ANC begins its campaign of sabotage

1964: Olympics bans South Africa

1966: 'Father of apartheid' Hendrik Verwoerd is stabbed to death in parliament

1987: British PM Margaret Thatcher labels the ANC as terrorists

1990: ANC ban is lifted

2008: USA takes ANC off terror watchlist

1948 Nelson Mandela joins the ANC P.121

1958 Winnie Mandela arrested for protesting P.121

1960 69 people killed in a massacre at Sharpeville P.104

1960 Oliver Tambo forced into exile after the ANC is banned P.383

1963 Miriam Makeba's speech to the UN P.90

1964 Nelson Mandela receives life sentence P.282

1976 Hector Pieterson shot and killed during the Soweto Uprising P.215

1977 Steve Biko killed in police custody P.326

1984 Desmond Tutu is awarded the Nobel Peace Prize P.356

1990 Nelson Mandela released P.231

1993 Chris Hani murdered P.231

1994 The first elections are held after the end of apartheid P.156

TIMELINES

475

TIMELINE 9 ~ IMPERIALISM AND COLONIALISM

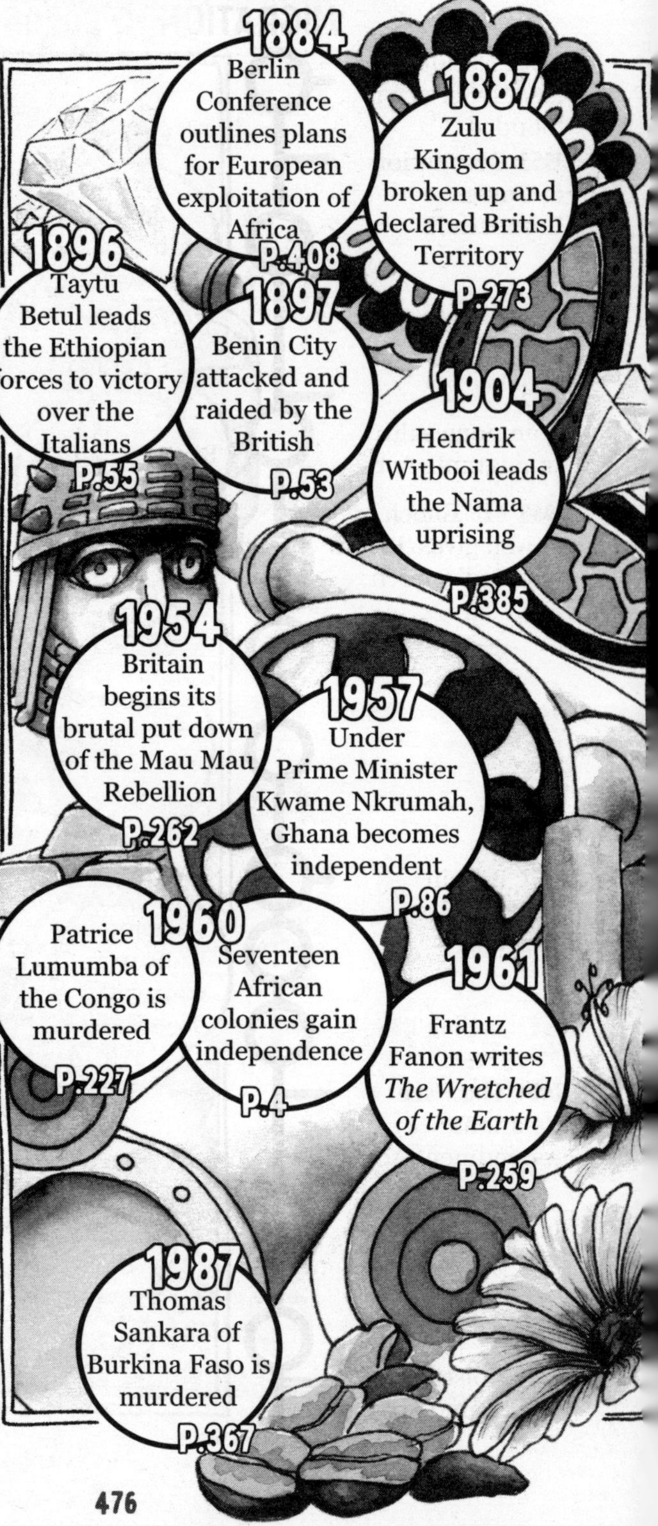

1884
Berlin Conference outlines plans for European exploitation of Africa
P.408

1887
Zulu Kingdom broken up and declared British Territory
P.273

1890: British South Africa Company under Cecil Rhodes starts claiming swathes of Southern Africa

1896
Taytu Betul leads the Ethiopian forces to victory over the Italians
P.55

1897
Benin City attacked and raided by the British
P.53

1904
Hendrik Witbooi leads the Nama uprising
P.385

1908: Belgian government takes control of the Congo from King Leopold when his atrocities become public

1954
Britain begins its brutal put down of the Mau Mau Rebellion
P.262

1957
Under Prime Minister Kwame Nkrumah, Ghana becomes independent
P.86

1960
Patrice Lumumba of the Congo is murdered
P.227

Seventeen African colonies gain independence
P.4

1961
Frantz Fanon writes *The Wretched of the Earth*
P.259

1962: Algerian War of Independence ends

1980: Rhodesia gains independence and becomes Zimbabwe

1987
Thomas Sankara of Burkina Faso is murdered
P.367

TIMELINES

476

1948 : National Health Service is founded

1953: Coronation of Queen Elizabeth II

1962: Commonwealth Immigrants Act

1968: MP Enoch Powell gives 'Rivers of Blood' speech

1987: Britain elects its first Black MPs

2001: The Race Relations Amendment Act

2022: Colston Four found not guilty

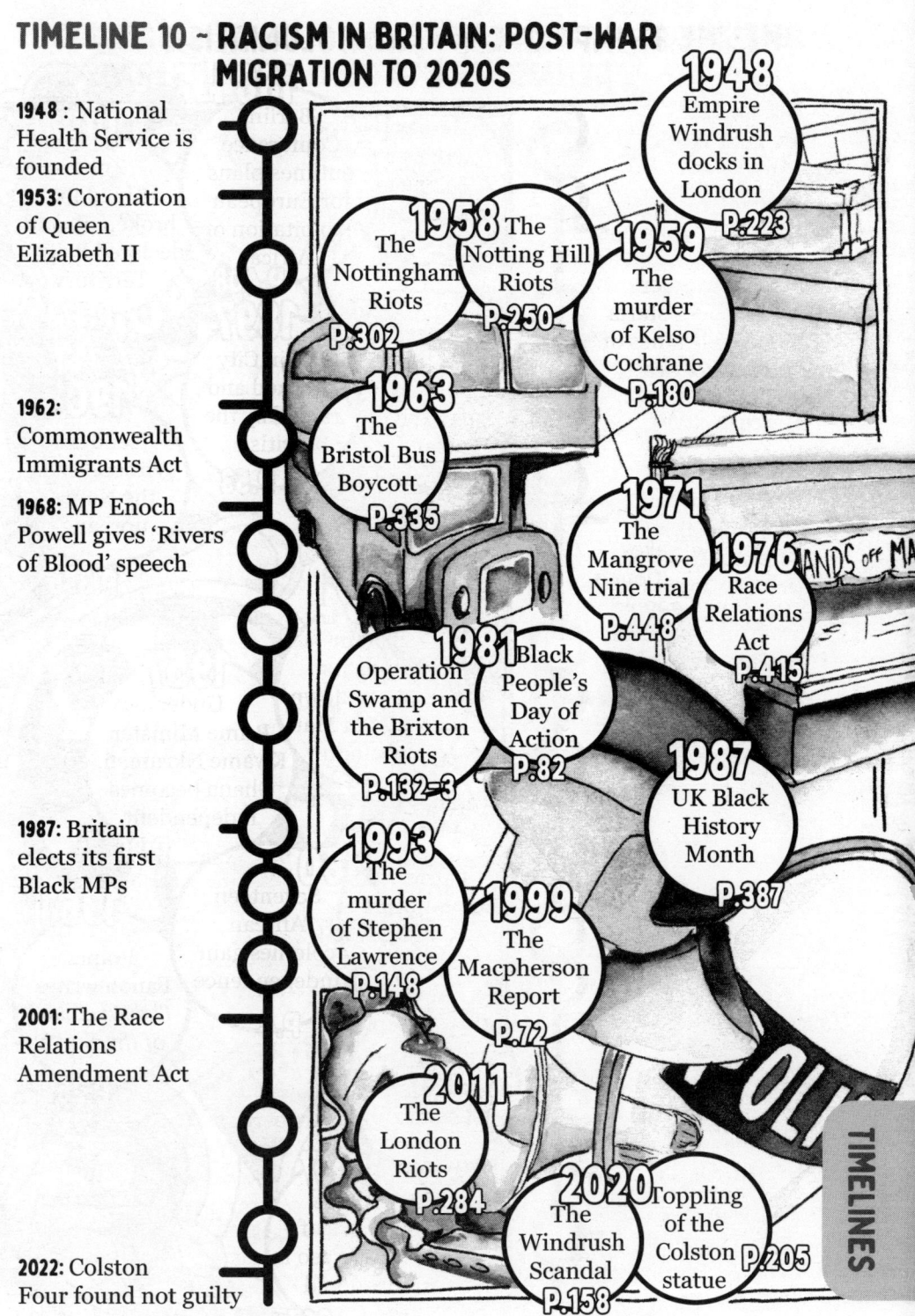

1948 Empire Windrush docks in London P.223

1958 The Nottingham Riots P.302

1958 The Notting Hill Riots P.250

1959 The murder of Kelso Cochrane P.180

1963 The Bristol Bus Boycott P.335

1971 The Mangrove Nine trial P.448

1976 Race Relations Act P.415

1981 Operation Swamp and the Brixton Riots P.132-3

1981 Black People's Day of Action P.82

1987 UK Black History Month P.387

1993 The murder of Stephen Lawrence P.148

1999 The Macpherson Report P.72

2011 The London Riots P.284

2020 The Windrush Scandal P.158

2020 Toppling of the Colston statue P.205

TIMELINES

477

TIMELINE 11 ~ BLACK CREATIVES: FROM THE HARLEM RENAISSANCE TO THE BLACK ARTS MOVEMENT

1918: End of the First World War

1924: Van Der Zee becomes official photographer for Marcus Garvey

1929: Painter and mentor to James Baldwin, Beauford Delaney, moves to New York

1940: Richard Wright's *Native Son* published

1963: Alabama church bombing

1916 James Van Der Zee opens his Harlem studio P.439

1923 Bessie Smith moves to Harlem P.324

1927 Harry Belafonte born in Harlem P.80

1928 Richmond Barthé sculpts a bust of Toussaint L'Ouverture P.38

1937 Langston Hughes sent to report on the Afro-American soldiers in the Spanish Civil War P.44 & 85

1943 Sidney Poitier moves to New York P.93

1948 James Baldwin moves to Paris P.279

1950 Paul Robeson founds Black newspaper *Freedom* P.130

1958 Alvin Ailey founds Dance Theater P.402

1959 Lorraine Hansberry's *A Raisin in the Sun* opens on Broadway P.93

1963 Nina Simone pens 'Mississippi Goddam' P.324

TIMELINES

478

TIMELINE 12 ~ BLACK CREATIVES: STEM

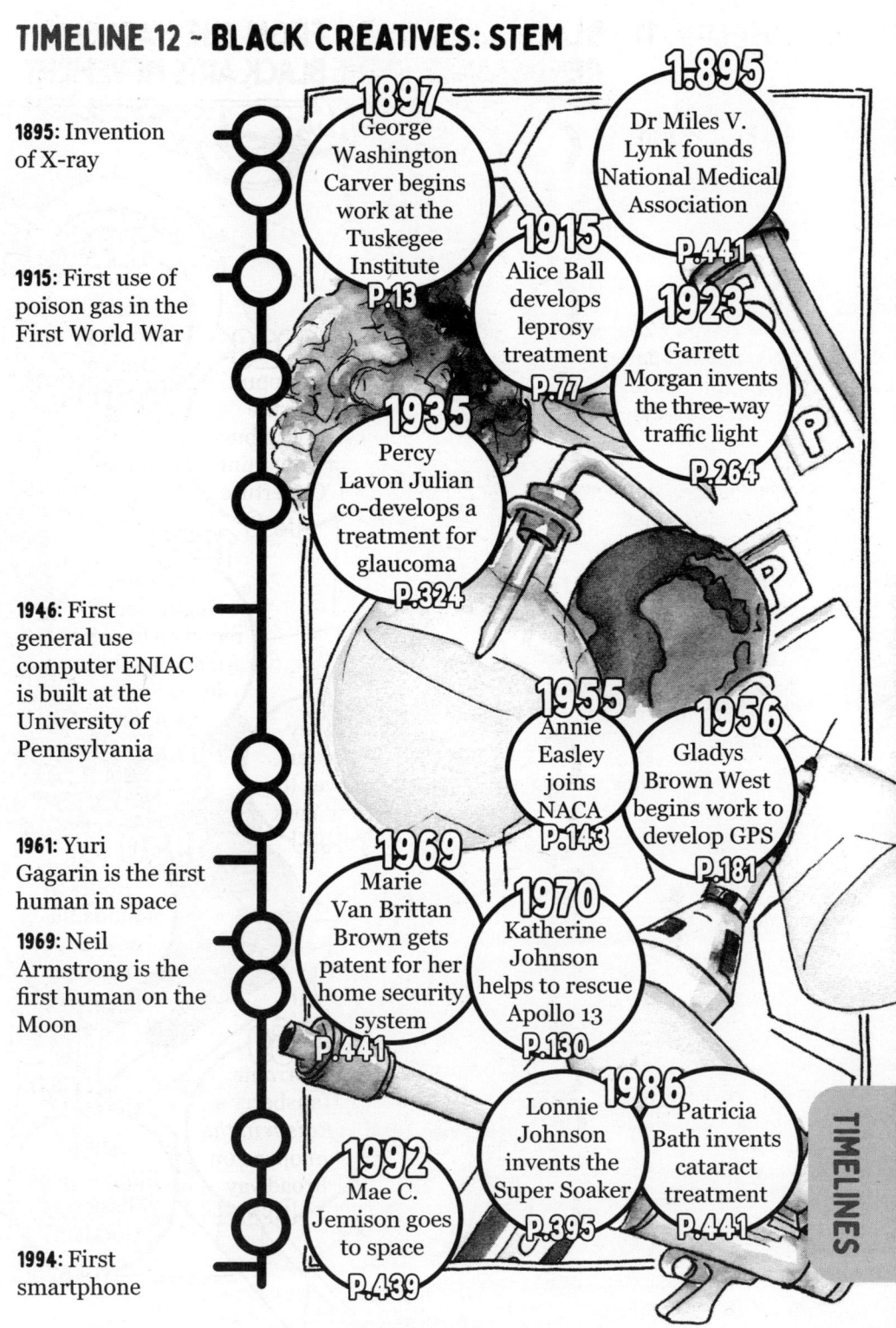

1895: Invention of X-ray

1915: First use of poison gas in the First World War

1946: First general use computer ENIAC is built at the University of Pennsylvania

1961: Yuri Gagarin is the first human in space

1969: Neil Armstrong is the first human on the Moon

1994: First smartphone

1897 George Washington Carver begins work at the Tuskegee Institute P.13

1895 Dr Miles V. Lynk founds National Medical Association P.441

1915 Alice Ball develops leprosy treatment P.77

1923 Garrett Morgan invents the three-way traffic light P.264

1935 Percy Lavon Julian co-develops a treatment for glaucoma P.324

1955 Annie Easley joins NACA P.143

1956 Gladys Brown West begins work to develop GPS P.181

1969 Marie Van Brittan Brown gets patent for her home security system P.441

1970 Katherine Johnson helps to rescue Apollo 13 P.130

1986 Patricia Bath invents cataract treatment P.441

1986 Lonnie Johnson invents the Super Soaker P.395

1992 Mae C. Jemison goes to space P.439

TIMELINES

GLOSSARY

Academy Awards: Based in the US, the Academy of Motion Picture Arts and Sciences celebrates and curates the cinematic industry. The annual **Oscars** ceremony distributes its awards for excellence in all aspects of film-making.

AIDS/HIV: Acquired Immune Deficiency Syndrome is the advanced stage of Human Immunodeficiency Virus. The virus attacks the body's immune system and can be spread through blood and other body fluids. In the late 20th century, before treatments were developed, it took a particular toll on the **LGBTQ+** community and compounded prejudices that they already faced.

Amnesty International: A human rights organization governed by its members and funded by charitable donations. It works to expose and rectify abuses of human rights around the world through research, campaigning and legal challenges.

ANC, African National Congress: The South African liberation organization founded in 1912. Initially non-violent, following the Sharpeville massacre they took up armed resistance to apartheid. After the end of apartheid the ANC was elected as South Africa's ruling political party.

Apartheid: The political and legal system of racial and ethnic segregation that existed in South Africa from 1948 until 1991.

BAFTA: Annual awards of the British Academy of Film and Television.

Bar: The examinations required of all holders of a degree in law who wish to become a practising barrister/lawyer.

Baron, Baroness: A title granted to people awarded an honorary peerage which entitles them to sit in the UK's **House of Lords**.

BCE: Before Common Era is the academic and scientific alternative to the term 'Before Christ' for dates on the Gregorian calendar.

Black Legion: A white supremacist terror organization formed as a splinter group from the **Ku Klux Klan** during the Great Depression period in the US.

British Empire: The group of countries (colonies and territories) that the British ruled.

Cash crops: Crops such as cotton and tobacco that are grown to sell for large profit, rather than for use by the grower.

CBE: Commander of the British Empire. Award granted to civilians in recognition of distinguished service to community or in a particular field of work.

CE: Common Era is the academic and scientific alternative to the term 'Anno Domini' for dates on the Gregorian calendar.

Census: An official population count as carried out by a government of its citizens. It can also include further details on race, gender, religion and sexuality.

Chancellor (Germany): Head of the German Federal Government.

Chitlin' Circuit: A collection of venues in the US that hosted Black performers and audiences during the height of the segregation era.

CIA, Central Intelligence Agency: Created in 1947, the CIA serves US interests through the collection and dissemination of information internationally.

Colony, colonialism, colonial, colonist, colonizer, colonization: Land or territory occupied and controlled by a group of people of another nationality. The legal and cultural structures of their homeland are retained and imposed over existing systems and traditions and Indigenous culture is suppressed. Historical treasures and profits from natural resources are sent back to the imperial core. Instances within the book are mostly those that began during the Age of Discovery (fifteenth to seventeenth centuries).

Colour bar: A semi-official system in which particular opportunities and access to certain spaces are denied to People of Colour.

Colourism: A bias of skin tone where Black people of lighter shades receive privilege based on their proximity to whiteness.

Commonwealth: An institution based on countries that gained independence from the British Empire. Some members still hold the British monarch as their head of state.

Communism, Communist: A political and economic philosophy in which resources, industry and social institutions are state-owned and managed for public benefit rather than private profit.

Confederate: The forces in the American Civil War of the eleven southern states of the Confederacy. They attempted to secede from the Union which threatened their right to continue the institution of slavery.

CORE, Congress of Racial Equality: Civil rights organization founded in 1942. It sought to use non-violent tactics to bring about the end of racial segregation in the US.

Coup d'état: The overthrow of a government, usually by violent means.

Crown Prosecution Service: A public agency responsible for prosecuting criminal cases in England and Wales that have been investigated by the police and other authorities.

Cultural Studies: The critical examination of everyday life through the study of art, the media, group identities, politics, cultural events and traditions.

Dame, Damehood: Dame Commander of the Order of the British Empire (DBE) awarded to women who are pre-eminent in their field and have made a sustained national impact.

Declassify: The process by which governments remove or reduce the security status of information previously considered too sensitive for public access.

Decolonization: A movement that recognizes and seeks to address intellectual legacies of colonialism. It challenges the domination of Western forms of knowledge and the marginalization of Indigenous knowledge.

Desegregation: The process of dismantling Jim Crow or apartheid legislation.

Diaspora: A population with common ethnicity living outside of the country of their ancestry. It includes voluntary migrants, those who may have been forced from their country of origin and their descendants.

Doctorate, PhD: A postgraduate qualification based on research and usually completed over the span of four years. Graduates are awarded Doctor of Philosophy (PhD) and can use the title 'Dr'.

ECHR, European Convention on Human/ European Court of Human Rights: The European Convention on Human Rights is an international legal code established in 1950 that protects political freedom and human rights. The European Court of Human Rights is one of three institutions responsible for legally enforcing the ECHR.

Enlightenment: The European philosophical and intellectual movement of the 17th and 18th centuries. Also known as the Age of Reason, it promoted reason and science over superstition, and advocated for individualism and liberty.

Fascism, Fascist: A right-wing, nationalist philosophy, characterized by a single charismatic leader in a highly militaristic regime which practises violent opposition to democracy, socialism and those deemed as 'unworthy'. The term itself derives from the Latin 'fasces' (a bundle of rods) and was used by Italian Fascist leader Benito Mussolini to name his party – Partito Nazionale Fascista.

FBI, Federal Bureau of Investigation: The national intelligence and security service of the United States of America. It has domestic law enforcement powers.

Feminism, Feminist: A political and social movement that rejects social and political inequality between the sexes. Feminists support equal rights for women.

FGM: Female Genital Mutilation is a non-medical procedure that alters and/or injures the genitalia of female minors. Such procedures can result in medical complications.

Folklorist: A person who studies and collects everyday aspects of popular culture, including songs, rhymes and games.

Genocide, genocidal: The pre-meditated extermination or forced expulsion of a group of people based on a characteristic such as ethnicity, race or religion.

Gestapo: The secret police force that operated in Nazi Germany.

GLAAD: An organization originally founded in 1985 as the Gay & Lesbian Alliance Against Defamation. The name was changed to GLAAD in 2013 to reflect its advocacy for all LGBTQ+ people.

Grand Slam: The name given to a set of major championships, matches or competitions that take place in a particular sport in a calendar year.

Guineas: A British unit of currency that was discontinued in 1816 but remains in use in some aristocratic circles. It was so named because it was made from gold bought on Africa's Guinea Coast. On one side of the coins was the head of the King and on the other the symbol of an elephant and castle – the trademark of the Royal African Company.

Guggenheim Fellowship: The John Simon Guggenheim Memorial Foundation, established in 1925, annually awards 175 Guggenheim Fellowships in recognition of exceptional scholarship by individuals working in any discipline. They are awarded via an annual competition open to citizens of the United States and Canada.

HBCU: Historically Black College and Universities: The group of institutions founded before the 1964 Civil Rights Act to offer higher education primarily to African American students.

Houses of Parliament/ House of Commons: The UK body where the 650 elected **Members of Parliament** sit to debate and propose legislation and governance.

House of Lords: The UK's upper legislative body charged with examining the laws proposed by the **Commons**. Its members are unelected and are drawn from the church, the aristocracy and new members who have been granted honours.

HUAC, House Un-American Activities Committee: An investigative committee of the United States House of Representatives established in 1938 to investigate alleged **communist** ties and activities of American citizens and institutions. Its remit moved to the House Judiciary Committee in 1975.

International Court of Justice: Based in the Peace Palace in The Hague, Netherlands, the ICJ is the **UN**'s court. Its fifteen judges are charged with settling disputes between nation states using international law, and with issuing opinions on particular international legal matters.

IMF, International Monetary Fund: Founded in 1944, the IMF's original forty-four member states sought to create an international institution to stabilize the global economy and prevent catastrophic economic events that could lead to conflicts. Now with 190 member states it is responsible for issuing national loans and shaping economic policies of nations.

Imperialism: The act of a country extending its power over other countries. Through military force or political influence the imperialist country comes to dominate or colonize other territories, and to benefit politically and economically.

Indentured: Poor people and prisoners who were signed up to work without pay for a period of seven to nine years. They were often very badly treated, but once their time was up they were free again.

Indigenous : People with an historical and continued presence in a land, with social systems, culture and language that pre-date the arrival of colonial or settler societies.

Jim Crow: A set of state and local laws in the late 19th and early 20th centuries through which racial segregation came to be practised in the Southern United States.

Knight, Knighthood: Knighthood of the Order of the British Empire (KBE) awarded to men who are pre-eminent in their field and have made a sustained national impact.

Ku Klux Klan: An American terror group formed in 1865 by veterans of the defeated Confederate army. The Klan has enacted a campaign of violence and terror across the southern states of America with the intention of maintaining white control and supremacy and is still in operation.

Law Lord: Formally known as a lord of appeal in ordinary, a law lord was one of twelve judges that carried out the legal responsibilities of the **House of Lords**. This became the responsibility of the Supreme Court of the UK in 2009.

Legion of Honour: The highest honour that can be conferred upon a French citizen whether military or civilian. The honour has five classes: grand cross, grand officer, commander, officer, and knight, or chevalier.

LGBTQ+: Shortened version of the acronym LGBTQIA+, representing lesbian, gay, bi, trans, queer or questioning, intersex and people on the asexual spectrum.

Library of Congress: The US national library which holds a vast collection of various media.

Lynch, lynched, lynching: The summary and extrajudicial killing of Black people by racist mobs.

Magna cum laude: An academic honour that translates as 'with great distinction' and is awarded in US institutions to those graduating with an average grade score of at least 3.7 out of a potential 4.0.

Marxism, Marxist: The theoretical framework of 19th-century philosopher Karl Marx. It was used to analyse class relations and the constant conflict between the powers of labour and money that characterize capitalism. Marxist theory formed the basis of both communist and socialist ideologies.

Master's degree: A postgraduate qualification taken over a year. Either taught, research-based or a combination of both, it can follow an undergraduate bachelor's degree and precede a **doctorate**.

MBE: Most Excellent Order of the British Empire, an award granted to civilians in recognition of contributions to art, science, public service and charity.

Mentioned in Dispatches/MiD: Report of meritorious action by a member of the armed forces, preceding award of a medal.

Metropolitan Police: One of the forty-five police forces that operate throughout the UK. The 'Met' polices the Greater London Area.

Miscegenation: Sexual relationships or marriages between people considered to be of different ethnicities or skin colours.

Middle Passage: Britain's Transatlantic Slave Trade consisted of three sections: outward Passage involved the journey of slave ships from Britain to the coast of West Africa to trade for or capture African men, women and children. Middle Passage was the transport of these enslaved people to be sold in American and Caribbean colonies – during which they suffered terrible conditions, sickness and sometimes death. Homeward passage was the return of the ships to Britain, carrying the valuable **cash crops** produced with the labour of the enslaved.

Missionary/Missionaries: A person who travels to a foreign country to promote a certain religion.

MoMA: The Museum of Modern Art in New York. Founded in 1929, it houses many of Western art's masterpieces.

MP, Member of Parliament: One of 650 people elected in the UK to represent the views of those living in their constituency in the **House of Commons**.

NAACP, National Association for the Advancement of Colored People: Founded in 1909 to advocate for the rights of the African American population.

NACA, National Advisory Committee for Aeronautics: American agency formed in 1915 to study military aviation in the First World War and to develop flight innovations.

NASA, National Aeronautics and Space Administration: The Soviet launch of Sputnik 1 in 1957 began the **Space Race** and the USA responded with the repurposing of NACA as NASA in 1958, with a focus on exploration and discovery.

Nation of Islam: Founded in 1930 by Wallace D. Fard Muhammad, the Nation of Islam (NoI) is an Islamic movement that promotes Black nationalism in the USA.

Nationalism: The ideology of loyalty to the nation or state before any personal interests, often alongside a belief in the inherent superiority of the linguistic, social, cultural and economic norms of the home nation over those of any other.

Nazi, Nazism: Nazi is the shortened form of the National Socialist Workers' Party that rose to power during the German economic depression after the First World War. Despite use of the term 'socialist' the party was far-right and **fascist** in its outlook.

Negritude: An anti-colonial literary movement originating from the French colonies and inspired by the Harlem Renaissance. Poet and academic Aimé Césaire began the movement around the redefinition of Black identity by Black people.

Nobel: A group of Norwegian prizes founded by inventor Alfred Nobel in 1901. Awards are given for outstanding international contributions in the fields of physics, chemistry, medicine, literature, economics and peace.

Oba: 'Ruler' in the Yoruba and Bini languages of West Africa.

OBE: Officer of the Order of the British Empire. Award granted to civilians in recognition of achievement or service in a regional or national role.

Oscar: The nickname of the **Academy Award** of Merit statuettes given annually since 1929.

Overseer: A person employed on a plantation to ensure that enslaved people were productive and obedient. Overseers employed violent and sometimes fatal punishments in order to maintain control and maximize profits.

Palme d'Or: The prestigious top prize of the annual Cannes Film Festival. Competition is open to all film-producing countries.

Pan-African, Pan-Africanist, Pan-Africanism: A movement to recognize and encourage cultural and political unity between the countries of Africa and the people of its diaspora. It grew out of the anti-slavery and anti-colonialist movements.

Partisan: An underground, armed resistance group operating in Europe that used guerrilla tactics to disrupt **Nazi** forces and their allies in the Second World War.

Passbook, Pass Laws: The 1923 Pass Laws restricted where non-whites could live, work or travel in South Africa. Regional laws were consolidated in 1952 and all Black South Africans over the age of sixteen were required to carry their passbook when in 'white' areas.

PhD: See – **doctorate**

Poll Tax: A tax that is levied on every adult in a population. It is a fixed sum that does not differ according to the financial circumstances of the individual.

Polygamy: The marriage to more than one spouse at a time. This is usually practised as polygyny which is the marriage of one man to multiple wives.

Post-Traumatic Stress Disorder, PTSD: A mental health condition caused by exposure to traumatic events or conditions. It causes flashbacks and symptoms of extreme anxiety.

Presidential Medal of Freedom: The highest honour awarded to civilians by the US president in recognition of their contributions to the country.

Protectorate: A country that exists under the protection of another country. Unlike a colony, a protectorate officially maintains its own government and status as a nation.

Pulitzer Prize: A prestigious awards scheme set up by American journalist Joseph Pulitzer in 1904 to recognize excellence in journalism, literature and drama. It has broadened its scope to include poetry, photography and music since its inception.

Quakers: A branch of Christianity that is specifically devoted to peaceful principles. Many abolitionists were also Quakers.

Rastafarianism: A religion, and social and political movement, founded by the pan-African Jamaican leader Marcus Garvey in 1930. Rastafarians believe in the Judeo-Christian God, who they call Jah. Some also view the late Emperor Haile Selassie as the second coming of Jesus Christ.

Reconstruction Era: The period following the American Civil War where southern states were tasked with restructuring their legislation, economy and society after the abolition of slavery.

Savantism: A rare syndrome in which an exceptional yet narrow talent is displayed by those with an otherwise debilitating neuro-developmental condition.

SCLC, Southern Christian Leadership Conference: Formed in 1957 and led by Dr Martin Luther King Jr, SCLC was a civil rights organization committed to non-violent direct action. It operated as a coordinator for other groups and campaign leader.

Sharecropper: Poor workers who in exchange for housing on and use of land must return a share of the crops to the land owner. In the US South many were freed Black men and their families who had no other source of income or shelter.

Segregation: A system that enforced barriers to social mixing in public spaces and institutions between people of different races and ethnic groups based on skin colour.

Sickle cell anaemia: An inherited blood disease causing painful episodes and organ damage that mostly affects people of African and Caribbean heritage. Inheriting one sickle cell gene grants some protection from malaria, but inheriting from both parents causes the disease. Screening programmes help people assess the risk before having children.

SNCC, Student Nonviolent Coordinating Committee: Established in 1960 as a peaceful organization that coordinated student civil rights protests in the USA. Its activities included lunch-counter sit-ins, voter registration drives and protest marches. It was dissolved in 1970.

Socialism, Socialist: Political and economic philosophy in which resources, industry and social institutions are collectively owned and managed under a fully democratic system.

Soviet Union: The Union of Soviet Socialist Republics was created in the aftermath of the 1917 October Revolution from the remains of the Russian Empire. Governed under a political system based on communist philosophy, the USSR spent much of the 20th century at odds with Western capitalism as played out through the Space Race, and the Cold War. The Soviet Union ended in 1991.

Space Race: The technological competition between the US and the **Soviet Union** in the mid-20th century.

SS: The Nazi organization responsible for ensuring national security and racial purity. Under the command of Heinrich Himmler it carried out the incarceration and murder of millions.

State Trooper: US law enforcement officers that operate across a state, responsible primarily for traffic and highways.

Stop and Search: The procedure carried out by some police forces of investigating people on sight based on a suspicion of criminal intent.

Suffrage: Suffrage, or political franchise, is the right to vote in public elections.

Summa cum laude: An academic honour that translates as 'with the greatest distinction' and is awarded in US institutions to those graduating with an average grade score of at least 3.9 out of a potential 4.0.

Supreme Court: The highest legislative body in the US, the Supreme Court is the final arbiter of the law at a federal (national)level. Its decisions overrule any state-level legislation.

Sus laws: A nickname given to a British law that allows the **Metropolitan Police** to stop and search anyone merely on the suspicion that they intended to commit a crime.

Truth and Reconciliation Commission: The body set up after the end of apartheid in South Africa and headed by Bishop Desmond Tutu. It was designed as a vehicle for all South Africans to come to terms with the violence and injustices of apartheid and to move forward in unity.

UN, United Nations: An international organization founded in the aftermath of the Second World War. Fifty countries wrote and signed the UN charter intending to prevent another global conflict. It aims to maintain peace, international law and human rights.

UN Ambassador: A high-profile person who is recruited by the UN to highlight causes and issues. There are messengers of peace, goodwill ambassadors and global advocates.

UN General Assembly: Body of the 193 UN member states that make policies and resolutions on international issues.

UNESCO, United Nations Educational, Scientific and Cultural Organization: Promotes international cooperation through knowledge sharing and protecting culture.

UNESCO World Heritage Site: An area or structure considered to be of international significance and deserving of special protections and preservation.

UNICEF, United Nations Children's Fund: Focuses on protecting the welfare and rights of children.

Union: The forces in the American Civil War under the supreme command of President Lincoln. Fighting to retain the union of the states, they were made up of the regular army plus volunteers and conscripts mostly from the northern states.

Windrush Generation: The group of West Indian people who came from the Caribbean to help fill job vacancies in post-war Britain.

White supremacy/supremacists: The idea that white people are a superior race with the right to dominate all other races.

YMCA: The Young Men's Christian Association was founded in London in 1844 to provide healthy activities and spiritual guidance for the young men flooding the cities during the industrial revolution. It has since become an interdenominational global organization and works extensively for global unity and human rights.

INDEX

Page references in *italics* indicate images.

Middle Passage 165, 483
Milam, J. W. 266
Mildred and Richard Loving vs. Virginia 204
Miller, Cheryl D. 34
minstrelsy shows 8, 169, 358
Minto, John 270
missionary/missionaries 106, 168, 232, 276, 348, 366, 483
Mississippi Freedom Democratic Party 453
MOBO Awards 376, 411
Mobuto, Joseph 227
Mohri, Mamoru 338
Molesworth Street, The Battle of (1981) 270–1
Molineux, Benjamin 144
Monkeypaw Productions 33
Montagu, John, Duke of 446
Monteverde, General Domingo de 20
Montgomery Bus Boycott (1955) 16, 335, 415, 428, 429
Montgomery Improvement Association (MIA) 429
Moody, Dr Harold 96
Moonlight (film) 75
Morant Bay Rebellion (1865) 363
Morello, Tom 372
Morgan, Garrett 264–5, 479
Morgan, John Hunt 264
Morris, Elijah 396, 397–8
Morris, Olive 229
Morris, Robert 390
Morrison, Susie 46
Morrison, Toni 117, *117*, 139, 170, 279, 447
Moscow, Hezekiah 404, *404*
Moscow, Mary 404
Moss, Thomas 457
Motley, Constance Baker 76
Motown Record Corporation 164, 423
Mount Stuart Primary School 424
Mouvement National Congolais (MNC) 227
Moxely, Elle 239
Muldoon, Robert 270
Murray, Anna 58
Murray, Lady Elizabeth 413
Myriad Editions 170
Myrmidon, HMS 232

NAACP (National Association for the Advancement of Colored People) 13, 71, 143, 153, 154, 179, 189, 216, 265, 267, 280, 317, 318, 345, 428, 429, 463
Nabrit, James 179, *179*
NACA (National Advisory Committee for Aeronautics) 136–8, 149, 479, 483
Nama uprising (1904) 385, 476

Narrative of Events since the First of August 1834 289
NASA (National Aeronautics and Space Administration) 34, 136, 137, 138, 149, 338, 395, 461, 483
Nascimento, Beatriz 249
Nation of Islam 68, 69, 73, 483
National Basketball League (NBL) 421
National Commission for the Protection of Human Subjects of Biomedical and Behavioral Research 145–6
National Council of Negro Women (NCNW) 145, 246
National Council of Women of Kenya 360
National Health Service 72, 415, 477
National Medal of Arts 81, 423
National Medical Association 462
National Women's Political Caucus 453
National Youth Administration 246
nationalism 172, 236, 481, 483
Naval Proving Ground, Virginia 181
Navy, Army and Air Force Institute (NAAFI) 113
NBA (National Basketball Association) 409, 463
Ndume, Dr Helena 257
Negro History Week 65, 387
Negro Registration Order 362
Negro World 296
Nelson Mandela Day 257, *257*
Nelson's Ship in a Bottle 187
Nemiroff, Robert 94
New African magazine 191
New Cross Fire (1981) 27, 82, 132
New Daughters of Africa 170
New York anti-slavery bill (1827) 192
New York Drama Critics Circle 93
New Zealand Rugby Football Union (NZRFU) 271
Newton, Huey P. 31
NFL (National Football League) 314
Nichols, Nichelle 338, 461
Nigeria 4, 7, 14, 53, 61, 100, 112, 122, 126, 187, 229, 232, 250, 253, 320, 333, 340, 373, 401, 403, 410, 421, 452
Njoroge, Ngethe 372
Nkrumah, Kwame 5, 86, 96, 202, 236, *236*, 375, 387, 476
Nobel Prize 17, 25, 117, 129, 250, 283, 356, 360, 475, 483
Nobunaga, Oda 106
Nollywood 61, *61*
Norman, Peter 369
North Star 59
Northup, Solomon 425, 442, 469

INDEXES

INDEXES

ACKNOWLEDGEMENTS

We are grateful to Cate Augustin and Gaby Morgan and the team at Macmillan for starting us on this journey and for their patience as we explored what this book could do. Thanks also to our agent, Charles Walker.

We thank our families, especially our children, for their forbearance as we spent day after day researching and writing (and in Kemi's case illustrating) this complex book. You will have lost count of all of the times we entered a room with the phrase 'Did you know?' before launching into the story of an entry we were working on. Your feedback was always honest, helpful and encouraging.

And profound thanks to our first readers, our mum Marion Olusoga-Ndebele and our step-dad Themba Ndebele. You generously shared your lived experiences and memories of key people and moments in Black history during the 20th century, suggesting overlooked figures and events, giving us insight into their impact at the time and since. This book is better for your input and support.

Finally, we would like to thank each other. Doing a group project is a challenge, doing it with siblings potentially even more so. The foundations of childhood meant that as well as our fair share of bickering (sorry Mum), there was also laughter, excitement and a shared sense of purpose in what became an intergenerational family project.

Yinka, David and Kemi

We are grateful to the following for permission to reproduce copyright material: